The Evil Side of a Racetrack

Michael John Horak

The Evil Side of a Racetrack

2100 NE 38th St.
Lighthouse Point, FL 33064

Retail price $30.00
ISBN 1-56825-014-2

Produced by Rainbow Books, Inc.
Cover and interior design by Betsy Lampe

This Book

is

Dedicated to the

Memory of My

Loyal and Faithful

Horse,

Michael John.

CONTENTS

Part III (An Update Summary)

Introduction

The American Race Horse is no longer an animal of Mother Nature. It has now become a type of machine. Man once raised and trained this fine animal for the sheer pride in doing so; that now has all but died.

I can still remember, in years gone by, the saying was, "It doesn't matter if you win or lose, it's how you play the game." Nowadays, it seems, the saying is, "No matter what it takes, whether drugs or bribe, winning is the only thing of any importance." Whatever happened to honesty, integrity, and good old American Horsemanship?

It seems that horsemanship and sportsmanship have taken a back seat to the drive to win at all costs. Over 79 percent of all horses being raced in the United States, be they of the Standardbred or Thoroughbred type, are being injected with a drug called *furosemide*, most commonly known by it's trade name, Lasix. The drug is a diuretic that helps control bleeding in the lungs of a horse, but it can also significantly increase the animal's performance over his previous start.

When horsemen realized the potential of the drug, they started lining up in front of the racing secretary's office to enter their horses that were now called, "Bleeders." New York is one of the few states that doesn't want their horses running on any type of drugs — only on Mother Nature.

It is also a proven fact that once any horse has been injected with Lasix, it is very difficult to detect any illegal drugs that a greedy horseman may have injected. One can only wonder what astronomically damaging side-effects these drugs will have on future generations of these fine animals. Because of the present generation's greed for wealth, men have taken to injecting dangerous drugs and using other means to ensure the outcome of a race.

In trying to prevent a few of these inhumanities, I

have had to abandon a lifelong dream of mine — having my own stable of good, sound horses racing well because of Mother Nature's care and not on Mother Vet's needles.

Each year, 70 million people wager over twelve billion dollars in the horse racing industry, be it on the Standardbreds or the Thoroughbreds, with these figures increasing every year. Out of this, each State takes sixteen percent on a daily basis. Part of this cut goes to the track itself, with the remainder to the local government. Most racetracks handle over one million dollars per day when they are open.

The majority of horse race track patrons know what occurs in the front yard of any race track, but obviously are unaware of the battlefield conditions in the backyard beyond closed doors.

It is a well known fact that in this world most things can be fixed for a price to ensure the final outcome, be it in government or in sports. It was at one particular track that I had an unfortunate, regrettable and disastrous experience. That track was Sportsman Park in Cicero, Illinois. Fortunately, I am very thankful just to be alive to write about these cruel and ugly events.

I really should not have been as shocked as I was, since it happened in Illinois, for this state has had its share of public scandals going back to the Annual Fall Classic of Baseball. In the World Series of 1919 between the solid favorite Chicago White Sox and the Cincinnati Reds, the Sox were vastly superior with their batting average of .351. The Reds had only one player hitting a .321 average. By game time, the gamblers had made Chicago 3-to-1 favorites. Cincinnati won the first game in a runaway by the score of 9 to 1; then going on to win the second game 4 to 2. During the last game of the Series, it was as though the White Sox players had brought their mattresses with them on to the playing field for an afternoon nap. The Cincinnati Reds won 10 to 5.

In June of 1920, a Grand Jury convened in Chicago and indictments were returned against eight of the Sox players. They signed confessions of accepting bribes of five thousand to ten thousand dollars each to lose the

Series; then, at their trial in 1921, the players' signed confessions mysteriously disappeared from the Illinois District Attorney's office. All of the players involved were suspended from baseball. The damage could never be repaired for the millions of children who loved this sport as it was intended to be.

Gangster Alphonse Capone, born in 1899, was allowed to rule the town of Cicero, Illinois, a suburb of Chicago, in 1924, with bootlegging, gambling and prostitution. The city officials were now living high on the hog with their two weekly pay checks — one from honest taxpayers and the other from "Good Ole' Al", as they called him.

During my life, I have noted that most states' evil and illegal practices have been somewhat curtailed, except for the State of Illinois. Two of their Governors, a State's Attorney, fifteen associate and Circuit Court judges were sent to prison. Most of them received eight to fifteen years and the sixteenth judge committed suicide rather than take his medicine. It goes without saying that they weren't there because they missed a day going to Sunday School! The governor of each state rules over its racing board. This fact does have a damaging effect on the integrity of racing when the governor is sentenced to prison.

Within a forty-five mile radius of Chicago, there are five major horse race tracks. Four of these tracks were well over fifty years old and in such terrible condition the attendance and pari-mutuel handle had fallen drastically. With huge losses occurring for the management of these tracks, amazing things soon happened. These four tracks' grandstands and clubhouses caught fire and burned to the ground within a few years of each other. Coincidentally, all of these tracks caught fire after their racing seasons were over. These tracks were Maywood Park, Hawthorn, Arlington and Washington Park.

They all collected their insurance money. Washington Park sold its property to a housing developer. The other three now have brand-new concrete and steel modern grandstands and clubhouses.

In some small but significant way, I want to tell of my

observations involving the savage cruelties performed on race horses by their owners and trainers. I also want to tell about the involvement of a major race track that has been and still is allowed to operate with corrupt officials who obtained such an extreme amount of clout, that the killing of a teenager on their track was quickly swept under the rug and forgotten within two days.

These same officials tried to silence my knowledge of their other illegal activities.

I honestly hope that, before I leave this world, I will be heard as a voice to help all mistreated and abused animals.

M.J.H.

Part I

Michael John resting on my shoulder with Mike's Lad looking on, both yearlings, on the Murphy's Farm, 1962. (photo by Mrs. Murphy)

Chapter 1

The Beginning of a Dream

Life had no meaning until I reached the age of fourteen. It was the beginning of a dream for me when I first began working with horses. I developed a love for them which has endured to this present day. At that time, I would visit the local race track in Denver, Colorado, where, after a couple of years, I would begin exercising Thoroughbreds. This was the happiness I had been looking forward to all my growing years.

Working for a racing stable with over thirty-five Thoroughbred horses for the next four years, gave me plenty of knowledge and riding experience. Then Uncle Sam sent me his usual greeting, and I was one of the "few good men" he was looking for. After three years, I found my body frame to be much too large and heavy for me to ever even consider riding any more Thoroughbred horses. The army pay didn't leave much money in my pockets either.

A month after my discharge, I started working for a trucking company. Within a short time, I was behind the wheel of an 18-wheeler, going down the highway and thinking of a way to get back into the horse racing business. In desperation and frustration, I thought about riding steeplechase horses or getting into driving in an actual race with the Standardbred type.

The latter ended up being my decision, though I knew it would be a very hard nut to crack. First of all, I would have to learn all I could about a type of horse I knew nothing about. The only time I even had seen one was in a 1944 movie, *Home in Indiana*.

Soon, in 1959, after months of driving a semi and putting most of my paychecks in the bank, I found an old-timer who had been in this racing game since he was a young "whippersnapper". He still had a few Standardbred horses in his stable, but had trouble keeping any worthwhile help that he could trust to jog and cool out his horses properly.

I put the facts of my plans before him over a Greek-style dinner at Rodity's Restaurant on Halsted Street in Chicago. He must have enjoyed the meal along with my telling him what I would like to do. I explained that I would work for him for free in my spare time from my trucking job in exchange for him teaching me the harness racing business. I knew that I wouldn't be getting much sleep in the following years and that this would also keep me from spending much of the money that I would need later. I learned very fast that no horse owner was going to let a "greenhorn" drive his horse on a race track. It was just like any other business: everyone wants a person with experience, but no one wants to take the time to give a person an opportunity. Yes, it was a Catch 22.

I decided that I would learn this business and go out and buy my own horse and equipment even if it killed me. I sure didn't like driving a semi! It just wasn't in my blood and every day was a drag for about the next six years. One cold February morning, I heard of a horse farm sale west of Chicago where they had sold all of their horses but had been unable to get a decent bid on two 11-month-old colts. This time of the year, most of the horsemen at racetracks weren't interested in any more young stock. They knew it would take at least two more years before they would be ready for the races.

After checking the breeding of the two colts and the kind of money the owner was trying to get, I thought that I would give him a couple of days to sleep on it. I figured that with cash on the table at this time, he might just mellow down some, and I would have my first possible future race horse. I knew that while he would be placed on a farm for the next two years, I would still be learning and saving money for his first race.

I dreamed of listening for the race track announcer's voice saying that the winner was Mike's Lad, trained and driven by Michael John Horak. It may have been just a moment of wishful thinking, but it made me feel good for those few seconds. So off to the countryside I went. There was the once proud-looking white rail fences standing in a foot or more of snow, then coming into view a huge red painted barn with a white, snow covered roof. It looked as if you would need a cab just to get from one end to the other. As I drove up to the main house, Mr. Thomas, the owner, whom I had spoken to earlier over the telephone, came out. He was dressed in a warm looking sheepskin overcoat. After a few minutes of the usual chitchat, we were at the barn door. He opened it slowly and we stepped inside. I felt as though I was walking into a mortuary. The cold gave me a chill as I looked down the aisle way which separated eighty horse stalls that were once full. They were now empty and very quiet. The long walk to the other end was almost over. I sensed the first sign of life and the sound of a small colt calling for his mother. This was the only time that there wasn't the sound of other horses around them, so they must have been scared of the quiet surroundings.

I opened the stall door in which both colts had been placed. They must have been very glad to see someone, for they both came right up to me instantly. As I began to stroke their foreheads and pat them on their shoulders, I knew I was hooked! I had just enough money to buy one colt and leave a little extra in the bank for a rainy day. Although I wanted to buy both, I was forced into sticking with my original plan of purchasing just the one.

A couple of hours later, I found myself shaking Mr. Thomas' hand, stating that I would return the next day with a closed in trailer for my colt as well as a check for the final payment. I really felt good driving back to my apartment, knowing that I was an owner of a fine little colt. I was already thinking of taking him to the farm the next day in the southern part of Illinois, 185 miles away, as prearranged with the owners there, who were very nice people and also had a love for horses. I knew that my colt would be well cared for there.

Bright and early the next morning, I headed back to the farm with my car and trailer. I had installed a soft two-inch rubber mat with straw on the floor to keep the young horse from slipping and a cushion for his small legs. The padding on the sides would be of great comfort for the little guy as well.

Soon I was in front of the big red barn again. A light snow was starting to fall. By the time I got the trailer door opened and the small ramp in place, I heard a voice yell out, "I see you made it just like you said!"

"Yep," I said, "I didn't get much sleep last night."

With very little difficulty, we got my colt into the trailer and closed the door to get him accustomed to the inside. We went into the house to finish the paperwork and for me to hand over a large amount of my life's hard earnings. After a cup of hot tea, I was now ready to roll. Opening the front door, the snow was now falling harder with larger flakes. The winds were picking up, biting into my face. Damn it's cold out here, I thought. Checking in on my horse, I hurried into my car and proceeded to turn it around the large driveway only to start spinning one of my car wheels that had slipped in a rut. I was soon able to force a couple of small boards under the tire, but when I got back into the car, I heard some banging noises coming from inside the barn. I knew it was the sound of the other colt left behind. Looking up towards the house, I noticed Mr. Thomas wasn't coming out. He couldn't possibly hear what I heard from that distance. I went into the barn where the noise was even greater. Running down the aisle way, I soon found out the problem — the little colt had his front legs over the stall door and was trying to climb over the four foot gate. He was then unable to get back down and was very frightened. It took me a few minutes to get him settled down, and in doing so, it occurred to me that even though I had tried to stop it, this colt would probably end up hurting himself to the point of being useless to anyone. My colt would also be scared along the road trip being by himself. So, once again, back to the farm house I walked, the snow falling at a steady pace.

I noticed right away that Mr. Thomas was glad to see me again. He read me like a book, for he too didn't want to see the colts separated at their young age. It didn't take much talking to make a deal for this second colt. Shortly thereafter, I registered this brave little colt's name as Michael John and named the first colt Mike's Lad.

With both colts together and happy again, I was finally driving down the bitter, cold highway. With only a few stops along the way and no snow in this part of the state, we reached the colts' new home for the next two years. The folks there were thrilled when I opened the trailer door, and they saw not one but two little colts. I stayed for a good old home farm supper. For the first time in a long while, I had a peaceful night's sleep.

Waking up the next morning, I hurried to get out to the barn to see my colts, only to see Mr. and Mrs. Murphy already feeding them. The colts little tails were wagging from side to side as they were eating the specially-mixed feed I had brought along with me. It consisted of fine-ground corn, oats, barley, vitamins, and molasses. This would ensure the growth of stronger bones, conformation and strength.

At least once a month, I'd be taking twenty bags of this specially mixed grain from Chicago to start getting the colts accustomed to the harness and training jog cart. Before bringing them back to the race track, I wanted one thing for sure — they would be trained slowly and carefully. They would get the feeling that it would be fun in doing so, without the quick rush that I have witnessed whip-happy trainers do. These trainers would, as a result, ruin many a fine yearling. It is a shame that the tables couldn't be turned for just one day, where the horses would become the trainers and vice versa. The horses would surely kick some rear ends!

Having given notice several months earlier to the trucking company, I left them in May of 1966 to pursue my lifelong dream. I figured that if it didn't work out, I would be back. I was assured that my job would be waiting, even though everyone there hoped that success would prevail in my new venture. It made me feel very good knowing that someone appreciated my loyalty as well as the long hours of work I gave them. I always believed in an honest day's work for a day's pay.

I waited with great anticipation for the first clear sunny day to hook up my new blue horse trailer and to make my final drive to pick up the now full-grown colts. They were three years old. The week in waiting was also a blessing for me. I was able to catch up on the sleep that I was never allowed to get while driving trucks five days a week, then being at the race track early each morning. The first few days I slept for more than twelve hours. I really felt good driving in the early morning sun with the cool sixty-five degree breeze blowing in my face. It was a far cry from the first trip I took there two years earlier.

It goes without saying that the Murphys hated to see the colts leave their farm. After serving me a delicious home-prepared dinner, they promised to drive to Chicago when the colts were entered for their first race. I informed them that if all went well, they would race sometime around the coming October, since it would take at least five months of serious training.

I thanked them over and over again for the extra special care and hard work they had put into raising my two colts. The results were standing before me. They were at least sixteen hands tall and well over 1000 pounds of strong muscular body under their shimmering coats and brushed out tails. Yes, I *was* very thankful that I had found someone who loved horses as much as I did. Well, I was finally off to the races for what was either feast or famine!

I previously prepared the colts' new home at the race track three days before by thoroughly cleaning out each stall, then spraying the walls with a fresh pine-smelling deodorizer and disinfectant. The next day, I spread a couple of bags of sawdust in the middle of each stall to absorb the horses "wetness" as quickly as possible. I then shook four large bales of clean straw over the complete stall, which made a very nice and thick two-foot-deep bed for when they wanted to lie down. I then put hooks on the wall to hang their stainless steel water pails and grain tubs. I also hung a rope net for hay to be placed inside, for easier eating.

With all of this completed, I unloaded my trailer which contained the new harness, blankets, race bikes, etc. into the tack room next to the horses' stalls. I also brought twenty bales of straw and hay, along with ten bags of specially-mixed grain. By the end of the second day, I was very tired. I knew that I could now unload the colts immediately, after the long road trip to the track.

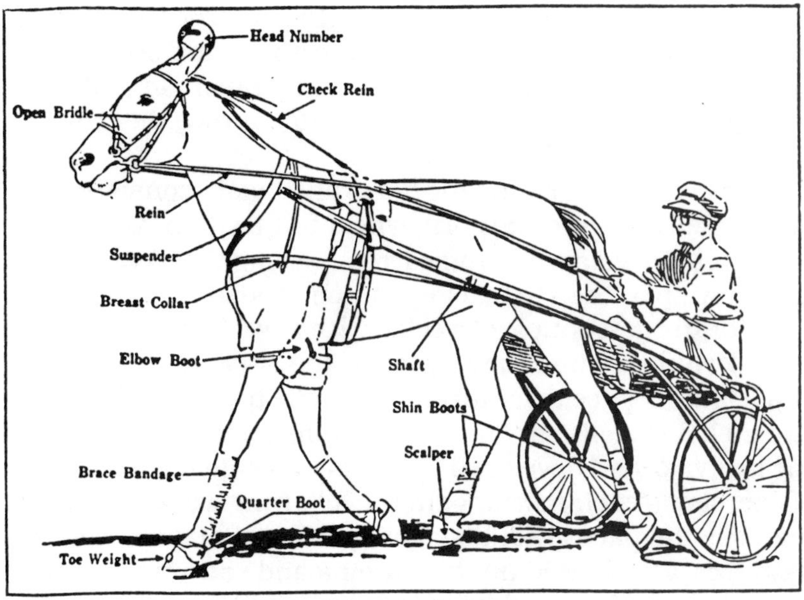

Race horse tack, Trotter.

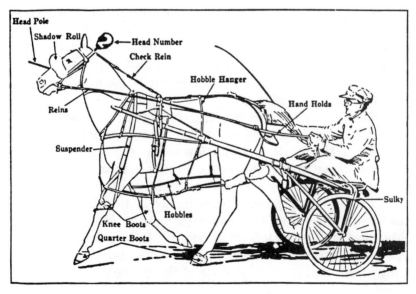

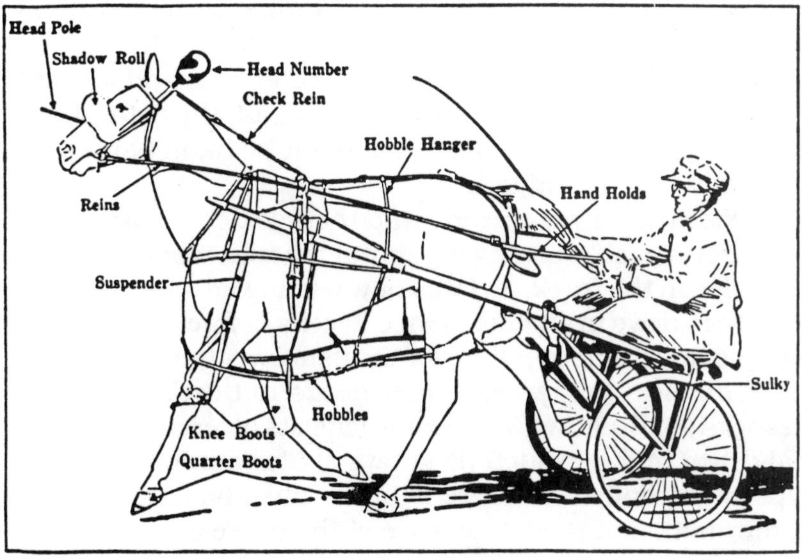

Race horse tack, Pacer.

I arrived at the track late in the afternoon. Within minutes, the colts were rolling in the straw and stretching out their legs. Standing still in a moving trailer isn't all that comfortable. If there had been a way to improve this condition, I would have done it.

The colts were eating the hot brand mash, consisting of hot soaked oats, ground corn, wheat bran, vitamins, a little molasses, sliced apples and carrots. Seeing this, I went out for my supper, then to bed for a much needed night's sleep.

For the first couple of weeks, with new shoes put on the colts, I would see how they jogged on the track. I let them run at a leisurely pace twice around the mile track which had a one inch dirt cushion. The light training on the farm during the last year had developed the colts into enjoying this type of exercising each morning. In the following weeks, I would increase the pace gradually, going three to four miles each day. This would build up the stamina and endurance of the animals. When I saw that they were handling the distance with ease, I would start using a stop watch, one day per week, for a mild one mile work out. Then by the third month, increase this to two work days per week with days in between for light jogging exercise.

By September, both colts were running fast miles of two minutes and ten seconds. To my surprise, Michael John was handling his workouts with much greater ease and wanted to go even faster. I thought that Mike's Lad, the better bred colt, would be a much faster horse but he hadn't shown it yet. Only time would tell.

With the leaves turning into their golden colors and a cool breeze each morning nipping at my face, while I trained the colts on the track, all I was now waiting for was my track license to drive in an official race. Weeks before, I had taken a plane to Columbus, Ohio, for the usual written test, which takes on the average about three hours, at the U.S. Trotting Association Building. This exam consists of testing a potential driver on how much he knows of Standardbred horses type of equipment, different horse bits, types of shoes, conformation of the horse, care of the horse and racing in general.

Finally, on the 3rd day of October, I was ready for my

first official race at a pari-mutuel race track. My license had arrived in the mail and I had already driven in more than twenty-five qualifying races months before without any trouble. I gave each horse a few more fast workouts and both colts were running in two minutes five seconds. Michael John, however, was still doing it much more easily than Mike's Lad. They were ready for their first race. At that time, the maiden races were going in at two minutes six and two minutes seven seconds.

I called up the Murphys, and invited them to see the first race. I had reserved a motel room for them on the 12th of October. Mike's Lad would run on the 12th and Michael John on the following night.

As I was jogging Mike's Lad for his first warm-up mile, past the well-lighted grandstand of Washington Park, some thirty miles south of Chicago, I could see all of the people from the other side of the fence where I once stood dreaming of sitting on a sulky, driving in a race like this. It had taken over seven years to fulfill my dream, so now it was up to me to make the most of my money spent and long hours of hard work. I let Laddie, as I called him, run a medium pace the opposite way of the track for about two miles. A quarter mile from the finish line I turned him around the right way down on the rail, this being the "rule of all Standardbred racing."

I started Laddie off slowly, letting him go a little faster as we neared the start and finish line. I had a very tight hold on the leather lines as I clicked my stop watch at the start. He was trying to go faster than I wanted him to, but talking with my voice and hands, I soon got him settled down. I went into the first half at a leisurely pace of one minute and thirty seconds. The second half in one minute and ten seconds all under a very tight hold. It was a very good warm-up mile for he wasn't even blowing even though the track had been rained on just a couple of hours earlier.

I brought him back to the barn, unhooking the equipment and putting a couple of blankets on him to keep him warm. Forty-five minutes later, I took him out for his last warm-up mile. It was a whole lot better for he and I both had gotten over our nervousness. This time I took him right to the top of the stretch, which was a quarter-mile from the line, and then I turned. He was full of energy. It was a good thing that I had leather hand-holds attached to the driving lines because they would have slipped right through. We went the first half in one minute and fifteen seconds and the last half-mile in one minute and ten seconds. As the air was biting my face, I felt as though I was flying with all of that power in my hands and plenty in reserve!

Taking him now back to the paddock for his race, which was carded number four, I noticed that the horses were now entering the track, in line for the first race. My groom, Charlie, whom I had hired to help me on the race night, was waiting for me. We quickly unhooked the sulky then backed Laddie into his open stall. We offered him a drink of water from his pail, but he didn't care for any. He wasn't even blowing, which meant that all of those slow jogging miles I had taken him out for all of those months had made a strong, fit animal. After Charlie had everything all cleaned up, and I checked Laddie over, I went out to see how the speeds were going in the second race, with the muddy track and all.

When I walked back from the fence, about 50 yards away, Charlie wanted to know if he could place a little bet on Laddie. I told him, "Not tonight. Let's just first see what I have when I get out there." I wasn't going to push him that hard his first time out. "If I can win easily, I will." He did draw a very poor post position, number eight.

Finally, I heard the paddock judge yell out, "Put your bridles on for the fourth race." After checking the sulkie's tires (about the size of the tires from a ten-speed bicycle), I got on and told Charlie, "Well, it's taken me a long time to get to this night!"

As we headed to the track in single file, the familiar sound of the bugle playing through the speakers high above the grandstand announced our arrival for the race. People were rushing down to the fence for a closer look at the horses and their drivers in their own colored jackets and white pants. My jacket was blue, with a silver diamond star on the front and back. Similarly, my helmet was blue with a small silver star on each side. Within ten minutes, this race would be started after the post parade; like the man said after mowing his lawn, "It won't be long now!"

As we made our turn back up the stretch to where the mobile starting gate was waiting, I couldn't help but look at the tote board to see what the odds were on my horse. It was no surprise to me — 80 to 1! I smiled and thought to myself, "Well, there aren't too many people who have faith in me, and this is my first and Laddie's first race."

A voice came from the mobile gate starter. He was sitting in a chair mounted at the top of a convertible Buick automobile. I heard him say, "Okay, drivers, you can bring them up." I thought, "That eighth post position looks a long way out from the rail. The shortest way around any track...Well, no use worrying about it now." I yelled, "Come on Laddie, Let's go for a little ride." I could sense that the other drivers had their eyes on me, knowing that this was my maiden "voyage".

Soon, I was behind the big, long arms of the starting gate that held the horses in line. It was moving down the stretch, picking up speed. Laddie's ears were straight up and my hands felt of sweat with the tight hold I had. Laddie's nose even bumped the gate, as if to say, "Let me go, and get that damn thing out of here!"

Just at that second, the long arms folded in forward and the race was up for grabs. With a very tight hold, I started to ease Laddie over to the rail, for there was no way in hell I was going to let a green three-year old bust out to grab the lead and maybe get hung out there three or four wide into the clubhouse turn. Before the turn, I got settled into the sixth place with horses parked on the outside of the front end. I checked my stopwatch and noticed about thirty seconds for that first quarter mile. In that heavy mud, I figured that was a might much, so I sat, as I had planned, without changing my position.

Halfway around the track, some drivers were already going to the whip for more speed. Laddie was trying to get away from the horse ahead of me. The driver was banging away at his horse with the whip, so down the back stretch I eased him out. It was some kind of feeling, passing up all of those tired horses at the top of the stretch. I was fourth on the outside, looking at the other three horses. The third and second were under fire from their drivers. The leader was doing pretty well. I thought, "Well, Laddie, coming in second place won't be to much of a disappointment." At the finish line, we were in second place, just two lengths from the winner. As I turned Laddie, I patted his rear, telling him that he had run "a mighty fine race, mighty fine."

I looked at my stop watch. It showed the mile in two minutes and seven seconds on a muddy track. Charlie was waiting at the paddock for me.

It was a pleasant walk back to the barn to give Laddie a hot shampoo bath. I then covered him with three blankets and walked out with three swallows of water every five minutes, until he was cooled out and dry. Then I wrapped his legs with cotton and bandages after a light rub with Absorbine.

By this time, Laddie was ready for his hot bran mash for he put his nose right to the bottom of the pail, and came up with a mouthful of sliced apples and carrots, along with his grain. With that, I took Charlie out for a thick prime rib dinner as well as the Murphy family. They informed me that they placed a little wager on Laddie, who paid $57.00 for every two dollars wagered, for second place. I didn't ask how much they won. They were just thrilled since this was their first time at the races. I reminded them that we had to do this all over again tomorrow night with Michael John. They laughed and remarked, "Let's hope that the outcome will be the same or better."

It was very hard for me to get any sleep that night, even though it was two o'clock in the morning. The excitement was just too great and I wanted to enjoy every second. I finally dozed off sometime after, but it was soon 6:00 a.m. At least I wouldn't have too much to do at the barn that morning, for later on that afternoon, Laddie would be taken out for a walk and Michael John would be taken to the blacksmith for a new set of steel shoes. They cost $28.00 for the set, which was more than I paid for my shoes!

I had Charlie come over for the 4:00 feeding to sit and listen to the radio and keep an eye on things while I went out for a bite to eat. Just as a precautionary measure, I had a few plans of my own that night. Seeing how it was starting to rain again, I knew that the track would be like a mud bath. Of course, not having my weekly check from the trucking company for the past few months, my bank account was looking a little pale.

I met the Murphys in the parking lot of the restaurant, handing them an envelope with a few dollars in it. I instructed them to bet it all on Michael John just three minutes before post time. I told them that there would be enough there for them as a bonus for all of the work and care they gave my colts on the farm. With that, we went in for a light dinner.

Dependable Charlie was waiting for us when we drove up to the barn area. Eventually, we started to prepare for the race. With all of this rain, things would be a mess out there tonight. I told Charlie that after the second warm up, we would take off the complete muddy spare harness and quickly put on the regular dry one that we would have ready in a plastic bag. That leather can get extremely heavy with all the rain and mud that will soak in it.

One thing I learned about the two colts was that Michael John was very sure-footed. His size and strength was a big asset over other horses on a muddy track. Michael John seemed to be enjoying his warm up. It was around sixty-eight degrees. For that time of the year this wasn't too shabby. The first warm-up mile went remarkably well, under a very firm hold, in two minutes and thirty-five seconds. Forty-five minutes later, we were on the track for his last warm-up mile.

I turned at the top of the stretch as usual and I could feel the power from Michael John wanting to run much faster than he was supposed to. We flew by the half-mile pole in one minute and ten seconds. Under an extremely tight hold, we crossed the wire in the second half in one minute and five seconds. We had a two minute and fifteen second warm up on a muddy track — I'll take that any time! I just hoped that no other horseman bothered to clock this warm up or Michael John would be bet down to less than even money.

Getting into the Paddock, just before the horses were coming out for the second race, without saying a word, Charlie quickly took off all of the equipment and the harness that I knew would be full of mud. He put the three dry blankets on him, covering the big frame of this fine animal. I checked out the third race. It went in only two minutes and eight seconds which told me that the mud was really slowing the speed of the horses down. As the horses were going out for the fourth race, we started to put the clean dry harness, new knee boots and new tendon boots on him. These boots are a great insurance protection for the knees and below. By the time we had the clean sulky attached, the familiar voice from the paddock judge came over the speakers saying, "Bridle up the fifth race." I said to Charlie, "It seems that I've done this before," as he was hooking the driving lines to the ring of the bridle bit. I put on my helmet and large amber glasses, which would be the only kind to wear during a muddy race like this one. I would only be able to see by peeking over the top edge of the glasses, due to all the splashing and flying mud from the horse's feet. As the number four horse left his stall, Charlie led Michael John out. I had drawn the number five post position. I was surprised to see so many people out by the fence in the grandstand and clubhouse. Finally, the rain stopped.

As we made our turn to head up the stretch, I neared the tote board, I took a sideways glance at it and saw number five at 80 to 1. Just simply amazing. Obviously, no one paid any attention to my last warm-up mile. I told my horse, "Well, Michael John, the sooner we finish this race, the sooner you get your hot shampoo bath and hot bran mash." I always believed that he understood me. His ears were standing taut and he was looking straight ahead as we neared the mobile starting gate. The judge called out, "All right, bring the horses." The gate started to move ever so slowly then picked up speed. I wanted to sit about fifth or sixth in the race for the first half-mile. There were at least four horses that were front runners judging by the race track program. In this mud I knew they wouldn't last if they got hooked up in a speed duel.

Soon we were at the sixteenth pole and the big Buick was giving all it had to speed away with the gates folding inwards. As expected, four horses were out to get in front before the clubhouse turn. As I got to the rail, I peered over the top edge of my mud-covered glasses. Near as I could guess, I was sixth or seventh. I knew that Michael John was thinking, "How about getting me off this rail and to the middle of the track." I kept yelling to him, "Take it easy, Old Boy!" Pretty soon it was too sloppy to even bring a stop watch in this mess. I would have to use my own judgment on when to pull out. One thing was sure — I wouldn't get boxed in back here. With the tight hold I had, there was plenty of steam on the kettle in my horse tonight.

As we went past the half-mile pole, the front four horses were still banging away with another horse going three wide. With the back stretch turn coming up, I decided to wait until the top of the stretch. With a quarter of a mile left in the race, I still had a good chance, unless those front-running horses had a pickup truck waiting to take them the rest of the way home. I now could see a lot of whips moving in the air. Michael John's nose was right on top of the driver's helmet in front of me. Coming out of the turn for home, I eased Michael John out. I didn't have to say a thing. Taking him into the middle of the track was the long way, but I wanted to play it safe. Those front-runners had to be very tired and that's dangerous as one could stumble and go down.

I passed so many horses coming down the stretch, I could have sworn that some of them were still out there from the last race. At the eight-mile pole, I now only saw one horse. I recognized the colors of red and gray of D. Busse. He wasn't in the front four and must have been the horse I saw going three wide in the back stretch. I waved the whip in midair as I flew by. The finish line was two lengths in front.

It was such an exciting feeling that I'll never forget it. I suppose that the first win is always the most important one. It sure was for me.

Easing Michael John to a complete stop, I sat there for a couple of seconds. The thought of what just happened suddenly flashed through my mind. To think that if I had not gotten stuck in that snow-covered rut on the farm almost three years ago, I wouldn't be sitting here now. I gave thanks for that.

I turned Michael John around patting his rear end and headed for the winner's circle for some picture taking. Jim Karubas, whom I had known for some time, and who owned a restaurant, was already waiting for a picture. He was saying, "Gee, why didn't you tell me that this horse could pace like that? I only bet $50.00 on him." I told him that I didn't know either how he would run in this kind of sloppy track. The old saying is, "Never tell all you know." I didn't want the Murphy family in the winner's circle for fear someone watching would follow them when they went to cash in the winning tickets.

I was then off to the detention barn for the after-race test of each winner. No problem. My horses are never given any type of drugs.

The time of the race was two minutes and six seconds. Charlie had all of the hot water ready as well as clean blankets and towels. Just as the night before, we duplicated the process, only tonight a bonus was waiting for us. When the Murphys drove up to my barn, they had a plastic bag with a lot of green lettuce in it, but not the kind found in a grocery store!

With Michael John eating his hot bran mash, I called Charlie over from where he was washing down all of my muddy equipment. I told him to put out both hands. In doing so, I placed a fistful of fifty dollar bills in them, telling him that I had these people bet $100.00 on me to win for him, along with some for me and themselves.

The odds probably dropped at the last minute from 80 to 1 to 31 to 1. Michael John paid $64.20 for every $2.00 wager.

5th, $1,400, pace, mile:
Michael John [Horak] 64.20 21.60 10.00
Irish Oaks [Busse] 14.80 8.20
Air Queen [Robinson] 4.40
Post positions—5, 3, 7. Time, 2:06. Hi Skipper, Adios Mickey, Little Queen, Red Angus, Justly One, Dolly Varden started.

My first win and Michael John's first win.

Chapter 2

A Rude Awakening

November, 1966: It started out to be a very sad and dark time in my life. I had gone to the track barn at 5:30 a.m., as usual, to feed the horses. An hour or so later, I started to get Michael John ready for a light workout on the track, as I had him entered for another race in two days. As I walked him out of his stall, I noticed a slight limp in his left front foot, and he was not setting it down firmly. I checked for any sign of swelling or heat, but found nothing. Still, he was favoring this leg. I put him back in his stall and went to get the track veterinary.

After waiting two days for the results of the X-rays that the vet had taken of Michael John's foot, I was informed that the worst possible thing had happened to my colt; he had a fractured sesamoid, the area just below the ankle. This I could not let myself believe, as there was no swelling or heat. These are known to be the first signs of a major injury as this. The vet then told me that he would keep this information quiet, and that he could give my horse a Butazolidin shot, a pain killer. He explained that for the next three days after the injection, the horse would walk as though he were as sound as a dollar. He added that it would be the best for me to sell him as quickly as possible, because Michael John would never race again. In shock, and unable to accept this diagnosis, I simply said that he should send me his bill and sent him away.

After recovering from this jolting news, I thought back on what could have happened to make this horse come up lame overnight. Then I remembered having the track horse-shoer put new shoes on him just the day before. With this revelation, I had a different blacksmith come over to see

Michael John. I asked him to take the left front shoe off my horse. He pulled out the first two nails — they were put in correctly; but as soon as he started to remove the third nail, my horse jumped into the air. I could see blood flowing from the foot where the third nail had been driven in. The nail had been hammered into the tender part of the horse's foot and not the toe nail where there would be no feeling.

The blacksmith said that he had never seen such a stupid thing done to a horse. I agreed and paid him, then he left. This information I kept to myself, but never forgot it. I soaked Michael John's foot, and put on a poultice to draw out the soreness. Within a week, I had a horse ready to race again.

Amazing! The morning following this incident, two trainers came to my barn saying that the vet had told them I might want to sell my horse; and if the price was right, they might be inclined to make a deal. I said, "Not today!" It was one week later that I learned that these same two trainers were friends of the blacksmith that caused the injury to my horse, and very good personal friends of the vet in the scheme. They were all out to get a good horse — cheap!

The vet sent me a bill for $429.00. This I took to him and told him that there was no way I would pay him one red cent. In the same breath, I told him to charge it to the dust and let the rain settle it. I also told him what I suspected, and if he still insisted on payment, he should take his case to the track officials. He quietly walked away and that was the end of that! Three years later, I learned that he was barred from race tracks for doping horses. What goes around, comes around!

My first encounter with these shady clowns almost put me out of business before I even got started. I suppose the temptation was just too great. It had probably been years since they had seen a good three and a half year old horse entered into a race and win with such ease under the poorest of racing conditions, without any drugs used. Most horses are put into their first races at the age of two. This is much too young for this animal. It's like putting an eight year old boy to work in a coal mine or digging a ditch, then expecting the same results as a twenty-one year old.

This is what greed will do. I asked myself, "What the hell kind of hornets' nest did I get myself into?" I had better learn fast, or I would be out in the streets selling pencils and chewing gum for a living very soon. Tomorrow I would be out looking for a Doberman Pinscher watchdog to protect my colts. It didn't matter about the cost. As the old Boy Scout's saying goes, "Be prepared!"

Claiming races at horse tracks are the same for Thoroughbred as well as Standardbred race horses. At each race track, over half the races are made up as claiming races starting with minimum at each track. At a major track, this could be around $5,000.00, with the best horses on the grounds for this meet reaching $45,000.00. The time a horse has been finishing his races would determine what class of claiming race a trainer would enter that horse in.

The reason for these claiming races is that the greater number of these horses do not have the speed to match that of the better bred horses, which run in the handicap or allowance races with much larger purses. Once a horse has been entered in a claiming race for a stated amount, he can be purchased by any horse owner who has a horse on the grounds of that track. With a certified check already made out, a claiming slip must be dropped into the claim box in the racing secretary's office, fifteen minutes before post time of the race the horse is entered in.

The person making the claim does not receive any of the purse money that the horse may win for that particular race, but, if the horse is injured in any way during the race, the expense for that injury falls on the owner who claims the horse after the race. Anyone claiming a horse from a race should know that it is one of the biggest gambles in racing. The horse could actually be lame, of poor breeding quality, or too old to be of much value. Once the horse is entered in a race, there is no way of checking to discover how sound the horse really is. Some trainers and owners get around this by just happening to meet up with the groom who takes care of the horse. By slipping the groom a few dollars or promising him a nice, new suit of clothes, you can learn much from a groom — much more than from a trainer, who is with the horse only a small part of each day. The groom would be there, when the trainer would have the vet over to give the horse an injection, be it a pain killer, Lasix or a vitamin shot.

What an owner would have to ask himself now is, "Can I correct this horse's problem? Does his breeding merit a risk after doing these checks and watching the horse's past races? "

Most owners, and their trainers, employ the same vet, thus becoming a very, very, friendly team. The prospect of cashing a wager on their horse could indeed influence a vet, to insure the outcome of a certain, well-planned race with drugs that he normally wouldn't inject into the horse.

I know of a case where an owner had a very well-bred Standardbred horse in a stable just three stalls from mine. He had bought his colt at a yearling sale, for $58 thousand and had put well over $40 thousand into trainers' pay and other expenses over the next two years. The horse had never come close to winning a race. Another year went by with no wins. By this time the horse was four years old and still a "maiden" (one who has never won a race). Each morning the owner would come to see the horse. The trainer could be heard saying very loudly that because of the horse's speed time in his last five races, he should be entered in $25,000.00 claiming races, or even lower.

By this time, the owner was running low on funds, but still believed in his horse. He wanted to give his "baby", Lincolnari, one more race. The horse again ran a poor race, finishing in 2:04 for the mile. Ten days later, Lincolnari was entered into a $20,000.00 claiming race. He was claimed while finishing last in slow time. It was interesting to note, however, that the former trainer and the new trainer were always seen together, going out to lunch, going out to the country for straw for the horses, etc. Just a couple of "Good Ol'e Boys."

I took notice of the entries for the week, following the sale of Lincolnari. It was no surprise to see this horse entered in a "conditioned" race rather than a "claiming" race. Anyone with a little understanding of a racing form would think from results of his past six races that he had no chance in this conditioned race, classified as horses who have not won more than two races in their lifetime. Their speed time averaged 2:01 for a mile race, about fifteen lengths faster than Lincolnari had been running. (Each second is equivalent to five lengths of a horse.)

My suspicions and curiosity aroused, I attended the races for that evening. It was not too long before my feelings proved to be correct. The program had Lincolnari listed in the number eight post position. A disadvantage, I thought, being on the outside. Many times I had not bet on a horse, just because of a bad post position. As the horses paraded down the track before the race. I noticed that Lincolnari looked very fit, very alert, and had his ears straight out. The tote board showed his odds as 60 to 1, ten minutes before post time. Then, three minutes to post time, just as I had suspected, the odds on Lincolnari dropped to 40 to 1, then to 30 to 1, until ,just one minute before post time, it reached 20 to 1. There had to be some big money put on this horse for the odds to fall so sharply!

Being near the $50.00 window, I placed a small wager on Number 8, just to satisfy my hunch that this horse's speed had never been fully tapped, and that he had never been "let out" by his previous trainer-driver. From the time the mobile starting gate opened up, I was wishing that I had bet more, as Lincolnari went right to the top of this field of horses. At the quarter-mile pole, he was five lengths in front with the drivers whip tucked firmly under his arm. He knew he wouldn't be needing it for this race. Lincolnari won the race in the fast time of 2:01 by ten lengths under a firm hold. Final odds were 12 to 1. The former owner had obviously been "sold out"! What a shame, believing in the horse as he did, that he hadn't hired a different trainer, instead of being talked into running his horse in a claiming race, only to have it "stolen" from him. This horse, in the next two years, earned over $195,000.00, with a time record of 1:56 2/5 for a one-mile race. Need I say more!

Horse doping has been going on for as long as there have been races where money can be made quickly. One drug that has contributed to this is Lasix. It is injected into a horse who is a "bleeder". This is a horse that, due to the stress of a race, will bleed in his lungs. Lasix is a proven drug known to prevent this. In years past you could find about one horse in a hundred who would be considered a bleeder. As soon as it was made known that other illegal drugs could be mixed in with Lasix, and that they would be very difficult to detect in the blood test given each winner of a race, more and more horses were reported to the racing officials as bleeders. They would then be permitted to give their horses Lasix injections by the track vet. There are now as many as fifty percent listed on some racing programs as Lasix users.

I read in the newspaper that four very high-priced, Thoroughbred horses had won their races with ease, but failed in the after-race drug test. It was also noted that all horses had been injected with Lasix, but there was something else in the bloodstream. After five months of trying to locate this illegal substance, the case was dismissed for lack of evidence. The four trainers, who were the Nation's leaders in the past, were pleased about this decision. No doubt about it!

For the people who go to the races, betting on claiming races is a very quick way to leave the track with an empty billfold before the seventh race comes around, as ninety percent of the first six races are of this kind. The reason for this statement is that most of these horses have one or another kind of a soreness or problem. This is why they are entered in this kind of race in the first place. When an owner finds out what part of his horse is hurting, he will then try to have the vet at the track inject the horse with a pain killer called Butazolidin or cortisone with an added vitamin B12 shot, and liver and iron to pep him up, and Lasix.

If this helped the horse to win or come in second, most owners that I know, if they did not want to lose this horse to other owners, would not give this horse any kind of shots for the next two or three races. The horse would then perform badly in these next races, and any other owners would lose interest. On the other hand, if he gave the horse the same shots, it, in all likelihood, would finish first or second and in the racing form would begin looking like a good horse to buy. The public would see him as a good horse to bet on, but a very poor investment would be noted by a wise horseman.

Once they are given these shots, ninety percent of these horses can never perform well without them, and only one in a hundred will ever be able to win against allowance horses in the better races, even though these horses are also given some kind of injection. The allowance horses have a much better blood line, and the cost of buying one is a hundred times higher. From the start, they are given much better care in their training, and when one comes up lame, in most cases, it is taken to a farm for a rest. This way, the horse is given a chance to heal Mother Nature's way, and is not left at the track for a vet to inject with different drugs. That would leave him crippled for life.

In harness racing, the purse is split up five ways. Fifty percent to the winner, twenty-five percent to the second place horse, twelve and a half percent to the third, seven and a half percent to the fourth, and five percent for fifth place. Once a horse has won, he must race in a higher class with better horses or go into a claiming race, where it can be decided in which price race to enter him. A horse finishing second at most major tracks can again race in this same class race. If he finishes second twice, he will have won the same amount as a winner, yet still stay in this same class, as in maiden races.

Recently, I was shocked and in total bitterness when I read in a local newspaper about the brutal and savage beating of a Thoroughbred horse. Former barn manager, Tommy Burns, 30, of Park City, Illinois, and codefendant Harlow Arlie, 32, beat the horse with a steel crowbar.

The horse's owner offered them $5,000.00 to kill the seven-year old chestnut gelding, worth $25,000.00 in insurance money. Of course, both pleaded "No Contest" to insurance fraud and animal cruelty at the Canterbury Farms.

Burns said that many Thoroughbred owners were in financial trouble, and had resorted to having their lame horses killed to collect the insurance money, rather than selling the animals at a tremendous loss.

Had I been their judges, I would have sentenced these two "lunatics" to be hanged by their feet at a busy Main Street corner, so each passerby could give them a whack with the same steel crow bar that they had used. This would be real justice, instead of being sentenced to prison, as they were.

The only good thing to come out of all this is that more investigating is still being done. This is just the beginning of many more Federal indictments out of Chicago, Illinois, and other states. It was also noted that, "This case is big. There are some big people involved." Assistant State's Attorney, E. Pooley, confirmed that other agencies were involved, but declined to name them.

Not long ago, there was another disastrous example of all this cruelty. The use of dangerous drugs, caused by greed to insure the outcome of a race, resulted in the death of four Thoroughbred horses at Mammoth Park Race Track in Oceanport, New Jersey. It involved the same stable and trainer.

Chapter 3
Vacation Time

Amazing at it may be, a couple of days after the first win, my little stable started to get some recognition by some other owners. They wanted me to drive their horses, whereas a week before, they didn't even know my first name. I thought to myself, "Don't these guys know that it's the horse that gets the driver over the finish line? For it's illegal for the driver to get off his sulky at the top of the stretch, and carry the horse over the finish line."

In other words, if the horse is properly trained and treated well, he will have a better chance of entering the winner's circle. So began my full time career as a harness driver, and the steady chicken dinners without the feathers.

Obviously, many of the horses I was asked to drive were poorly cared for. A good, hot-bran mash for a horse after a race was unheard of. The groom of these horses would put a gallon can of oats in their feed tub and leave. There was no way I could change this world overnight.

With the first signs of winter and a few extra dollars salted away, I planned to keep my promise to the colts, that if we had a few bucks, a nice, warm vacation would be had by all in sunny Florida. They must have understood, for they started to move their heads up and down. Of course, holding a couple of apples in front of them had nothing to do with this response.

So, now, on this cold, windy day in November with everything packed, we just waited for the semitrailer to arrive at the Maywood Park track in Illinois. I left Charlie in charge while I drove to the Paddlewheel Restaurant, three blocks away. I went there to get a couple of Greek-style chicken dinners, a couple of apple pies and some other goodies, for we had a 1,400-mile trip ahead. I now had two extra colts to feed since I had bought half interest in each from Jim Karubas, who owned a restaurant. I figured that if things got bad, I would at least have a place to get a bowl of soup and a sandwich. I hoped that it sure would never come down to that, since this business is, most of the time, "chicken, today, feathers, tomorrow!"

Two hours later, Charlie and I were following the horse van, with my four, and eight others, being driven south on Route 65 in Indiana. We took turns driving, stopping at times to feed and rest the horses. We had a man standing in the van, for the safety of the horses, looking over them.

With the semi drivers taking turns, we arrived in Florida after forty-one hours on the road and a temperature change of sixty degrees warmer under a sunny blue sky and palm trees. It was like I had turned the calender back some four months. I thought, "What a way to go."

My horses must have thought that they were in heaven, as they were running in the farm's pasture, lined with white wooden fences for their three months vacation. I would start driving other owners' horses at the local race track. The eighty-degree weather isn't too hard to take. It was really neat to turn on the television news each evening and see those little white flakes falling from the cold, windy, five-degree-below-zero skies in Chicago. A few times, I called Ted Glazos at his Paddlewheel restaurant, and Jim Karubas to let them know of the winners I had driven, while sweating under the sunny, blue skies. It did give me a thrill to rub it in about the weather, being my first winter in Florida. I wouldn't be shoveling any snow or getting stuck in a snowbank with a semi or a car.

Spring of 1967 arrived all too quickly and meant going back up north, where the decent purses were. The race tracks in Florida are very small. The main reason for going back, however, is that I saw many drivers holding back their horses, while having money bet on the horse in front of them. Almost every night, someone would approach me with some sort of a scheme to insure the outcome of a race. Soon after, they learned that I always gave an owner's horse the best possible chance of winning as I could. I wasn't getting rich, but I was able to sleep at night.

To some of the more stupid trainer-drivers, I would have to ask, "What part of 'no' don't you understand?"

With dandelions in full bloom in the infield of the race track, it obviously meant one thing to me — I was at Washington Park Track. It was located just south of Chicago in Homewood, Illinois.

Each morning, with the help of my loyal friend, Charlie, we would have the horses fed and ready for their workouts by 8:00 a.m. We used the new lightweight nylon harnesses, for I had sold all four sets of the old style leathers ones. The nylon could be cleaned in minutes by placing in a tub of warm, soapy water, then a quick rinse. It would be dry in no time. This saved me hours of saddle-soaping the leather harness and would be pounds lighter on the horse. While I was on the track, letting my horse jog at a slow pace for his first couple of miles, I couldn't help but notice the beautiful golden-brown shining coat on each of my horses. This was from being in the Florida sun, roaming free in the green pasture on the farm, compared to the other horses that had trained all winter in Illinois.

As other drivers would pull along side me, they would remark, "That Florida sun sure makes a horse look good!" Of course, I also had a nice brown tan.

It was a great expense, doing all this, but I knew that you only get out of life what you put into it. Yes, I was sure that my horses would give 100 percent in trying to get me into the winner's circle.

They did just that in the following months. They had earned me plenty of framed pictures for my wall. As I suspected, Michael John was at least ten lengths faster than Mike's Lad, or the two other colts, owned by Jim Karubas. I knew that I would have to make a tough decision down the road sometime, on what to do when there were no other "conditions" races that they would be competitive in. At that time, I had no intentions of throwing them to the greedy wolves, via the claiming races. I wouldn't think of this until the time would arrive. Maybe Laddie, at least, would develop more speed. It was in his blood line. Only time would tell. I knew that it would be nice if it did happen, but I was grateful for what he had done for me already.

By October, after many conversation with Jim, we decided to ship both of his colts to his brother in Kentucky and retire them. His children would take care of them, while taking slow afternoon riding sessions, for this type of horse is great with teenagers.

I would retire Mike's Lad and return him to the Murphy farm, where he was raised. The folks were very pleased to hear of this.

Michael John would be taken back to Florida for his usual vacation in November. In the spring, he would start training for the 1968 summer racing, while I started looking for another couple of yearlings. I thought that by the time I retired my horses, the new ones would be ready. I also knew that plans are easily made, but carrying them out is another thing.

Chapter 4

The Devil's Disciples

Spring of 1968: I shipped my horse back to Illinois for the summer and fall racing meets. The weeks went by swiftly, as the speed of the horses increased. I knew that it wasn't Mother Nature's doing, but the results of new drugs that were being used. The same horses that had been finishing their races in two minutes and four seconds, were now running in two minutes and one second. No, this was the doings of Mother Veterinarian.

In every race, one couldn't help but notice the large number of horses that were injected with Lasix, and Lord only knows what else.

In my first four races at Sportsman Park, Michael John finished no better than third. In his last race, I took a good look at the horse that was passing me like a wild animal on drugs. His eyes were bulging out from his eye sockets. I knew that this was very far from normal. I sure as hell wasn't going to use my whip to ask for more speed to try to keep up with this kind of a horse. I finished fourth and Charlie and I cooled out Michael John. I told Charlie that I would never race another horse at this track as long as I would live. After Michael John was given a couple of days to rest, we would get out of this "rat race track".

With Michael John on one side of my two-horse trailer, and the equipment on the other, my Chrysler Imperial pulled the trailer smoothly out onto the open highway, heading for Kentucky.

This was a nice, carefree trip during the last week of June. Leaving early in the morning, I had the big horses bedded down before dark. I left Charlie and my Doberman in charge, while I checked into a motel. Gee, I thought, I am sure tired. I think that most of it had to do with the stress and the knowledge that Sportsman Park officials must have been taking sleeping pills not to take a little notice around the back door of their race track.

The next day was warm and sunny. Just next to the barn area was a field of red Clover, which was owned by a track called Latonia Trots, ten miles south of Cincinnati, Ohio. Each afternoon I would let Michael John graze on the luscious, sweet clover which grew over a foot high. After his morning workouts, he was getting so frisky that I figured I'd better put him in a race soon.

I found an easy spot on the 28th of June. It would be a fun workout, compared to what he had been up against. Drawing the number one position would make it even easier. I told Charlie, "We won't make much from the purse of this race, and if the general public checks out the racing form a bit, they'll all be emptying out their cookie jars of mad money to wager on Michael John!" Charlie let out the biggest laugh I've ever heard. So did I. My dog even started to bark his approval. Yes, we needed to forget about that last track.

With this mile-around type of track, there would be little chance of any other driver trying to pin me up against the rail with a horse in front of me. I was now smart enough to know that where the track purses are small, the drivers greed grow large. I also knew that many of these drivers were "Good Ol'e Boys".

Turning Michael John for his second warm-up mile on this clear, warm night, it was a great temptation to warm-up a fast mile and let him get a new lifetime record. This thought only lasted a split second. I knew that because of the small purse money, Charlie wouldn't collect enough from our bet to buy a hamburger. So setting the line handholds up, in order to have a good, strong hold, we headed down the stretch for the start. A two minute and twenty-five second warm-up mile would be more than enough. He really took off, and was enjoying himself, doing the mile in two minutes and twenty-two seconds.

When Charlie put the blanket on him, he leaned over and whispered to me, "It's too bad we don't have an extra $20 thousand around to invest. I gave him a big grin.

With the sound of the bugle, we were on the track. I was really relaxed. As I headed up the stretch, as always, I looked to see how the public was betting. Knowing that Michael John should be bet down as a heavy favorite, which he was. I smiled when I saw the odds of four to five. This meant that Charlie would only get back $1,800 for my $1,000 bet. Ah!, I though. Just think of all the people we would make happy after the race. It would sure be nice if all my races were this easy.

The starter called the horses up and the track announcer could be heard saying, "The gate is rolling, and they're off!" Five horses went for the lead. Before the clubhouse turn, I was in seventh place. Practically lying flat on my back, holding Michael John back, I thought, "These guys are out to win a million dollars, the way the other drivers are using their whips, even before the half-mile pole." I then suspected that one of those five lead horses would soon get a long lead with the other four relaxing to start counting their winnings on the bets they had made.

As we turned up the backstretch, sure enough, a horse pulled away from the pack by some five to seven lengths. In doing so, he went way to fast for the first half. I eased Michael John out to the middle of the track. Passing the half-mile pole, I started passing up the four tired horses. The leader was now some five lengths ahead. Before the turn for home, I pulled along side the leader, who, by now, was using his whip as though the devil was chasing him. He looked at me in total disbelief, and yelled at me that most of the other drivers were betting on him. They would cut me in, if he won. "Sorry, George," I yelled back. "Not tonight. My grandmother is in the hospital, in need of an operation." With that said, I let Michael John out a notch, and we pulled away for a seven-length win.

Returning to the finish line, a roar of approval arose from the surprisingly large crowd. It did make me feel good every time I entered the winner's circle for a few pictures. After which, Charlie and I took Michael John back to the barn for his usual shampoo bath and hot bran mash late supper, then had our own.

We would be able to sleep late the next morning, for

LATONIA TROTS
I MILE
6-28-68
MICHAEL JOHN
PACE
2-07-0
M J. HORAK
OWNER
MICHAEL HORAK
DRIVER

Michael John winning at Latonia, Kentucky, June 28, 1968.

Michael John would be doing the same. Later on in the afternoon, I would put him on a 100-foot rope and let him graze in the red clover field. I always had a portable radio with me, so I'd be lying on the ground while Michael John would be enjoying this rare meal under the warm, sunny skies of seventy-eight degrees.

It never failed; whenever I would win a race without

using a whip, the following day other owners and trainers would be over to my stable or see me while I was having breakfast in the track's restaurant. They would want me to drive a few of their horses, and I usually accepted. Some, I would win, while others, considering how they were previously driven and abused, I would at least give them an honest drive.

After Michael John had his three-day rest, I put him back to light jogging miles. As sharp as he felt, I had him entered into the next Saturday's feature race. It would go a tad faster, but as he was feeling so good, I figured that without much trouble, we would again be visiting the winner's circle. At least that's what I was hoping!

Saturday afternoon, we gave Michael John his light lunch of a gallon can of sweetfeed. This consisted of oats, a little ground corn and molasses. We put the Doberman on a short rope next to the stall door and went out for our own meal.

Later, after Michael John's second warm-up in a very fast time of two minutes and fourteen seconds, I wasn't too surprised that a couple of other drivers, who were in my race, stopped by my stall. I had noticed them in the paddock with stop watches in their hands, when I was coming off the track.

It took them a while to get to the point, but I already knew what they had planned, and what they wanted to do. It all boiled down to me purposely getting boxed in on the rail, with the help of one of their friends in the race. The other three would be finishing in front for a big Tri-fecta payoff. They knew that with Michael John the overwhelming favorite, out of the money, their plan would be possible.

In a soft-toned voice, I told them, "Look. I'm no priest or saint, but I'm too late in this game to be in on fixing a race. So I'll just pretend that I haven't heard you. Let's leave it at that." In disgust, they left. Charlie quickly came over, wanting to know what that was all about. I just said that they wanted to know if Michael John was for sale. Charlie then said, "Hell, I could have told them what your answer would be!"

A few minutes later, the paddock judge was saying,

"Let's be putting on your bridles for the eighth race." In doing so, Charlie whispered to me, "Watch out for those two clowns." "I will," I answered, as we left for the race.

Looking at the tote board, my number five post-position, which I had been assigned earlier, showed odds as four to one. It seemed as though the number three was getting some heavy play at even money from his past three wins. I hoped that the people weren't overlooking the fact that those wins were against cheaper horses. The times of these past races were also slower than this race was going to be.

I had Charlie put a few bucks down, for we might want a hot dog after this race. As we lined up behind the mobile starting gate, I glanced over to the two drivers who want to cash an easy bet. As the mobile gate sped away, the two of them quickly went for the lead with the favorite following in third place. This left the fourth place for me. With the first half running too fast again, the situation was tailor-made for my horse to run under a snug hold. The favorite pulled out and easily took the lead at the top of the stretch. As I took after him, I could clearly hear the track announcer calling the horses. His voice got louder when he said, "Michael John is flying on the outside at the sixteenth pole." He was saying, "Michael John is in front by four lengths." "Yes!," I said to myself, "he did indeed feel as if he is flying tonight." The favorite finished second and the two clowns finished third and fourth.

Michael John came out of the race in good condition, and I was grazing him on the red clover the next day. This is the only track in America with a field like this, but very few trainers take the time to make use of it with their horses in the afternoons. The most number of horses out there at one time was eight. There were over six hundred stabled horses on the grounds.

With a few more drives, each night kept me busy. Some of the horses should have been retired years ago. I had to refuse to drive a couple of horses, due to bow tendons and swelling on the knee. All they would get in a race is hot and tired, and would finish last. I'd be better off watching television.

Then the entries came out for the following Saturday

races; to my disbelief Election Boy was listed. This horse caught my eye the first day I was on the track. He was only jogging at a leisurely pace, but had already broken out in a white lather and was blowing very hard. He was also favoring his left front leg. I just assumed that the horse, for the past couple of weeks, was being given a little exercise, trying to bring him back from whatever lameness he had developed. Apparently, this was not the case. Since I now saw the entries, one thing I knew for sure — anytime a horse is broken out with sweat and white lather, he is out of condition and hurting. A hurting, sore horse doesn't belong on a race track, let alone in a race.

Friday, when the racing form which listed all of the horses that were to race the next evening, came out, I quickly turned to the entries for the ninth race. Sure enough, there was Election Boy's past performances. He hadn't raced in three weeks. In his last race, he was leading the field until the turn for home. The form showed that he faltered in the stretch and finished fourth. His performance was about the same in the other previous starts. I knew that if he did start the next day, I knew where he would be at the first half-mile pole. Judging from the way he looked on the track a couple of days ago, the owner would, in all probability, have him withdrawn. I sure hoped so, for the horse's sake.

Saturday night, in the paddock, Michael John's last warm-up was excellent. It was under a clear, full-moon sky with the temperature around seventy degrees. This was perfect racing conditions and a fast track. Charlie had been quietly checking around the barn area to hear any news through the grapevine of Election Boy. He heard nothing, however. One thing about these local boys, they kept to themselves.

Surprisingly, coming into the paddock, broken out with white lather as usual, was Election Boy. I just shook my head, not believing my eyes. I did notice in the racing form, that two years earlier, he had raced as a two-year old, in stake races of very large purses. He had won three, but the torture on those underdeveloped bones had taken their toll. He now had to be racing on drugs. Bute, I presumed, would be the first. As poor as he looked physically, as well as the other six horses entered looking the same, I told Charlie to place the usual wager for one thousand dollars to win. I figured that Michael John would probably be the favorite. We could probably pick up a little coffee and donut money.

Following the sixth horse as we entered the track, with the sound of the bugle over the loudspeakers, I had another chance to notice Election Boy, number three. The driver was very nervous, and the horse already had a white lather sweat forming. He had a tight hold on his horse's reins. I had planned to stay away from him, until we hit the top of the stretch, in the event that he would go down or break stride. That would cause a serious accident.

As we headed back up the stretch, the tote board made me take a second glance. Election Boy was even money and my horse was three to one. What a shocking surprise that was! Somebody must have known something that I didn't. Well, I thought, it's too late to worry about it now. The judge in the mobile starting gate was saying over the car's speaker, "O.K., gentlemen, bring your horses up to the gate."

Soon, with all eight horses pacing slowly behind the gate at the top of the stretch, we were picking up speed as we neared the starting line. The track announcer informed the people in the stands that the gate was rolling, and "They're off!" With Election Boy bursting to the front, I didn't pay any attention to the others. At the half, I pulled out of sixth, as Michael John had been anxiously awaiting this moment. The first half went in a blazing fifty-eight and four-fifths seconds. I passed four horses with considerable ease, with only Election Boy still in front by two lengths. He was all broken out as though someone had sprayed his whole body with shaving cream. But the shocking thing was that the driver still had a firm hold.

With speed left for the stretch, I pulled along side, thus causing him to use his whip. As he did so, the horse responded and started to pull away with me asking Michael John to catch him. Trying as he did, there was no way I was beating that horse to the finish line tonight. I knew that it would be Election Boy going into the winner's circle. Michael John finished second in a race that went in one minute and fifty-eight seconds.

Heading back to the barn, I patted Michael John for doing a great job. I also told him that it was pretty hard to beat Old Mother Vet's drugs.

Charlie had the buckets with the warm water ready, and came over quickly to unhook Michael John from the sulky, patting him while doing so. He said, "One mighty nice race, Michael John. Mighty nice, indeed! You made Election Boy think that the Devil was chasing him down the stretch."

We cooled off Michael John, and wrapped his legs with cotton after a light rub of Absorbine. I then gave him his hot bran mash. Next, Charlie and I went out for our late-night supper, giving the Doberman a large can of Alpo dog food and a few biscuits.

The next afternoon, lying out in the clover field, Michael John was enjoying himself, not knowing that he was in the fastest race he had ever been in. A couple of owners came over wanting me to drive their horses and wanted to know if I had set a price tag on Michael John, even though they knew that the answer would be two letters, "N.O."

One thing was for sure, I wanted to see, during the next few days, what kind of condition Election Boy would be in when the drugs wore off. I didn't see him out walking with his owner in this nice, red clover field. As I had suspected, Election Boy wasn't able to walk out of his stall. The vet told me that he would be retired to a farm. "Thank Heaven for that!" was my reply.

I was very disappointed with the State of Kentucky for legalizing drugs to be administered to Thoroughbred and Standardbred horses. This state should have been setting an example about drug-free racing, like the state of New York and three others. Kentucky has always been noted for its beautiful, picturesque race horse farms, where many champions are raised. It's enough to bring a tear to your eyes, to see these fine animals being injected with Lasix and other drugs. Even now, young, two-year olds are being abused in this manner. I promised myself that when I raised my next yearlings, their races would be in a drug-free state, or I'd go back to driving a semi.

For the next three weeks, I left Charlie in charge to just take Michael John out in the clover each afternoon. I would be going to different farms in Kentucky to see what kind of prices they were asking for yearlings. After my return, we would head back to Washington Park, Illinois, for the fall meet before shipping to Florida.

The trip around the farm-lands of Kentucky was very educational and enjoyable. Seeing million-dollar stallions and yearlings that I could never afford, it made me feel like a kid in a toy store with only a dime. Seeing all of those new, brightly colored bicycles and electric trains, left me very sad when I had to leave empty-handed, but I did plan on returning one day.

We were then on our way to Washington Park to maybe make a dollar or two.

Chapter 5
Good Times

The few weeks' rest did Michael John a world of good. With only a couple of workouts, he was very sharp. In his first four starts, he finished one in third place, two in second, and won a race on September 25th, 1968, with odds of six to one. These brought me a few extra dollars of spending money, which one can never have enough of.

Maywood Park Track was only forty-five miles north. After a two-day rest, we were on the road again for their fall race meet. This track was called a "bull ring", as it was a half-mile in circumference. On this type of track, many a time, the best horse may not win. It is very easy to get boxed in on the rail. Any horse that drew the number five or further position would have a great disadvantage. Mainly because the race started at the finish line, the sharp turn at the clubhouse is only one sixteenth of a mile ahead. Many good horses had been parked out, three or four wide, thus going a longer distance than the horses on the rail. As we were all taught in school, this would be the shortest route around a circle. Most horses, when parked out for more than the first half-mile, end up in the race as an "also ran", and would be very tired, I might add.

The thing that I was really counting on was the fact that Illinois had many rainy days. As sure-footed as my horse was on a muddy track, it would be worth a chance before leaving.

The whole month of October, turned out to be like the climate in the Sahara Desert. Not a drop of rain fell from the sky that month. The first three weeks in November turned out to be a carbon copy of this.

By then, I had now raced my horse six times on this dry, white, dusty crushed lime rock-covered track that was mixed in with the sand and soil. When the heavy rain did

MICHAEL JOHN
MICHAEL JOHN HORAK
OWNER
SEPT. 25, 1968
2-04-4
WASHINGTON PARK
MICHAEL HORAK
DRIVER-TRAINER
Kuprion photo
TENTH RACE—1 MILE. PACE. Non-winners of $4,000 in 1968, non-winners of $600 at this meet. Purse $2,200. Mutuel Pool $28,718.
Horse ¼ ½ ¾ Str Fin Driver PP Odds
Michael John 4 4 2½ 1¹ 1½ M Horak4 6.30
Baby Talk 1 1 1½ 2½ 2²¼ J Mathews2 5.30
Pam Arden 3 3 3² 3² 3³ L Rapone1 2.20
Senator Glowaway 6 6 6¹ 5² 4¹ K James5 8.30
Dutch Queen 7 7 8² 6¹ 5h F O'Mara6 17.50
Ann Louise Adios 5 5 4¹ 4¹ 6²¼ J Ackerman3 9.00
Witch Doctor 9 9 9 8⁵ 7²¼ A Petty8 33.00
Brother Byrd 8 8 5½ 7¹ 8⁹ N Willis7 10.90
Homer Dares 20 20 7¹½ 9 9 G Wentz9 4.00
Time, :30⅕, 1:01⅗, 1:33⅘, 2:04⅘. Track fast.
4-Michael John $14.60 $ 5.20 $ 5.80
2-Baby Talk 6.40 4.40
1-Pam Arden 4.40
Quinella Numbers 2 and 4 Paid $29.20; Quinella Pool $37,581.
Attendance, 7,316; Total Mutuel Pool $626,008.

fall, the track would have a firm footing for the horses. This would be all well and good, if it rained, but even the little water truck that sprinkled water over the surface didn't help keep all of the dust down during a race. I would rather have had a little nice, clean mud instead. I did manage to win two races and finish no worse than fourth in the remainder.

With December just around the corner, I was satisfied enough to just head south for the winter in a day or so. Then as fate would have it, a short delay in my plans surfaced the next day as I was packing.

Chapter 6

Thanksgiving Day Wonder

While I was packing my equipment, the peace and quiet was suddenly broken by loud yelling from the horse stall next to mine. Quickly stepping into the shed roll of the stable, I could see two guys having harsh words with Dory Tammen. He was trying to convince the other two that he would pay the money that he owed them. I had known Dory for years, and knew that he owned a seven year-old mare named Liberty Queen. The horse had never won a race, thus forcing him to accept a job driving a tractor grader between races to smooth out the surface of the track. The pay for this service, in itself, wasn't enough to mention. In a few days, he was about to lose the only thing he cared about. I know how I would feel about losing my horse. The amount of money that he was to pay these two men, really wasn't all that much, so I calmed everybody down by paying them myself. Peace was restored once again. Dory and I had a conversation for an hour or so, much of which I had already known since long before. I had already seen his mare race.

In her race the week before, when Stanley Banks, her driver, took her to the front, he had driven her under a mild hold, letting her open up some ten lengths over the other horses. In the first half-mile, with blazing speed, as they neared the three-quarter mile pole, she started to falter, crossing the finish line last. This was about the same way all of her races went for the past three years. I couldn't figure out why some driver wouldn't try something different. What would they have to lose? If he could beat just one horse in a race, it would be a vast improvement.

After Dory had me examine his horse, I thought I had seen everything. The straw looked as though it was the same as Columbus left. The moldy hay and a dirty bag of oats looked just as bad. I thought to myself, "Dory, you would have been better off if you had given those guys this horse, and threw in the dirty bag of dirty oats as a bonus," but I would never do that to anyone who liked horses as much as I did. His working for the track proved this to me. I knew that he was just down on his luck, trying to get back up after being knocked down so many times. I agreed that I would try to help Liberty Queen's chances to at least finish in the money, within the very short time that I would be at this track. I also reminded him that a couple of small miracles would be greatly appreciated, but I would still have a go at it. This was with the understanding that I never wanted to see any veterinarian near his horse. I knew that, in the past, she had been given different drugs, trying to obtain more staying speed. These only made her wild and uncontrollable in a race.

The next day, I took her on the track for a slow mile, just to see what kind of pacing stride she had, and to see if she had the proper shoes. They looked worn so thin that it was a wonder that they hadn't fallen off. Obviously, they would have to be replaced with a different type, as she was cross-firing (her left, rear shoe was clipping the right, front shoe), at full pace.

While the blacksmith was making these changes, I cleaned out her stall completely. I put in four bales of my own straw, fresh clean hay, and placed three bags of mixed grain in Dory's tack room. On her return to her stall, Liberty Queen quickly laid down in the two-foot deep bed of straw, and rolled a half-dozen times. I thought, she never had it so good.

Later, I took her out for a long leisurely walk to get her accustomed to her new, thirty-eight dollar steel shoes, which I paid for, as Dory's credit around the track was just a tad on the slim side.

The first time I put a rubber tub of hot mash in her stall, she refused to eat. She probably never had mixed grain, molasses with boiling water added to it, apples and carrots sliced into it. I handed her a few pieces of apples, and she was soon enjoying a first-class meal.

Checking her bridle, I removed the harsh, steel bit that

was causing her mouth to be painfully sore. I attached a new leather bit which would greatly reduce the problem. It would also be more comfortable in a race.

A couple of days of light jogging miles, proved my judgment to be correct. On Thanksgiving night, I had her in the only race that was available — non-winners of three races. There are never any races listed of horses over five years old, or seven and still a maiden. It was a wonder that management even gave her a stall. I suppose that Dory's promise to drive the tractor grader on the track helped.

I was awakened around five in the morning Thanksgiving Day by strong, gusty winds and rain splashing against my bedroom windows. The first thing I remember saying out loud, was, "Oh, no. Not now!"

I quickly dressed, not even taking time to have a spot of tea. I then drove to the track three miles away. Along the way, I thought that it seemed that all of those clouds were holding their tears over the past two months when I could have benefited by them. It seemed that they finally broke down for a good crying session. My windshield wipers were having a terrible time, trying to do the job they were meant for.

To my surprise, Dory was already awake and feeding Liberty Queen, so I checked in on Michael John and prepared his breakfast. The rain was making much noise on the steel roof. It would make the horses a little nervous, but a small tub of grain would keep their minds off the storm and settle them down.

I could tell immediately that Dory was also very nervous, due to this sudden, unpredictable rain storm, especially when he asked me, "Do you think the races will be called off tonight?" I assured him that these officials would never do that even if they had to put each horse in a row-boat and have the drivers paddle them around the track. As he started to force a laugh, I added, "Haven't you ever heard of a Boat Race (A slang for a fixed race)?" Dory was now feeling better. Maywood park was giving a complete Thanksgiving dinner in the clubhouse to anyone connected with racing at their track, at no cost. That really put the frosting on the cake.

By 11:00 a.m., Dory was on his way. I told him that I would stay with the horses, and have dinner when he returned. The rain never let up for a moment. This was the only time I've seen so much rain in such a short time. I was hoping that it would stop soon, for Dory had mentioned that Liberty Queen disliked a sloppy track.

When Dory returned, he was carrying two large plastic bags while trying to run to the barn. In the still-heavy downpour, the weight of the bags made him look like he would fall down any second, so I ran to him and took one from him. When we were inside the tack room, I started to laugh. I said to him, "You didn't leave me any food over there. You have it all here!" He had packed up what looked like half a turkey, two chickens, a loaf of bread, pies and anything else that wasn't nailed down, as it looked to me. He reasoned that it would be tough that night to make any money, so, with the picking so slim, God helps those who helps themselves. With his now fully-packed refrigerator, and a couple of cakes on the shelf, I got up and told him that I would walk over to see if he left a few crumbs for my dinner. I also told him to keep a close eye on the horses.

As the track lights were turned on for the evening's sporting events, the rain had still not yet let up. I decided to use Michael John's new nylon harness, due to the fact that the condition of Liberty Queen's was dirty, worn-out looking.

After many adjustments with the harness and sulky attached, I put on my rain wear blue suit, and helmet, with amber glasses. I patted Liberty Queen on the head under the shed row. With the rain still falling, I told her in a nice, quiet voice, "Look, old girl, for your warm-up miles all you'll have to do is jog one mile at a slow clip, then go to the paddock where Charlie will be waiting for us. As high-strung as you are, it wont take much to warm you up. Maybe with all your warm-up miles, before a race, you didn't have any steam left. Well, tonight, we'll find out."

I didn't mind a little rain as we jogged on the track, but this kind of slop could make you start saying, "What have I done to deserve all of this?" At that split-second, Liberty Queen, with her ears straight out, tried to run off with me. It was a very good thing that I had the hand holds set up as far as I did. Lucky for me, I was near the outside track rail fence, or I would never have been able to hold her. I eased her, heading to the rail, hoping that she herself would slow up. She gave me some anxious seconds before the rail was inches ahead, then she stopped. When we turned, I told her, "Just save a little of that kind of speed for the last quarter-mile of the race tonight, and we will be eating a mighty fine meal."

Charlie helped me, but he couldn't understand for a moment why I didn't take her down on the rail for the usual warm-up mile. Hurrying as we spoke, I told him that this would be all the warm-up that she would get tonight. I had noticed that everyone else was doing fast warm-up miles as though it were summertime under sunny skies.

I thought to myself, "Tonight, it's not how fast you can go, but how long you can last." With all that deep, sloppy surface, it was going to be a very tiring track tonight. I backed Liberty Queen into her number six stall. This section was quiet for the time being, as all of the other horses were still out in the rain getting covered with white rock-colored mud.

I got Charlie over to the inside of the stall, and placed $600 into his hand. I told him, "Look. We've got about as much of a chance, as a snowball in hell, but I just can't help feeling that this rain may be the advantage I need to come even close to having a shot to win. With all of those guys on the track going the way they are, they might out-smart themselves. So, $200 will go to Dory, $200 for you, and $200 for me." Charlie stood there for a few seconds and looked at me as though he were in shock. He said, "Michael John, you're pulling my leg! I know this mare as well as everyone else does. She'll get you to the half-mile pole and stop." "Charlie," I said, "that's what I'm counting on. I should be able to get an easy lead, so let's keep this quiet. In a minute, I want you to walk out of here nice and slowly for the grandstand, so you'll be ready to bet this money as we approach the starting gate, just as you always have done. Tonight, with all of this rain, we'll probably go right to the starting gate, so I want you to leave now. Dory will be coming from the track garage soon. He will help me out to the track." I added, "If you run into him, don't tell him about the money that I'm betting for him. He's a nervous wreck the way it is."

As Charlie left, a few of the horses were coming into their stalls next to mine. They looked terrible. It was as though they were water-logged.

The general remarks from many of the drivers in the race were, "Michael John, how did you get stuck with a charity case?" Or, "It's too bad they don't have a half-mile race for poor Old Liberty." I would laughingly reply, "Well, it's Thanksgiving Day, so I'm just giving a donation of my time tonight. So, don't you guys splash too much mud on me as you go by, after the half-mile pole."

I was sure glad to hear the paddock judge, Frank, yell out, "On with the bridles, you'll be going right to the starting gate tonight. You all should know the reason. Try to stay dry." A few loud laughs could be heard. As Dory came running in with too many questions for me to answer, I just said, "Everything is mighty fine. So, give me a hand and I'll see you back at the barn, after our little 'Singing in the Rain' show is over. Keep calm, O.K.?"

I was wondering where all of that rain was coming from. It hadn't eased up one drop since the time it woke me this morning. Well, I thought, just keep me awake for another ten minutes more, and I'll know if all of this work was in vain. We paraded in front of the grandstand, then turned and headed for the mobile starting gate. I thought, I do hope that car has good mud grip tires on it, because if Liberty Queen is trying to run off with me, she would probably try to go over the starting gate.

I couldn't see anything through my glasses, so I was already looking over the top of them. I was trying to catch a glimpse of the tote board to see the odds. When I saw that my odds were 40 to 1, I knew that Charlie hadn't made his bet yet, and like always, kept quiet. In the next few minutes, he would be putting down the money. By the time the clerk had time to spread the word, the race would be started and the machines would be electronically locked.

The starting judge was now calling for the horses to line up. I only wished that Liberty Queen would have just one-tenth of the power left in her at the turn for home. My arms were beginning to ache from her pulling. I let her put her nose up against the wing of the slow-moving gate, as we had less than a quarter-mile before the starting line, and one-eighth of a mile to the clubhouse turn. I knew that I must be on the rail before this turn, so I would be able to back up this field speed for as long as I could, before anyone would get wise and try to pass me before the half-mile pole. Anything after that pole would be considered a bonus. With each step, my chances would improve greatly. If there was anything short of this, I would have been better off staying at home watching "Laugh-In" on television.

The gate was now picking up speed, and as usual, Liberty Queen's nose was pressing the gate as though she wanted to push it out of the way. I kept telling her, "Take it easy, and settle down." You would be amazed at what a few soft words will do to relax a very nervous horse.

At the sixteenth pole, I glanced to my right, and then to my left, in order to check the others, in the event that any of them were going to the front. I didn't want to get caught up in a speed duel in the first half. Seeing that most drivers had their horses a foot or so away from the arms of the gate, I was satisfied. Just at that time, the gate started pulling away. I could hear the engine of the car, being pushed to the maximum, due to the sloppy track surface.

Liberty Queen looked as if she was going to keep up with the big Cadillac. As I looked over the top of my glasses, I was able to see that I was about four lengths in front, with the clubhouse turn just ahead. I then started to ease Liberty Queen to the rail, under an extreme hold. So far, it seemed that things were going my way. The main question to me, was, "For how long?" I had to continue to slow down the speed, at least for the half. Going up the back stretch, I had to be out in front by at least ten lengths, for I couldn't hear any of the other horses behind me. With all of this rain, it was almost impossible to even see the rail. This, also, was an advantage of being in front, for Liberty Queen wasn't getting any mud splashed into her eyes by other horses. Those horses behind me had to be getting a mud and lime bath. That alone would make them slow up. Those fast warm-up miles the other horses did earlier, surely didn't help.

Turning into the home-stretch for the first time to complete the half-mile of the race, I figured that any second

I would hear the sound of the rest of the horses starting to make their move to pass me. Going past the grandstand, it was electrifying to see, at a quick glance, that not one person had come outside, or near the fence to watch the race. It was because of the heavy down-pour. A funny thought flashed across my mind, "What if all the people had gone home, and the rest of the horses were flagged off the track at the first quarter pole, due to the weather? What if there was an accident?" All I could hear was the track announcer saying that Liberty Queen was cruising down the back-stretch.

Going around the clubhouse turn for the last time, I still hadn't heard anyone behind me. From this point, every yard would be a bonus. Halfway up the back-stretch, things started to come to life. From all of the noise, it sounded as though all seven horses were spread across the track, about three to four lengths behind me. I still didn't want to ask Liberty Queen for the remainder of her speed until they were along side.

Going around the back-stretch turn, heading into the turn for the home-stretch, I knew that the only way any horse would ever catch me, was for him to have wings and start flying in the next second. I eased my firm hold on the driving lines, and the old gal took off down the stretch. The noise from the rest of the field was no longer to be heard as we crossed the finish line. Slowing her down at the club-house turn, we headed back to the winner's circle. I was able to see a few of the exhausted horses crossing the finish line.

With no one at the finish line to take a photo of us in this rainstorm, I headed back to the paddock, where Dory was waiting with the pails of hot water ready. Needless to say, for a man nearing sixty-five years old, he was jumping up and down as though he had won a million dollars. I then happened to think of Charlie. I knew that he would be around in a few minutes, after cashing in the winning tickets. Then Dory could have some cheering to do!

Charlie arrived as we were rubbing Liberty Queen down with clean towels after her hot shampoo bath. Putting blankets on her, then clipping them together, Dory started to walk her inside the paddock barn, where a vet would take a blood sample as a drug test. Every winner must do this.

One good thing — she was able to be cooled out right away in this barn. Just when we were trying to locate a large piece of plastic to cover the blankets on the horse, to get us back to the stable, another strange thing happened. The noise of the rain splashing on the roof suddenly stopped. It happened so quickly that we all froze. It was like someone shut off the shower in the bathroom. It was unbelievable, just as Liberty Queen winning her first race at seven years old!

"O.K., guys," I said, "let's get all of this equipment back to our barn, just in case the rain decides to start again." As we opened the large barn door, it was like stepping out into a different weather zone. The air was very clean and had a crisp, cool feeling about it.

As the three of us took our slow walk with Dory leading the way with his horse, his steps had a little spring in them, as he seemed to glide along the path under the dark skies.

While I rubbed Absorbine on the legs of this happy horse, I knew that I would have been proud of her even if she had finished second or third. After wrapping her legs with cotton and bandages, she was eagerly awaiting her hot bran mash, late night snack. While she was eating, I told Charlie, "O.K., now we can give Dory his bonus surprise in the tack room. It was only then that I learned what the final payoff was. As Charlie mentioned it, he was emptying out a plastic bag with a lot of money. He counted out $3,800, saying to Dory, "Michael John had me bet $200 to win on your horse for you." We all made a little for ourselves and Charlie handed me my share. Then waving Dory's share, I said, "Be sure that you guys thank Liberty Queen. I'm now ready for some fun in the sun."

Dory was still speechless at that time, not knowing what to say. So, I broke in and said, "If you really want to thank me, I would like to see you take your horse down to southern Illinois and pay the Murphy family to take care of her, until next spring, when I return from Florida. Then we'll have another go of it. I'll make the arrangements, if that sounds all right with you." All he could say was, "Thanks."

As a little add-on, I reminded Dory to pay-off any bills by tomorrow, for it was easy to see that all of the wolves would be flocking over to cash in, knowing about his win.

"Well, Charlie," I said, "we can start finishing our packing tomorrow and leave on Sunday, instead of waiting around until next week as planned. Frankly, I thought I'd have to race that old gal twice, just to finish second, so I could get Dory a few dollars!"

Chapter 7

On the Road Again

December 2nd, 1968. The strong northeast winds coming across Lake Michigan brought on the "Lake Effect" snow just as we had completed loading Michael John and eight other horses and their equipment into the van. The radio broadcast predicted six to eight inches of snow that night, and the temperature in the teens. I always get chills when I hear these kind of reports!

Charlie, and the other two grooms, would take turns riding in the van, to look after the horses. A buzzer alarm system was installed in the semi-tractor, so the driver could clearly hear it. If the caretaker deemed it necessary for the driver to stop, he would only have to push the mounted push-button switch, above the door.

This would be a 1,400 mile trip to Florida, where, as I had seen on the television that morning, it was going to be around eighty-three degrees under bright, sunny skies. What a nice, warm feeling. It gave me something to look forward to during the next three and a half days.

As I was waiting in my car for the semi-van to start rolling (with my dog sitting in my back seat) I couldn't help but feel sorry for the 1,200 horses that would be remaining, and would be expected to actually race each night. They would run during an extremely long and cold winter, with some nights the wind-chill reaching forty degrees below zero. The track would be frozen so they would put salt on it to keep it from icing. This is a very risky situation on uncertain track surfaces, not to mention the damage that the cold winds would do to the horse's lungs. Many nights after a race, the saliva from a horse's mouth, would become frozen to the bridle bit and even the horse's nostrils would freeze closed. The stalls in the barn would be extremely cold. In one hour, the water pails would be frozen solid.

The really stupid thing that I've seen many a so-called horseman do is taking barber's electric clippers and shearing all the horse's hair off. They do this because in these extremely cold winter nights, a horse will break out in a sweat during a race. His coat of hair will stay wet, unless he is properly rubbed down with clean, dry towels, and has blankets quickly put over his entire frame. The majority of trainers would much rather clip the hair off, than buy towels and do a little extra work, especially those trainers who do not own their horses.

The only sure bet in horse racing on these cold and windy nights is that the Governor of Illinois would be home keeping nice and warm watching television, even though he is the head of the Racing Board. He surely wouldn't want to see horses being abused. He might lose a couple of hours sleep. One might ask, "For God's sake, where are some of the officials from the Humane Society?" Could it be because of the state collecting huge profits from its percentage of each night's pari-mutuel handle? Were they given notice not to make waves at any of the state's race tracks? I have always wondered why, when on a number of times that I've called them, I always received the same old line that the person in charge of that section is out. I was always told to leave my name and phone number. It is about the same as, "Don't call us, we'll call you — when it snows in July!"

No! I don't feel sorry for the horsemen, whose cruelty to these horses is inexcusable. Why do they put on all of those heavy-duty warm clothes, gloves and face-masks, if the cold wouldn't hurt anyone?

I've always said, "If the horseman can't make enough money in eight months of racing, he'll never make enough in the remaining four.

The windshield wipers were going full-blast by now. With those little white, fluffy flakes streaming down from the foggy sky, it made driving pretty miserable. I started to follow the semi along the Tri-State Tollway, heading east into Indiana on route 65 to Indianapolis. Thank heavens there was no snow! The dry pavement was simply marvelous.

I noticed the van pulling into a large lot behind a restaurant. This would be a welcome relief for the horses and all of us from all of the bouncing on the highway. After the horses were given water and grain, we had a light lunch, then I took my faithful dog for a little walk.

We were rolling down the road to a farm, outside of Nashville, for a rest. The weather was fifteen degrees warmer with cloudy skies, but still very comfortable driving and a lot less stressful. It looked like it would be all down-hill now.

Before I knew it, around 3:00 a.m., we were cruising on the by-pass of Atlanta. A thought crossed my mind. "Wouldn't Clark Gable be amazed at how this city has expanded in the past twenty-nine years, since he arrived to see the first showing of my favorite movie 'Gone with the Wind'?" For a few seconds, I almost thought that I might see the Tara Plantation around the next bend in the highway.

By the next day, we were in the middle of Florida, with the temperature at seventy-two degrees. There was a clear, blue sky and all of the windows in my car were halfway down. We were driving past large groves of orange trees, laden with fruit soon to be picked. The smell of fresh oranges filled the air. At our next-to-last stop, a quart of orange juice would certainly quench my thirst. The taste would spoil you from ever drinking orange juice bottled from concentrate.

At last we had arrived at our destination, Pompano Beach, Florida. Just minutes later, the horses were being carefully walked down the ramp of the van. Seeing the lawns of green grass, and swaying palm trees, I had always wondered what goes through the horse's minds, when a moment like this comes into their lives. When they feel the warm breeze of seventy-eight degrees, they must be elated.

While Charlie walked my horse around the race track, I checked in at the office and obtained my pre-arranged stall and tack room where Charlie and the dog would stay. Charlie was the only other person that this well-trained dog would let near him. He was well worth the $800 that I spent on him.

Having the horse fed and bedded down, we went out for a late supper. Then I dropped Charlie off at the track and went to the apartment that I had rented before. The next week, all I did with the big horse was graze him on the grass and walk him around the race track in the warm, sunny afternoons, after the training of all the other horses was completed.

Also at this track, they had a swimming pool for horses. There was a ramp which gradually descended into the deep water. It had a walk-way so that you could keep hold of the horse's head with a rope or leather leash attached to the halter. This way you would be able to walk with the horse while he swam in the circular pool.

That morning, I took my horse for his first swim. I thought that I might have a little trouble getting him into the pool, like many other trainers had. Not Michael John. He knew that by now, whatever I did for him, would be all right. I led him to the ramp and he walked down into the water and started swimming like a duck in a lake. After six times around, I gave him a warm shower, then rubbed him dry with five towels. I added a couple of blankets, then took him back to his stall. I kept him there until the afternoon. I then walked and grazed him in the grass and noticed that he was really getting frisky with his life of leisure.

After Christmas, I had put him back into training for a few easy races. After always being up north for Christmas time, the past two years just didn't seem like that time of the year. This was especially true when I went on a deep-sea fishing boat and the music on the radio was interrupted by a weather report. It said that the remainder of the afternoon would continue to be mostly-sunny and the temperature would reach a high of eighty-four degrees. "It's no wonder that Santa has trouble sledding down here — no snow!" I had jokingly remarked to a few youngsters who were looking forward to presents that they might receive.

Chapter 8

Incredible Similarity

A week before Christmas, I was approached by Mr. L. Toth and his eighteen year-old son. He owned a horse called "Rarity", and kept it in the stall next to mine. In the short conversation that followed, I learned that they had shipped her in from Canada on November 2nd. They had raced their mare in three races, finishing very poorly in each race, even though the winners were timed in slow time. They had also wagered most of their extra money, especially in their last race. She was in with a class of horses that her warm-up mile time should have been almost fast enough to win this race. But instead, she finished last.

My curiosity was immensely aroused when they told me that the morning following her last two races, a complete stranger became interested in their horse. He asked if they wanted to sell her, even though he admitted seeing how she had finished her previous races. He had stated that he was looking for a mare with her blood-line. He said that he had known of this bloodline as he used to live in Canada, but now lived in Kentucky.

This five year-old mare had cost the Toth family $83 thousand as a yearling. They had started to race her at the proper age of three. Earnings up-to-date were $46 thousand dollars. With all the races in Canada, this was satisfactory, due to the medium amount of purse money regulated at their tracks.

Then came the nitty-gritty of the matter. Mr. Brian Lareau stated that at the present time he was prepared to give them a check for $10 thousand. When Mr. Toth told me this, my immediate reaction was, "What a con-artist!"

What all of this led up to was that Mr. Toth asked me

if I would watch his horse from the backstretch fence while the rest of the family were in the grandstand for the Saturday night races. He just couldn't believe that his horse was racing as badly as indicated. I had nothing important planned for that night so I agreed. I found myself with binoculars in hand, feeling that I was on an investigative report. In a sort of way, I did want to find out why an expensive, well-bred mare was racing as though she were a mule. Obviously I wasn't a "Sherlock Holmes", but I did have a few things over him. I knew a few things about horses and I didn't drink nor did I smoke.

Watching other horses go by in their warm-up miles on this 23rd day of December, a full moon was brightly shining in a clear, starlit night sky. The temperature during the afternoon had reached a comfortable eighty-one degrees, only dropping now to seventy-four degrees. I thought for a moment of how cold it was up north and wondered if the people there were shoveling snow!

As I was thinking of this, I spotted Rarity coming onto the track from the colors of the driver's jacket. She looked fit and alert as she jogged past the small plank stand bolted on the outside fence for the track personnel who wanted to view their horses. This driver paid no attention to me, which put my mind at ease. I was glad that he hadn't been forewarned that he was under suspicion. After three slow miles, everything looked normal. Still no cause for alarm. Maybe, I thought, the Toth family just didn't have the horse they figured her to be. It does turn out that way sometimes. It sure happened to me with Mike's Lad.

Just when I started to give this driver a vote of confidence, he went and did a stupid thing. He turned Rarity to start her medium warm-up mile, then took his whip in hand and laid the full length of it upon Rarity's back. She reared up in the air from the sharp pain and started pacing down the backstretch toward the far turn. They then went to the top of the stretch turn in front of the grandstand. The quickness of all this almost caught me off guard, as I had only seconds to start my stopwatch for the first warm-up mile. I really hadn't planned on using it for the usual slow warm-up mile that I would normally take with their horse.

With my binoculars clearly focused I noticed that the driver tucked his whip under his arm while going past the grandstand. Many people had gathered early to watch other horses going through their pre-race warm-ups. Then, as before, going up the back-stretch, the driver did the same identical thing. He was driving this mare right out of her shoes with this killing speed. I glanced at my stop watch which showed her first half-mile in one minute and eight seconds. Nearing the three-quarter pole, he again used his whip twice more before tucking it back under his arm as he headed down the stretch. He completed the mile in two minutes and eleven seconds. It was a good thing for him that he stopped at the clubhouse turn and pulled Rarity in the direction of the paddock. If he had driven past me, I might have lost my cool, for he was abusing a horse and running a disastrously fast warm-up mile. If I thought I could have gotten a pass into that paddock on such short notice, I sure would have tried. It seemed as though the only thing these officials did right at this track is to allow only those people who have a horse racing that night to gain admittance to the paddock. So, all I could do then was to see if Mr. Toth and his son, Raymond, would notice the poor condition their horse was in and cancel the last warm-up mile, or even the race itself.

I then noticed that the horses were coming out for the first race. Rarity would normally come out after the third race for her second warm-up mile, for she had drawn the number two position in the sixth race. A little breeze was starting to come out of the east; as I looked up in the clear sky I saw that the full-moon was still out. It reminded me of the song, "Moon Over Miami."

The winner of the third race was heading to the winner's circle while I trained my binoculars on the paddock gate. The horses listed for the sixth race were coming onto the track for their warm-up miles. Five horses had already come out and I hoped that maybe Rarity would escape any more torture tonight and be taken out of the race. My hopes were suddenly destroyed, as I saw that depraved driver's colors coming onto the track. I felt helpless. The only thing I could do was clock her warm-up mile, then tell Mr. Toth about it after the race. I knew that he had to be hoping for some kind of miracle tonight to at least finish second if not win. For I also found out earlier that just as in Dory Tammen's case, Mr. Toth had sold his racing sulky for money he needed desperately.

The driver took Rarity around the track at a fast pace, then turned her the right way of the track for her last warm-up. I already knew what his intentions were after seeing what had previously occurred. This clown had to be getting paid by Brian Lareau, to make sure that Rarity finished a poor race. With a couple of extremely fast work-out miles in her before a race, it would indeed ensure these results.

It was then no surprise to me to see this mare taking the same torturous warm-up mile in two minutes and six seconds. Any of the paying customers who had witnessed this blazing warm-up mile, would probably have started getting all their money ready for the sixth race to bet on, what looked like, a "sure thing". The only sure thing that night for anyone betting on Rarity would be that their pari-mutuel tickets would make a nice covering on the floors of the clubhouse and grandstand.

I didn't have much longer to wait for the results of the sixth race as the sound of the bugle came over the loud-speakers announcing that the horses were coming out for the race. I felt sorry for the Toth family, for all of the money and hard work they invested. I knew that they had as much of a chance of winning that night as a snow ball in a heated oven, to put it mildly.

Ten minutes later, the track announcer could be heard saying, "The gate is rolling." It came around the clubhouse turn of this five-eighths mile track, then half-way up the backstretch, picking up speed to draw away from the field of nine pacers. Folding the long arms of the two gates inwardly, it was then driven to the outer fence of the track as the horses raced by the mobile gate. The starting judge, sitting in a comfortable chair, would follow the field and observe the race for any infraction of the rules and regulations of the track. From my past experiences in racing, it is not too difficult for me to believe that on many a race, this judge takes a little cat nap, or on some other occasions, he may even have a small wager. Maybe, by chance, the driver of the horse wagered on should happen to accidentally, on-purpose, bump another horse, causing him to go off stride. In doing so, it would interfere with the other horses. It is very easy to win a race this way, especially if the judge might win a few green-backs. Obviously, we all know, he surely wouldn't dream of disqualifying his choice should he happen to win the race.

As I had expected, Rarity, displaying a burst of speed, was quickly leading by five lengths. Approaching the back-stretch turn, I had an excellent view of this first quarter-mile. I was watching the driver already using his whip. When he went past the grandstand, his whip would be neatly tucked under his arm, as though this horse was doing all of this pace on his own, without asking. It seemed like a smart way to get a horse beat and tired without causing anyone to believe the driver would actually be doing so. Any horse, Thoroughbred or Standardbred, can only be used for three-eighths of a mile at their top speed. Some may be able to go that other one-eighth, but not many.

With Rarity now leading the other eight horses by seven lengths going past the stands, I could almost picture the people who wagered on her thinking, "I knew that horse was a good choice. I wish I had bet more on her." This thought would be short-lived, however, for as Rarity was half-way up the backstretch, nearing where I was standing, I could see she was beginning to shorten her stride. Those over-excessive work-outs were taking their toll on her. I was only hoping that she wouldn't fall due to fatigue.

Turning for the homestretch, it would be only a couple of seconds before the field of horses would pace by her as though she was standing still. I gave a sigh of relief, as I watched her stagger across the finish line last. At least no more damage was done.

Quickly, I stepped down the plank stairway and ran back to my barn. I wanted to have a few pails of hot water ready for Rarity's bath. I also put a heater in a pail to have some boiling water for her hot bran mash, something I knew that she had never had before. I had previously prepared all of the ingredients in her grain tub. After what she had just gone through, this should be appreciated.

Upon hearing the car doors slam shut, it was easy to understand the disappointment of the disastrous race they had just witnessed. I had only a couple of minutes to talk to Mr. Toth, as the driver was bringing Rarity to the barn in a slow walk. I thought he would have at least gotten off the sulky and walked her back, for she was exhausted. I didn't want to be around to hear what kind of lies this driver would probably tell as to why he finished so poorly. I could already guess. I went over to help Raymond unhook his horse and remove the old leather harness that had certainly seen better days. After using the five large pails of warm water and rubbing Rarity down with clean towels, I put three blankets on her. I told Raymond that after four swallows of cold water, she would be ready for him to walk her around the barn area to cool out. He could then give her small amounts of water every ten minutes. With that, I went to see how Charlie and my horse were doing before going to bed.

The next morning, after Michael John's swimming session, Mr. Toth and his wife came over to tell me that Mr. Lareau had just left, making his offer at only $5 thousand this time. He told them that he wouldn't want to race her after watching the race last night, but felt that he might mate her to one of his stallions in Kentucky. He explained to the Toths that this would be his final offer. He must have already known that these people were walking on very thin ice and that it was melting fast, as he slowly drove away from their barn, hoping to be called back.

I could plainly see that Mrs. Toth had been crying as her eyes were red. I couldn't blame her. So when they asked me if I would drive Rarity in her next race, I really couldn't refuse, even though I thought that at this stage, what possible chance would I have at getting anywhere near the winner's circle. I was no magician. A flashback of Liberty Queen came across my mind, and before I realized what I was saying, I agreed. Surely, the hot sun must have been getting to me!

Well, one thing was going for me — when a horse or person hits rock-bottom, there's only one way to go, and that's up.

I looked at the condition sheets for the races that horsemen would enter their horses in during the next couple of weeks and that Rarity would be eligible for. January 4th was the earliest date available. With this information, I informed the Toth family that we would have a tough nut to crack, sort of speaking. I told them that with a little co-operation from Raymond, we might be able to improve upon her last effort, adding that I wouldn't sell them out.

I suggested that we first give Rarity a three-day rest, taking her out in the afternoon for walking and grazing. The warm sun would be good for her. Then for the next five days, Raymond and I would take her swimming in the pool, right after I took Michael John for his morning swim. The last three days, I would jog her for a couple of slow miles to see if she had any problems. After all, she had just gone through a very painful experience. I then also mentioned that she would have a set of new shoes the day before the race, so I would take her to my blacksmith. With all of that said, I asked them, "How about you folks coming with Charlie and me for a Christmas dinner?" Raymond's eyes lit up with glee, saying, "Hey, dad, wouldn't that be just dandy!" Everyone was now in a much better frame of mind as I left.

Everything had gone as planned. Rarity seemed to be back to her old self and each day she was showing vast improvement. So, all in all, I was pleased with her progress. One can only do so much in such a short time. I just hoped that I had done enough. With her warm-up miles for this upcoming race, it would be a complete opposite of what I had witnessed in her last. I had hoped that I was doing the right thing with these changes. As far as the Toth family was concerned, when they awoke on January 4, 1969, that day would be a day that they would never forget. They had all of their eggs in one basket, and the burden was on my shoulders not to break these eggs tonight.

It would now be impossible to even consider taking Rarity back to Canada if she finished poorly. The temperature up there was around thirty degrees below zero. The weather change from eighty degrees to that extreme cold would kill her in a day. Also, no trucks would be going to

Canada until May, in all likelihood.

Knowing that I had to do something to settle these folks down and relieve some of the stress that the next twelve hours would obviously bring, I took them out for breakfast, while Charlie looked after the horses. Actually, they were taking a chance on me. After all, a few weeks earlier, they never heard of my name. Fate, sometimes good and other times, very evil, brought us together.

The only way I could possibly let them know that I was going to give one hundred percent of myself in tonight's race, and take a little pressure off their minds, was to put my money where my mouth was. I had always known that "Money talks, and B.S. walks!"

As we all packed into my car at the restaurant, I counted out $1,000 and laid it on the dashboard. Then, I told Mr. Toth, "I want you to go to the fifty-dollar window, and bet this money on your horse, five hundred to win, and the remainder to place. If we don't cash any tickets tonight, you don't owe me a cent." I told him, "On the other hand, if we get lucky, we'll split it fifty-fifty." I also added, "I want you to know here and now, if I see that she can't keep up with this field, I won't abuse her with a whip. That's the one thing that I never believed in."

The quietness in my car was such that you could have heard a pin drop. I guess these people were in total shock for the next few minutes. To break the silence, I remarked, "One thing is for sure; this is one night that you won't be sold out, even it if kills me."

On the way back to the track, it was agreed that Raymond would take Rarity for a leisurely walk, after which he would wax my sulky and clean my nylon harness that we would be using. This would keep his mind occupied from being so nervous. I couldn't blame him. I was a bit nervous myself. This wasn't just any race where I was the only person involved. These people got themselves in this position because of a few greedy people who wanted to steal their horse from them. I already knew the feeling.

Another thing that was also making me a bit nervous, was that since the entries were printed for tonight's races two days earlier and included the driver's names, no one had approached me. I asked myself, "Could it be that after the abuse she was given in her last race, these clowns figure that it would be impossible for Rarity to finish anywhere near the first six horses?" I did hope that this was their way of thinking.

The tall, aluminum poles, spaced around the race track with the huge lamps attached, would generate a source of illumination to convert this darkened area into daylight. Within minutes, this procedure would be completed, announcing the arrival of the clientele who patronize this establishment. A very few would still enjoy small success in their wagering. The majority would be seen slowly walking to the parking lot with much lighter billfolds and purses. Some can be heard saying to their companions, "I knew that number eight would win. Just think. I could have had a $600 daily double. Instead of listening to you guys I bet your number one who finished dead last. That's the last time I'm going to the track with anybody."

The hustle and bustle at a track is enough to drive anyone to drink.

I told Raymond that with Rarity in the seventh race, we would start with a leisurely three-mile jog, after the second race. We would follow this with a moderate warm-up mile with a speed of around two minutes and thirty seconds, after the fourth race. I also told him that once we were in the paddock, not to talk to anyone and not to leave the horse alone, not even for a second.

As the sound of the bugle could be heard for the second race, we proceeded to hook up Rarity for her easy and relaxing outing. The weather was cooperative that night, with a pleasant temperature of seventy-three degrees, under a clear sky with a mild, warm southern breeze. This was ideal for an evening at the races, one would have to think. This was especially true if they had watched the weather report on television earlier showing that Chicago was having near-blizzard conditions and a temperature of five below zero. The horses would still be going to the post as usual at 7:30 p.m.

Rarity went her three miles with ease under a firm hold. As I was bringing her to a stop to turn into the paddock, she must have remembered what had happened to her in the last race. She started to actually rear up as though she were going to be hit. I began to talk to her, and got off the sulky. I then patted her forehead and calmed her down. There is one thing about any animal, I've always said, They never forget any abuse.

Raymond was at the paddock, waiting. He quickly helped me unhook Rarity. We then placed one blanket over her and put her in the number one stall for the number of the post position she had drawn. Raymond commented that he approved of how things were going. I liked to hear that. I said, "Let's hope we obtain better results."

With the fourth race now on the track, I put the bridle on Rarity, talking to her as I did. By the time we had the sulky hooked up, the race had finished. With Raymond leading, we headed onto the track for this important warm-up mile. I knew that if I could control her easily enough, we just might have some sort of chance of salvaging something from this race.

I let her jog slowly past the clubhouse, then the grandstand where I stopped her to turn for the warm-up mile. Turning her there, I figured, might be better than doing it in the backstretch where that clown used the whip on her.

It helped, for she started pacing as though she were off to a Sunday afternoon picnic. She picked up speed on her own as we neared the starting line, under a comfortable hold. I clicked my stopwatch and noticed that a couple of drivers were looking over Rarity with more than a casual glance, as they went by me. This concerned me a bit.

At the half-mile in one minute and fifteen seconds, I could feel the pressure from the reins in my hands. Rarity was trying to go much faster. This was the first real sign that I was hoping for. Coming down the stretch, it seemed that her feet were barely touching the ground as we finished the last half-mile in one minute and ten seconds. "What a nice mile," I told her as we headed towards the paddock.

I whispered into Raymond's ear, "She's on the iron and hitting on all eight cylinders!" As we put her into the stall, she wasn't even blowing. That was a very good sign indeed.

The horses were on the track for the sixth race, so we

still had another fifteen minutes before our race. Raymond went to the bathroom. He was gone for only a minute, when the driver who had been watching me on the track, approached me. In one motion, he placed, what looked like five to ten$100 bills into my driving jacket pocket. In a soft-tone voice, he said, "All you have to do is finish back of the pack in your race." With a very quick glance around the area I saw no one but a shoulder of someone behind an empty stall, with what looked like a camera. I stepped back a foot, looked this stupid thief in the eye, and said, in a very stern voice, "You have three seconds to remove that money from my pocket or all hell is going to break loose, here and now!" I continued, "You can also tell your buddy with the camera to leave, for there will be no photo session tonight!"

He must have felt that I meant what I said, for he quickly removed the bills. I didn't look because I wanted to see the camera man who was turning his back and heading in the opposite direction.

I made sure he didn't leave anything else in my pocket, as he was saying, "You'll finish last anyway." I made a sudden move to him and he took off like a scared rabbit. Just as Raymond was returning, he asked, "Any problems?" "No," I said. "Everything is just like peaches and cream." Soon, we heard the paddock judge say, as he walked by, "Put your bridles on for the seventh race."

Stepping onto the track, the sound of the bugle informed the race-goers that the horses were now on the track and post-time would be in ten minutes. Parading single file down the middle of the track in front of the grandstand, I caught a quick glance of Mr. and Mrs. Toth standing near the fence. I knew that they must have been very nervous at this stage of the game.

Turning Rarity around at the clubhouse turn, I was able to see that very little money had been wagered on her, for the odds were forty to one. That would change drastically after Mr. Toth placed his wager. I figured that Rarity would close at about ten to one. The regular patrons had already lost their confidence in management. With the small purses, the horsemen just naturally take it easy with their horses down here in the winter, for the one hundred times larger purses up north in the Spring. It is a proven fact that many horsemen or drivers who may not want their horse to win a certain race, because it would be more profitable to place a wager on a prearranged horse in the same race, where the returns could be ten to twenty times greater. The act of greed is performed as easily as falling off a log.

Rarity started to pace a little faster as we went around the turn at the top of the stretch, so I took her to the outer fence. I brought her to a complete stop just to settle her down. In seconds, we would be slowly pacing down the stretch to where the mobile gate was waiting for the track announcer to inform the patrons, "It is now post time."

I timed it perfectly. I then heard the starting judge over his speaker call out, "Gentlemen, bring up your horses." As we neared the long arms of the gate, I felt the tightening of the reins in my hands. Quickly, I took a firmer hold on the reins and said to her, "Take it easy, old girl. I don't want you in front until the last half of this mile. Nobody pays for the first half."

Seconds later, I glanced over from my rail position, and tried to see who might bust out for the lead. The speed of the car had reached about thirty miles per hour as it started to pull away faster while folding the two long arms of the gate inwardly. I had all I could do to keep Rarity from running off with me. Obviously, she hadn't forgotten being whipped by that so-called driver in her last race.

I was amazed that only two horses were bolting out for the lead. In doing so, Hickory Daredevil, the number three horse driver, came across and over to my sulky. His wheel guard bumped my right wheel so hard that it lifted me up an inch or so out of my seat. I thought that Rarity would surely go off stride and fall quickly. Bracing myself, she went about her business. I yelled at the driver a few unkind words, while hoping that the judge, who was riding in the mobile gate, witnessed the infraction. I did feel that this was an unavoidable accident at the time. As he passed me, Lovetta Dream, the number four horse, did likewise, but never attempted to go for the lead. Both drivers were slowing down the fast pace of the race. At that point, it was understandable. In an honest race, I was in the golden spot, but just at that second,

Prairie Scott, the number two horse, pulled along side me. The driver seemed to be content without attempting to go any faster than me. This is what I call down and dirty "County fair racing". I had experienced a few of these types before. I said to myself, "Have patience, and I will pay thee all."

As the two front horses picked up a little more speed, they left about a two-length gap in front. I still kept a firm hold on Rarity to see if this driver along side me would go on and try to take over the third spot. He, also, had a firm hold on his horse. Then I knew that I was in for it, and what his game was. His interest had to be with the two up front and with me pinned next to the rail, he would control the outcome of the race. I would have to take some drastic action as we were nearing the backstretch turn. The two in front had a four-lengths lead and that was what I was hoping for. Easing my hold, I yelled at Rarity, "O.K., old gal. Let's go!" In a fraction, we were in the open, leaving the stunned driver whipping his horse to try to keep up.

With the stretch turn up ahead, and nearing the two horses who had their own way for three-quarters of this race, I figured I would have no other choice but to go to the outside as we straightened out down the stretch. I could feel by my reins that I had plenty of horse left too, at least to beat the outside horse. He had to be getting very tired being parked outside for this entire race, unless he had a spare engine installed in his horse.

Just as I was making my move, I heard one of the drivers yell out to the other, "He's going to the outside." It was a good thing that I wasn't near these two clowns, for they both started to drift out from the rail very quickly. Had I continued my same route, they would have taken me to the outside fence or my horse would have been knocked down. This I am sure of every time I think of this race.

I pulled up Rarity as quickly as I dared to, almost stopping her. I headed her back to the rail for these two clowns left enough space to drive a semi through. The remainder of the horses were very close behind with two other horses now along side me, fighting for the lead. They were the number eight and number six horses. I didn't see what happened to the number three or four horses at that moment. My concern was the present. Not knowing how much I took out of Rarity or how she would finish the last one-eighth mile, I had no plans on using my whip. That wouldn't' have accomplished anything.

I kept urging her on, shaking the reins as we passed the sixteenth pole. I wanted to jump off the sulky and carry her across the finish line, for I knew I had a horse right along side me. The driver was hitting his horse repeatedly with his whip. Just as I knew the finish line was within feet of me, I eased myself from the seat of the sulky and lunged forward as hard as I could. This would help to take the pull and weight of the sulky off Rarity's body, passing the finish line in doing so.

I had no way of knowing what the results were for my head was under my outstretched arms holding the loose reins giving Rarity complete movement of her head. Straightening back into the sulky as I began to ease Rarity to a stop at the clubhouse turn, the driver of the number six horse, Perfect Image, asked me, "Did you win it?" I could only say, "I don't know, but it's damn close." That driver was Glen Garnsey, one of the very few people that I have total respect for as a horseman and gentleman.

Heading back to the finish line, the "photo" sign was still lit on the tote board, for the judges still hadn't posted the winner. I got off the sulky and took hold of Rarity while waiting another minute or so. This race would become history. The Toth family were just as one would expect. They were yelling, "Did you win! Did you win!" I yelled back to them through all of the noise, "It's too close to tell." Some of the people involved with the eighth horse had already walked out onto the track to get their picture taken with what they though was the winner. Figuring that they had a better view of the finish line, I patted Rarity on the head and neck saying softly, "You did real good. It's a good thing we put a little back-up money on you for second place, old girl."

Just as I said that, a loud roar arose from the crowd as the winner was flashed on the tote board. The track announcer was saying that the winner of the seventh race was a brown five year-old mare named Rarity. Mr. and Mrs. Toth came running out of the gate, onto the track, over to me. It was a good thing I had a firm hold of the horse, for she jumped up and was a little nervous with all of the activity in the winner's circle.

They were both saying, "We saw you get bumped at the start, are you all right?" They said, "We were frightened that you might go down. What the hell was that stupid jerk doing out there." All I could tell them was that he was probably trying to make some money the easy way. I said, "Now let's get our picture taken and get your horse back to the barn after her drug test." It was too bad that Raymond was at the paddock for he would have liked to have been in the picture. Then I whispered into Mr. Toth's ear, "You did bet the money?" His grin from ear to ear answered my question. I said, "See you at the barn."

It was a slow jog past the grandstand where many patrons were still standing at the fence, clapping their hands and giving their approval. I didn't know if they were doing this because they had won a bet on Rarity or they appreciated a good race. At least some parts were good. I later found out that the number three and four horses finished fifth and sixth place, just like a team of mules. Not the horses, the so-called drivers I had in mind.

Raymond was filled with ecstasy as he came over to help me unhook Rarity at the paddock, asking about his folks. "Were they in the winner's circle?" He said that he was at the top of the stretch and saw all of the trouble I had. He said, "You sure kept her on her feet, Michael John." Smiling, I looked at him and said, "It's a good thing I did. I wouldn't have appreciated it if the other five horses behind me would have made me part of the track's surface!"

"O.K.," I said, "let's get the harness off inside the paddock stall, and give this winner a well-earned bath. Then we'll take her back to her barn for a hot bran mash."

When we walked Rarity to the barn, Charlie and the Toth family were still jumping for joy. While Raymond finished taking care of Rarity, Mr. Toth handed me an envelop with all of the money he received from our wager. He told me that Rarity had paid $16.20 to win and $8.00 to place, for every $2.00 wagered. I then placed in Mr. Toth's hand, his share of the $6,050.00, while saying, "This money, plus half of the track's purse, should be able to buy our late-night supper, right?" We all laughed.

By that time, I even had Charlie jumping like a two year-old colt, when I gave him half of my winnings. He kept saying, "I didn't think you would bet a dime on your chances tonight." "Sometimes we all do crazy things," I remarked.

Rarity was enjoying her specially-prepared dinner and with all of the equipment cleaned, it was now our post time for dinner. I took Charlie aside, asking him to stay with the horses. "I'll bring you back a meal with all the trimmings," I told him. I'm sure that he understood what I was trying to tell him, without alarming the Toth family. I had a strange feeling that a few people would be very displeased with the accomplishments that had occurred that night.

Chapter 9

People Love a Winner

Losers are soon forgotten and fall by the wayside of life. I was learning that more and more with each passing day and this day was no exception. I was rubbing Michael John down with two towels, after his morning swim. Red Scott walked over to me and said, "That was one hell of a good drive last night. I thought for sure, when you got bumped, it was curtains for you." As he shook my hand he said, "The finish of the race was a gutsy move, I might add." I thanked him for his compliments.

As he was looking at Michael John, he said to me, "Your horse looks like a million bucks. I've heard that you spend a lot of time and hard work on him, and I can see the results." Momentarily, I figured he was just setting me up for some kind of con or something else along that order, so I was naturally on my guard.

Placing three blankets on my horse as we talked, I put a clamp on to hold both ends together in front of Michael John's neck. I asked Red if he would mind talking while I walked my horse around among the trees to dry him off. He said, "Better yet. Why don't we walk over to my stable eight barns away? Then I can show you what I'd like for you to consider."

With that, I said, "Sounds good to me!" I had to take a firmer hold on Michael John, for he was feeling his oats, jumping around as though he was again going to be released in a clover pasture on this bright, sunny morning of seventy-five degrees. It wasn't too hard to take for a January 5th day.

By the time we arrived at his stable, I had a general outline of the situation. The horses that he was contracted to train, all belonged to Raymond Galt, whom I later found out sold a beach-front strip of land in North Fort Lauderdale, Florida, for around $40 million in 1947. It was sold with the understanding that the name "Galt Ocean Mile" not be changed.

I quickly understood that of these ten horses, not one of them cost less than $100 thousand. Yep, I thought, This guy's credit should be worth the price of a cup of coffee.

Red Scott's problem was in the fifth stall. As we started to walk towards it, I handed the leather line to one of the grooms that Red had called over to walk my horse while we looked at a quarter million dollars standing on four legs. We found a beautiful, golden-brown, three year-old colt with well-developed conformation with a black mane and tail. He was just a tad on the stocky side. This was probably because he hadn't been on the track except for only a few miles.

Scott was short of dependable stable help as well. The colt, named Bye-Bye Sam, needed someone's personal training. He was nominated for the Messenger Stakes race in five months, for three year-olds only. This race is the equivalent to the Thoroughbred's three year-olds only classic, The Kentucky Derby, run every first Saturday in May.

It seemed that this colt had not raced as a two year-old, and very little training had been put in him. This made him very green, and would require many hours each day of patient care to be ready for this big day. It comes only once in a horse's lifetime with the owner paying a large sum of money to

Bye Bye Sam at three years of age in Pompano, 1969.

enter in this prestigious race.

With a handshake, Mr. Scott said, "I'll call Mr. Galt in Illinois about you taking over training of Bye-Bye Sam." This would be a serious challenge for me, especially when there was no room for error.

Now Michael John and I were both jumping in stride on our way back to the stall. I thought to myself, "Would Red Scott have offered me this horse if Rarity had finished last? I doubt it very much."

Telling Charlie and the Toth family about the past hour's events, we went out for breakfast, even though it was past ten o'clock. On the way, Raymond smiled, saying, "By the way, no one came around to buy Rarity at a discount price this morning!" Laughter from my car, could be heard as we headed down A-1-A along the Atlantic ocean. There were pelicans flying overhead in a "V" formation, looking as though they were motionless in a slow glide through the light breeze.

The Toth family stated that this would be their Christmas and New Year's day to celebrate. This was because they were so overwhelmed with last night's miracle, which was how they referred to that race. Seeing all this happiness made me feel a warm glow of delight and gratification.

Working all morning with Bye-Bye Sam, it was quite obvious that I would have to start on him as though he had never been trained at all. I wished I had owned him; he wouldn't have been so neglected. I was sure that he would keep me busy these next winter months. One thing I knew for sure—this colt, with close to two hundred fifty thousand dollars already invested in him, had a lot of extremely fast blood in his system from his sire. I only hoped that I could give him a chance to show it to a field of horses behind him on a race track, crossing the finish line. The Messenger Stakes would do for a start.

Bye-Bye Sam was so rambunctious when I finally got him hooked to a jog cart (a training bike) that each morning I would have to walk him to the track to settle him down. This relieved the stress within him, for he was indeed a very nervous colt. I could only imagine some of the abuse he must have gone through. I did hear of a couple of busted up jog carts that were new before he was hooked up to them. They would make for some mighty fine fire wood up north.

After a week of two-mile per day leisure jogs, I was able to put on a set of shoes that would suit him far better. The next week's sessions started to show a slight improvement. After all, "Rome wasn't built in a day". Patience will also come into play every day.

I also started Bye-Bye Sam on hot bran-mash with the usual delicious Washington State apples cut into quarters with the seeds taken out and sliced carrots. Once he got a mouthful of this delectable meal, he would have his head out of his stall each early evening, waiting for me. He would be shaking his head up and down as if to say, "What's taking you so long?" That was when I knew that I had won his trust.

Driving a few other owner's horses every evening, except Sundays, plus getting Michael John ready to start racing in March, with a few races for Rarity on the side, I kept very busy. Rarity's next race was so easy I thought I would be arrested for taking the money from the track.

In February, I was jogging Bye-Bye Sam four miles each day and taking him for a swim twice a week in the eighty degree sunny weather we were having. On some days, the wind would kick up its heels at around twenty to twenty-five miles per hour and the temperature would only be around seventy degrees. There would be no swimming sessions when this occurred. Mr. Galt came down from Illinois saying that he was pleased with the progress I was making. He wondered if his horse would be ready for the big race. I assured him that everything possible was being done, without the help of any drugs. Then, to my surprise, he came back from the tack room and wanted to know who was going to eat the four bushels of apples and three bags of carrots. I replied that those were going to be sliced into his colt's hot bran-mash — three apples and three carrots each day. I told him that I had bought them from the Publix supermarket.

His only reply was, "Oh!" I would have appreciated it if he had said, "Thanks." It wouldn't have cost him a penny.

Chapter 10

The Last Treacherous Saturday

The last Saturday in February, I entered Michael John in his first race after his three-month vacation. He was feeling very frisky and in tip-top condition. Pompano Park still hadn't raised any amount on the purses for 1969, thus making it very difficult for the horsemen to pay their bills. When the opportunity presents itself, most likely, certain horses would win where as their past performance charts would indicate that they would finish in the "also ran" category. In their following race, they would join in with the "also ran" club. Strictly, "Button, button, who's got the button?"

This is why I would never in a million years go to any race track and bet more than one race, and only a small wager at that, unless I was driving the horse or knew the owner well enough to trust. As always, one could beat and win a race, but one will never beat the races.

Charlie and I were having dinner at the track's restaurant when the evening's programs arrived. At a glance I knew right away that four of the eight horses entered in my race were very well-bred and were worth a few greenbacks. The question was, how many would actually try to win? All four had raced six times this year and each had won one race, finishing the other races third or fourth. Then my eyes caught the name of the driver who was on the number eight horse. This was the clown who had tried to stuff the handfull of one hundred dollar bills into my jacket the night of Rarity's race. I hadn't seen him around the track since then, so he must be small potatoes. He didn't own this horse he was to drive. I thanked my lucky stars that night when he stuffed the money into my pocket that I didn't reach up and take it out to hand it back to him. His friend would have taken a picture of me doing so. They would have had me with the brass ring in my nose, no matter which way I had chosen.

I can just imagine being in front of a judge trying to explain a picture of me holding a hand-full of money, saying, "Your honor, I was handing the money back to this person, not taking his bribe." His remark would have been, "If and when I believe that story, my ears will grow long and I'll be called Peter Rabbit. GUILTY AS CHARGED! Next case." His comments would have made the six o'clock news for the humor of the days events. At least that clown gave Charlie some good laughs when I told him the whole story the day after. I kind of liked it, after I thought about it. Thank heavens that I spotted the damn camera man.

I tapped on my program to catch Charlie's attention. "Remember the camera guy in the paddock?" Charlie's head bolted upright, "Where is he? I'll break his neck." "Calm down, Charlie," I told him, "He's not here, but take a look at the program. His friend is driving the horse next to me tonight." Charlie then asked, "Do you want me to ride shotgun with you?" I answered, "No, besides the track officials would want to discourage such practices, maybe?"

Looking over his past five races, no matter what post position he was in, he has always gone for an early lead. So I figured that I would just head over to the rail where, for the first quarter, I'll be seventh or last until the half-mile post. Then I would pull out, going up the back stretch. I would have the field in full view in the event this clown had any mischievous tricks up his sleeve.

The biggest joke is Pompano Park's classification of horses. They are supposed to be evenly matched horses depending on their races won, money earned and gender. They surely must have had an amateur making up the races each night. An example was an owner with a record of a two-minute mile and his mare had earned $9 thousand. She was entered into a race that was listed for non-winners of $3 thousand in the last six starts. When the entries were posted for this race, this owner was shocked that his mare had to race against a male horse with a speed time record of one minute and fifty-six and three-fifth seconds with earnings of $180,524. This horse had been racing against the best horses in the nation. With this kind of classification, it was quite possible that this owner's horse, shall I say, had been kept on a tight rein in his last few starts so as not to earn the three thousand dollars. The door would be opened for him to race against these pigeons, obviously after going to all of this trouble and time. He would naturally want to cash a large wager, at decent odds. The only way that the patrons would lose interest and their money would be for this driver to do a few stupid drives and finish last. You would be amazed at the general public. When they study their racing forms and scratch off any horse that has finished worse than fifth. Thus the odds grow on these kinds of "sleepers" (horse set up to win at a later date). Another long-shot is born. The old saying is, "The favorites have a hard time of winning, but the long-shots win very easily."

Saturday night's race was no exception to the rule. Four of the horses had earned well over one hundred thousand dollars with the best record of one minute and fifty-seven seconds. This is why I had asked before, "How many would actually try to win?"

There was no way in hell I could beat this class of horse, unless the officials let me put my horse and sulky on top of a truck and have the driver drop me off at the winner's circle. One thing was for sure. It was another beautiful night for racing, even though the chances of making a dollar would disappear like an ice cream cone at a Sunday afternoon picnic in July.

As Charlie was helping me hook up Michael John to the sulky, he whispered into my ear, "You're not really going to bet on this horse tonight, against all those bearcats?" I gave him a warm smile and said, "Charlie, me lad, I do think that you're learning to read a racing program." Continuing, in a lower voice, "If those bearcats do fall asleep in the stretch thinking they're going to have easy pickin's, I'll be right on their backs. But just between you and me, we'll have a hard nut to crack tonight." With that statement I sat on the sulky and headed Michael John for his second, last warm-up mile. Under a firm hold, I clicked off my stop watch in two minutes and eighteen seconds. I was very proud of him, even after his vacation, to pace so effortlessly.

Parading in front of the grandstand, with people crowding up to the fence to catch a closer view of the horses, might help decide their choice of horse to place a small wager on. A smile came across my face as I was slowly turning my horse to head back up the stretch. It was then I heard a couple of ladies yell out, "We're betting on you, Michael John, that's my son's name!" I wanted to yell back, "Save your money," but there were too many people around. I thought that maybe a miracle would happen and I'd see those ladies at the winner's circle. With Michael John's odds at fifty to one, this would be a night at the races they would never forget.

Soon, the familiar voice could be heard from the mobile gate saying, "Bring your horses up." Slowly approaching the gate, I looked over the field of horses. The number one was the solid favorite at odds of two to five. This meant that if a bet were placed on him of five dollars, only seven would be collected had it won. This indeed would be a very poor wager, especially since he had just gotten into this lower class of horses from what he had been racing against. I figured that he would finish fourth or fifth. This would leave the race up to the other three better horses in the field to decide. The clown next to me, with the number eight horse, had a very good chance of winning by going to the lead quickly, then slowing down the pace until the last quarter. My thoughts were interrupted as the mobile gate started to pick up speed. Michael John's eagerness forced me to take a firmer hold on the reins for I wanted to get him over to the rail before the first turn. The gate pulled away, and I grinned when I saw that I was having no problem of setting behind the fifth horse. Not seeing the eight horse trying for the lead seemed very unusual. That front runner must have been last as we neared the first quarter pole. After that, I was able to see how that race was unfolding. The favorite had the lead by some three lengths, with the next three choices close together as though they were triplets.

At the half-mile pole, the positions were unchanged. Still, there was no sign of the number eight horse, for the number six was behind me. I was able to see at a quick glance over my shoulder. Just then, the stupid driver on the number one horse started banging away with his whip for no reason, unless he was planning on losing this race. On the turn, I could see that he had plenty of horse left with a firm hold leading very comfortably. The whip would only make his horse shorten his stride, which he started doing. His three musketeers passed him, as if prearranged.

Nearing the three-quarter pole, I pulled out to see what I could salvage. Passing the one horse was easy now. His so-called driver did a complete job in letting the judges believe that he really tried to win. Of course, most judges wouldn't know which end the horse's tail was , unless it was pointed out to them. I always wondered, "How in the world do they obtain their jobs? It must be political," I reasoned.

Turning into the stretch, it was quite obvious that the three good old boys were going to be eating steaks tonight. They would be leaving the bones for me and whoever was behind me, for they started to pull away as though a bee had stung them. I made an attempt to keep close, to no avail. Easing across the finish line, led me into a false security. Nearing the clubhouse turn, like a bolt of lightning, some horse was closing in on me on an angle, as though out of control. I pulled up the lines as tight as I dared, to stop my horse, but not in enough time. The driver's left frame that holds the wheel, hit Michael John's right leg. The impact almost made him go down. Having a strong grip on the driving reins may have helped prevent this dangerous incident. As I was jumping off the sulky to settle down my horse, my blood started to boil. I noticed that number eight was the so-called runaway horse. The driver said that one of the reins had slipped out of his hands. It seemed to me to be too convenient that it was the right line that slipped while he pulled on the left line that took his horse and sulky into me.

From a quick glance, I could see a small gash midway on the outside of the cannon bone and another gash on the ankle. Thank heavens that I always put knee boots and tendon boots on any horse I race. These saved my horse that night from possibly becoming a cripple for life. I walked with the horse to the outside fence to further check the damage.

Seeing that he was walking fairly well, I kept going up the back stretch where the tractor driver opened up one of the gates to the barn area. In those sudden anxious moments, I let that clown of a driver know what I thought about his "losing a rein" story. I let him know that he better start saying a lot of prayers that my horse would come out of this planned accident without any side-effects.

Charlie came running just as I was walking through the gate, carrying the blankets and water pail, asking a lot of questions. I told him that everything was all right. I said, "You walk Michael John back to the barn and give him his shampoo bath and I'll be back in a few minutes with some bags of ice from the gas station up on Atlantic Boulevard".

Running to my car, I was out of the stable area in a minute. Fifteen minutes later, I was returning with the ice. This was about the only time I ever speeded with my car. I slowed down near the stable gate and continued to my barn. Charlie had also been working fast, for he was putting the warm rinse water on and then scrapping it off. I grabbed a couple of clean towels and started to rub and talk to Michael John to calm him down. This was the only time he had ever gotten hurt in a race. Charlie was then telling me that the number eight horse's driver was almost laying completely backwards, holding his horse in last place. He had no intentions of finishing any where near the leaders, only near me. "You are so right, Charlie," I said. "After you put on the blankets, put the ice and water in a tub so you can set his foot in it, while I return with a vet." Just as I was about to leave, lo and behold, the vet's white pickup was driving to the barn. He said that he had received a phone call from his truck that I might be in need of his services. He said the call came from someone who witnessed the accident from the clubhouse.

While he was taking the X-rays of the full leg and ankle, my thoughts suddenly flashed back to Illinois. I almost said out loud, "Oh no, not again!" I hoped that I could trust this vet.

After the vet left, I put Michael John's foot in the deep tub of ice water to reduce the swelling that had formed. While Charlie held on to the horse's halter, I started to prepare the hot bran mash. We were just a might off our usual schedule. Two hours later, after drying the leg and ankle, I placed a large amount of healing salve over the wounds, then wrapped a thick sheet of sterile cotton around the leg and put a bandage over it to hold it in place for the night. Only then I realized that it was two in the morning.

"Let's get a snack and then go to bed," I told Charlie, "after I check on Rarity." As we drove to the restaurant, I again started thinking of the race. I said to Charlie, "You know, I should have had you ride shotgun with me tonight, after all. That damn clown deliberately threw that race, just to get even with me for not taking that fistful of money in the paddock. He must have lost his pants that night when Rarity won." I continued, "I almost lost my horse!"

Those judges and track officials must have taken their mattresses with them to the track that night, like some White Sox baseball players in the World Series, for a little nap.

The next morning, the Toth family were waiting for me, for they had heard about the incident only an hour before. It didn't take them long to ask, "Did your winning with Rarity have anything to do with this?" I replied, "None whatsoever. It was just an unavoidable accident." That eased their minds. For I kind of figured that as soon as they heard of it through the track's grapevine, the worrying would begin. To calm things down just a little more, I said, "Let's all go out for breakfast. Charlie and I only had a sandwich after we were finished at two o'clock this morning." I went to check out my horse who was standing by his stall door with his head out of the top half of the open door. I gave him a light meal for he had plenty to eat the night before. I said, "Later I'll take off the bandages after I see what the X-rays look like."

As the Toth family were getting into their car, Charlie came up to me and whispered into my ear, "You know you'll go to hell for lying. Telling those people it was just an accident." "Not me, " I said, "I had my fingers crossed!" As I grinned at him I said, "That's why I didn't go over to that driver's tack room and box his ears. Then the Toth family would know for sure and that would make them feel very upset."

Returning from the restaurant, I still had a few hours before the vet would arrive with the X-rays. Good or bad, the tension was nerve racking, to say the least. I tried to ease my mind by reminding myself that he did not favor the right leg while walking back to the barn. This alone should have convinced me to keep calm. Saying and doing is like summer and winter!

It was best for me to keep busy until the vet showed up. I had Charlie stay with Michael John while I prepared Bye-Bye Sam for his usual five miles of jogging. Leaving, I yelled to Charlie, "If the vet gets here sooner, come out and find me, cheers!"

Three hours later, Bye-Bye Sam had a clean stall, cooled out with a shampoo bath and ate a meal fit for a "horse king". Still, no vet. Since it was one o'clock in the warm afternoon, I was warm enough even without the stress. Taking a bottle of freshly squeezed orange juice from the refrigerator, I forced myself to sit down and listen to the radio while waiting, no matter how long it would take, even if I had to cancel driving a couple of horses that night.

Four glasses of juice later, the white pickup came into view. As soon as the door opened, I looked at the vet's face for a quick answer. Only when he reached out his hand to shake mine, did I give a sigh of relief. The vet then told me that there were no fractures, and soaking the horse's leg in a tub of ice water for an hour or so each day would make the swelling go down within four days.

"Well, " I told the vet, "thanks for everything and also your quick response last night." As I handed him a $100 bill, I said, "Keep the change."

"Charlie, you look after everything, and I'll get a few bags of ice. Then I'll be here for the rest of the afternoon. I'll be soaking Michael John's leg and listening to some soft music on the radio. See you tonight, I have two horses to race in the second and eighth races. We should have no difficulty, the competition is weak."

It's strange how something or someone could change a person's plans. Just twenty-four hours ago, I hadn't a care in the world. I was enjoying my career, then some clown comes into the picture and tries to ruin everything because of his greed for money and a lack of desire to earn it himself.

While sitting there holding my horse while he stood in the rubber tub of ice water, he must have also felt that something was very different that day. I knew he was hurting. I wondered if he knew how he got hurt and that I had nothing to do with it. Even though had I taken that bribe and Rarity had finished last, then this clown would have been trying to win the race instead of trying to destroy a horse. "Well, Michael John," I said as I started to give him a few light pats on his shoulder and his forehead, "what goes around, comes around. In a couple of weeks I'm going to take you to a nice farm for a long vacation, in a couple of weeks, just a few miles from here to heal your wounds and forget about this ever happening." I told him, "From what I've seen of this country fair-type race track, I'd rate it second to, yep, you guessed it, Sportsman Park. I would love to see both closed down." I would have gladly paid to be given the opportunity to drive the first bulldozer to help tear these scandalous track buildings down for a quiet and peaceful grass-covered meadow, with trees and flowers. It could be a cemetery for all of the horses that have died there, due to the abuse done to them by the personnel.

Michael John started to nod his head up and down as though he understood every word spoken. "Maybe he did," I thought. For that, I said, "Here is a red, delicious apple." I thought, "If only people were as good as horses."

Pompano Park would be closing its scheduled race meets at the end of April. The two weeks remaining would be enough time for my horse to be ready to be shipped to the farm. I probably wouldn't have raced him here again anyway. It would almost be certain that I wouldn't ever race another horse of mine on this track again, unless hell froze over.

Tonight would be the end to all of the frustrations of the past twenty-four hours. I had a delightful evening, winning both races with considerable ease. This was solely due to the fact that these two colts outclassed the other horses in their respective races.

In their previous races, eight days before, they were

entered with the same competition. They were also heavily favored to win, but both finished last, in two minutes, with the same driver. Their winning times were one minute and fifty-eight seconds, as though they were twins. Obviously, Mr. and Mrs. Lawrence, the owners, were very displeased with their driver's unprofessional drives. That was why he was watching television while I was getting my picture taken. It gave me a thrill to see the owners and their family bolting into the winner's circle, jumping for joy with hugs and kisses for everyone. Holding a few winning pari-mutuel tickets was the frosting on the cake.

With the usual hand shakes, I was invited to have dinner the following night at the Top of the Home Restaurant. It was on the seventeenth floor of the Home Bank Building in Hollywood, Florida — strictly lobster and two-inch porter house steaks.

Bye-Bye Sam was quickly developing into the class racehorse that was expected of him for the amount of money spent. During his training miles, I was clocking in at two minutes and ten seconds. Confident that he would be in extraordinary physical condition for the next month's Messenger Stakes race, I informed Red Scott of his progress. Hearing this remarkable news, he stated that he would phone Mr. Galt in Illinois. Maybe now I would receive a word of thanks, I thought. If Bye-Bye Sam should just happen to win, he might break loose with a can of Pepsi.

The Top of the Home Restaurant had indeed lived up to its expectations as one of the finest eating establishments in Florida. The surrounding scenery from our window view table on the seventeenth floor was magnificent. We could see the giant royal palm trees and the bougainvillea trees fully laden with clusters of brightly-colored flowers of pink and purple.

Our meal started off with a jumbo shrimp cocktail, which had been served in a 12-inch porcelain clam shell designed dish. It was filled with crushed ice with a dozen shrimp placed around and over the edge, along with a glass dish of cocktail sauce. This was followed by a bowl of steaming hot minestrone soup and a Caesar salad. Much later, two uniformed waiters wheeled to our table the main meal. Lobsters and porterhouse steaks on sizzling broiler platters. After everything there was strawberry short-cake.

The conversation during this delicious meal centered around Mr. and Mrs. Lawrence's racing stable of thirty-seven horses. They were without a regular driver and would be leaving at the end of the meet for the spring and summer race track in Canada.

Before the evening came to a much-too-soon close, I assured them that I would give their proposition complete consideration. Mainly, if my horse's injury healed quickly and how Bye-Bye Sam would do in his up and coming race.

Someone must have been looking over me, I thought. Michael John recovered enough for me to take him to the farm and I obtained a foreman position for Charlie there. He would take my Doberman with him for the long summer and fall, until I returned to Florida from Canada. I decided that it would be a good opportunity to see this great country plus make a few dollars and look for some yearlings that I might purchase.

Bye-Bye Sam won the Messenger Stakes race in a very close photo-finish. It could have gone either way. Canada, here I come!

Chapter 11

Magnificent Territory

Taking a leisurely, scenic route to Canada was a most enjoyable and relaxing trip. This was the only time in my life that I wasn't following a horse van or had to be somewhere on a certain day. With Michael John, Charlie and my Doberman on the farm, some of the stress was relieved from Michael John's injury.

There are many horse farms that I would have had second guesses of boarding any of my animals, for they too have problems of obtaining responsible employees. They also cut corners in the feeding and care in order to have a larger profit margin. The cheaper the help the poorer the class of workmanship you will receive. That is a proven fact.

Arriving in Nashville, Tennessee, on the second day, put me over halfway to my destination. A four or five-day stopover would enable me to see the Grand Ol'e Opry show and do a little sight-seeing.

A week later, I was driving east of Detroit, Michigan, on Route 401 with only two hundred miles more to go. I felt very rested and hoped that I would be of useful service in driving Mr. Lawrence's horses to the winner's circle.

Driving into the stable area of the Greenwood Race Track in Toronto, Canada, I was immediately impressed with the magnitude and landscaping. Whoever was in charge knew their business. I drove over to the Lawrence's stable and received a warm and friendly welcome. They had arrived the day before, and were still in the process of getting organized. At first glance, I could see that this was no fly-by-night outfit. Looking down the shed roll, I could see forty stalls with neatly painted equipment trunks next to each door. Each set of harnesses were in brightly-colored zip-up bags with the letter "L" in the middle, all hanging above each trunk. "Yes," I said to myself, "this is what a lot of honest work will bring."

In the following months, it was quite obvious to me that these Canadian people were truly great horsemen and horsewomen. They took pride in their stables and horses, win or lose. Over 300 races later and a lot of fishing in between, the geese were already gathering for their long flight south for the winter. The once-green leaves of trees were dressed in their autumn colors of red and gold, as though they were going to her majesty's ball.

This could mean only one thing. It was now post-time for me along with the Lawrence family and a stable of horses to start preparing for Florida. This had been a memorable experience that I shall certainly never forget. Even though the purses were small, there was very little "hanky-panky" going on in those six months. I saw no lame horses going to the post to race. This was one of the main reasons that I would return to race my own horses in the summer and autumn. The Lawrence family were pleased with my accomplishments and we both made a few extra dollars more than we had figured.

Chapter 12

The Turning Point

Ten days later, I was driving into the farm yard where Charlie was walking Michael John to the wooden fence pasture. He was turning him loose for his day-long time in the grass under a sunny blue sky. His coat was a golden, reddish-brown, with a nice shine. I knew from this quick glance that Charlie had taken excellent care of him in my absence.

Charlie waited for me at the gate while I ran towards him, carrying a small bag of apples. There was no doubt that Michael John recognized me as I reached out an apple to him. With one bite, the first half was being chewed up. Shaking Charlie's hand, he informed me that the horse was now completely healed and was running like the wind. I gave a big sigh of relief as I told Charlie that I wouldn't be taking him back to Pompano Park for the races. Instead, I would leave him here until the Spring. Then we would start training in Kentucky. In four months, he would be ready for the big-money races. Meanwhile, I would drive horses for the Lawrence stable to pass these winter months by (and do a little fishing).

I could tell from Charlie's face that he wanted to be back in the action of the race track, and not the peace and quiet of the farm. I hurriedly told him, "Spring is right around the corner and if I should happen to be driving a class of horse that has a better than normal chance of winning, I'll drive out and take you to see the race. Maybe we'll even put a few dollars on it so we can win enough money for a Greek-style broiled chicken dinner!" That brought out a roar of laughter.

As Charlie opened the gate to release Michael John, he

took off like a jet with his tail straight up in the air. I was so thrilled at seeing this demonstration of his soundness that I had almost forgotten putting his foot into the tub of ice-water just some seven months before. I know of many so-called horsemen that would have had him in a race within two weeks, with the help of Mother Veterinarian's needles.

Through the entire winter months of driving horses at Pompano Park, not one horse looked good enough for me to wager any of my money. The majority of them had been "raced out" with over forty-five races each year. This was without getting a rest for a few months on a farm. The remainder of these horses were placed in classes over their ability to be competitive in, due to management's classification system. It is no wonder that the Dog Races at Hollywood Park have a greater attendance with a larger mutuel handle than Pompano Park. Even for a novice, by watching his or her third race, they could easily see that all that glitters is not gold. This is because of the driver's unprofessional acts during a race.

For the many hours per day that I was putting in other people's horses, the cash register was making very little noise. It obviously left no doubt in my mind that it would be impossible to obtain any high-class yearlings unless I salted away a huge bankroll. I was driving other people's horses at the usual ten percent. To cash in a decent wager, one must drive a horse that is in a class where he has a good chance of finishing in the money and not be raced every week of the year. As it is, the only time a horse is sent to a farm is when all of the injections have failed to help his lameness.

Years before, when I first started in this venture, horse racing season always started on Washington's Birthday, February 22nd and ended in November. Then some bright clown went to the Governor of Illinois, stating that with the football and baseball seasons also over, the general public had plenty of loose money just burning holes in their pockets. They were looking for some kind of action to bet on. Thus, with the Governor assigning the winter dates, this would be advertised as the only game in town. The American race horse would now be racing twelve months per year unless the temperature reached forty-five below zero. Only then would the night's races be postponed. I would like to know the clown's name who wrote that clause into the official ruling. He wanted to make sure that the State of Illinois would not lose one night's paycheck from the mutuel handle during the winter months. It's a lead pipe cinch that on these cold nights, it would be very easy to predict where he would be — sitting home watching television and eating hot popcorn, never caring about the poor horses suffering in the cold, blowing snow.

Another reason for the horsemen to be racing their two year-old horses was that the race track officials wave a few dollars for two year-olds' races. It's no wonder that the majority of these two year-old horses aren't around when they should become four. There are just too many states that want to conduct races the entire year with not enough fresh, sound horses to fill their cards. There will never be enough horses, especially in this day and age. With all of the abuse, illegal drugs and being over-raced, most horses are so fatigued that during races they would stumble and, in some cases, break a leg. When this happens in front of the grandstand or clubhouse, where the patrons would see the evil side, the race track officials waste no time in having their employees place large sections of canvas around the fallen horse until a trailer arrives to haul him off the track.

Yes, these states have quite a racket going on. These tracks receive thousands of dollars each night that they have races, with not one penny invested. With so much easy loose-money lying around from race tracks alone, it's no wonder that some people will go through any expense to get elected to a public office. This is where their grubby fingers will stick like glue to those green-backs which the public likes to throw into the air during their day at the races. It's not in my blood to be a crooked politician or a Governor. My only choice was to ship Michael John to Kentucky, and in the next four months have him in razor-sharp condition. If I was successful in winning at least three races before the fall yearling sales, I would have my one or two high-class colts. It would either be feast or famine.

The cards were already dealt. I wish that I could have

seen in advance how my well-planned time table would work out. If no Joker would show up in the deck, I'd have a fair chance. Otherwise, this project could be all but destroyed. My new title would be "Mike the Pear Driver!" One thing was for sure. My hands would be very clean washing dishes if it ever came to that stage.

My new Merhow blue, two-horse trailer arrived on April 4th, 1970. I called Charlie to have Michael John ready for his trip to Kentucky around six in the morning. Along with his horse the farm people wanted me to race for them, Charlie would receive a weekly check for trainer and caretaker services. It would also be good for my horse to be riding with another horse in the trailer.

April 5th, in the afternoon, we made our first rest stop for the horses near Ocala, Florida. This is called "horse country", and there are many farms of high standards. So for a few dollars, we unloaded the horses for the remainder of the day to run in the pasture.

The next morning we were fully refreshed and had a home-cooked farm breakfast. We were back on Route 75. This was a million times better to ship the horses this way, rather than in a crowded semi trailer van that would be on the road for three to four days without taking the horses off for rest and relaxation. Our next farm stop would be a few miles north of Chattanooga, Tennessee, the next day. It would be like a breeze on Route 75 into Lexington, Kentucky.

On April 7th, about three in the afternoon, we pulled into the barn area and quickly unloaded the horses into their stalls. That would be their home for the next four months. If all went well, we would be racing at Washington Park, in Homewood, Illinois, where I had won my first race. If not, I would cross that bridge when I got to it. The temperature was a mild sixty-seven degrees under a sunny, clear-blue sky, compared to Illinois which was around thirty-nine degrees. This was why I elected to train here. Besides, no one knew me here, so they wouldn't be watching to see how my horses were doing, as the rail birds would be doing in Illinois. All that the racing form would show is that my horse hadn't raced since April, 1969. If I could get him back in condition, I would. If I couldn't, I would retire him. There wouldn't be any need for Mother Vet's needles to keep him racing until he would drop on the track.

By the Fourth of July, Michael John was training better than he had ever done in his life. His feet seemed to float through the air and his racing stride was so smooth a glass of water could be sitting on his back and not a drop would spill out. I only hoped that the next month would go that well, for I would be into serious training miles. Michael John must be able to break his own record plus have a little speed in reserve in order for me to take him to Illinois.

Charlie would always train his horse the same day. This was a great advantage for both of us, for horses will always work better with another horse along side. We would take turns being parked on the outside of the other, for a harder workout mile.

August 2nd, we timed the horses workout miles so that the final one would be around one in the afternoon. This was when the other stabled horses would be finished and the help would be all gone to lunch. The temperature was near eighty-five degrees but cloudy. It looked as though it was going to rain later on. The track was dry and fast. As we walked to the track, I told Charlie that I was going to give him a ten-length lead. I told him to go as fast as his horse would go without a whip. If I could catch him, we would start packing for a trip up north. Charlie smiled and said, "Michael John, I'll be back at the barn when you'll be just crossing the finish line. Don't forget, we went in two minutes and four seconds last week and we were side by side at the finish." He asked, "Are you sure you want me to start ten lengths ahead?" I said, "Charlie, does a cow give milk?"

As we jogged by the then-empty grandstand, I nervously looked around to see if anyone was near who still hadn't left. I didn't want anyone watching the horses' workouts. Not seeing anyone, I told Charlie that we should start as usual, then turn at the top of the stretch and let the horses go at the wire of this mile-long track. I also told Charlie to check his watch and try to get to the first half in one minute and two seconds or better.

As I let Charlie get ahead of me, he yelled out, "I'll see

you back at the barn." His horse was going very good. With his ears straight up, he was off. When he was at the start, I gave a quick glance. I guessed that I was about ten to twelve lengths behind him. "Perfect," I thought. Michael John must have thought that I had fallen asleep to let that other horse get so far in front. By then, he was pulling the reins trying to catch up. I was talking to him out there as we were by ourselves without the yelling of other drivers. This was common in races and made it much easier for me to control him.

I looked at my stopwatch when Charlie passed the half in one minute and two seconds. I was then about seven lengths back. It felt as though I had tons of horsepower pulling at the reins. Going up the back stretch, nearing the far turn, I picked up two more lengths. As Charlie turned for the home stretch, I saw him shake his driving lines asking his horse for more speed. When I reached the same spot, I called out, "O.K., Michael John, you can go now!" Never in my years of driving horses had I felt the power in my hands as I experienced with a firm hold that day.

I was closing in on Charlie, as though he had stopped to get a drink of water. As I flew by him, I yelled out, "Charlie, I've got to go; I'll see you at the barn!" I was laughing as I went the final eight of the mile workout in two minutes. I was simply shocked when I looked a second time at my stopwatch. Impossible, I thought. I'll see what Charlie has on his stopwatch when I crossed the line. I pulled up to the outside fence and quickly got off the sulky. I patted Michael John, thanking him for such a nice birthday present he had given me three days early. Charlie pulled up yelling, "Do you know how fast you went?" He was holding out his watch for me to see. Saying nothing, I wanted to see what he had. Lo and behold, I was correct with my time. Charlie's watch showed two minutes and two-fifth seconds. He said that he was about ten lengths behind when I crossed the finish line. In a low voice I said, "Let's get back to the barn and give these two good horses their shampoo baths and hot bran-mash. Remember, mum's the word, I don't have to remind you." I said, "We'll talk over a thick prime-rib dinner when we're finished."

The horses were both eating their special dinner and came out of their workouts in superb condition. Two hours later, I put the Doberman on a short nylon rope between both stalls before we went out for our dinner. Again, I patted Michael John with a word of thanks.

While we were eating our delicious dinner, I went over my plans again, now that we were knocking at the door of a much larger payday. "Charlie," I said, "I think that we should give the horses the next two days of grazing in this warm, blue-grass country. I would then reconfirm my stalls application and slip into Washington Park by August 6th. I told Charlie, "With a couple of days rest and a few jogging miles, I'll find a race for your horse and mine. Of course, you know what to say when anyone asks about the horses." Charlie was still chewing a large piece of steak, but quickly added, "Michael John, if you told me that a turkey could pull a boxcar, I'd put a harness on that bird and find some pigeon to make a bet with."

It was a wonder that we didn't get thrown out of that restaurant with all the laughter. It really helped me relax for a few minutes, "Charlie," I said, "you and Michael John really made my day!"

Chapter 13

The Crossroads

Arriving at Washington Park main stable gate on August 6th in the early afternoon, I was informed that three stalls were allotted to me in barn thirty-three. They were at the south end of the stable area. Within minutes, it was quite obvious that management hadn't spent one penny in the stable area. The water was the worst problem as it was still the water from the old well system. All of the horsemen were promised that it would be changed over to the city water supply. I filled one pail and it looked like I had a bucket full of dark-orange Kool-Aid. This was caused by the old, rusted water pipes. The smell of the water was like rotten eggs. No horse would drink that garbage. I located the feedman's truck and he dropped off enough hay, straw and sweet feed grain for the week. He would then return in a few days time.

While Charlie was fixing up the stalls, I called up a bottled water company and ordered twenty-five gallons of water. I explained to them that it was an emergency and that the driver would be given an extra twenty dollars if he got there "like now, or even sooner!" Not taking any chances with this company, I unhooked the horse trailer after we finally put the horses in their stalls. We also put in four bales of straw for them to roll in and a couple flakes of baled hay to nibble on.

I then went to the local grocery store and brought back ten one-gallon jugs of spring-filtered water. Later I'd get a large refrigerator so we could mix a bottle of cold water with a bottle that would be placed in our tack room. Then the water wouldn't be too cold for the horses to drink. They could get sick if the water was too cold especially after a workout or race. All animals must have a sufficient amount of water to prevent them from becoming dehydrated. I only saw a few trainers hauling-in small drums of water from the outside of the track. The others said that if their horses got thirsty enough, they would drink anything. "Real bright trainers," I thought.

With my refrigerator installed and the second shipment of twenty bottles of water stacked in the tack room, this problem was solved as quickly as it had arrived.

On August 9th, I had entered Michael John in a race where the conditions should have favored him, as he hadn't raced in over a year. Of course, there was always a chance that the racing secretary would add on an "also eligible" clause for horses etc. that he would want in the race. Sometimes, an owner or trainer would go to his office saying that he had a certain horse that he would like to race but he was just one or two thousand dollars over the winning limit. He would know that this would be a race for easy pickings for a win.

Lord only knows what transpired behind those closed doors. Most of the time, an amazing feat would occur, as I found out the next day when the entries were posted for the racing program of August 11th, 1970. At first glance, I knew all of the horses from races from the previous year. The exception was number one, a horse named Forli, with driver Williams. I only slightly knew of him from the high-class horses he always seemed to be driving for different owners. He would then ship off to another track. I thought, "Maybe Charlie knows something of this horse," as I drove back to my barn trying to place him. At least I drew a favorable post position, the number three.

I gave the entry sheet to Charlie to look over and he only knew what I already did but stated one quick way to find out any information. That was to go over and have a cup of coffee at the track restaurant right about this time. The trainers would be there that had a horse in a race. Getting up from sitting on a bale of straw, Charlie said, "I think I could use a cup of coffee, I'll be back shortly."

I had finished waxing my sulky when Charlie returned with a very disgusted look. He threw the entry sheet to the ground. "You're right when you said that Williams seemed to be driving only high-class horses. Well, I don't know what he drove before, but he sure has a good one now. He had won with this horse the last time out in two minutes and one second." He told me, "Every other horse's time in your race is around two minutes and four to two minutes and five seconds. I think you'd better wait for another race, this is some kind of bearcat. From what I've heard, he's entered in a stake race at Yonkers' race track in New York next month. You may also be interested to know that he got into this race on the 'also eligible' clause because of being a younger horse. He's a four year-old, and we both know that he is in his prime."

"Well, Charlie," I told him, "when the cards are dealt, we either play or fold our hand. You know that we have come too far to roll over." I couldn't help from laughing, as I said, "Charlie, there's one thing for sure. We'll get a bushel basket full of odds. The track management might even put larger numbers on the tote board, just for this race." That brought out laughter from Charlie. I then told him, "Besides, when the programs come out and all of these hot-shot horsemen see how over-matched Michael John is, there won't be anyone in the paddock shoving hundred-dollar bills into my pocket, telling me to hold my horse back from winning." That put the frosting on the cake. Charlie was feeling pretty good. Deep inside of me, though, I was plenty worried, but trying not to show it.

The morning of the race, I took Michael John for a long walk and let him roll in the tall grass in a field along Halstead Street on the east side of the track. I then took him back to a blacksmith I could trust to put on a new set of shoes. Even the blacksmith was talking about my race. That race seemed to be getting more attention than any other in some time. The talk was all about Forli. He was saying that all Forli had to do was to show up at the paddock and the photographer would take his winning picture there to save time. Then the track officials could give him his check for the race!

The more I studied the program, the more I started believing in this "wonder horse." Then I jokingly stated, "I should get a discount for the shoes you're putting on my horse, for all he's going to do tonight is wear them down for nothing." The blacksmith looked up from his bent position as he was putting the last shoe on. He said to me, "Just think, you'll be getting a good workout tonight, then we'll all bet on Michael John next week in return." I said, "Maybe next year," as I paid him thirty-five dollars for his services. I said, "Cheers, George," as I left, leading Michael John carefully back to his stall.

Chapter 14
Tension

It was August 11th, 1970. Early supper-time for Michael John consisted of a gallon of oats with a handful of ground corn and two sliced apples. This I gave to him at four o'clock in the afternoon, after Charlie had fed his horse. I told him to watch Michael John and the dog, and I would bring him a couple of sandwiches and a piece of apple pie after I had a light lunch.

In the tackroom, I handed Charlie two envelopes marked "Number 1" and "Number 2". Both had money inside. I told him, "I want you to bet one minute before post time. Bet all of the first envelope to win and all of the second to place." As Charlie was looking inside each, he gave out a great, "Holy Cow!" He said, "Michael John, are you sure you want to bet all of this?" I replied, "Yep, you got it."

I added, "For tonight, don't go to the grandstand. There are too many people from the stable area that might recognize you and follow you to the betting windows, so slip over to the clubhouse. Your share of the bet is included. If I can at least finish second, we'll be in good shape. Cheers now, I'll be back in an hour."

I returned at five fifteen and gave Charlie his lunch. Then I opened a couple of cans of Alpo beef dinner for my faithful Doberman.

While Charlie was eating, I started to check over the equipment I was going to be using. This included the nylon harness, knee boots and tendon boots. I also added a set of blinkers that would fit over the bridle. They would keep Michael John looking straight ahead, thus he wouldn't be able to pay any attention to a horse that might be closing in on either side of him. After the incident in his last race, he just might remember and shorten his stride if another horse drew along side.

Animals are much smarter than we people give them credit for. They never forget a wrong.

At six forty-five in the evening, Charlie had Michael John hooked up to the sulky. He was waiting outside for me as I finished putting on my driving silks and helmet. Taking hold of the reins near the bridle, Charlie said, "Well, this is the night you have been waiting for. Good luck." He patted Michael John. I started walking away from the barn, saying, "We'll need all we can get!"

Just then I turned left onto the black-top roadway to the track which was about two blocks away. My thoughts were suddenly interrupted by the sound of the engine of a dark blue Oldsmobile or Buick being started. It was parked about twenty yards to my right. I noticed that the car started to move slowly in my direction. I stopped my horse on the shoulder of the road to wait until the car passed, but as it drew along side the engine was turned off and the driver rolled down his window. I was completely flabbergasted when I recognized that it was, of all people, Phil Langley, the Superintendent of Racing at Sportsman Park. If it weren't for his father, Peter Langley, setting him up as Racing Secretary before he passed away, this clown would have probably ended up as a bum on West Madison Street in Chicago. I had always classified him as "two-faced". While shaking your hand he'd be stabbing you in the back.

He started off by saying, "How is your horse for tonight's race?" I gave him an answer that he would never forget. I said, "Phil, if you're going by the Racing Secretary's office, how about telling them for me to leave the track lights on a little longer after the races. With all of those tough horses I'm in with, I'll be lucky just to finish before breakfast time!" As he and his passengers broke out laughing, I was able to get a better look at the other four people in the car. They were dressed in dark suits, with short-brimmed hats as though they had just stepped out of an old Al Capone gangster movie. I quickly branded them all as "The Unholy Five."

I think that Old Phil forgot himself for a minute, when he said, "You have a few classy horses to race with, especially Forli. We came out to watch him WIN!" This was an answer that I'll never forget. This statement made me very nervous to say the least. He then said, "We've got to go now, you take it easy." As they slowly drove off, I was still thinking of Phil Langley's last bold remark, "We came out to watch Forli win!"

I have always wondered what the reaction would have been if I had told Phil that I had worked Michael John in blazing speed and that I was going to do my damndest to win that night. I was positive that these five clowns didn't get all dressed up and drive over fifty miles just to come out here to buy a few boxes of popcorn.

The walk to the track was to relax my horse. Instead, I needed it for myself. Never have I had such an experience of this kind. It did rattle me, but I knew that I had to put it aside for the time being. I had a more important three hours ahead of me.

I stopped Michael John at the entrance of the track to let him look around for a few seconds. There were only a few horses on the track at this early part of the evening. The lights hadn't been turned on yet. The sky in the west had a bright orange glow with a warm light breeze. The temperature of seventy-four degrees made this ideal for racing. With that in mind, and trying to get back to the business at hand, I sat on the sulky, talking to Michael John.

As we slowly jogged around this mile-long track for the third time, I said, "Well, big fella, let's turn and go a nice mile." The second that we started down the stretch towards the start, he was already on the iron and forcing me to take a firmer hold on the reins. The first warm-up mile was fantastic. I only hoped that his last one would be equally sharp. The surface was a lot deeper than normal, giving it a more yielding cushion for a horse's legs. The speed time of all the races would also be a tad slower, with most of the front-pacing horses having the difficult task of keeping the lead the entire mile, unless a driver was aware of these track conditions. This would help a horse like Forli because of the fact that he comes from behind and his late drive in the last half-mile. I like this cushioned track and so does Michael John. We headed for the paddock.

After putting a couple of blankets over my horse, it was about fifteen minutes before the first race. As my race was the fifth, I would take Michael John out for his last warm-up mile after the second race. Charlie would be leisurely walking to the clubhouse if I gave him an "all clear" sign. He would be watching my last warm-up mile on the platform of the backstretch fence.

Minutes later, as all of the horses for my race were in their stalls, I was able to get my first look at this great horse, Forli. "Yes," I said to myself, "he does look like a million bucks, standing proud." He was about the same size as my horse. I only wished I owned him. I'd have a real team then. He also had the new, lightweight nylon harness and was sporting a brand-new sulky. There was no doubt about it. These people came to get their picture taken in the winner's circle. I also noticed that other drivers walked past me to look at Forli. I have to give credit where credit is due. At that split-second, I thought, "Finishing second to Forli would be no disgrace, now that I've seen him."

The first race was over. The only thing I was interested in was the time of the race. It did go two seconds slower than these same horses went the week before. If the second race did likewise, I would warm-up my horse accordingly.

With the horses on the track for the second race, I started to put the bridle on Michael John. All of the other drivers were also getting their horses ready for the last warm-ups. Ten minutes go by mighty fast when you're busy and nervous. I planned to let all of the horses go ahead of me so I would be last, warming up my horse when these drivers would be headed back to the paddock and unable to see my warm-up mile.

Turning at the top of the stretch, I felt as though I was driving a bright-blue Lamborghini Countach automobile down the stretch, almost forgetting to click my watch. Michael John was never this razor sharp in his life. I thought before that he had reached his peak. That year's layoff may have been a blessing in disguise. I had a tight hold on the reins as we blew by the half-mile post in one minute and five seconds. We were heading up the back-stretch. I had a quick glance at Charlie. I knew that he was also looking at his stopwatch. No other horses were on the track as I turned for the home-stretch. I had all I could do holding Michael John from going too fast and being obvious of his sharpness of speed to anyone watching very carefully.

As I crossed the finish line, I pressed my stopwatch. It read two minutes and eight seconds. I started to ease around the clubhouse turn and onto the backstretch where I would send Charlie and two envelopes to the clubhouse. While I was sponging off Michael John in the paddock, he wasn't even blowing. He only showed signs that he might have been out for a light buggy drive in the park.

The driver and groom next to me jokingly said, "Michael John, it looks like you'll be coming in after all of us will be back at our barns. You must be practicing tonight." My reply was, "You wouldn't have a long rope that I could hook on to your sulky so you could pull me down the stretch?" A few others heard this remark and got a jolly laugh from it. I was pleased with their jokes as it helped relax me a little. I could feel my heart going "pitter-patter" as I was putting on the blankets and clipping them together. By the time I had taken off the knee boots and tendon boots to clean and replace them, I heard the paddock judge call out, "Put your bridles on for the fifth race." Without Charlie helping me tonight, I didn't have one second to sit around and worry.

It was the moment of truth. The sound of the bugler over the loudspeakers of the grandstand informed the large crowd of patrons that the horses were coming onto the track.

The clubhouse fences as well as the grandstand were filled wall to wall with people. There must not have been anything worthwhile to watch on television that night or it was an exceptionally nice, warm night to be out in the fresh air to lose a few hard-earned dollars. I took my usual glance at the tote board and was forced to take another. I thought that my eyes were playing tricks with me when I saw that I was posted at ninety-nine to one, and could go even higher!

Forli's odds were one to five, meaning that a patron would only make one dollar for every five wagered. Ninety-nine to one was as high as the numbers would show on the board. If a horse's odd were higher than that and won, the mutuels would be paid accordingly.

I was very shocked because I had driven some horses that a mule could have beaten, and they were never posted at these large odds. I said to myself as we headed up the stretch where the mobile starting gate was waiting, "If those odds stay this high, I could buy this race track." I almost laughed out loud. Three minutes later, the starter's voice came over the car's loudspeakers, "O.K., gentlemen, bring your horses up to the gate."

With all of the horses pacing slowly up to the long outstretched arms of the gate, the big Buick started to slowly roll down the quarter-mile stretch, picking up speed with each second of the clock. I had my hands full trying to keep Michael John's nose off the gate. I wanted to take him back and get over to the rail quickly. Glancing over to the rail, I noticed that Forli was at least two lengths from the gate as we neared the eighth-mile pole. Maybe he was going to make a faster running start just as the gate would pull away. I would have liked to have had him in front of me at the start. At the sixteenth-mile pole, the sound of the Buick's engine told me he was at maximum speed and pulling away while folding the arms of the gate inwards.

At the start, it looked as though everybody wanted the lead at the first turn near the clubhouse. I was able to ease Michael John over to the rail with the number two horse in front of me. The mobile gate kicked up a lot of dust, so it wasn't until after the turn that I could see where the other horses were placed. At the quarter-mile, I saw that Forli was sitting under a firm hold in fifth place. I was seventh with two horses having a clear view of the entire field behind me. The time of the first quarter-mile was a slow thirty-one seconds. If the speed didn't pick up quickly, I would have had to move sooner than I wanted to. Those front horses would have had plenty of reserve speed for the home stretch, if they cut out a slow first half with no one to force them faster.

I leaned over to the left so I could see the leader and time his half-mile time. When he passed the half-mile pole, I was amazed at the unheard of slow time of one minute and one second. I said to my horse, "Hell, Michael John, we almost went that fast in our warm-up mile." I pulled him out from the rail as I said this. I went out just a little wider for I was sure that Forli would be taking out when he saw me pulling near. To my surprise, he wasn't a bit concerned with me. He was probably thinking that I was just giving my horse a work-out as fast as I blew by him. I would have given me a little more respect if it were me sitting in that sulky.

Turning for home, there were only two horses in front with their drivers using their whips as though they were swatting flies. At the eighth-mile pole, I easily passed these two horses, quickly obtaining a two-length lead. My mind was only on one horse. Where was he?, I thought. I put both reins in my left hand and took a quick look to the left then to the right. Sure enough, all hell broke loose as we neared the sixteenth pole. I saw a horse moving faster than any other horse I had ever seen at the almost end of a race. I could see the finish line with less than a sixteenth-mile left. My mind was working like a Swiss watch. I was thinking, "Could I last before this steam roller would brush me aside?" He flew by the two horses that I had passed. With every yard, he was gaining on me. I asked Michael John for more speed, holding both reins with my left hand, and with my right holding my whip, while I had the tip it of touching the ground.

I was hoping that I wouldn't have to ask for more speed than he was already putting out by himself. There was just a couple of more feet to go. Forli was near my sulky wheel. Had Williams driven a smarter race, and wasn't so overwhelmingly confident of winning, I would have been very hard-pressed in winning this race. Just as I crossed the finish line, he went by me like a gust of wind.

I slowed Michael John up enough to let the other horses go by as someone yelled out to me, "Where have you been hiding that horse?" When it was clear, I headed him to the outside fence to turn him back to the winner's circle. I stopped Michael John for a few seconds to reach out to pat him on his rear-end, thanking him for an ultimate experience.

Slowly walking around the clubhouse fence, I spotted Charlie deep in the enormous crowd, not wanting to draw attention to himself. He gave me a nod and a huge smile to let me know that the bets were made. Entering the winner's circle, a roar of approval arose from the thousands of people who had pushed their way to the fence to see a happening. I was emotionally aroused as the photographer snapped a few keepsakes for my photo album. When the tote board lit up with the mutuel pay-off prices, a tremendous applause came from the crowd. Michael John paid $68.40 for every $2.00 wagered and $20.60 to place for every $2.00.

I didn't think that ninety-nine to one would last. The two-dollar bettors love a ninety-nine to one shot. Charlie's bets did drop the odds somewhat. It goes without saying that the chalk players (those who only bet favorites) would be hard to get along with, by losing on Forli. As the old saying goes, "You can please some of the people some of the time, but you can't please all of the people all of the time."

I had already given Michael John his shampoo bath and had been walking him around the barn area when a cab drove up to my entrance of the barn. I started to laugh when I saw Charlie stepping out, calling me over, saying that he needed thirty dollars for the cab fare and tip. Bewildered by this statement, I knew that he must have had a good reason for this act. I handed him a couple of twenties. When the cab left, he then told me that he had gone to at least six different mutuel windows after the race, cashing only a few tickets at each. This was to not draw a crowd to watch him at one window collecting a large sum of money. It would cause a lot of excitement and probably draw a few undesirables who would then follow him to the parking lot. This is why Charlie told the cab driver that he sprained his ankle and he had to get to the stable area where he had a dozen horses, but was sort of low on ready cash.

For a promise of thirty dollars for driving about a half-mile to take a horseman back to his stable, the driver wasted no time in helping Charlie into his cab. I had a good laugh saying that that was a very smart move. With no one around, Charlie unfolded from his newspaper a black plastic bag, saying, "You know what's in here?" He handed it to me. I handed him the lead shank to walk Michael John a few more rounds before giving him four more swallows of

Michael John's last race.

our bottled water. I put the bag away and got the hot bran-mash ready.

Michael John's hoofs were packed with a special mud mixture to draw out any heat if it occurred. I rubbed down his legs with Absorbine and wrapped them with a thick roll of new cotton and bandages. Placing his tub of mash on hooks in his stall, I turned him loose for his much-awaited meal. He wasted no time in pulling out a mouthful of sliced apples and carrots covered with the hot bran from the rubber feed tub.

Handing Charlie my car keys, I told him to get me a Greek-style broiled chicken dinner and whatever he wanted. I told him that for that night, I would stay with the horses just as a precautionary measure. I would add up our profits while he was gone and feed the Doberman, who was anxiously awaiting her supper.

Chapter 15
Shattered Dreams

One week after Michael John's big upset win, the race track's gossip vine was still buzzing with the news of the amazing accomplishment. Frankly, I was enjoying every minute of it, for now I was getting a little respect as a horseman after all of those years. Every afternoon, when I would take Michael John out for his walk in the vacant field near my barn, there always seemed to be someone walking by and saying, "Howdy." Maybe they had a couple of dollars on the big fellow.

In the mornings, I would help Charlie train his horse. I felt he needed another three weeks before he should be entered into his first race, which I definitely wanted him to win. It would make Charlie look good as a trainer in the eyes of the owners in Florida. I had always given him a share of my winning bets for his loyalty, but winning with his trained horse would be my bonus to him that no money could ever buy.

Many times, for example, I would see people handing a small amount of money to a so-called friend to take to the track to bet it on a horse they liked, only to find out later that the horse had won at long odds. The friend would somehow arrive at the track too late, because of a train blocking the crossing or a traffic jam, etc. They obviously kept the winnings and just said they were sorry as they handed the amount of money back that was to have been bet. I call these people, "Fair weather friends" or "Rice Christians". As long as you give them food, they will come to your church.

The following week, I started to take Michael John to the track for a few slow jogging miles in preparation for his next race which would be within eight to ten days. The week-long rest restored all the energy he used in his previous race. I was still unable to comprehend the logic that the owner of Forli had shipping him from this track the next day after the race. It was quite understandable that he would have had easy pickings in his next race. In all probability, he would be racing against the same horses, without Michael John. From the way he dusted them off in the stretch, it would be like taking candy from a baby. It was very puzzling, without a doubt.

Wednesday, August 28th, 1970: after a couple of good-spaced workout days, I entered Michael John in a race on the following Saturday night. His past winning money was salted away for the purchase of my next yearling colt which I would buy in Kentucky at the fall sales. One or two more wins would fulfill my ambitious dream.

August 30th, 1970, I picked up the entries' sheet for Saturday night's races. Michael John drew the number six position in the eighth race. Looking over the other horses entered, I figured our odds would be about four to one. The majority of the patrons would probably be betting on my horse, especially after winning over Forli. This made Michael John a favorite.

I went to my apartment around seven thirty, after having a light dinner, to watch my usual television program, *Dallas*. I haven't missed too many episodes. After the news, I went to bed for a good night's sleep.

A sudden banging on my door awoke me. The continuous pounding led me to believe that maybe the building was on fire. I quickly jumped out of bed, slipping on my pants as I hurried to the door. Unlocking it, I said out loud, "Charlie." I could see, even at this quick glance, that he was very distressed. "What's wrong?" I asked. Gasping for breath, he said, "Michael John's been hurt. Come on, I've got a cab waiting." Not bothering to put on shoes, we ran to the taxi. I yelled out, "This is an emergency, get us to Washington Park race track. There's a hundred dollars in it for you!" As the driver was burning rubber, I told Charlie to calm down and tell me what he could.

He said that he was awakened by the sound of a horse that seemed to be in pain and the sound of a horse kicking his stall. As he stepped outside, two big guys were by the stall door of Michael John. When they saw the light come on from the tack room, they both yelled out, "Let's get out of here." Charlie then saw a third man coming out of the stall. In the same breath, he said, "They killed our dog." At that instant we were pulling into the stable area of Halstead Street. Charlie was saying, "I left a couple of guys from the stable next to ours to look after Michael John and asked them to call a vet."

The cab made a cloud of dust as we slid up to my barn door. I handed the driver a one hundred-dollar bill and gave him a quick, "Thanks."

Almost falling down as I entered, the first thing I saw was my dog lying on her side. There was nothing I could do for her. As I met Charlie's friends, one was inside the stall trying to settle my horse down. He had been tied with two ropes. One rope to the left side of his halter and the other to the right. Then the ropes were tied to each wall of the stall, making it impossible for my horse to turn. He could only kick the back wall. That is what Charlie heard.

I could see three or four one-inch wide welt marks across his back, about a foot long. The same kind of marks were on his left stifle, about a foot and a half above his hoof. I started talking to him as I patted him to calm him down. I was thinking in those few minutes that he must have gone through a living hell. Had I been in that tack room with a gun, there would have been three bodies along side my dog. Yes, these lunatic losers must have waited since my race, in the event that I might have suspected something might happen after my winning. Then, I did relax my guard. I still blame myself for that, but how long can a person keep a twenty-four hour guard on his horse. The only ones that do are a few that make a lot more money than I have, with more horses in their stables.

Fifteen minutes later, the vet drove up. It was then three in the morning. In a few minutes he was injecting a pain reliever into Michael John. With some help he brought in his X-ray equipment. He took a dozen or so pictures, after which he handed me a large can of healing salve, and we both gently placed it on the welts of my horse. An hour or so later, the shots must have been working, for he was much more relaxed.

In the meanwhile, Charlie had wrapped our Doberman in a new blanket and placed her in the back seat of his friend's car. I figured that as soon as the pet cemetery opened, I would buy her a nice coffin. I didn't know what else to do but try to find these maniacs. I told Charlie, "We don't know the names of these people, but I have a very good prime suspect as to who gave the orders to destroy my horse." I told him, "Without you coming out from the tackroom, my horse would also be dead."

On September 1st, 1970, nine o'clock in the morning, I prepared a small amount of hot bran-mash with sliced apples for Michael John, for I hadn't left his side for a minute. After a few slow mouthfuls, it looked as though his left stifle received the hardest blows. From what I could figure out, it looked like they used a flat, long, tire-iron or crow bar.

I sent Charlie back to bed around five o'clock in the morning. When he got up, I would go to the racing secretary and security office to make out a report.

At eleven thirty-five, I returned from making out my report. Judging from those clowns' reactions, they wouldn't call in the police because, as they put it, "Any bad publicity for Washington Park Race Track will lower attendance and it is already low, without making it any worse." They did say that they would look into the incident. I reminded the so-called track officials that my Doberman was still wrapped up in a blanket if they cared to drive to my barn within the next fifteen minutes. After that, I would take her to the pet cemetery. I then left their office.

At ten minutes after four in the afternoon, Charlie's friend dropped me off at my apartment to clean up and change clothes. In an hour, I was driving back to the track. The first thing I asked Charlie, was, "Did any track officials stop by?" Just as I suspected, the answer was, "No." I remember using some nasty words in reference to the management, after which Charlie said, "The vet stopped by and checked out Michael John." He said, "He will be back tonight around seven o'clock with the X-rays."

"Well, at least someone was doing something right," I thought. I said, "Charlie, get us both something to eat, I'll fix up both horses' dinners while you're gone. This has been some kind of a horrible nightmare."

The vet arrived as promised. He said that the back showed no fractures, but considerable damage was done to the left stifle. He said, "Only time will tell if he will ever race again for he may favor that leg. If he is not raced, there shouldn't be any pain, once the swelling goes down. The best thing to do for him is to take him to a farm in a couple of weeks. I'll give you some pills when you're ready to go, so you'll have them if he shows signs of pain."

When Charlie returned with my meal, I gave him the bad news of the Vet's visit. I planned to take Michael John to a farm in Kentucky as soon as possible. Florida was out of the question at that time, because of the great distance. I wouldn't want him to travel much until all of the soreness was gone.

I told Charlie, "Why don't you call that owner to get his O.K. and I'll race his horse in Kentucky. Besides, their track will make this place look like a dump. Just tell him of the workouts and that his horse will win at first asking down there."

After much careful and loving care in the next month, we were finally leaving that "hell hole". In all of that time, not one track official stepped one foot in the direction of my barn. Maybe one day something unpleasant will blow their way.

Chapter 16
Struggling Comeback

With the tragic, brutal beating of Michael John firmly embedded in my mind, never to be forgotten, I was left in a state of shock and absolute disappointment. I realized that I must continue to fulfill my lifelong dream, for if I should relinquish it, what else was there left for me?

October 3rd, 1970: I was driving my car with the trailer carrying both horses. Charlie and I arrived at the farm in Kentucky in the early afternoon. I made a few extra rest stops and drove at a slower speed than normal so Michael John wouldn't be bounced around in the trailer. I had also put in a few one inch-thick sheets of foam padding on the inside of the trailer walls that he would be leaning against. This all made the trip much more comfortable for him.

Carefully unloading both horses, Charlie took his colt to the wooded fenced-in pasture and let him run. As he kicked up his heels and did a few playful bucks into mid-air in glee, it was obvious that he was enjoying himself.

I put Michael John in his extra-large stall that was well-bedded down with straw and had a fresh stainless steel pail of water. I also put in a rubber tub filled with a gallon of mixed-grain. This settled him down immediately.

I made arrangements for Michael John to stay at that farm until the following spring. Then I would decide if I would retire him. In my mind, I had already done so, but at that time, I was still very much upset about the entire incident. Time would eventually heal him and me both.

Charlie and I left the next morning with his colt for the local racetrack to see what we could salvage from all of this tragedy. It was against my better judgment to race in Kentucky. This was due to the widespread use of drugs being used on race horses, but under the prevailing circumstances, I had no choice. If I wanted to keep my promise to my loyal and faithful friend, we would just have to get his colt in superb condition. That way, he would be able to overcome the added speed of the drugs which might suddenly appear from the other horses in this race.

The one thing that was going for us was that Charlie's horse was named "Political System". I disliked this name for it always reminded me of crooked politicians and lawyers. I had told Charlie earlier that this wouldn't stop me from getting into the winner's circle. It got a little laughter from the both of us.

What followed were two speed work-outs and many jogging miles within the next three weeks. The owner of the horse flew in from Florida to watch Political System in his first race. Charlie was just a tad on the nervous side, for it was sure, without a doubt, that he wanted to be in the winner's circle after the race. And so did I.

To relax him, I told him in one quick sentence, "Charlie, if any of those drivers want to win against your horse tonight, they better start growing wings on their horses within the next twelve minutes." Just then, the paddock judge called out, "Put your bridles on for the fifth race."

The paddock was close to the grandstand entrance so Charlie would have plenty of time to put our wager down. As I got on the sulky and headed for the track, I leaned to the side and whispered, "Charlie, I'll see you in the winner's circle. Be there. Cheers, now."

Heading towards the starting gate, I noticed that our odds were only five to one. Apparently, there wasn't much speed in this field for a first-time starter to be at such unheard of short odds. My only concern at that time was that the colt would race well without any difficulties.

As the starting gate pushed away, I eased over to the rail from my number six post position. The first quarter-mile went in thirty seconds. This was just a little too fast for that class of horse. So far, I had made the right move by going to the rail and sitting seventh in this field of nine horses. When the front horse passed the half-mile pole in fifty-nine seconds, I wanted to take out my comb and fix my hair for the camera man, had I been able to. All I had to do now was wait until the three-quarter pole before I pulled out for the home-stretch drive. I noticed that all of the drivers in front of me were already flaring away with their whips. They surely would have trouble finishing this race. I glanced behind me at the two remaining horses. They were in no hurry. Maybe they were writing in their diaries of that evening's outing.

My arms were hurting something terrible, holding Political System firmly, waiting for the precise moment. I left a gap in front of me, thus enabling an easy out into the middle of the track. There were three horses across that were about finished. Going four wide, they were now behind me. Only two horses stood between me and Charlie's secured future. I let out with a couple well-spoken words as we passed the eighth-mile pole.

Like "Gone With The Wind", the two stopped using their whips, knowing that this was not going to be their night. Crossing the finish line, under a firm hold, I knew that Charlie had trained this colt magnificently.

In the winner's circle was a jubilant Charlie along with the owner and another man. I later found out that he had also flown in from Florida for he was interested in buying an un-raced colt and wanted to see his first race. I figured that he was impressed by his reactions and handshakes. He noticed that I hadn't used a whip under a firm hold with plenty of horse left. I looked like I was out for a Sunday afternoon drive in the park. I sure needed a little laugh after a race for a change.

After Political System was cooled down, and eating his hot bran-mash, we ended up in a first-class restaurant for a late dinner. It was then that Charlie was asked if he would like to continue his foreman's job at the farm. Political System would be sold in the morning when the papers would be available, at an amount that was very much more profitable than before the race. The horse would be sold to a first-class racing stable that would never allow any illegal drugs to be used.

Charlie and I were saddened by the sudden change of events, but realized that he would be firmly set for the remainder of his years with a small house on the farm. He would have maid-service and would be using his brains to have others use their backs. The colt would be given three days of rest before being shipped to Ocala, Florida.

I watched Political System being loaded with another horse that was purchased, and with a few hardy handshakes, Charlie and a great horse were leaving on their separate ways. It brought a tear or two to my reddened eyes, but when I thought that I had done something worthwhile for a good friend, the tears soon changed to a smile.

Chapter 17
Start From Scratch

For the next two months, I stayed on the farm to oversee Michael John's recovery. I was trying to decide what my next move would be. It was the most difficult decision of my life. I had some money salted away, but not enough for a top bloodline yearling. Those clowns in Illinois prevented this. I was at least fifty thousand dollars short of my goal. I could go the longer route by buying a mare and paying a breeder farm to mate her to their best proven-speed stallion.

I knew that there was no way I would ever get that kind of money driving other owner's horses. They all thought that they were champions. I couldn't blame them but ten percent of nothing was not my cup of tea. It is very unpredictable betting on horses that are unknown to me, even though I may be driving them. When I put my money down on a horse, I want to know what makes him or her tick. I can't take promises to the bank.

There was only one road that I could possibly take. Going back to driving a semi, eighteen-wheeler was about the only other thing I knew how to do. Thirty-five thousand dollars per year would buy me a cup of hot chocolate along with medical and paid vacation. It seemed that this was my only choice until something better arrived on the scene, or I located a yearling or mare. Which ever would be located first, I would buy. After that, the money I made from driving the semis would be used to raise the colts until they would be ready to race.

In February, 1971, I had no use for my driving whip as I was rolling down the highway in Indiana in a semi, diesel eighteen-wheeler. I was driving through the blowing snow and freezing temperatures. It was not exactly like lying on a white sandy beach in Tahiti, but somebody had to do it.

Making short trips from Wisconsin to Illinois and Indiana on the toll-way system, went as smooth as could be expected. With the spring weather around the corner, I knew I should pull through. I would be able to catch up on my radio listening with the triple speaker that I mounted in my tractor cab along with the air conditioning for the summer months.

April 19th, 1973, with two years already gone by and my bank account growing bit by bit, things weren't as bad as they probably would have been had I not made this decision. Michael John had healed completely, but due to his age I retired him to the farm that Charlie was still foreman at. I knew that he would live out his remaining years in peace.

I noticed that all of the local Chicago television stations were having a field day announcing that Judge Taylor sentenced ex-Governor Otto Kerner to three years in prison with a $50 thousand fine for conspiracy, income tax evasion, mail fraud, and making false statements on income tax returns. He was also fraudulently dealing in race track stocks. A special panel of the Court of Appeals called the transactions bribery and found that Kerner gained $159,800 from stock sales and that they were out of pocket only $15,079. The opinion told of "devious and complicated devices" used to conceal the governor's role in the bribery. Checks had been laundered — the opinion twice used that term — that Kerner did not have to endorse the $150,000 check received in the final payoff. On the witness stand, Kerner projected an aura of untouchability that did not impress the jury. After all of his appeals were exhausted, on July 29th, 1974, he arrived at the Federal Correctional Institute in Lexington, Kentucky. He was driving his Mercedes and dressed in a dark blue suit to become prisoner number 0037-223. On March 6th, 1975, Channel Two in Chicago announced that ex-Governor Otto Kerner was suffering from cancer and was immediately released from prison by the United States Parole Board.

On July 1st, 1975, four years of driving that semi had given me a two-week vacation and enough money to start looking for my future in racing. I had been thinking of that with every mile down those long and dark roads of the highway. It kept me from falling asleep at the wheel.

Chapter 18

The Overmatched Race

I always wanted to see some high-class horse races and the only places to go are Belmont Park and Yonkers Race Track, both in New York. With my suitcases packed, I boarded an Eastern Air Lines flight on July 2nd, 1975. I arrived at eleven o'clock in the morning in plenty of time to drive a rented car to Belmont Park in Elmont, New York, a few miles off Laureton Parkway.

At the entrance to the grandstand were large posters announcing that on July 6th, the Great Match race would be between a three year-old colt named "Foolish Pleasure" and a three year-old filly named "Ruffian". It also stated, "See history made!" Little did the people involved with the making of these posters realize that history would truly be made with a disastrous ending.

Belmont Park management had made up the conditions for this race. It was to be run at a distance of one mile and a quarter on the dirt track. The purse of $350 thousand was to be divided with the winner receiving $225 thousand. The runner up would receive the remaining $125 thousand. They booked it as "No real losers." The New York Racing Association had hired help to hand out pins and buttons with a picture of Foolish Pleasure on some and Ruffian on others. CBS had spent over a quarter of a million dollars for the television rights.

My first reaction were that a good sound colt and age will always win over a filly of same, unless one plus one is changed to add up to three.

Two months before, Foolish Pleasure had won the prestigious Kentucky Derby going the distance of one mile and a quarter in two minutes and two seconds in a field of fifteen horses. He was eleventh at the first quarter, eighth at the half and still some twelve lengths from the leader at the mile marker. He moved up to fourth place only three lengths behind the leader. He then went down the stretch passing all and pulled ahead to win by two lengths ridden out in a hand ride. It was a powerful race.

Two weeks later, he finished a fast-closing second in a shorter race, the Preakness Stakes. It was one mile and three-sixteenths long. The third leg of the Triple Crown races came three weeks later in the Belmont Stakes. The race was one mile and a half. Foolish Pleasure again finished a strong closing second just missing the win.

Foolish Pleasure had raced in seven races of one mile or more in his fourteen lifetime starts and had won eleven, finishing second twice and third once. His total earnings were $971,107.

Ruffian was a truly great filly as her record would indicate. She ran strictly against other fillies. She was always able to obtain an early lead with no real pressure from the opposition.

Any horse, filly or colt, if not pressured in the first quarter or half-mile of a race, will run more relaxed. This will lengthen their stride allowing them to run a much faster race than if on the other side of the coin. If they were pushed faster than the normal speed by the use of a whip, their muscles would tighten up and they would shorten their stride. In some cases, they would take a misstep and stumble, falling to the ground. This would sometimes happen from over-exhaustion, from being abused, or by just being asked for more speed than is there.

Ruffian had raced all five races as a two year-old, winning all five. These races were sprint races of three-quarter of a mile or less. After her fifth race, "The Spinaway", Ruffian suffered a hairline fracture of her right hind leg, in September, 1974. In my estimate, she wasn't given enough time off from the race track to properly heal. She was raced on April 14th, 1975. Judging from all normal standards, she had to have been put back into training sometime around January, 1975. Surely, not much time for healing. After the excessive pressure used, it had to cause some sort of stress on this undeveloped two year-old. More time on a farm to heal and recuperate would have made her into an even more productive mare after her racing days.

Up to July 2nd, 1975, Ruffian had won all ten of her lifetime races, with total earnings of $313,439. Ruffian had raced in only three races of one mile or more. The other seven races were three-quarters of a mile or less.

With a hairline fracture just ten months before, I would have been very much concerned even in a mild work-out, let alone a match race with a superb three year-old, well-built colt.

On July 5th, 1975, I was so caught up in all of the talk about that match race, I was up at the crack of dawn. Eating a waffle and sausage in the track's restaurant, I was waiting to see the two horses on the track. Over a dozen reporters were also waiting for them. I made a guess to myself that both would be jogged once around this one and an eighth-mile oval then taken back to their stalls for a rub-down. It wasn't long before someone came in and said, "They're on the track!" I left half of my waffle and was in between a group of reporters with cameras hanging from their necks hurrying out the door to the track.

Foolish Pleasure was first on the track and was allowed to take a leisurely gallop, then walked back to the stable. I would have to believe that with all of those reporters around snapping just one more picture, it might cause Foolish Pleasure to be a little nervous of all that activity so early in the morning.

When it was announced that Ruffian would be worked for three-eighths of a mile and ridden out a half-mile, tongues were starting to move briskly. It was as though this was unheard of at this late stage, with a grueling race just thirty-six hours away.

I didn't have my stopwatch with me, but rest assured, someone was bound to yell out Ruffian's work-out time. Sure enough, a loud voice that could probably have been heard in California, said, "She worked three-eighths in thirty-five seconds, finishing the half in forty-seven." A few whistles could plainly be heard. This extremely fast work-out just might have left her race here, or maybe she was a super filly after all.

As Ruffian was walked to the exit gate of the track, I was not a least bit surprised to see her broken out with white lather and blowing very hard. She looked like she ran twice the distance she actually did. I always believed in the old saying, "When something looks too good to be true, it probably is." In any case, I wasn't going to put one penny on that kind of race.

July 6th, 1975, at about 5:50 p.m., the sound of the bugle came over the loudspeaker system. Over 50,000 people stood up stretching to get a view of two great horses as they stepped onto the track. A roar of applause from the patrons seemed to make the support beams quiver. As the two horses paraded past the grandstand, I took a good look at the odds to see how this huge crowd had figured on making a little coffee and donut money. With Ruffian at two to five and Foolish Pleasure at four to five, even if they did win, the only big winners would be the State of New York and that race track. If all went well, both horse owners as well. Obviously, there would be "win" betting only.

With my binoculars focused on both horses as they neared the starting gate, a chilling weird feeling swept across my mind like a bolt of lightning. I remember lowering my binoculars thinking that I might have been pressing them too closely to my eyes. The feeling lasted for only a split-second. It wouldn't be until after the race, that I would think about this incident, due to the results of the race.

I took a quick look at both jockeys. I had no doubt, in a race of this magnitude, they were the best experienced riders available. I noticed that Jacinto Vasquez, who had ridden Foolish Pleasure in ten of his races, still elected to ride Ruffian. Bravilio Baela had ridden Foolish Pleasure only once before which was his fifth race. He won with ease.

I thought this to be a mighty strange prevailing occurrence, especially with thousands of jockeys riding at so many tracks. Here was a match race, where as the same jockey had ridden Ruffian in eight of her ten lifetime races and also ridden Foolish Pleasure in ten of his fourteen lifetime races.

The track announcer had just notified the patrons that

"The horses are at the starting gate, it is now post time." The noise of the crowd rose to the occasion. The weather was a perfect day for racing. It was warm and sunny with a mild breeze cooling down the temperature of eighty-four to a comfortable feeling.

It was announced earlier, that Ruffian had drawn the inside post position. Instead of using the number one stall, management decided that with only two horses starting, they would put Ruffian in the number three stall and Foolish Pleasure in the number four stall of the starting gate. This would have both horses leaving the gate away from the inner rail for the safe start of a much open race.

The tension in the air was as thick as molasses in January up in Canada. Ruffian was already standing in her stall while Foolish Pleasure was being led into his. Bravilio Baeza was sitting straight up and relaxed as though a board was taped to the back of his five foot five-inch frame. In a matter of seconds, the track announcer was saying over the speaker system, "Ladies and Gentlemen, we are ready for the greatest match race in history." As if on cue, I could hear the noise of the starting gate as it electrically sprang open.

It caused immediate amazement from the huge crowd, for it was Foolish Pleasure who burst into the lead. With the race starting out of the chute in the far back stretch, it was very difficult to see the horses for the first quarter-mile without the use of binoculars. The majority of the people had to rely on the voice of the track announcer. When he called out that Foolish Pleasure had taken the lead at the start, they had thought he was blind in one eye and couldn't see out of the other. Someone was tugging at my arm wanting to use my binoculars, as he had a big bet down on Ruffian. I quickly told him that Ruffian was moving up. Nearing the first quarter-mile pole, she was about one-half length in front. Nearing the half-mile pole, tragedy struck.

At that split-second, no one could have known what happened in the back-stretch. Ruffian was suddenly being taken up and jockey Vasquez managed to guide her to the outside fence before dismounting. Meanwhile, jockey Baeza, knowing that Ruffian was pulled up, took Foolish Pleasure in hand and completed the race in two minutes and two and four-fifths seconds. That was just four-fifths of a second slower that his time for winning the Kentucky Derby, carrying the same jockey weight of one hundred and twenty-six pounds.

No one knew of the seriousness of the injury of Ruffian. The track announcer stated, "At the present time, all anyone knows is that Ruffian is lame." Within a minute, a horse ambulance arrived and Ruffian hobbled aboard. It drove off the track very slowly.

It wasn't until I returned to my hotel room, that I learned from the television news, that Ruffian's both sesamoid bones in the ankle of her right fore-leg shattered. She was now in Doctor William O. Reed's Equine Hospital. Dr. Reed and four other surgeons operated on her for three and a half hours.

More than two hours after her operation, Ruffian was lying on her side in a padded stall used as a recovery room. Ruffian was still in shock and very weary after expending much energy in her head to head dual with Foolish Pleasure. She was dehydrated and had "contaminated wounds". She had almost died before reaching the operating table. The spirit that made Ruffian such a great race horse was working against her. She was a fighter.

What the doctors were hoping for was that Ruffian would remain calm after getting to her feet. Injured horses, especially spirited ones, in most cases will injure themselves further as soon as they stand after an operation.

The final act in the disheartening drama began at one forty-five in the morning. Dr. Reed came out of the building and told others of the operating team. He told them that they had serious problems. Ruffian was beginning to thrash around on her side dislodging her cast. Eventually smashing it to pieces.

Dr. Harthill consulted the trainer, Frank Whiteley, then phoned the filly's owners Mr. and Mrs. Stuart Janney. They told the doctor, "Don't let her suffer anymore."

At two-twenty in the morning, a massive dose of phenobarbital was administered into the stricken filly. Ruffian died almost instantaneously without any pain. Ruffian was buried in the infield of Belmont Park Race

Track, at the foot of the flag pole.

The most mysterious part of that complete incident, was that Ruffian was never insured, until two weeks before that match race. The owners refused to disclose the amount of the insurance policy they had bought. Another insurance broker stated one day before the race that he would be thrilled to insure Ruffian for $1.5 million.

On July 9th, 1975, I checked out of the motel and drove up-state to be closer to Yonkers Raceway, where I spent four of my evenings watching some mighty fine pacers and trotters.

The remainder of my vacation was spent seeing a few Broadway plays, trying to somehow forget the Ruffian race.

The race had left me devastated and in disbelief that people would put any horse in this hazardous position, where they would over-exert themselves trying desperately to win.

Chapter 19

Nightmare

Be it an honest mistake or a well-planned case of greed, I'll never know. Therefore I must simply call him "George". Money can and will destroy many a friendship. Dealing with a person I had previously considered a true and honest friend since my boyhood days, I should have had more confidence in him. But, apparently due to the prevailing circumstances that became involved, I was naturally forced to alter the high regards I had placed on his integrity.

March 14, 1978: I had returned home from a twenty-six hour, miserable and nerve-racking road trip delivering a semi-load of new auto parts from Detroit, Michigan to the Chevrolet plant in Janesville, Wisconsin. I drove through a blinding snowstorm accompanied by intense cold and gusty winds.

The huge snow plows had all they could do just to keep one lane open each way on the Northwest Tollway in Illinois. Over twelve inches of snow had fallen and continually made me wonder if Spring would forget to make herself present.

Many a time, I had to force myself to roll down my tractor window to let the sub-zero wind blow against my face to keep me awake. The music from my radio was enormously helpful in preventing me from sleeping at the wheel. There were so many trucks and cars that had slid into the ditches, the Tollway looked like a hundred used car lots. Still many a car or truck would speed by me only to join the other impatient drivers for a very long wait to be towed out of a ditch. All I could do was beep my air horn to let them know I would send help from the next truck stop garage and say, "Cheers! Next time drive a little slower."

I had no sooner gotten into my house, shaking off the

snow from my sheepskin jacket and taken off my boots, when I went straight to the bedroom and dropped onto the bed. With my clothes still on, I went out like a light.

Some fourteen hours later, I returned to life. I was still drowsy, thinking that I had fallen asleep at the wheel and possibly destroyed my semi and caused a terrible accident. A few seconds later, I was almost back to normal. I headed to the kitchen to have some hot oatmeal and a cup of tea. The clock on he wall showed that it was ten minutes past nine. Being that it was as dark as the Ace of Spades outside, I smiled. This was a very nice time to be having breakfast. I put the telephone plug back into the wall that I had removed just seconds before going to bed.

The hot oatmeal and raisin toast hit the spot. I was being brought back to a human being as the telephone started to ring.

Immediately, I recognized the voice of my life-long friend George. He had been trying to reach me all day. I told him that I was having a winter holiday playing in the snow and having a jolly good time. Jokingly, of course. He then just had to rub it in that he had burned his feet on the hot sand of the beach due to the sunny temperature of eighty-nine degrees that they had that afternoon. He then stated the urgency of his call. He had heard of a well-bred four year-old filly that could be bought at a moderate price. He knew that I was in the market for one or two to mate with a stallion in Kentucky. During a half-hour or so of conversation, I heard how he watched her burn up the race track in a blazing workout. He said that she would, in all probability, be put in a race within the following week and that I should fly down. I told him that I didn't need much of any kind of excuse to leave this ice box. I told him that as soon as O'Hare Airport would open, I'd call him to let him know when to pick me up at the Fort Lauderdale Airport. Hanging up the receiver, I gave out with a "Hot Dang!" while looking out the window towards the street lamp. I could see the snow flakes still falling past the bright beam of light. Back to bed I went.

Awakened by the light from the window, I knew that the morning had arrived. My first thoughts were on the weather and I was delighted to see a suddenly clear blue sky. I could see trees that were heavily-laden with snow above huge drifts of two or more feet of snow.

I was surprised to hear the phone service had not been interrupted due to this late winter storm. I called Eastern Airlines for reservations on their earliest flight to Florida. Giving my credit card number, I would soon be in the air, then eat dinner and walk the streets that night in a temperature of seventy degrees warmer than where I was. I thought, "It's a shame Columbus didn't have this kind of transportation."

Next I called George. I left a message on his answering machine to pick me up at seven thirty that evening. After an hour of shoveling snow from my sidewalks and brushing my car of the heavy, wet snow, I started to pack my suitcase and prepared for a quick change of climate.

True to his word, there was George awaiting me. As I stepped off the plane, I saw that his skin was deeply-tanned as I once was. With the usual hand-shakes, we walked through the terminal for my luggage. We talked of the four year-old filly named Ocala Star Craft. He had been obtaining more information on her.

My first question: "Was she on drugs?" I didn't receive the quick response of an answer I was hoping for. His voice changed to a tone that left me a little doubtful of his answer of "no". I then asked him if he was able to contact the caretaker of the filly for he would know everything about her. He would especially know if there were a few "greenbacks" placed into his hand. He then stated that he would take care of that point first thing in the morning, for there wasn't much time left. She was entered in the tenth race at Pompano Park on March 17th, 1978, just two days away.

When he told me that the name of the trainer/driver was Sterling Buch, a chill went through my system. I had been stabled next to him once at Washington Park and had witnessed his kind of treatment of horses. I told George, "Had you known of this person when you called me, I would still be shoveling snow!" At least I wouldn't be wasting my time here. Just the mention of this "Jughead's" name was all I needed to know. "One thing is for sure," I said. You have now put me on my guard one hundred percent. As long as

I'm here, we'll see the rest of the show and I'll get a few days at the beach." I told him, "I hope you have a nice restaurant picked out."

The next two days were spent on the beach with a gallon of fresh-squeezed orange juice, under a bright sunny sky. It started to turn my "Casper the Ghost-like" white skin to a pink reddish complexion. I was also getting well-rested.

After an early dinner, we arrived at Pompano Park for the evening races. I wanted to watch Ocala Star Craft's warm-up miles. After seeing these, I would have a very good idea of what kind of condition this filly was in. I wasn't too enthusiastic over George's sudden interest in telling me only the good qualities of this filly. He said that buying her before the race would be thousands of dollars less, in the event she would turn in a fast winning race as she indicated by her last work-out mile a week before. Of course, as he also stated she wasn't on drugs, but no owner would come out and tell him that she was if indeed she were.

I had already formed the opinion that my so-called friend George got himself into a bind and needed some quick money for a bail-out. The owner of this filly would probably slip him some blood money under the table if I bought her. I hoped that I was wrong.

After the third race, Ocala Star Craft entered the track for her first pre-race warm-up. I followed her with my binoculars looking for any tell-signs of lameness. Her driver Buch took her at a leisurely pace for two miles then turned her the right way of the track for a faster pace along the rail. I didn't even bother to use my stop watch for it was quite obvious to me that she wouldn't be putting much wear on her shoes tonight. She wasn't pulling on the driving lines and was still going at the same pace as before.

After the sixth race, Ocala Star Craft was again on the track for her last warm-up mile. This time I noticed Buch had a whip in his hand. Strictly a Jughead, I thought. As he started, he was already tapping his whip over the filly asking her for more speed. She responded at the half-mile pole. What I had expected was starting to happen. She was already breaking out with white lather and blowing hard. She ran the first half in a slow one minute and twenty-five seconds, coming down the stretch finishing her mile in two minutes and forty seconds. It was a very strange warm-up mile for a filly who always had shown, by her past performance charts, was always in front by a dozen lengths or more at the start of a race. Then again, I always did think this driver was weird. As she passed by the grandstand and headed back to the paddock, I turned to George, "When you watched her work out last week, was she in the condition that she is in now—broken out with white lather?" His reply was, "Not quite as much." I explained to him, "Had you mentioned this important fact to me before, I wouldn't be here at this time, for this filly has been injected with drugs and has to be lame. There is no way I would buy her to raise a colt from." I also saw a slight hike in her pacing stride nearing the half-mile pole and that she was favoring her left front leg. I knew that if this driver was smart he would take her out of the race when he got back to the paddock, but knowing how stupid he was, this wouldn't happen.

The bugle sounded that the horses were coming onto the track for the tenth race. There was no announcement of any changes. The thought of Ruffian flashed before my mind. Surely the same results wouldn't happen again. I didn't have enough information to go to the track officials, for Ocala Star Craft to be withdrawn from this race. In any event, it's their job to be on the look-out for horses that are unsound. I realized that if they took every lame horse out of a race, there probably would be only two or three horses in each race. I had no choice but to sit and hope that someone up above was looking out for these poor animals, for no one was down here.

I looked at the tote board and to my surprise Ocala Star Craft was now the overwhelming favorite. This was caused by someone putting $500 to win on her the very second the board was open for wagering. Her morning line had listed her at twenty to one. With this kind of move, she would indeed be what I call a "phoney favorite" and the general public would be led to believe that she was what they call a "hot horse" that was set to win. Why else would she have dropped to even money? These people will never learn that in any race the big smart money is never put down on a horse until one minute before the start.

When a phoney favorite has been set up by a gambler of another horse in the same race, their horse may have been listed at eight to one on the morning line but would now be at thirty to one. So when he placed his large bet, the odds would be dropped to around twenty to one. This, as any two year-old could see, is a very shrewd $500 investment. Especially as the person knew that Ocala Star Craft was lame. Whoever put that quick money down knew how to add two plus two.

My curiosity was aroused enough to check out the odds on the rest of the horses, watching for any drastic changes.

With five minutes to post time, Ocala Star Craft listed as number seven on the program was being bet as though she were the only horse in the race. Her odds were now at two to five. Making two dollars on every five dollars wagered, is not my cup of tea. Obviously, whoever set this ingenious plan into motion had to be very pleased with himself with the first phase, plus doing a few other things to ensure the outcome of this race, even without the owner's knowledge.

The track announcer was telling the patrons that the horses would be going to the starting gate in three minutes. Keeping a close watch on the tote board, the only horse that had a considerable odd change was the number five horse, Caviar Choice. His morning line was fifteen to one but was now at forty-five to one. I took a quick glance at his past performance chart. He looked terrible. He always finished in the "Also ran" column with slow speed times. This kind of record would stop anyone from putting even a wooden nickel down.

I nudged George, "Let's get a Pepsi." Walking, I asked him if he had $50 or so that he wouldn't mind wasting. Reaching for his billfold, he said, "What's up?" I quickly told him that we were going to stand by the $50 window. I explained that if the number five horse's odds start to drop, we would play out my hunch.

The track announcer called out that the horses were nearing the starting gate and it was then that the odds changed. Number five was now thirty to one and number seven was two to one. All I said to George was, "We have a live horse. Bet him if you don't mind making a fistful of money."

No sooner had we placed our bets, the track announcer started saying that the horses were all in line on the track and that the gate was rolling. We had just gotten outside for me to look over the field of horses as the gate slowly went by. Sterling Buch already had his whip straight up in the air while the others had theirs tucked under their arms. The number five horse looked very alert and the driver had a firm hold. That was for the most part a very good sign that he had come to race and should be competitive.

The mobile starting gate was picking up speed as the voice of the track announcer could be heard in an excited voice saying, "They're off and racing." Ocala Star Craft was quickly drawing off to a five-length lead, with Bold Name second. Big Brother was a close third and Party Ahead fourth.

The first quarter went in a blazing twenty-nine seconds with Ocala Star Craft opening up her lead to ten lengths. Big Brother was trying to keep close, Bold Name pacing third and Party Ahead closing the gap for fourth place. Caviar Choice was moving into fifth position.

I felt my arm being tugged while I was straining my eyes through the binoculars, not really believing what I was seeing. This was not the same Ocala Star Craft I had witnessed just an hour before having a difficult time just finishing a mild warm-up mile. I knew that it was impossible to switch horses. Even if two horses looked like twins, each horse is tattooed as yearlings on the inside upper lip with a registered number that cannot be changed. I had to believe that she was injected with some kind of drug while in the paddock. This is illegal and everyone knows it — or is supposed to know it, but greedy people will always say, "Rules are made to be broken."

For the split second that I was thinking of this, I felt my arm being tugged on again. Lowering my binoculars, George was almost screaming, "What did I tell you, Michael John? Isn't she the fastest filly you ever saw?" As I started to raise my binoculars, I don't know what made me say, "They don't pay off for leading the first part of a race."

The wild and emotional crowd was electrified as well as I was to see this filly pacing with such a commanding lead of fifteen lengths, nearing the half-mile pole. As the track announcer was straining his voice, he could barely be heard over the noise of he crowd, who were hysterically jumping up and down. They were all trying to get a glimpse of the horses going by. Passing the half-mile pole, Ocala Star Craft was cruising by twenty lengths. Doctor Ainhart took over second place with Caviar Choice along side in third. Bold Name was pacing in fourth place.

Like a sudden bolt of lightning from the sky, Ocala Star Craft abruptly stopped then reared into mid-air on her hind legs. She jumped at least two feet off the ground. When she came down she kept her left front leg in the air about a foot above the ground. She didn't even attempt to set it down.

It was plain for me to see through my binoculars that her whole body was shaking as the white-lathered sweat poured from her. She was obviously in terrible pain.

With the enormous lead she had, the other drivers had ample time to guide their horses to the middle of the track without much difficulty as they continued the race. I shuddered at the thought at what might have happened had Ocala Star Craft not had that twenty-lengths lead.

Even after the last horse went by, Sterling Buch still sat on his sulky doing nothing. It was as though he were waiting for a taxi-cab! Finally, he got off and started to unhook the filly from the sulky without bothering to check why she was still holding her left leg off the ground. What a stupid Jughead. He must have gotten his license from the Flea Market.

Minutes later, a tractor pulling a large trailer arrived with six or seven track maintenance men. They proceeded to load the crippled filly carefully into the trailer. I also noticed that a pick-up truck with a veterinarian's name on it was also there. Well, at least she was in better hands than before.

I was so engrossed with this incident, that I had completely forgotten about the ending of the race. I knew that when Ocala Star Craft stopped, the crowd's noise subsided spontaneously. That was mainly due to the shocking experience they had just witnessed. I lowered my binoculars and took a good look at the people around the area. The crowd was a bit more subdued. Most people were still bewildered by the sudden change of the bright side of what has been called "The Sport of Kings". They were presented with the reality of what does happen when lame horses are put on a track to race.

I walked over to where George was drinking something from a plastic cup. He looked up and said, "I was just coming back, I got so damn thirsty. How bad was the accident?" I looked at him sharply and told him, short and to the point, "That was no accident. That was greed and stupidity." I then ordered a Seven-Up to settle me down as I was still upset. George was asking me if I had seen the finish of he race. Saying, "No," I then learned that my hunch was right. Number five, Caviar Choice, did win, paying $55.20 for each $2 wagered. I was so disgusted, I handed my $50 win ticket to George and told him, "Take this and enjoy yourself for your trouble in looking for a filly and the long distance telephone calls." He quickly said, "Are you sure, Michael John?" It didn't take much coaxing for him to hurry to the mutuel window to collect the gift money.

He dropped me off at my motel. It had been a very long and terrible day. I only hoped that Ocala Star Craft didn't damage her previous injury any worse than it was. I hoped to hear the next day that this nice filly was retired.

I spent the next ten days basking in the warm sun at the beach. I consumed a half-gallon of ice cold fresh-squeezed orange juice each day. The tapes I had brought along of The Best Tunes of the Big Bands were very relaxing. It was only then that I fully realized the toll that the long hours of driving over the road had taken on me. I'm sure it did the same to many other semi drivers that caused them to take different kinds of pills to keep from falling asleep at the wheel. This I knew would have damaging effects on the human body and I wasn't about to go in that direction. Very soon, I thought as I looked up at the blue cloudless sky, I will have my small stable of race horses and the mental tension and stress of over-the-road driving would become nothing more than a page in history.

Before leaving for Chicago, I drove my rented car back to Pompano Park Race Track's restaurant. That would be the quickest way for me to find out the condition of Ocala Star Craft. Within minutes, I was smiling as I learned that she was retired to a farm. I had to control myself from jumping up and down for joy as I was delighted to hear the news. It had made my day, knowing she would not suffer any more abuse at the track!

Chapter 20

Calm Before the Storm

March 28th, 1978: Within minutes, the Eastern Airline's jet would be landing at O'Hare Airport ten miles northwest of Chicago. Looking out the window, I could plainly see that very little of the snow remained now that the temperature had risen to the high fifty-degree mark in the past few days.

The taxi driver filled me in on the weather and the local news as he sped along the freeway. Thirty minutes later, he pulled up in front of the Paddlewheel Restaurant. It was on North Avenue, three blocks East of Maywood Park Race Track. Ted Glazos, the owner whom I had known for many years, quickly came out to help me with my luggage. Walking inside, he said, "It was a good thing you called me from the airport to say that you were on your way." He jokingly continued that he wouldn't have recognized me due to the dark tan I was sporting. There were only a few customers left from the lunch hour as we went into his office.

Immediately, I told him that we could forget about Ocala Star Craft and the events of the trip. The only thing I had accomplished was what he could see — my suntan.

Ted had owned eight Standardbred horses years before and had remarkable success with them. He enjoyed every minute of this sport. As each horse reached the age he felt they should be retired, he sent them to a well-managed farm for their remaining years for a life of leisure.

Along with Jim Karubas who still owned the Alpine Restaurant, we drew up plans to form a racing stable. Thus, we would be able to purchase a higher-class of horses. Going on the theory that it takes money to make money, my bank account was now ready for the venture.

The chef interrupted the conversation stating that he had prepared our Greek-style salads with black olives and cheese. Talk about perfect timing. In walked Jim Karubas. We all laughed as we said, "He must have smelled the special main course dinner the chef was about to start."

With that statement, we left the office for the East dining room where the waitress had our table neatly set up. She was placing bowls of steaming hot creamy chicken and rice soup, along with our salads and fresh hot loaves of baked bread.

While eating these tasty morsels, my thoughts suddenly flashed back to when I used to watch Michael John eat his hot bran mash meal. I felt my eyes becoming watery as I then heard Ted's voice say that he would like to fly with me to Baltimore, Maryland, in May for the spring yearling sales that we had previously talked about. Jim also stated that he would like to come along as he could use a vacation.

Our waitress brought the small cart on which were three prime ribs each well over an inch thick on hot broiler platters. There were also dishes of vegetables and a large bowl of steaming potatoes. Later, fresh-baked apple pie with a scoop of ice cream was served with coffee to end a very delicious meal.

I knew beforehand that the State of Maryland, primarily noted for its Thoroughbred horses, wouldn't have such an enormous Standardbred selection as New York or Kentucky. We knew that if we did find a few yearlings we liked and I knew of their bloodlines, we wouldn't have to be bidding against the larger stables. Most of the time, they went to Kentucky. We all agreed that if it looked like the exceptional colts were not to be had, we would buy one stallion and a couple of mares and raise our own yearlings a lot cheaper.

This was not just an idle remark. Even a year before, I had gone many a night just to watch a coal-black five year-old horse named "Phase Out", race without the use of any drugs. He won a large number of his races and always closed fast at the end of the race to be in the money. I knew that his owner also had the Donner Packing Plant in Milwaukee, Wisconsin and was planning to retire him to stud. He was even thinking of then selling him if the price were right.

May 31st, 1978: Just as Jim Karubas had said that he needed a short vacation, that was all we accomplished in Maryland. There were hundreds of yearlings to choose from but, to speak in auto terms, they were all in the class of Volkswagens and I was looking for a few Buick V-8-class yearlings. They cost the same amount of time and money to raise, but I still haven't ever seen a Volkswagen keep up with a Buick in a race. The sun was almost out of view as I pulled out of the parking garage of O'Hare Airport. Jim lived in Westchester about ten miles to the south, so I headed in that direction on La Grange Road. It was eight-thirty when I handed Jim his suitcase. I told him to keep in touch even though it was a long reach. Ted had his car at the restaurant six miles to the east. Twenty minutes later, I was pulling into the parking lot. Being away from home for a week, Ted wanted to check out how business was, then hurry home. I would stay and have a light lunch before going home for a hot shower and a much-needed night of sleep.

I sat down in a booth and ordered a turkey club sandwich on toast and a pot of tea. Drinking part of my glass of water, I noticed a newspaper that had been left on the counter. I went over and checked to see that it was *The Chicago Tribune*.

There was nothing much of interest on the front pages. Then I thought that maybe Phase Out had raced the night before or that he might be racing tonight. I probably wouldn't be watching his race, though, as tired as I was. His name wasn't in the race results of the races from the night before so I started to look at the horse's names from the seventh race on. Only the lower-class horses race in the first six races and the last race.

I started to run my finger over the horse's names listed in the eighth race. Not finding Phase Out, I continued to the ninth race. I went past the number six horse, Marco Direct with driver Connel Willis who had helped me obtain my driver's license some twelve years ago. I paused and smiled. Here was a true loyal hard-working horseman who never abused any horse.

I moved my finger on past the remainder of the horses

and started into the tenth race entries. I stopped cold and dead still before moving my finger back to the ninth race. Not wanting to see what my brain was telling me, my mind had to be playing tricks on me from the long airplane trip and lack of sleep. "This can't be so," I told myself as I slowly moved my finger back to the eight horse. I then saw it just as clear as the morning sun. The name of the number seven horse was Ocala Star Craft. Unbelievable. I was still thinking and even saying to myself, "This horse is crippled and on a farm in Florida. This has to be a different horse with almost the same spelling." Again I studied over the name. I wasn't positive until I saw the drivers name was Sterling Buch. I was now thoroughly convinced. He was living up to all of my expectations of his stupidity.

Instantaneously, I thought of the filly Ruffian. I didn't have the solid facts and information that I had on this filly Ocala Star Craft . There was no guess-work involved in this case. Some way, somehow, I had to find a way to stop this crippled filly from racing that night and forever after. My main difficulty was that she was at Sportsman Park Race Track and the Director of Racing was Phil Langley. I thought to myself, "This is going to be a hard nut to crack."

Chapter 21

Preventable Disaster

Immediately, I phoned Sportsman Park. Seconds later, a lady answered. Telling her that it was an emergency seemed to make no difference. She said that she would take my message. If I wanted anything more, she told me that I would have to come to the track personally, if I wanted to talk to Phil Langley or make a complaint.

Realizing I was wasting time, I told her who I was and of the crippled filly in the ninth race. I hung up the receiver and handed my waitress a $10 bill, telling her, "I have to run." It was now nine fifteen. The quickest way possible to the track six miles away was to take First Avenue South from North Avenue. There would be very few stop lights along this route. Without breaking too many traffic rules, I slid into the east parking lot of the track. At nine forty-five, I paid my way into the clubhouse and hurriedly walked along the fence which separates the track from the patrons, always watching the horses that were warming up after the last race. I was looking to see if Ocala Star Craft was there. Passing through the gate into the grandstand area to the east end where the paddock was, took another couple of minutes. Walking between the large crowd of people just as I reached the paddock gate where the horses enter, I saw a tall haggard-looking horse coming in from the track. I couldn't see any numbers from my angle, but I could see the horse was blowing very hard and covered with white lather sweat. This had to be Ocala Star Craft. My next glance gave me my answer, for this horse was still favoring her left front leg, just as she had done in Florida on the night of March 17th, 1978. I almost broke down and cried as she was driven by me into the paddock where Mr. Stupid finally got off the sulky and backed her into her stall. He left her hooked up, only removing her bridle and put a halter on her that would hold her in the stall. He then went for a drink of water, not offering any to Ocala Star Craft.

I walked up and down the paddock looking for any track official or Mr. Frank Pennino, the paddock judge. I went over to the racing secretary's office hoping to see Phil Langley, but no one was around. Where in the hell are the personnel who operate this track?, I thought. In frustration, I quickly went back to the paddock. The state pays a veterinarian to be on duty in the paddock for the entire race program. If he claims that he was here after the eighth race, he must have been invisible, I thought.

With three minutes left before the horses were to leave, Ol'e Frank put in his appearance. He only said, "Get your bridles on for the ninth race." I went along the five-foot fence to where Frank Pennino was standing and called him over. He responded with, "What do you want? I'm busy!" I told him that a vet should check out the number seven horse Ocala Star Craft . I explained that she was lame and told him about the Florida race. It seemed to be going in one ear and out the other. The real shocker came when he looked at me in a cold freezing look and yelled out, "You take care of Michael John, we'll take care of this track." Then, in the same breath, he yelled out, "All right, number one, take your horse out!" I walked over to where the number six horse was being led out but Connel Willis was already at the far end of the paddock. I would see his horse on the track as he went by. Standing next to the track fence, I waited for Willis. His colors were red and white, making him easy to pick out as the bright light above the track turned the dark of night into the light of day. As he got within my voice's range, I yelled out, "Watch out for the number seven horse. She's dead lame and a front runner." From the look on his face, I could tell that he heard most of what I yelled out, but before I could say anything else, a large hand was pressing on my shoulder.

Quickly turning, I saw that it was Eugene Oliver. If anyone ever saw him, they would see that he never missed a meal, at least five of them per day. He weighed only 350 from the over 400 he used to weigh. The track had hired him as a security guard. They must have had him watching over the food in the track kitchen before. That is probably why he was losing weight. Now, when I was stabled at that track, he would always go by the barns looking for a hot horse to bet a couple of bucks on. I never paid much attention to him before, but now he was putting just a little too much pressure on my shoulder. In turning to him, I asked, "What's with the strong arm?" He then said, "You're not supposed to be yelling at the drivers on the track." I gave him a quick explanation of my action. I also told him that he should use his two-way radio and have Phil Langley paged before this race started. All this Rolly-Polly would say was that it wasn't his job to be looking out for lame horses.

I turned to see where the horses were so I could point out how badly Ocala Star Craft was favoring her left leg. I lowered my binoculars to ask Oliver if he'd like to take a look but he was gone. The track announcer had just given notice that the horses were nearing the starting gate. Post time would be in two minutes. I rushed back to the racing secretary's office just on the chance that Frank Pennino contacted Phil Langley or that I might contact the state veterinarian. That was like looking for a needle in a haystack. Not one track official was around. It was as though it was a Sunday evening and the track was closed. The patrons were not aware of the disastrous possibilities that could occur. I was completely baffled and discouraged that I had failed. I slowly walked among the noisy crowd of people, working my way to the wire fence that looked over the track surface. I noticed that there was very little loose top soil on the track to act as a cushion for the horse's feet. This would be extremely painful on a horse's tendons and stifles. If a lame horse was asked to race on that kind of surface, there would be more damage to the horse as well as greater pain. The speed time would increase for the mile and that's what the race track management would like. Never mind the many serious accidents that have happened at this race track. They don't care about the jockeys and the harness drivers who have been killed during a race, with many others crippled. Their only reply is, "That's the hazards of racing."

They also fail to mention that this track has had the most accidents of any other in the nation. I've always stated, "Accidents just don't happen, they are caused."

The track announcer interrupted my train of thought as he said, "It is now post-time." I took a glance at the tote board. It was impossible to believe that Ocala Star Craft was again the favorite with her odds at even money. The track program had her previous races and dates listed in order as every other horse. However, they failed to inform their readers that she was taken off the track in Florida by a horse ambulance because she was so lame, she couldn't even take one step to walk into the van. She had to be lifted by leather straps with the use of a hoist.

In any other business this would have been classified as fraud. With over $100 thousand already wagered on that race, the majority of people's pockets would be mighty empty of that green stuff. The stuff people commit murder for, after this boat race (the favorite won't win).

The mobile starting gate moved past the paddock fence where I was standing with my binoculars focused on only one horse, Ocala Star Craft. She was already broken out with white-lathered sweat and was favoring her left front leg badly. Her head was bobbing up and down. The so-called starting judge who was riding in the seat above the gate that overlooked the entire line of horses had to be blind not to see the difficulties Ocala Star Craft was having due to her lameness. Even at that late stage of the race he is authorized to call for a restart before reaching the one-sixteenth mile pole ahead of the starting point. Instead, the mobile starting gate began to pick up more speed as it went around the clubhouse turn of that five-eighths mile oval. The mobile gate was heading up the backstretch nearing the point of no return. I was only hoping that Sterling Buch would do one smart thing in his life by slowly taking his filly away from the gate and stay in the rear the entire mile. With this class of horse, there was no possible way she could out pace the field of better horses and obtain any kind of a large lead. It didn't matter how many injections of drugs she had been given. She was just too lame. The sweat was pouring from her body as the long arms of the gate folded inward and the car sped away. Not only did he not do a smart thing, but Sterling Buch also started using his whip trying to cross over in front of the first six horses.

Nearing the backstretch turn, I could clearly see that four of the other drivers had taken a very firm hold of their horses in order to give this dummy plenty of room to clear. Surely, they had to know how lame she was. I gave a sigh of relief for this race could have been over had they not taken that drastic move.

Nearing the top of the stretch turn, the field of horses were coming into my line of view. Ocala Star Craft was leading by only one length with Louis Misty pacing second and Manor Born third. Connell Willis had Marco Direct in sixth place under a firm hold. He would make his move after the half-mile pole. Then, it hit me. "That's the same place that Ocala Star Craft stopped in her last race!" I stood there not wanting to believe she would do the same thing for the field of horses were tightly bunched together single-filed along the rail. I couldn't understand why these drivers didn't pull out on the stretch and go around that filly, for Sterling Buch had been using his whip for most of the first quarter-mile. Nearing the clubhouse turn, the positions were still unchanged.

At the approach of the half-mile pole, Connel pulled out of sixth place along with the other two that were in the rear. Passing the half-mile pole on the turn and heading up the backstretch, I could feel my heart pumping faster. My forehead was wet from sweat. Maybe they can get around the filly if only that dummy would stop using that damn whip, I thought. Connel was almost along side in second place with three horses bunched up close behind him.

Then, in a split second it was as though someone had fired a cannon directly at the field of horses. Ocala Star Craft came to an abrupt halt, trying desperately to hold her left leg off the ground, causing a chain reaction. The second horse on the rail behind Ocala Star Craft tried to pull up only to have the horse behind him knock him from his sulky. He fell into Connel's horse, knocking him from his sulky. I released my hold on the binoculars and climbed over the fence along with a couple of other guys from the paddock. We ran across the infield to the backstretch. At first glance, it looked like a bloody battlefield. I saw only one horse standing. To get out of the way, its driver took him around the turn and headed down the stretch. I started unhooking the harness straps on the first fallen horse I came to. It was entangled with two other horses along with broken pieces of their racing bikes and harnesses. The wheels looked like lids from tin cans. Connel was being helped by some of the stable hands who came over the fence from the barn area. Finally, an ambulance pulled up, with another coming up the backstretch.

With the blood all over the horses and drivers, it was hard to tell how deep the cuts and gashes were. I took off my dress shirt and tied it around a horse's lower part of his leg. It stopped the fast-flowing blood from about a two-inch gash that was probably caused by another horse's shoe in fighting with the tangled harnesses and broken pieces of his sulky while trying to get up off the ground. It was amazing that out of all this mess no one was killed and no horses were put to sleep later.

From a quick glance, it looked as though four of the horses would need the rest of the year off to heal their wounds. Now Ocala Star Craft would be retired as I thought she had been. The two ambulances were taking five of the drivers to McNeal Hospital in Berwyn, next door to Cicero. Talking to the stable hands later, someone said that Connel Willis's knee was shattered and he was in great pain as he was put into the ambulance.

While we were picking up a few pieces of broken equipment off the track, I heard over the public address system that the horse I saw walking away from the accident to get out of the way by going down the stretch and finishing the mile race was declared the winner. They said that all of the place and show money that would normally be paid to the second and third place finishers would be added to the only official finisher. They added that no refunds would be handed out due to the unfortunate accident.

A huge roar of boos, blasphemous remarks and profane language arose from the crowd. I could see, even at that distance, that people were throwing anything that wasn't bolted down onto the racing surface. It had turned into a small riot. Needless to say, the patrons were disgustedly angered by the decision. I don't know how long the disturbance lasted, for I left by the stable gate entrance on Laramie Street where my car was parked.

Driving home, I forgot all about being tired and that I left a good club sandwich to go to waste. I stopped at a restaurant in just my white T-shirt and dress pants that were just a little dirty from the track surface.

It then dawned on me: Would Frank Pennino report to Phil Langley that I had warned him that such an accident might happen as it did or would Eugene Oliver mention my conversation with him?

I personally thought that Sportsman Park officials should have called the race a "no contest" event and refund all money wagered for that accident race. Frank Pennino had fifteen minutes to contact the other judges as well as Phil Langley. Eugene Oliver failed to notify anyone, to my knowledge, of Ocala Star Craft's previous race and her lameness. He maintained that I never spoke to him. This liar is so crooked that when he dies they will have to put him in the ground with a cork-screw.

I shall never change my opinion that Sportsman Park officials were indeed guilty of negligence and endangering the lives of every driver and horse in that race. Obviously, it's understandable why this race track has so many unnecessary accidents. If any of those drivers filed a law suite against this race track, I would positively be in court to testify about that accident to help their cause.

Chapter 22

Stupidity or Payoff

June 12th, 1978: Connel Willis was still in the hospital recuperating from major surgery only to have more operations within weeks of each other. This was due to the serious damage that was done to him in the accident. The other drivers came out of the race a little better and were still being treated.

I always wondered how much it cost Sportsman Park to keep the newspapers from telling "the rest of the story", as Paul Harvey says on his radio program. All I could find was a few lines that said that a minor accident had caused only one horse to finish the ninth race and that a few of the drivers were taken to the hospital for check-ups. Nothing was mentioned of the fact that no one from the Animal Humane Society ever came to the track before or after the accident. It also didn't mention why the state veterinarian wasn't in the paddock. After all, he's there for his pay check on pay-day!

I did notice from the race results in the sports section that the next night's attendance and mutuel wagering was considerably lower than usual. I do believe that quite a few patrons left the track very displeased about the scandalous way the officials ride shotgun over this track. Long before, I stated that I would never race a horse at this track again. Since then, this bloody track has deteriorated even more due to the present management.

June 12th, 1978, 1:00 p.m.: I withdrew $2,000 from the bank in the event I might want to place a small wager on a horse. Had it not been that Phase-Out was entered for the ninth race that night, I'd be staying home watching television.

Phase-out had won his race the previous week in the remarkable time of one minute and fifty-seven seconds. I was out of town selecting two high-class mares. I left a sizable check for a down payment until I returned in a month with the final payment and my van.

6:00 p.m.: Jim Karubas had watched Phase-Out win and was ready with his checkbook when I had dinner at his restaurant. I told him I would watch the horse that night and see if his owner had driven down from Milwaukee, Wisconsin. If so, I would make them an offer to see if it would catch his interest. Jim said, "My night chef has the night off, but I will try to find some way to slip away and meet you at the paddock." As I was leaving I said, "Don't forget, we're going to Milwaukee next week."

9:00 p.m.: I parked my car in the lot west of Laramie Street as usual. I took a leisurely walk through the clubhouse entrance, buying a program while heading to the paddock at the east end of the track. The weather was cooperating very nicely with a light, cool breeze and a temperature around seventy degrees. The sky, glittering with an abundance of stars, made this a beautiful night for watching a champion win another race.

The horses were coming on the track for the fifth race. Just as I had planned on being here, Phase-Out would be taking his last warm-up mile. I watched his trainer put on his bridle. I stood at the wire fence that separated the paddock from the patrons in the grandstand. I then saw a truly magnificent animal standing well over sixteen hands high with perfect conformation and very muscular looking.

I could plainly see that this horse had been given special care from the day he was born. I was right when I told Jim and Ted, "Be prepared to write a few big numbers on your checkbooks, as I am. This horse won't be bought cheap." I was so amazed by this horse, it wasn't until I saw him being led out of the paddock that I realized the fifth race had already been run, even though the track announcer had called the entire race. I didn't care. What I had seen was far more enjoyable to me.

I took out my stop watch and binoculars and walked a couple of dozen yards to the fence that was facing the race track. The trainer had his driver silk jacket on and was now taking Phase-Out around the back stretch turn going the opposite way of the track. In a few minutes, he was turning the right way of the track near the clubhouse turn for his slow start. He picked up speed going up the back stretch. At the three-eighth pole, he eased the big fella out a notch. I could see that he had a hand full of dynamic speed heading into my view at the top of the stretch. He was pacing effortlessly as he began his journey down the stretch and around the clubhouse turn. I checked my stop watch at the half-mile pole. One minute and ten seconds, under an extremely firm hold. It looked like money in the bank. It always made me happy to see a well-trained horse performing so splendidly without the use of a whip or drugs.

Coming into my view at the top of the stretch turn to complete his mile, Phase-Out was hardly blowing as though he were out for an evening in the park. As he was pacing down the stretch, I used my binoculars to make sure I would catch his time at the finish line. I was simply amazed as I looked at the time for his warm-up mile. It was in two minutes and sixteen seconds.

When the trainer got off the sulky and patted Phase-Out, he was smiling as he walked by me into the paddock. Then carefully backing Phase-Out into the number three stall with the help of a groom, they unhooked the sulky and removed the harness and bridle. They put a halter on him after a damp sponge-bath. They then covered the horse with a couple of blankets, or "coolers" as horsemen like to call them.

There was one thing different in his race. There were only four other horses entered against Phase-Out . Not one of them had the race time speed to out pace this fine horse. Obviously, there were no other owners at that track who wanted to settle for second or third place, so they elected to wait for an easier race with less purse money.

Phase-Out, like my horse, always raced from off the pace staying fifth or sixth until the half-mile. Then, when asked, he would show a burst of speed equal to none and be in front in the stretch drive where it would all pay off. With such a small field, this race would be the easiest he has ever had for there would be less chance of traffic problems as there could be with a nine- or ten-horse field.

Up to that point, I hadn't looked at my program that I bought just to give it to Ted at his restaurant the day after. I wanted him to also come up to Milwaukee where we could make the owner a legitimate offer for Phase-Out.

The horses were now on the track for the seventh race. I pulled my program from my pant's pocket and folded it to the ninth race. I was casually looking at the past performances of the first two horses. There was nothing there that I hadn't already known. As I started to skip down to the number three horse, Phase-Out, like a bolt of lightning I got the shock of my life. I had to take a closer look. It was printed there that driver's name who would be driving Phase-Out that night was Darryl Busse. Of all of the other drivers at that track, the owner couldn't possibly have made a poorer choice. Hell, had I known that something had happened to his regular driver, I would have been in Milwaukee paying him to let me drive this horse. Especially in an easy race as this was.

I had always classified Darryl Busse running in a dead heat with Sterling Buch for the stupid award trophy of the century. The facts speak for themselves. Nothing could ever change my opinion of him as a person or horseman even if he had won a billion races. It would still boil down to the way and how he won them in my judgment.

I only wish the owner had driven down to see this race. It's a sure bet, I'd be talking to him into making a change so as not to endanger his horse's life. This may sound like an extremely harsh statement but I have observed how cruelly Busse operates his stable of other owner's horses. I've seen his methods of winning races for many years. Of course, there are horse owners who are no angels themselves, and could care less how their horse wins a race. To them their horses are like used cars. They buy a little insurance and if they drop dead, they collect the money and buy another horse.

Before I realized it, Frank Pennino was walking down to where I was looking at Phase-Out. In a couple of minutes he would be yelling out to bridle up for the ninth race. I was a little surprised that he hadn't been fired due to the accident he could have prevented. After I thought for a second, though, I realized that that would not happen. This is Sportsman Park.

He noticed me instantly and gave me a cold and bitter look. If looks could kill, I'd be dead. But I didn't get the opportunity to remind him of my warning about the Ocala Star Craft race, for he abruptly turned and headed back in the direction of the office.

Just as I was hoping that Phase-Out might get lucky due to Busse not showing up on time, my expectations faded as I saw him wearing his colored driving jacket of gray and red trim. Busse walked over to the number three stall and the trainer immediately began to talk. Judging from the way he was holding both hands outwards, I could only come to the conclusion that the trainer was telling Busse of his last fantastic warm-up mile. He was probably saying that Phase-Out was razor-sharp. Busse wasn't paying much attention and seemed disinterested. I then heard someone else call out for the drivers to be ready to go out in one minute. The bridles were already on the horses and the drivers were waiting for Pennino, but he didn't return.

My concern was, "Do I bet or don't I?" After all, betting on a favorite is something that I rarely do and only on a special horse. The problem was that the one thing I would never do was bet on a horse that Darryl Busse was driving knowing I would end up in the poorhouse. The one outstanding point in this case is that with such a high-class horse as this and a smart trainer overlooking the race, I didn't think that Busse would be playing any games that night in this race. I figured that the owner might have something to say after the trainer called him on the phone after the race.

I was thinking of all of these points as the horses started to leave the paddock. With the sound of the bugle over the public address system announcing that the horses were coming onto the track for the ninth race, I walked over to watch the five horses parade by me on their way down the stretch in front of the grandstand and clubhouse. In ten minutes, they would be going to the starting gate that was waiting on the straight-a-way of the back-stretch.

The thought had crossed my mind that any time a driver has an overwhelming favorite in a race on a horse that belongs to someone else, the temptation would be enormous for him to guarantee that his horse would not finish in the money. This is especially true when all the driver would be getting for a win is a handshake and a couple of hundred dollars. If he gave in to the temptation, his pockets would be bulging with hundred dollar bills from a few high-roller gamblers. These people get mighty friendly with the drivers that drive in most of the races each night, and pay well for that kind of information.

I decided to wager only $1,000 that night instead of the two I had planned. I figured that with the odds at three to five, the profit would cover my expenses to Milwaukee the following week. There was no use in getting greedy. At least I stopped worrying about the driver change. After all, all Busse had to do was sit on the sulky, keep a firm hold on the lines, and pretend that he was a wooden dummy. Phase-Out was smart enough for both of them to win that race.

That made me laugh out loud as I made my way through the crowded grandstand area. There was one thing for sure, the $50 windows are never crowded with lines of patrons waiting to make their wagers. I picked up my twenty tickets and I was a might tempted to buy another twenty. That flash was all I had for I said to myself, "No, no, no!"

I heard the track announcer say that the horses were nearing the starting gate as I hurried to my favorite spot near the top of the stretch across from the paddock. Standing near the fence over-looking the track, the five horses were about ten yards from the out-stretched arms of the starting gate. It slowly started to move around the back-stretch turn and approach the top of the stretch turn. The horses were about five yards from the gate as it headed down the stretch. I had my binoculars on Phase-Out and Busse as they came into my view. It was as though I was sitting in the sulky. They were very good glasses. Then, even without the binoculars, I would have noticed that Busse wasn't looking straight ahead at his horse or the starting gate like the other drivers were doing. Instead, he had his head turned to the right looking almost sideways at the fence near the paddock as though he was trying to find someone. He was still looking as the gate went by my position and slowly headed down the stretch when the announcer gave out with his usual last call, "The gate is rolling."

I felt very uneasy for the next few seconds. Something wasn't right. Busse hadn't paid any attention to the trainer in the paddock and for damn sure wasn't out there either. Well, I thought, It's too late to worry now. The horses were going around the clubhouse turn heading for the back-stretch as they started up the straight-a-way. The mobile gate was picking up speed as it neared the starting pole, with less than an eighth of a mile before the start. All five horses had their noses up to the moving gate. Then, with a quick burst of speed, the long arms of the gate folded inwards as the car pulled away from the horses and headed to the outer edge of the track.

I was totally shocked to see Busse using his whip on Phase-Out from the very first second of the race. That horse never in all of his past races had been taken to the lead at the start of a race. Certainly, no one ever used a whip on him from the start like this lunatic was doing.

Going around the back-stretch turn and heading into my binoculars's view, Phase-Out was out in front by three to four lengths. The other four drivers were following in single file along the rail. None, of course, were using their whips at that very early stage of the race — they wanted to win. Coming around the turn and heading into the stretch, Busse was still banging away with his whip. Each blow made Phase-Out's head turn. He was feeling the severe pain from the beating.

I lowered my binoculars when he was near the closest point to me. I yelled out at the top of my lungs, "Busse, you whip-happy stupid jerk!" That was all I had time to yell for he was then out of range of my voice. Leading by five lengths going down the stretch, many people in the crowd that had bet on Phase-Out probably figured they had won with that big of a lead and only five-eighths of mile left. It seemed like a piece of cake. It's no wonder why the patrons usually go home broke. I knew better. Every time Busse hit Phase-Out with his whip he would shorten his stride. Just as every time a human would be hit, he or she would flinch and try to draw away from the oncoming blow.

There was no way that Phase-Out would finish the race. I thought, "What in the Hell was that so-called judge doing in that mobile starting gate that was following the horses. They should be looking for any infractions of the rules or any type of abuse."

Phase-Out had just passed the half-mile pole when the other four horses all pulled out from the rail at the same time and moved towards the middle of the track to pass Busse. They knew he had finished off his horse and were giving him plenty of room in the event Phase-Out went down due to exhaustion and stress from the beating. The accident of two weeks before had to still be in their minds.

All four horses passed Phase-Out as though he had stopped. Busse then held both driving lines straight out loosely and flapping them up and down. He was driving as if he were trying to convince the track officials that he wasn't holding the horse back. Well, if they believed that, I'd like to sell them the Brooklyn bridge! Any dummy would know that Phase-Out was finished at the start of the race.

The four horses approached the top of the stretch. They were tightly bunched and making a race of it. Then I felt sick in my stomach as I watched Phase-Out coming into the stretch turn some twenty lengths behind. He was struggling just to keep from falling. I yelled at Busse, "Get off before you kill that horse!" I was mad along with a number of other people at the fence who realized the damage he had done to a horse that ten minutes ago was the best horse at that track with his gifted speed.

I followed his movements down the stretch with my binoculars. Many of the patrons were throwing their programs in the direction of Busse as he slowly went by, crossing the finish line. I silently gave thanks that Phase-Out hadn't fallen. Any other horse would probably have gone down before the half-mile pole. I would give anything to find out the true reason why Busse sadistically bludgeoned this fine animal. Personally, I knew why, but until I had proof, I couldn't do anything about it. I would be very much surprised if the track officials requested Ol'e Busse to review the race films with them the next day for an explanation of such unprofessional and unethical conduct. The only way this would happen is if the races were postponed the next day due to a heavy snow storm. That was my thinking, anyway, of this race track.

I walked to the gate where I noticed that the trainer was waiting for Busse to return with his badly-beaten horse. I was glad to see that the owner hadn't seen this race for it could have caused him to have a heart attack. The trainer slowly walked onto the track to take the reins from Busse as he slid off the sulky. I couldn't believe that neither said a word to each other as Busse started to walk quickly to the paddock. I was horrified to see the exhausted condition Phase-Out was in. He was gasping for a breath of air and blowing like a steam engine. There were numerous long whip welt marks on both sides of his body and across his back. I heard the few people who were standing at the fence yell at Busse. They were saying that they would have liked to use the whip on him.

Busse was heading into the paddock so I crossed over to that side where I knew he would be passing me. When he was about ten feet from me, I yelled out to make damn sure he heard me. I yelled, "Busse, you gave that horse a lousy drive. If I couldn't drive any better, I'd tear up my license. He hurried by me quickly without saying a word. I didn't get the opportunity to ask him the one important question, "Busse, how much money were you paid to keep Phase-Out from winning?" With him running off that way, he answered it. I knew that some day I would learn the truth. I am a great believer in the saying, "What goes around comes around."

There was only one race left as the majority of people were passing the paddock heading to the Cicero Avenue parking lot. They were throwing their pari-mutuel tickets on the blacktop pavement along with their hopes and dreams of wealth. That reminded me of the $1,000 I wagered. I pulled out the tickets and let them fall along side of their playmates. I started to walk along the track fence through the grandstand area for there were only a few people around. The remainder were at the windows making bets on the last race trying to break even.

Chapter 23

Gestapo Headquarters

Midway through the grandstand area, I was approached by two track security men. One was Eugene Oliver who stood out like a hippopotamus as compared to his partner. He was about five and a half feet tall, weighing about one hundred and thirty pounds. Oliver spoke first saying, "Michael John, the officials would like to talk to you. For a few minutes at that precise moment the only possible conclusion I could think of was that they were finally investigating the Ocala Star Craft accident.

Looking directly at Oliver, I asked him, "Did you contact Phil Langley or any of the judges about that lame horse that started a riot a couple of weeks ago?" Receiving no answer, I said, "You guys must have had your hands full. Did anyone get hurt?" He was getting a little nervous judging by the look on his face. I must have hit a sore spot. He then spoke out sharply and said, "Everything will be ironed out in the office." Never in this world had a person given such a short and true statement. No one else besides all of the security personnel, Sportsman Park race track officials and Phil Langley knew of this conspiracy by their leader. They knew the final depraved and disastrous ending that meeting would bring.

Had I only had a hint of the true nature of my visit that was already planned, I would have broken an Olympic record for the mile run in leaving the track and headed for the nearest bomb shelter!

I started walking in the direction of the racing secretary's office, but Oliver quickly said, "Not that way, the meeting is in the security office." I said, "O.K.," as they both followed a few feet behind me with only a few patrons to walk between or around. Nearing the office that was next to the clubhouse entrance, with his two-way radio in his hand, I heard Oliver try to keep his voice down. It wasn't low enough for me not to hear him say, "We're bringing Horak in." I turned and asked him, "What was that all about?" Softly he said, "I just wanted to make sure the officials had arrived."

There was something in his tone of answer that made me very uneasy. Something just didn't seem to jell so I took slower steps. Oliver had to notice my actions, for he then said, "I want to see a horse in the last race that I bet on." I supposed that was all I needed to hear for the next thing I knew, I was at the security office door. There was a large window next to the door and the blinds were drawn closed. So was the window on the south side. I had noticed this as we had approached from the door's direction.

I opened the door and slowly stepped in. There was only about four feet of floor space with a five-foot high counter and a four-foot swinging gate that separated the office. It contained a large desk and chair with three or four other chairs against the two side walls. There were a few filing cabinets but no Phil Langley, Frank Pennino or any of the other officials I knew. I still couldn't grasp the meaning of all that. It was probably because I was starting to get sleepy for it was past my usual bedtime, but the cards were already dealt. Eugene Oliver was the only person I knew. There were three other men in the office besides the little fellow with Oliver. Behind the desk sat a stocky-looking guy dressed in a dark suit and a brown shirt. I almost thought he was Al Capone's son.

The other two were standing to the right of the table. Both had to be well over six foot tall and weighed over 200 pounds and were also dressed in dark suits. These five guys looked like they all met at Zayres to buy their clothes. Oliver and his partner were identically dressed as the others.

My relaxed feeling now made me think that all these copy cats needed was to be holding machine guns, then they would be ready to make a movie in Hollywood. Frankly, I had already formed an opinion of those "ham-and-eggers" that they had been watching too many gangster movies on the late show after the races.

My humorous thoughts were suddenly interrupted by Oliver who had pushed something hard into my back. He said, "Go through the gate to the front of the desk." I turned around enough to see him holding a very large hand gun. At first glance, I couldn't tell what kind it was, but I said, "What the hell do you think you're doing with that gun!" Then, bringing his gun into full view, he said, "Just do as I tell you." Stepping through, I saw one of the other guys holding a hand gun along his side. I again turned to see Oliver having a difficult time in squeezing sideways through the four-foot opening.

I walked up to the front of the desk and looked directly into the eyes of the man sitting behind the desk. (I was later able to learn this was Steve Bajovich and the other two were Joseph McCarthy and Daniel Groth. The little fellow's name remains a mystery.)

Bajovich straightened up in his chair. He looked at me and said, "We've had many complaints about you causing trouble at the paddock." I immediately replied, "The one thing I tried to do is stop trouble from happening. Just ask Oliver about me telling him to call Phil Langley on his two-way radio to stop Ocala Star Craft from racing because she was lame." I continued, "You surely know what happened by now." Before I had a chance to continue, the telephone rang. While he was talking in a low voice, I could hear the track announcer telling the patrons that the horses were lined up behind the gate for the tenth race. The announcer could be heard saying that the gate was rolling.

I was trying to hear what Bajovich was saying, but all I heard was, "Yes sir." He looked like a puppet dancing on strings. I knew that it had to be Phil Langley pulling those strings. I slowly turned enough to see how close Oliver was to me as well as McCarthy. Only Groth was standing near the desk. I knew I had to get out of there. Oliver lied about the officials and there was a lot more to it than I could figure out at the time. I surely didn't care to find out in that office with the cards stacked against me. I thought that if I could make it to the door, I'd be all right. There were still enough people outside. My hopes were quickly shattered as I saw Groth stand in front of the door. Whatever they had planned for me, I wasn't prepared for it.

Bajovich was stalling. He was waiting for something. I watched him carefully as he was still softly talking. The track announcer had just said that the horses were at the sixteenth pole. Bajovich said one more, "Yes sir," then slammed the receiver onto the telephone. He then looked up at the ceiling, then sharply lowered his head. At that second I felt a strong arm around my neck pulling me backwards. The pressure was cutting off my air. I tried to catch my breath but it was impossible. I then felt myself falling backwards and hitting the floor. Someone was sitting on my chest with his grubby hands around my throat. He was choking me to the point that my mind was going dim. I had one free arm so I took a swing as hard as I could muster hitting Oliver somewhere in his face. It was good enough that I made him loosen his choke hold. Then I felt someone's foot kick me in the side of my ribs three to five times. In the process, I was being turned over facing the floor. My arms were being hand-cuffed together behind my back. I yelled out as many swear words that I knew as those Gestapos continued kicking me completely over my body.

Then, as if on cue, everybody stopped and the room was quiet. No one was saying anything. I laid on the floor motionless. I thought that they were tired and through with me. That was the longest and quietest minute I'll ever remember.

It was just too long for something terrible not to happen. I didn't finish the last word when I felt a crashing blow on my left exposed elbow from a very hard object. The pain went through my body like a jolt of electric current. I felt like I was falling through the sky at a frightening pace and speed into total darkness.

I had no idea how long I had spent in another world, but gradually my senses were returning. I was feeling a tremendous amount of unbearable pain over my entire body. I then realized that I was sitting in a chair with my arms over the back with hands cuffed together. I could feel the tightness of them pressing into my wrist. My mind was still not clear. I was hearing voices in the room but I left my head lowered to try to understand what was going on and how long I had been there. It couldn't have been ten minutes later, when I heard loud noises from outside of the room. Instantly, the door sprang open and a young man was pushed into the room falling through the gate entrance. He landed on the floor with his hands handcuffed behind his back. The two bullies then kicked him at will. I found enough voice to yell out, "You better stop. He has a witness." Bajovich was furious as he jumped up and in a loud voice said, "Why the hell did you bring him in here? Didn't you see that the blinds were closed?" That statement made me think that obviously those S.S. Storm Troopers had made more plans for me for after the crowds were gone. Like some kind of accident happening, there was no way they could turn me loose then, after all of the damage they had already done.

Bajovich sat down in disgust and picked up the telephone. I desperately wanted to hear what he was almost whispering to the person on the other end. I'd bet all the tea in China, it was Phil Langley. The two brave bullies were now dragging the young man to where I was sitting and sat him in a chair next to me. I could see that he had been badly beaten, as he slumped in the chair. I was thinking, If Adolf Hitler were alive, he would have decorated Bajovich and his perverted mentally deficient S.S. Storm Troopers with Germany's highest award for bravery, The Iron Cross. They were only armed with guns and Black-Jacks, while I was armed with a large pair of binoculars and a stopwatch. I also had a billfold containing a little over $800.

The pain from the tightening handcuffs was then far greater due to the swelling from my damaged elbow. I yelled out to Bajovich that he had better get somebody over to loosen them or I was about to start a riot. He motioned Oliver to check on me as he was still on the telephone. Oliver wobbled over and looked behind my back. He told Bajovich that the swelling was tightening the one wrist. Bajovich told him to take the hand-cuffs off me after he finished getting his orders over the telephone. One of the other morons yelled out, "I wouldn't do that. Leave them on." Oliver laughed and confidentially said, "He won't be using that arm any more!"

After he had caused even more pain in removing the handcuffs, I had to struggle to bring my left arm around. The pain caused me to become dizzy. I stopped for a minute then tried again. Seeing just the damage that the handcuffs had done by cutting into my wrist and making it bleed, I said to myself, "Oliver, when you die, I hope that it will be a long and painful death."

The swelling from my elbow was already entering into all of my fingers. I knew that Oliver had been right with his statement.

The young man next to me called out that his cuffs were hurting him after he had a good look at my wrist. His cuffs were removed. I later found out that his name was Richard White and was twenty-two years old. He had graduated that afternoon from college. To celebrate the occasion, his grandmother treated him to an outing of dinner and an evening at the races. While she was sitting in the grandstand, Richard White in his haste to make a two-dollar wager accidentally bumped into a lady. While he was saying that he was sorry, the two security bullies happened to be a few yards away. They hand-cuffed him and brought him in with me. I told him, "It was a good thing that she didn't fall when you bumped into her. They probably would have shot you!"

The office door opened and two policemen from the Cicero Station walked in. A couple of minutes later, we were told that we were being charged with disorderly conduct. I stated that my damaged elbow required medical attention in a hospital. The policemen said, "After you post the $35 bond, you can go yourself."

With the help of Richard White, I was able to get up from the chair. Standing there, Oliver started to place my billfold into my rear pocket. One of the police officers wanted to know what he was doing with my billfold. He did do a magnificent job of lying when he said, "It fell out of his pocket when he stumbled to the floor hurting his elbow." I asked the officer if he could get my billfold and count how much money was inside. I told him that there should be a few dollars — over 800. After a quick glance, he said, "I don't know what amount you had before, but you have seventy dollars now."

The officer walked over to Bajovich and Oliver asking if they knew anything of the missing money. He also asked them if they had anything else of my personal effects.

Looking the officer in the eyes, they both said, "NO!" With that, the officer told me that without any witnesses, there was nothing he could do.

I walked over to where Bajovich and Oliver were standing. "I see you Gestapos are a bunch of thieves also," I told them. "I'll give you a guaranteed winner you can bet on. There will be serious repercussions from your actions of tonight, no matter how long it takes me. That is a promise" Those two blooming idiots didn't have the brains of a flea. Even a woodpecker is smarter, for this bird knows how to use it's head.

Ten minutes later, at the Cicero Police Station, Richard and I were told that it would be a few minutes before the paperwork would be completed. We were then put in separate rooms until such time that I was released, about four hours later. Richard White was released after only twenty minutes. Asking for an explanation from the police was like asking Phil Langley why he gave the order to cripple me.

I asked the desk sergeant if an officer could take me to the hospital after letting him see my swollen arm and the deep gashes the handcuffs had made. As if he were reading it from a written note someone had given him, he said, "There weren't any cars available," and that I should get a cab. When I asked if he would call one, he said, "We're not allowed to do so."

I walked outside at four a.m., hurting badly. I walked about five blocks before a Morton cab pulled along side. Within minutes, he had me near my car I had left at the track. I was surprised that the car was still there. Had Bajovich known it was mine, he would have had it sold by this time.

I drove in the direction of the hospital while thinking, What could they do that I couldn't? Besides, I remembered waiting five hours just a few months ago to have my hand x-rayed, soaked in ice and bandaged. I went to a Seven-Eleven store that stayed open 24 hours. I bought two large bags of ice cubes and headed home. I had to cut my shirt off for I couldn't bend my arm. I put all of the ice in the sink then added some water. It took some time for me to get used to the cold water, but soon I had my complete arm soaking as I leaned across my sink.

At six o'clock, I wrapped the entire arm with four towels. I dropped onto the bed, crippled and totally exhausted. I thought, "Now I know for sure how Phase-Out felt after his race."

I soaked my left arm for two hours twice daily for the next three days but the swelling still hadn't gone down. I knew that normally in that length of time there should have been some improvement unless there were serious complications.

June 16th, 1978: At ten a.m., I checked into the McNeal Hospital in Berwyn, Illinois. I was assigned Dr. Aldo Ray. I had so many x-rays of my body taken that I thought I would glow in the dark. My entire arm to my fingers were placed in a hard cast. The ulnar nerve had been permanently damaged and there was a severe fracture. This would prevent me from ever using my left hand in a normal way. I may be able to retain forty percent use of my left arm the remainder of my life. This report shattered my mind. I thought, "Eugene Oliver, I'll never forget your statement at Sportsman Park."

The pain killer shots I had received were helpful. Eight hours later, I stepped outside. The heat of the day hit me like a furnace. The ninety-five degree sun was was still up for another hour. I hadn't eaten in the past thirty hours due to my sore ribs and worry about my elbow. Had it been just bruised, I could have forgotten part of the anger I had against Sportsman Park but that had changed with the medical report. These next hot summer months would be pure agony with my arm in the cast.

As long as I was in Berwyn, I drove to see my life-long friend Mr. James Balodimas and his good wife Bertha. Strange as it may seem, he also owns a restaurant on the corner of Sixteenth and Harlem Avenues. All three of my good friends are Greek and have restaurants.

I knew that James and his wife would be surprised when I entered their restaurant. I had breakfast there the morning of Phase-Out's race. Bertha was almost in tears when I walked in for she said that she saw the difficult time I was having getting out of my car. Then James came out from the kitchen. About an hour later, I mentioned some of the problems I was having. James went back in the kitchen to prepare for the three of us one of his special Greek meals. I was unable to even lift a spoon with my left hand so James cut up all of my food. He gave me strict rules that I was to eat all of my meals there until the cast was removed.

In this cruel world, it's almost impossible to find absolutely wonderful friends like the Balodimas family. I felt terrible that I had to impose on them, but they would have it no other way. Thank heaven, there are a few good people around in this world.

Jim and Bertha Balodimas

Part II

Racing days are over.

Chapter 24
Seeking Justice

July 20th, 1978: The old cast was removed and there was very little improvement. Five hours later, I was leaving the hospital after numerous x-rays and a new hard cast. Sportsman Park officials steadily maintained that they had no knowledge of the damage that was supposedly done by their security guards. They also remarked that I probably fell down a few stairs or out of bed.

I had expected some sort of a statement like that since I knew the type of people I was dealing with. Therefore I thought it best to retain a lawyer and see if a jury would believe their preposterous story.

September 25th, 1978: Talking to over forty different lawyers in the past two months would definitely discourage anybody. I soon realized the fact that whenever I informed each attorney of Sportsman Park, they treated me like a leper. I was told to take whatever they offered me even if it was only $500. I came away with an embittered attitude towards the legal system.

I eventually retained the legal services of the Law firm of M. Burken. My only concern was that the office was only a couple of miles away from Sportsman Park. This thought crossed my mind, but I thought, "Naw! He wouldn't sell me out. Even Columbus took a chance." Time would tell.

During the next few weeks, I spent many hours in Burken's office explaining the events of June 12th. In October, he filed a lawsuit against Steve Bajovich, Eugene Oliver, Joseph McCarthy, Daniel Groth, The National Jockey Club and The Fox Valley Trotting Club, Incorporated. All of these organizations operated from Sportsman Park, in Cicero, Illinois. The amount asked for damages was $500 thousand.

After the lawsuit was filed, we learned that the law firm of Garretsen Santora and Bishop of 33 North Dearborn Street, Chicago, Illinois was assigned to the case to represent Sportsman Park.

Within a month, Mr. Burken called to tell me of their offer of $5,000 to dismiss the suit. I told them to "Buy a new suit and we'll see them in court!" I would have enjoyed knowing the amount of a bonus that law firm had been promised by the race track if they could close the case without taking it to trial. I knew that Sportsman Park realized that if the case went to court, things might be exposed that would indeed cause bad publicity for them. That would lower the attendance even more.

December 20th, 1978: The hard cast was finally removed. It had caused me to lose thousands of hours of sleep. It was replaced with a soft-type cast made out of a medicated bandage called a gelo-cast. That gave me much more comfort. The swelling was gone but any quick movements caused a sharp pain. I dreaded taking the pills my doctor had prescribed that would be helpful.

February 5th, 1979: Still experiencing severe pain and swelling in my elbow, I had to obtain a second opinion of Doctor Karmel Mikhall, an orthopedic specialist.

I had met my attorney that morning at the Maywood Court House to answer the disorderly conduct charge that Sportsman Park used to cover up their real purpose of having me brought into that office. I thought, "They had to stop me from talking about the Ocala Star Craft accident. Their plans would have succeeded had it not been for Richard White mistakenly being brought into the same office. These Gestapos with their guns and blackjacks fear nothing but a witness."

My case was called at nine-thirty. Eugene Oliver was there to represent Sportsman Park. He must have been confident that I would be given a fine thus making him look mighty good in the eyes of the track officials when he returned. When it was his turn to talk to the judge, he made it known, loudly and clearly, that I was a very dangerous individual. The judge let him continue with his rapid fire of charges for the next twenty minutes. Finally, the judge interrupted Oliver by saying, "Of all these ridiculous charges that you have seen fit to waste this court's time on, I find Not Guilty!" Oliver wasn't smiling any more. As I thanked the judge, round one was over. I knew that the other fourteen rounds wouldn't be that easy.

The next three years were spent in obtaining depositions from the personnel of Sportsman Park, with the progress moving at a snail's pace. The remarkable aspect of all of their depositions was that not one person told the same story in regards to the night of June 12th, 1978. It would be very interesting to see if they do the same with a jury that would decide their guilt or innocence.

I began to notice an enormous change in my attorney's attitude. My phone calls were not being returned nor was I kept updated about my case. I could only second guess, but to this day I still believe that Mr. Burken only took my case to collect a quick settlement, doing as little leg-work and paper-work as possible. Like most law firms, they looked at me as an easy meal ticket, with no concern of how I was to make ends meet in the future. All that this lawyer was doing was giving me another problem. I had to worry about him and wonder if he would take a bribe from some Sportsman Park official. Some lawyers are like vultures and prey on helpless individuals. I have noticed that the majority of attorneys have a saying, "Trust me. If you can't trust your attorney, who can you trust?" I soon discovered that I could only trust myself. This lawsuit was going to be a long and hard-fought up-hill battle with no holds barred.

I had given Mr. Burken all of the information on Richard White that I had. He was my only witness. I was flabbergasted when he told me, "There's no need to waste time and money looking for him." He didn't think his testimony would be of much help in court.

September 14th, 1982: A pre-trial hearing was set for September 17th, 1982 to find out how far apart both sides were in settling the law suit. Burken sent his junior partner for the hearing. He couldn't possibly have known anything about my case as he was with the firm for only two days. I thought this to be a very unprofessional decision.

I put together all of the so-called legal advice I had been given over the past four years and arrived at the same conclusion over and over: That Mr. Burken was *ordered* not to make any waves against Sportsman Park. I dismissed him after he informed me that *he* would only be able to collect the original offer of $5,000.

Chapter 25

Second Law Firm

James Balodimas's son Chris introduced me to Bennett Alban. His profession was a corporation and business attorney and he was related to the Balodimas. I was impressed by his firm's offices on the thirtieth floor of the First National Bank building in the Chicago loop. I knew that the rent must have been tremendous. The furnishings alone would have bankrupted most businesses.

Quickly, I formed my opinion of Mr. Bennett Alban. I judged him to be one of the smartest attorneys in Chicago or he was a bigger gangster than Al Capone, using his pencil rather than a machine-gun to steal from his clients.

Our first meeting lasted about two hours. We arranged an appointment with another lawyer named Paul Kagan. He said, "Paul will be able to handle your case due to his vast experience with lawsuits." That statement sounded too good to be true. I asked myself, "How many times have I heard that before?"

October 2, 1982: From the beginning we had regular meetings. We went over and over the complete case, and had depositions taken from me and the four guards at Sportsman Park. We were still unable to locate the little guy that was with Eugene Oliver on the night in question. Sportsman Park officials refused to reveal his name. This gave some truth to the rumor that he had been sentenced to twenty years in prison for selling illegal drugs at the track. I could see why the officials would want to keep a cover on that scandal. They had more at that time than any other race track in America! I knew that I would have to keep a watchful eye and ears opened at all times, also that the key to my success was to locate Richard White and obtain a deposition from him.

At the time I had given Mr. Burken the address of Richard White, he was living with his grandmother on the South side of Chicago. Had Mr. Burken followed that lead, there would have been no problem. By then, however, Mr. White was no longer at that address. No one in his neighborhood seemed to know what became of him. He had just vanished into thin air. I prayed that no harm had come to him since he was a witness of mine. Chicago has been known for its many secrets that lay at the bottom of Lake Michigan, wearing cement boots.

October 12, 1982: I drove to Chicago's loop to keep an appointment with a private investigator to try to find Richard White. I gave him a $1000 retainer that day. I felt confident of his ability to produce results, even more so than my new attorney.

It was time for more action. On the following Sunday morning, I was up before the birds. I had a waffle and ham steak along with a cup of hot tea, stirring in a teaspoon of honey. I dressed in my best dark-blue suit and new shoes. I then loaded my Canon A-1 camera with film and placed two extra rolls in my pockets. I hurried out of the house, being extra careful not to bump my left elbow. At that time, I was still only wearing the soft Gelo-cast bandage on the entire arm. Any bump or sudden motion would have me pay the price with pain.

There was a cloudless sky and the slight trace of sun was just about to rise, as I backed my car out of the driveway. When I arrived at Sportsman Park, the sun was shining brightly. There was a crisp, cold breeze that reminded me that there would be no sun tanning that day, especially with the temperature around forty-five degrees.

I knew that on Sunday mornings there would be only one track guard on duty. He was there to open up the main gate of the grandstand to let the clean-up crew in to sweep the floor area of trash and the thousands of dollars of losing pari-mutuel tickets from the Saturday's racing program.

After a half-hour of listening to the car's radio, I watched the track guard open the gate as though he were half asleep. He then slowly walked in the direction of the racing secretary's office where he would probably finish his nap. Casually, I walked into the grandstand and began taking pictures of the complete layout of the track. I took extra pictures of the track security officer's office that I had named the Gestapo Headquarters. A chill went through me as I walked within a few feet of it to obtain pictures of the inside. The blinds were open. Sundays must be their rest day from inflicting severe physical pain on their patrons.

After finishing my third roll of film, I walked slowly through the grandstand area. I passed the paddock just as some of the crew were entering. They did just what I figured they would. They waved to me, thinking that I was one of the track officials checking out the track before going out for a Sunday breakfast. I thought I should have been given an academy award for my performance and picture taking.

Driving back home, I was enjoying my daydreams of the reactions from the track officials when they would view my photographs in court. I always knew that one picture was worth a thousand words. The thought had crossed my mind many times that I could also end up with a neat pair of cement boots before I had my day in court.

It had been four years of waiting for an honest lawyer to get my case rolling, and it still seemed like it was at a standstill. Two weeks after that Sunday, I had two copies of each picture developed and enlarged to eight by ten size. I took one set to the bank and placed them in a safe deposit box. The other set went to Kagan, my attorney.

I checked in to the Michael Reese Hospital to have a third opinion on my damaged elbow. It was becoming impossible for me to obtain a complete six or eight hours of peaceful sleep. Whenever I rolled on to my left elbow, the pressure of the weight caused me to suffer an acute attack of excruciating pain. One week later, I was back home. I made another appointment with Dr. Karmel Mikhall. He informed me that I must face reality. It would be impossible for any kind of operation to help me. As he put it in layman's terms, "Once a water glass has been broken, it will never be the same." Almost to the word, two different doctors at the hospital stated the same remarks after all of their tests were completed.

I had over sixty appointments in Dr. Mikhall's office during the previous three years. It had been a very frustrating experience. Whenever the swelling returned in my elbow, Dr. Mikhall would inject it with cortisone. The needle was so painful that I had to get by on the pain-killing pills.

During my appointment in the spring of 1983, Dr. Mikhall revealed that there had been no improvement. Not being able to flex, stretch or extend my arm normally would make it impossible for me to ever control a horse with the reins. This was due to the lost muscle substance and numbness in my fingers. My left hand grip was very weak. Dr. Mikhall put me on a new medication — Darvocet-N-100, a non-narcotic. He stated that as a last resort he would consider an ulnar nerve transplant operation.

December 14, 1983: Chicago was experiencing one of the most severe and coldest winters it ever had. The temperature was fifteen below zero with the wind-chill factor lowering it to forty below. Incredible as it may seem, the harness races went on as scheduled. I called the animal Humane Society to refresh their memory of their purpose and to inform them that if they would go to the track, they would find at least 500 cases of animal cruelty. There would be many horses unable to get a drink of water because the pails were frozen blocks of ice. I was simply told that my message was being recorded and that the matter would receive top priority, then a polite, "Good-bye." I was left with the feeling that all my words went in one ear and out the other. No harness racing was ever canceled the entire long, cold winter, even though very few people attended.

The spring of 1984 brought out the familiar sight of dandelions that were then in full bloom. They changed the meadows from their white blankets of snow to blankets of golden yellow flowers. I received a letter from the private investigator. My hands trembled, fearing to open it, thinking that if he hadn't found Richard White by now, the chances were slim to none that he ever would. If I had noticed the postmark I would have known that it had to be good news inside. It came from Los Angeles, California. Slowly I pulled the one-page letter from the envelope. The first words to reach my eyes were, "I have located your witness, Richard White. He has been living here since November of 1978. I shall contact you with full particulars next week, May 16th, 1984."

Immediately, I called my lawyer, Mr. Kagan with the best news I had in six years. True to his word, my investigator met me at James Balodimas's restaurant. I was almost shocked when I saw him getting out of his car for it was a rare event for me to see a person that I put faith in do all that he claims he will do. I paid him the balance of his $3,500 fee and three days later, I was on a plane for California.

Richard White picked me up at the airport. We had dinner and I brought him up to date on all the events that followed that terrible night in 1978. I assured him that, for his safety's sake, I would only give my attorney his address. I told him that he would probably want a deposition from him in the near future.

I also made it clear that I would pay his expenses when it came time for him to appear in court on my behalf, if that day should ever present itself.

Chapter 26

Cold-Blooded Murder

July 24th, 1984: Rodney Harris was a well-educated, black youth celebrating his seventeenth birthday. While putting eight hours in on his steady summer job, his father and mother were preparing a delicious dinner party. They were expecting a few relatives who would also bring some specially-prepared food. Ice cream, cake and cookies would be the dessert to follow the dinner. A dozen of Rodney's close high school classmates were also invited.

At five o'clock, the usual "Happy Birthday" song was sung with a lot of cheering. Everyone sat down to enjoy the magnificent meal placed before them. By eight o'clock the table had been cleared and Rodney's parents presented him with his birthday gift. They gave him some spending money and told him that he could go to the harness races at Sportsman Park with his best friend, Martin Osborne and two others. Martin owned a well-kept Oldsmobile so the transportation was no problem. They promised to return by eleven thirty. None of the teenagers had ever seen a live horse race, just what they had seen from television. They knew it would be different.

At nine o'clock, Martin handed the $1 parking fee to the attendant at the Sportsman Park entrance. The majority of parking spaces were already filled, leaving only room at the far end of the lot. The boys didn't mind the long walk to the grandstand. After all, it was a beautiful, clear and warm night. The parking lot had ample overhead lighting attached to tall poles which turned the darkness into daylight.

The four teenagers started walking towards the grandstand, all still dressed in slacks and short-sleeve sport's shirts with their brown leather shoes as they had gotten ready for the birthday party. Walking between the rows of parked autos, they were laughing and talking as they neared the grandstand entrance. Within thirty yards of the entrance, they all suddenly stopped, for there parked before them was a 1979 Chevrolet in immaculate condition. It looked as though it just rolled off the assembly line. Standing near the auto, over-looking such a rare item, no more than thirty seconds had passed. A loud voice suddenly disrupted the calm by yelling out, "Police! Put your hands up in the air and lean over the car. You are under arrest!" Martin Osborne quickly said that they had just stopped to look over the sharp-looking car. The person who yelled at them, "Police," was actually a heavy-set security guard for Sportsman Park. The guard was holding a large hand-gun as he yelled out, "Keep quiet and do as I tell you."

The teenagers, knowing they had done nothing wrong, put their hands on the car next to the Chevrolet and leaned forward to be searched. Rodney Harris was closest to the guard with Martin Osborne next to him, The guard stepped up behind Rodney to search him as Martin again tried to explain that they were just looking at the car. The guard raised his gun and hit Martin with the barrel, causing Martin to yell out with pain. The guard was sounding like a raving maniac as his loud voice rang out for Martin "... to be quiet or I'll blow your head off!"

He then started to search Rodney Harris, putting the barrel of the gun in the back of Rodney's head. Only two or three seconds passed before the silence of the night air was instantly shattered by what sounded like a cannon being fired. Martin stood up quickly, only to see Rodney falling to the ground with the guard holding his gun downwards at Rodney. He was face-down on the black-top surface of the parking lot. He then looked at Martin and yelled out, "See what you punks made me do?"

To this day, I believe that those other three teenagers owe their lives to the five people who happened to be walking in the direction of the grandstand. They had heard the gunshot and ran over just as the guard was raising his gun to Martin Osborne.

The three teenagers were sent home after giving the

Cicero police their statements. The guard was allowed to go to the police station when he was ready to make out his report of the "incident" as they called it. He said that he first had to talk with the track officials, probably to outline a believable story for an accidental shooting.

The shooting of seventeen-year-old Rodney Harris occurred after the second race, but Sportsman Park's racing schedule for that night went on as planned. None of the paying patrons knew of the murder that just took place.

At the Cicero police station, the security guard stated that he saw four boys attempting to break into a 1979 Chevrolet, so he ordered them to lean over the car to be searched. He said that the boys willingly submitted. He said that as he was about to search the first boy with his loaded gun placed in back of the boy's head, the boy suddenly turned, causing the gun to accidentally fire. The report was signed by Eugene Oliver.

Two days later, the *Chicago Tribune* had three small lines on the bottom of the fifth page of their newspaper. It read, "Accidental shooting at Sportsman Park Race Track, Rodney Harris died instantly. No charges to be filed against Eugene Oliver, the track security guard."

Investigative reporter Pam Zekman of CBS television, Channel Two in Chicago, noted that Oliver's written statement didn't coincide with the medical report. It said that Rodney Harris died from a bullet wound from the middle of the back of his head which came out the middle of his forehead. Oliver said that the boy turned his head when the gun went off accidentally. If that had been true, the bullet surely would have entered the side of his head.

I watched the news on television each day for the next month, waiting to see if that Gestapo Lunatic Eugene Oliver would ever be charged with the murder of Rodney Harris. It was not to be as yet!

Had Oliver driven through a red light and received a traffic ticket, he would have to appear in court. But as he had killed a helpless teenager in cold blood at Sportsman Park Race Track, he didn't even get a slap on the wrist and no court appearance. Obviously, murder is legal at this race track.

This was a travesty of justice. I drove to the State Attorney's office in Chicago to see Richard J. Daley who, at the time, held the office. His father, before he had passed away, was Chicago's mayor for many years. I was told by Mr. John Kogut, Cook County Assistant State Attorney, "This office did not recommend any charges be filed in the shooting. The case has been closed — period!"

It took me until September to find Martin Osborne. After I proved to him that I wasn't working for Sportsman Park officials, he gave me the facts on the "cold-blooded killing" which was the way he saw it.

A month later, I made an appointment at Operation Push Headquarters on the South side of Chicago off the Dan Ryan Expressway. I brought along Martin Osborne. I had hopes of meeting with Reverend Jesse Jackson, but instead was led to a room to speak with Reverend Reddick. I left him with the video tapes of Pam Zekman's news report and newspaper clippings. I drove Martin home with the feeling that the day was a total waste.

Nothing ever did come from my meeting, I was later to learn. I never found out if Jesse Jackson even received a copy of my report, so as to have this killing reopened for a complete investigation. The facts sure merited one.

With Christmas only twenty days away, and the first light snow falling outside, I settled in for the night and drank a glass of warm milk. After watching the television program, *Dallas*, I received a phone call. It was Kagan. "What a surprise," I thought. In all of the time I had known him, he had not called me once. These lawyers must think they are some kind of Gods. They sure don't like to keep in touch or earn their money. I had begun to have a little faith in him and thought perhaps he had some good news. I thought that maybe he had found the fifth race track guard. After much small talk, Kagan got to the point. "Michael John," he said, "if you could loan me twenty thousand dollars, I could get your case to court in two months. I know the judge who will be there, and we will have a good chance." This really stunned me. I was speechless. He was saying, "Are you there? Are you there?" I finally answered, "Yeah, I'm here." When I regained my composure, I asked, "How come you told me that the earliest we could even get this case on the court docket was three to four years away, with the trial anytime after that?" Kagan quickly remarked, "Well, that's Chicago for you! If you are willing to pay, you can get almost anything done." He continued, "This will be good business for both of us, and after I win the case, you'll be able to deduct the loan from my fee. How about dinner tomorrow night so we can go over this case more. O.K., Michael John?" I told him that I would get in touch with him by Monday. I gently put down the phone and said, "Another fair weather friend."

If I had known Bennett Alban's number, I would have been getting him out of bed. But, as it was, I would have to wait until Monday to see him at his office. I was so furious and frustrated. Six years and two different law firms, and still not one day closer to having my day in court. I had to talk to someone, so I called my friend Ted Glazos, even though it was late in the evening.

After hearing about my latest telephone call, he too was shocked. We both agreed that I should speak with Bennett. Ted's feelings were that someone didn't want my case to be heard before a jury. I might cause too many waves. I agreed.

Sleep didn't come to me that night, nor the next few nights to come. I just kept thinking, "I may die trying, but I'll not stop 'til justice has been done."

The salt trucks had been out all Sunday night, trying to keep the ice from forming on the wet, snowy pavement. Bright and early Monday morning, my car was headed down the Stevenson Expressway. There was very little traffic at that early hour. Two hours later, it would be bumper-to-bumper, without me in it. After having had breakfast, I had a wait of two hours before Bennett's office hours began, so I walked down to State Street looking at the Christmas decorations, wondering if I would live to see the Yule Tide of 1985.

After the long walk down State Street and over to Dearborn, I arrived at the National Bank Plaza. While on my way to the thirtieth floor by way of the elevator, I wondered how Bennett could afford to pay the rent there, if he ran his office the way he set me up with that Kagan crook that he called a "good lawyer."

My first impressions of Kagan were correct, but that was all in the past. My main concern was to find just one lawyer who knew his way around a court room without having to study a road map in the process.

Two years had passed since I last saw Bennett. I sat in his outer office and waited. At 9:55 a.m., he arrived. As he walked by me, he didn't seem at all surprised to see me. I thought this was very strange. Twenty minutes later, his secretary informed me that Mr. Bennett would see me. All he had to say about my bitter encounter with Kagan was, "Too bad!" Just mentioning that I wanted him to file a report of the matter to the Chicago's Bar Association made him quiver, but he remarked that it would be just a waste of time. He said, "I think I know of a law firm you can rely on. Let me get back to you in a couple of days. Meanwhile, I'll see Kagan in my office with your file today."

I wasn't at all satisfied with the meeting, but I was in no position to be picky. I thought that if the third law firm didn't work out, I'd hire a dishwasher. An honest one would be a lot easier to find than an honest lawyer. I left Bennett's office after three o'clock. The traffic was heavy. One thing about driving in Chicago — just let a few snowflakes fall, and traffic comes to a crawl.

It was after four-thirty when I called Ted Glazos from my home. He wasn't too pleased on hearing about what had transpired. He simply said, "Hang in there, Michael John! When you've hit bottom, there's no way to go but up, me lad." We ended our conversation with a chuckle.

Chapter 27

Third Law Firm

Two weeks later, Bennett called saying that he had obtained my file and a written release. He asked if I could be at his office the following morning and he would have a lawyer there to discuss my lawsuit. The law firm he had chosen was thirty-five miles out of Chicago. The one good thing about that, I thought, was that it was far away from Sportsman Park.

I called Chris Balodimas to give him an update on events of the past few weeks and asked if he would like to come along with me to Bennett's office. At seven-thirty the next morning, we were a block away from his office having breakfast and waiting for nine-thirty. The office opened and we met the lawyer. His name was David J. Fares. We reviewed the complete file of papers and records. While doing that, he noticed the four different statements in the depositions of the four guards. That was the main reason for him accepting the case. Since most of the paperwork had already been done, I assumed that he would want the usual thirty-three and a third percent of the money collected as most other attorneys do. I

Attorney David J. Fares

also assumed that Bennett had discussed that with him and might even have tried for less. I trusted him to do that. Perhaps it was a stupid thing for me to do since I was to regret it later. From then on, my motto was, "Trust your lawyer only as far as you can throw him!"

December 22, 1984: It was a Saturday morning and Chris Balodimas called for me. We drove to Creswell and Fares law firm office, on 233 West Joe Orr road in Chicago Heights, Illinois. We were to complete the paperwork involved in his takeover of my lawsuit. It was noted that Kagan had possession of my file for eight days after he had been discharged from my case. What he had done in those eight days with the information is not exactly known but it became known that in the following months that Sportsman Park lawyers had the California address of my main witness, Richard White. It was very strange that for six years his whereabouts was unknown to them. Then suddenly, out of the clear-blue sky, the information popped into their heads. It was amazing. I wondered how much money Kagan received for selling parts of my file record.

February, 1985: I learned that two lawyers from Bishop's office flew to California and obtained a thirty page deposition from Richard White. They did this without informing my attorney as the law requires. By whatever means, they received the kind of statement they wanted. Had my lawyer been present, they would not have had their "pickings" so easy, I believe. Mr. Bishop was out to win this case for Sportsman Park any way he could. No matter what it cost.

Mrs. Pam Zekman, the investigative reporter from CBS, was doing some research work on different kinds of lawsuits, two of which mentioned Eugene Oliver's name. That seemed strange and almost unheard of in such cases. As one of these cases was mine, Mrs. Zekman contacted my lawyer, Mr. Fares. He had notified me that a reporter from CBS had sent him a letter requesting a taped interview at his office to be shown on television at a future date. The date would be later so as not to jeopardize our lawsuit against Sportsman Park. I consented.

One week later, Pam Zekman and a television crew arrived in Fare's office to tape the interview. Four hours later, they left with the understanding that it was not to be televised until after my trial, if that day should ever arrive.

April 7, 1985: Another strange event happened that day. Early in the morning, I had backed my car out of the driveway. After having made a few slow stops, I noticed that the brake pedal was easing towards the floorboard more than usual. I thought that I was still a little sleepy and was imagining it, so, sipping on my hot tea, I let the matter pass. About half-way to the store, going about forty-five miles per hour, I noticed that the light ahead had been green for some time and would be turning red before I reached the intersection. I began to press on the brake pedal. After touching the pedal for the third time, it went to the floor. I had no brakes! Still going twenty-five miles per hour, I was just a half a block away from the intersection.

Someone upstairs had to be looking out for me because there weren't any cars in front of me and no traffic as yet crossing the intersection. I was looking in both directions and still pumping the brake pedal. I was also looking for a place to crash into in the event of any cross traffic. As I entered the intersection, I heard the air horns of a semi-truck. It became larger as it neared. My car was rolling across to the lane he was in. I don't think he bothered to slow up, for just as I crossed his lane, he zoomed by me, missing me by only inches and leaving me with the dust blowing into my open window.

I guided the car onto the shoulder of the road as it slowed down. Still a little shaken, I sat there for some time. After regaining my composure, I got out of the car and opened the hood to check for possible causes of break failure. Finding none, I crawled under the car to look at the inner wheels and received an awakening. The brake lines going to each wheel were wet from brake fluid. As I took hold of each, slightly bending them, I saw what had caused the problem. Each had a quarter-inch cut in it so that when the brake pedal was applied, the fluid would pour out. No fluid, no braking power.

Someone almost succeeded in trying to dispose of me! Had I been going just a tad slower through that intersection, the truck would have made my two-door Buick look like a bicycle.

Wiping my hands on a towel I had in the back seat of the car, I walked to Ron and Bud's Shell Service Station, two miles away. The cold morning air helped to relieve my frustration. I walked next door for a cup of tea, while Bud went to tow my car in. An hour later, while they had it up on their rack, they noted that it was no child who did all of the damage. The four wheel lines were cut, as was the main line to the master cylinder. By the time the repairs were made and the car was completely checked over, it was mid-afternoon.

Due to the possible threat that might be taken on my steady girlfriend's life to force me to drop my lawsuit, I had no other alternative but to discontinue our relationship until the case would produce the justice that I sought.

As soon as I arrived home, I began to pack for a move to safer quarters. I wasn't about to sit in my bedroom each night waiting to see if the same clowns who damaged my car would make a return visit.

After two weeks in a motel, I found a small house six miles away. With the help of my friend Jim Karubas, we moved everything in a rental truck. My lawyer was informed of my move and I also gave him my new telephone number. That didn't seem to be necessary, as he had not called me even once in five months to update me on my lawsuit.

The following Christmas, I bought him a cordless telephone, costing me one hundred and fifty dollars. At least he wouldn't have an excuse for not calling me. Hell, he didn't even send me a Christmas card! Once again, I was losing sleep wondering if, after almost seven years of waiting, I was ever going to get the case to court.

Without telling Fares, I employed the services of another law firm. I wanted to check on what, if any, paperwork had been filed in the court records and to inquire about when the case might get into court. By giving them my court file number, I thought it would be easy for them to get the information. I asked them to call me as soon as they had some information for me. I was worried. For all I knew, the case could be in the "dead" file and forgotten.

Three weeks later, I was informed that the case was still

on the court docket, and that very little had been done or added in the past year. It was well worth the five hundred dollars I had to pay for that information. I knew then that my case was still alive. I thought, "Perhaps now I could get a few night's sleep." I thought that it was things like that which made a person wish for the old wild-west days of quick justice! A person could be his own judge, jury and hangman. The only bad thing in this case would be that a little more money would have to be spent on cable. With Oliver and his excessive weight, the rope might break when the trap door was sprung!

That day should have been recorded in the history books as a sad day for humanity and Sportsman Park officials. Their attorneys should have been given the "Fickle Finger of Fate Award" for the unjust way they treated Mrs. Harris after her son Rodney was murdered by track guard, Eugene Oliver. It was only after paying the bills for his funeral and waiting until household bills grew out of proportion that she asked for a settlement from damages inflicted by Mr. Oliver for one of his barbarous acts against human beings at that race track.

Mrs. Harris, wanting to put the tragedy out of her mind, and not being financially able to wait the seven to ten years it might have taken for her to have her day in court, accepted the track's offer of a meager sum of money — the amount I promised not to reveal. Any price for a life is not enough. One thing was sure. Her attorney came out smelling like a rose. I was shocked that he accepted their offer so quickly, especially when he must have known that in a trial by jury, the amount of settlement could have been ninety-nine times greater. This shooting was clearly a case of negligence on the part of Sportsman Park but because of the negative publicity for the track that a murder trial would have they took advantage of Mrs. Harris with a quick payoff. If it did go to trial, then maybe the State Attorney would have taken the time to check into that murder case.

As it stands, Eugene Olive is still working for Sportsman Park and is now head of security. A person would have to wonder how many killings this maniac would be allowed, before he would have to answer for them in a court of law.

I have always wondered about what strange, magic power he must hold over Sportsman Park officials for them to have given him the title of Director of Security.

I know of no other business or race track other than Sportsman Park where the employees are permitted to conduct evil crimes such as murder, acts of brutality and stealing from the patrons. Obviously, it is quite possible that those employees have knowledge of the management officials who committed like-wise evil crimes. That would prevent the employees from being brought into court to pay for their crimes against human nature.

With all of that in mind, I wrote a short and to-the-point letter to my attorney, Mr. Fares. It stated that there was poor communication between lawyer and client. It also said that I wanted it understood one hundred per cent that no deals or settlements were to be considered and that I was prepared to wait another seven years for a trial if necessary.

My worries then were two-fold. I not only had the worry of Sportsman Park antics, but also of my lawyer getting lost in the cement jungle. I had one thing to say about the other side, though. If Sportsman Park's lawyer, Mr. Bishop couldn't win this case with all of the breaks he had so far, he should apply for a job with the city, picking up cigarette butts off the streets of Chicago. Of course, they might have even turned him down for that job.

I know that Sportsman Park officials were counting on a win after years of waiting. They knew that my lawyers were unable to find the court house doors without falling on the sidewalks, as though they were covered with snow and ice in July. I'm sure they were also thinking that I might be so disgusted by then that I would accept the few bread crumbs they would throw me.

July 20, 1986: That was a day I'll never forget. It began as a normal day. I was out for a while, had supper at a local restaurant then drove home. I turned on the television to watch the six o'clock news. All of the networks were carrying the same story that sixteen judges had been indicted by a Grand Jury for misconduct and bribery. Police and Court bailiffs were also indicted. The operation was called Graylord and had been under investigation for several years.

On December 13th, 1983, a Chicago police officer fatally shot himself hours before he was to appear before the Federal Grand Jury investigating Graylord charges. A few years later, a former Cook County Circuit Court Judge also committed suicide. He was carefully dressed in slacks, shirt, sportscoat and a favorite pair of cowboy boots. He placed framed photos of his wife and two children around himself and fatally shot himself in the temple with an unregistered thirty-eight caliber revolver.

On hearing all of this, I realized that my ex-lawyer Kagan had been telling me the truth. He said that if I would lend him $20 thousand, he would lend it to the judge and get me a favorable ruling in court.

It was a small wonder why I was still waiting to have my day in court. At that rate, there might not be any judges left in Chicago. I just needed one honest one. The State of Illinois could look forward to having the dubious record of the most judges, two different Governors and one State Attorney all sent to prison. It just might be a source for a tourist attraction!

The Governor, whoever he may be at a given time, is also the President of the Illinois State Racing Board. He, with other board members, grant the racing dates for that State. It is quite obvious that none of them ever got out to the track on a cold, frost-bitten, windy night with fifteen below zero temperatures and a wind-chill factor of thirty-five below in December or January to watch the so-called horse racing under these extremely cold conditions. This is a perfect example of cruelty to these animals. A person could see their nostrils and mouth covered with icy, frozen saliva after each race. Some of their lungs have been very affected by the sub-zero weather as well as their legs from pounding on the frozen ground of the track. Yes, Governor and Board members, it's much better for you on those kind of nights to be home in your easy-chairs next to the fireplace eating popcorn and watching television.

Every October, since retiring my horse Michael John to a farm in the south where it is always sunny and warm, I would load a large trailer with Michigan apples and fifty pound bags of carrots and make the trip down to visit him.

By leaving at that time, I could get there before winter would put her frozen blanket of ice and snow over the frozen ground.

I can remember October 25th, 1985. At about 4:00 in the morning, after having had a hot bowl of oatmeal and raisin toast, I went outside into the dark, chilly morning. With the aid of my flashlight, I gave my car its daily check over. I had been doing that ever since the brake lines were cut. Finding nothing wrong, I quietly closed the hood and loaded a few articles of clothing in the car. I then drove off slowly so as not to wake up the neighbors. It was six miles to where the trailer was stored.

Having attached the trailer, I drove down the toll-way and arrived in Indiana before the first rays of light began to appear. The sight and smell of the thousands of bushels of Michigan apples that had been trucked into Munster in the past week and the turning of the leaves into their fall colors helped relieve some of the bitterness I had been feeling the past seven years and four months. After buying as many apples and carrots my small trailer could hold, I headed towards Portage and Chesterton just to admire briefly all the large different-colored trees. Some were completely yellow, others solid red. They looked like round bundles of rainbows. After filling my ice cooler with a bottle of water and a few jars of orange juice, I set the cruise-control of my car at fifty-four miles per hour and prepared for the long drive south.

Around midnight, I stopped for a night's rest just within striking distance of the farm. It was good to be able to rest well for a change away from Chicago and the concerns it held for me. I was up the next morning and back on my way. I soon arrived at the farm.

My horse was already in his pasture of deep grass. He must have smelled the apples for he came running up to the fence where I had parked. He was jumping up and down like a kid waiting for his Christmas presents. One quick look showed me that he was being well taken care of. Seeing that and Michael John's reaction to my coming with the apples and carrots brought tears to my eyes. I was so grateful that I had found someone I could trust.

I spent a month at the farm with Michael John. I paid his board bill for the next year then reluctantly said my good-byes and started my trip North. The return trip was somewhat sad, but reasoning brought me back to reality. I wanted justice!

Winter was here and the first snow had fallen. With the holiday season nearing, Christmas decorations were beginning to appear throughout the city. As was my custom in the winter-time, I emptied the icy water from the bird bath, cleaned it well and filled it with bird seed. I enjoyed looking out of my bedroom window, watching the birds arrive to partake in a feast. Of course, the squirrels had to be fed with a spread of peanuts and walnuts on the ground. Otherwise, they would jump on the bird bath and scatter the feed looking for the cracked corn that was mixed in with the seed.

Little acts like that helped to divert my thoughts from the Gestapos at the track and the injustices done to me, so that I would not be tempted to take illegal action against those who "did me dirt!"

Chapter 28

Jury Selection

One day, about a week before Christmas, I returned home to find a letter from my lawyer in the mail box. I put it aside thinking that it was one of those few letters I had received from him asking for more money to file this or that. After bathing and dressing for dinner at a restaurant, I opened the letter. After reading the first few lines, I was so startled that I had to sit down quickly. I was being informed that a trial date had been set for me on January 27th, 1986, at the Daley Center, Chicago, Illinois, room 2202. I read and re-read the letter, still in silent disbelief. "Was it really true?" I thought. If so, why hadn't Fares called me? He must have already received word of the trial date and certainly knew of my anxiety regarding the whole ordeal. After a few minutes, I called my witnesses to find out if they had been notified. They had not. I thought it strange that Fares had not notified them.

Forty minutes later, one of my witnesses, Ted Glazos and I were having dinner together at his restaurant discussing the manner in which Fares had been handling my case. We thought it was very unprofessional. Even with the new cordless telephone I had given him for Christmas, he hadn't bothered to call me. I told Ted that there would be no Christmas presents for Fares from me under his tree that year. I also said that I would call him the next morning at nine-thirty for sure. Three hours later, after a delicious meal and enjoyable conversations, I drove home excited and feeling wide-awake. I knew that sleep would not visit me that night.

The next day, I was able to contact Fares at four-thirty in the afternoon. I asked him for an update and inquired about a meeting with my character witnesses. I suggested bringing them to his office on Saturday of that week. He agreed with me. I thought, "What else must I do for this man?" Over three-quarters of the paper-work had already been done before he took over the case, and still he had not "taken the bull by it's horns." I knew one thing for sure, the opposing lawyer, Mr. Bishop would not be "letting the grass grow under his feet." He was probably already planning how he would spend his bonus money from his victory of the suit against Sportsman Park.

Fares sent me another letter stating that he would rather have me bring the witnesses in after the holidays. We set the date for January 11th, 1986. I made the necessary phone calls for setting up the meeting. Ted Glazos couldn't seem to make contact with Fares by telephone. When he told me that, I said, "What else is new?"

Christmas and New Year's dragged by, with each day making me feel more tense. It was like being David going up against the giant, Goliath, as written in the Bible. However, I didn't have a sling-shot with a rock. My only armor was the truth of what had happened. Just a handful of words. "Would it be enough for victory?" I thought. I had spent many sleepless nights wondering.

I was up early Saturday morning, January 11th, and off to Jim Balodimas' house. We then picked up Jim Karubas. From there, we all had breakfast at Ted's restaurant. An hour later, we were riding in my Buick and in high spirits.

It was amazing. Fares was there waiting for us! He met with me first, then with the other three separately for about ten minutes each. We commented on that as we drove home. They had no idea of what kind of questions would be put to them on the witness stand other than their name. It appeared to them as if Fares was just trying to lose the case. I had no comment for them at the time. It was nearing post-time so I just figured that I'd let the "chips fall where they may." What else could go wrong? I was to find out later!

January 27th, 1986: I awoke at three-fifteen in the morning with a sharp pain running through my arm. I had accidentally rolled over onto my damaged elbow. Even my padded elbow-guard didn't help. I got out of bed and took two pills that Dr. Mikhall had prescribed for me. I took two instead of the usual one because after having waited seven years and seven months for my day in court, I wasn't about to let elbow problems interfere with it. I put the elbow in a pan of ice-water until four in the morning. I then wrapped the entire arm in a towel for a half-hour, then the Gelo-cast bandage had to be wrapped from above the wrist up over and above the elbow. By five o'clock, the pain had somewhat subsided.

I ate a breakfast of hot oatmeal, a warmed-up slice of coffee cake and a glass of orange juice. I then turned the television to a cable station for the latest weather report. It was to be five degrees below zero with a wind-chill factor of twenty-five below. Driving to Daley Center in Chicago was not in my plans. Taking the train seemed safer even though the eight-block walk from the train station to the Center would be a cold one. I laughingly thought that it might have been a blessing. I'd save some money on ice soaking the elbow.

My dress for the first day of trial was a plain pair of slacks, a tan sport's shirt, a sport's coat, black shoes and a heavy overcoat with a new knitted scarf that Mrs. Balodimas had made for me, also, a warm pair of gloves and rubber boots.

At seven o'clock in the morning, I closed my door quietly and began my walk to the train station through a foot of snow. I was really feeling the cold and thought that I should have worn two pair of socks. "That would be number one on my list for tomorrow," I thought.

Arriving at the station, I had twenty minutes to warm my feet before the train arrived. Making only four stops along the way, we pulled into Chicago station at eight fifteen a.m. Before walking the six blocks to my destination, I stopped for a cup of tea, finished my journey, and walked into the lobby of the Center at eight fifty a.m.

Fares arrived at five minutes after nine and informed me that the day would be spent picking a jury of twelve people. All I would have to do was sit at a table about twenty feet from the jury box and listen. I thought, "Well, that's nice to know, Mr. Fares. Why couldn't you have informed me of this days ago! Very good communication between us!" We were sitting in the court room at nine-fifteen looking at the walls with Sportsman Park lawyers at a table two feet from us. Bishop looked like a nervous two year-old colt being harnessed for his first race. Or was it that he already knew the verdict? He sure was moving around a lot, in and out of the courtroom while we were waiting for the judge.

By eleven o'clock, we still didn't have a judge. At eleven thirty-five, we learned that the judge assigned to our case four days earlier, for some unknown reason, was in Miami, Florida! Everyone was dismissed and we were told that a new judge would be assigned the next day. I looked over at Mr. Bishop to see his reaction and to my surprise I saw a smile cross his lips. I nudged Fares and asked, "What's this all about?" He didn't know.

On the train ride home at two thirty-five in the afternoon, I was pondering over what I had heard and wondered which side was to benefit from the change in judges. I knew that I was disappointed because the judge who had been originally assigned to the case was black. I figured that since a seventeen year-old black boy had been killed by Eugene Oliver at the track, this might help our side. Lord knows, I needed something besides the truth to help me. This seemed to top the list of events working against me, and I still hadn't had my day in court.

By that time, I was quite frustrated. My friend Ted even noticed it when I called him to relate the day's events. He and my other witnesses wanted to be at the trial. They had been informed that they would not be allowed in the courtroom to watch until after they had testified.

I then went out to eat and stopped in a drug store for much-needed sleeping pills. I just had to have some sleep. I was in bed by eight o'clock, after swallowing three pills with water. They were the first I had ever taken. I put extra padding around my arm and closed my eyes, hoping for some sleep.

It was five in the morning when I next looked at the clock. I realized that I must have slept. I removed the wrapping from my arm, but left the Gelo-cast bandage on.

I went into the kitchen and prepared myself a bowl of hot Cream-of-Wheat and toast with jelly. Already, the morning was looking better than the day before. I then got dressed in a white shirt and a dark-blue suit. I checked the weather report and learned that it was a little warmer than the day before. It was five degrees above zero with a slight breeze. I put on my scarf, overcoat and a new pair of rubber boots over my dress shoes. I left at six fifty-five. When Fares and I met, I remarked, "Let's hope that today's judge doesn't end up in Hawaii. This is getting to be too much for my nerves!"

We took the elevator to the twenty-second floor to Courtroom 2207. The Honorable Willard Lassers was to preside. The court opened at nine-thirty sharp. The bailiff called for all to rise. I thought, "Am I really going to see the beginning of my trial? Praise the Lord!" Just as I finished uttering the last words, a very distinguished-looking gentleman entered, wearing a long, black robe. It was Judge Lassers. My first impression of him was that he ran a "tight ship", with no nonsense allowed. I was hoping that I would be right. Court was now in session!

The first order of business was to choose a twelve-member jury. By eleven o'clock, two had been picked. A ten-minute recess was called. Lunch-time rolled around with only three jurors in the box. A slow process indeed! It was especially true since Bishop refused to accept as juror any person who had been to a track to bet the horses. It was obvious where his instructions were coming from.

During the lunch break, I took Fares and his assistant to Rodiety restaurant on Halstead Street, hoping to get him loosened up. I could see that he was "tighter than a drum". The meal was excellent but the company was a wash-out. He was acting as if it were his first major case. I thought that if he didn't change, Bishop would be spending the bonus money sooner than he had planned, for winning the case for those Gestapos.

At one-fifteen, the court was called to order. By three-fifteen, with only five jurors chosen, a tenminute recess was called. After resuming the process of questioning the prospective jurors, something strange took place. The bailiff and judge exchanged some words in private, after which a quick recess was called. There was a hush in the courtroom. One could have heard a pin drop. Bishop was not smiling. I looked to Fares for an answer but he just shook his head. Whatever it was had to be something important. Thirty-five minutes later, the lawyers from both sides were called into Judge Lasser's chambers. Twenty minutes after that, everyone in the courtroom was told that the panel of twenty-six would be excused. The story was that the third juror chosen was an employee of the insurance company that had Sportsman Park as their client. I thought, "The odds of this happening legitimately would be astronomical. Another strange event and another day wasted!" After the courtroom was cleared, Judge Lassers made the statement that a new twelve-member jury would be chosen from a different twenty-six-member panel the following day.

I called my friend Ted that evening to report the news. His reply was, "That's impossible! Tell me it's just a joke." I explained it again slowly and said that the whole justice system was looking like a joke or else someone had their hands in the cookie jar. At the speed things were progressing, it looked as though Ted wouldn't be needed until spring. The one consoling thought was that it would, at least, be warmer then.

January 29th, 1986: At five minutes past five in the morning it was bitterly cold. I was wishing I could stay in bed as I was unable to see out of the frost-covered windows into the darkness of night. The weather channel showed figures of ten below zero with a wind-chill factor of forty below. I could see how it would be very easy for one to accept an all-expense-paid trip to Miami this time of year. I too would have rather been there than where I was, walking to the train that morning. Running through my thoughts were the poor horses that had to race under those frigid conditions.

Arriving at Daley Center at nine o'clock that morning, and not seeing my lawyer after a ten-minute wait, I took the elevator up to the courtroom. There, like two buddies, were Bishop and Fares. They were talking as if they were at a picnic social together. It unnerved me a bit, but I recovered quickly. The pace at which the trial was progressing made me feel as if I had been stuck in the starting gate three days after post-time. This was the third day the members of the jury selection panel would receive their $17 for their pay there.

It was nine-thirty in the morning, and the only thing going according to schedule was the calling of the court to order by Judge Lassers. Again, jury selection had begun. Bishop was still ruling out anyone with knowledge of racing or who had ever gambled at the track. At times, the way he bounced around the courtroom made him look like a puppet on a string.

One example of his questioning was of a business woman who was a college graduate. He was about to accept her as one of the jury, then asked her if she had ever attended the races. She replied that she had not but might in the future. He smiled and thought that perhaps she would make a good juror. He then asked about her hobbies. She revealed that she boarded a quarter-horse on a farm twenty miles west of Chicago and that she spent her week-ends grooming and riding this beautiful animal. A sad look crossed Bishop's face and he excused her from duty. Judge Lassers immediately called a ten minute recess. It was obvious why. In anyone's eyes, this woman would have made an excellent juror. I was told later that my judgment for the quick recess was correct. When court resumed, Bishop seemed more subdued, but too late for having that nice lady sit in the jury box.

Lunch hour arrived, and only two people had been chosen. For some reason, Fares wanted to have lunch alone. I followed him some distance just to make sure there was no "hanky-panky" planned. He stopped at Wendy's for a hamburger just two blocks from the Daley Center. I waited to see if Bishop followed, but he may have already been inside. I left for another place for a club sandwich and a glass of milk.

At one-fifteen that afternoon, jury selection continued. By five o'clock, there were still only five jurors in the box with seven to go. I almost fell asleep during the process, with Bishop's stalling tactics and refusal to seat qualified people.

January 30th was spent in the same manner. Ten jurors were picked with four yet to be chosen. Two would be used as alternates if any of the original twelve would be unable to attend the complete trial.

January 31st, 1986: Snow had been falling since midnight and was well-over a foot deep with drifts of two feet in spots. As a bonus, there were more sub-zero temperatures on that day. Walking was difficult but I was determined to let nothing keep me from having my day in court. For a few moments, the fear entered my mind that maybe the trial would be delayed due to bad weather. I thought, "Could anything else happen to cause another delay?" My determination to get to the train station canceled out my fears. It was six o'clock in the morning and there wasn't a car on the road. I had left an hour earlier because of the weather. The thought of watching those fluffy, white flakes fall from the sky from inside a living room with a large bay window sitting next to a blazing fireplace kept me warm.

It was ten minutes after seven when I finally plowed my legs inside the train station and I was "plum tuckered out". With a forty-five minute wait for the train, I was able to get my wind back. The trains seemed to be the only means of transportation that was still running well. I was happy to have made that my means of transportation to and from the court. There were still eight blocks for me to walk once in Chicago, but much of the snow had already been plowed by the street cleaners during the long and cold night.

I was in the lobby of the Daley Center at eight-fifty. I wanted to talk to Fares before he entered the courtroom. I thought that it might be a little more private there. I knew that he should have been showing up there any moment. The lobby of the Daley Center was completely glass-enclosed. Watching the people hurry through the blowing snow with the slow-moving traffic on Randolph Street gave me something to occupy my mind while waiting.

Twenty minutes later, I observed Bishop's huge frame coming through the door. He was covered with snow. I raised my newspaper above my face so he wouldn't notice me. When I didn't see him walk to the side of me to where the elevators were, I lowered my paper a few inches to see where he did go. Did I ever get the shock of my life. My little lawyer Fares was brushing the snow off Bishop's overcoat, having a difficult time reaching his shoulders. Those two attorneys were acting as though they belonged to the same law firm! It was obvious to me that they had a pre-arranged breakfast meeting.

I waited ten minutes before taking the elevator. The long ride up settled me down somewhat. I realized that, no matter what happened from that point on, it was too late to express my feelings on the very poor choice I had made trusting Fares with my life. If he had already sold me out, I hoped he received more than 30 pieces of silver, since the cost of living has risen since Judas' time.

When the elevator opened, I immediately saw Fares in the empty hallway. He was hastily putting a few papers in his briefcase, and he acted a might nervous about it when he noticed I was there.

I sarcastically asked if Bishop and his "gang" had arrived. Zipping up his briefcase, he said in a low voice that he hadn't seen anyone. He added that it was late and we should be inside like everyone else.

Entering the courtroom, Judge Lassers was already waiting, unruffled. His short and to-the-point statement pertaining to completion of selecting jurors left no doubt in anyone's mind that he was a little unhappy about the slowness in jury selection. His eyes were focused on the one and only Mr. Bishop, Sportsman Park's ace lawyer.

The little speech must have helped. By 11:45 that morning, the jurors had all been selected. Much can be done when one strikes a match. An hour and a half for lunch was then called. At 1:30, the trial was to begin with the opening statements. I got goose-bumps just realizing that it had finally happened. A cold chill went through my body. "Is this true?" I was about to have my day in court, after seven years seven months and 17 days of agonizing waiting.

STATE OF ILLINOIS)
) SS:
COUNTY OF COOK)

IN THE CIRCUIT COURT OF COOK COUNTY
COUNTY DEPARTMENT-LAW DIVISION

MICHAEL J. HORAK Plaintiff, -vs- EUGENE OLIVER, STEVE BAJOVICH, JOSEPH McCARTHY, DANIEL GROTH, NATIONAL JOCKEY CLUB, INC., AND FOX VALLEY TROTTING CLUB, INC., Defendants.	No. 78 L 17696

REPORT OF PROCEEDINGS had in the hearing of the above-entitled cause, before the Honorable Willard Lassers, Judge of the said court, on the 31st day of January, A.D., 1986, at the hour of 1:30 o'clock P.M., Court Room 2207, Daley Center, Chicago, Illinois.

APPEARANCES:

MESSRS. CRESWELL & FARES,
BY: MR. DAVID J. FARES,
233 W. Joe Orr Road
Chicago Heights, Illinois 60411 756-4000,
appeared for the Plaintiff;

MESSRS. GARRETSON & SANTORA,
BY: MR. RONALD T. BISHOP,
33 N. Dearborn Street, Suite 730
Chicago, Illinois 60602 263-6635
appeared for the Defendants.

\- - -

GUS G. PALOIAN COURT REPORTING SERVICES

Chapter 29

Opening Statements

The following excerpt is from the original 1,325-page official court transcript of this case. These are the opening statements from January 31st, 1986.

JUDGE LASSERS: Good afternoon, ladies and gentlemen. We are now ready to begin the next phase of the trial and that will be the opening statements. We are going to hear first from Mr. Fares on behalf of the plaintiff, then we are going to hear from Mr. Bishop on behalf of the defendant. Mr. Fares...

MR. FARES: Thank you, your honor. Your honor, Mr. Bishop, ladies and gentlemen of the jury. As it's already been explained to you, my name is David Fares and I am representing the plaintiff in this cause, Michael John Horak. This is a case where my client was unjustifiably harassed, detained, assaulted, battered and arrested. The result of all those things, he suffered an injury in the battery that continues to bother him and give him great pain to this day; and more importantly than that, has thwarted or stopped his ability to be a horse driver and a horse trainer.

At this time, I'd like to tell you a little bit about what our job is in regard to this thing. When I say "our", I don't mean me or the Judge or Mr. Bishop, I mean you. All of our jobs bring justice in this courtroom. In regard to me specifically, I have certain evidence that I have to present. In giving this opening statement, I'm not attempting to be argumentative. I have an opportunity because we as lawyers have to present evidence in disorder from time to time, to try to tie everything together for you so you have some idea of what I intend to prove in regard to this matter. I will attempt to that as fairly and honestly as I can for you and indeed that is Mr. Bishop's duty to his client as well.

The Judge, as you well know, is here to monitor and preside over the trial, to rule on objections, to show no bias to either party and to do his best job to bring this case to justice. And then there is you, the members of the jury, have been through, what is this Friday, two and a half days of jury selection. You have a lot waiting already, and I think you have some idea from just the questions we were asking as to what your job is, and indeed your job is to bring justice to this courtroom, just as it's my job and Mr. Bishop's job.

A long time ago, years and years ago in England a group of people got together and decided the best way to determine if somebody —

MR. BISHOP: I'm objecting. This is not what the evidence is going to show.

MR. FARES: I will be brief in this regard.

JUDGE LASSERS: Let's move on.

MR. FARES: Thank you. In regard to this, as to the best way to tell if somebody was telling the truth is to have his neighbors judge him. And that system slowly developed into our jury system until 1776 when it was incorporated into our Constitution and became part of our law. So here you sit today as a jury, in order to look at these witnesses and make a determination — and indeed you people who have been chosen are the experts in that regard —

MR. BISHOP: Objection, your Honor. This is closing argument. This is not what the evidence is going to show.

JUDGE LASSERS: Why don't you move on, Counsel.

MR. FARES: If I may, I think I have an opportunity to discuss with the jury what their duty is in regard to this matter.

MR. BISHOP: Object to statements, speeches in front of the jury.

JUDGE LASSERS: Let's move along now. It is the job of the jury to find the facts and to decide the case in accordance with the law as the Court gives it to the jury.

MR. FARES: Along the lines of what the Judge says, it is also important — and you stated when I asked you questions, you have a willingness to believe these witnesses, to listen to them as they put the evidence on, to pay attention to the exhibits as they are put in and to make your decision. And when you do that judging, that means that you have that willingness to listen and —

MR. BISHOP: If the Court pleases, I still must object.

MR. FARES: I need to object to Mr. Bishop's constant interruptions.

JUDGE LASSERS: Let's move on.

MR. FARES: I'm sorry, Judge.

JUDGE LASSERS: Go ahead, move along, Mr. Fares.

MR. FARES: That willingness to believe is what judgment is. This is what you are doing here. Judgment equals a willingness to believe. And so when this case is over and you come to the jury box, to the jury room to make your decision, you have to take those facts as you heard them with that willingness to believe and ask yourself what happened in regard to Michael John Horak and that is all that we ask of you as the Plaintiffs in this cause, that you have a willingness to believe.

If you enter it with a pre-disposed judgment or a negative eye, then in that case your opinion is pre-disposed to a negative judgment. And that is not what justice is all about.

As I've already talked to you about a burden in this case

numerous times, I don't think I need to reiterate that. The Judge has told you the order of proceedings because we as the Plaintiffs have the burden to carry the preponderance of the evidence. We as the Plaintiffs are allowed to go first in opening statement, in putting on our evidence and in closing arguments of this case. This is because we have the burden.

I will get to the long awaited facts of the incident. This incident occurred on June 12th of 1978. I think before we get into that specifically, you have to know a little bit about the parties and what I intend to prove about the parties in regard to this matter. Number one, there are four defendants: Eugene Oliver, Dan Groth, Joseph McCarthy and Steve Bajovich. The last three of those, McCarthy, Bajovich and Groth, were employed by Fox Valley Trotting Association. That's another defendant in this case. Fox Valley Trotting Association ran the meet at Sportsman Park. What we mean by that is in running the meet they were the ones who got the horses to run and organized it and put in on. The owners of the track were National Jockey Club. National Jockey Club employed only Eugene Oliver. Fox Valley Trotting employed the other three. They were all agents of one or the other of those two entities, National Jockey or Fox Valley Trotting.

Mike Horak is the plaintiff in this case. He is bringing this action, as I earlier stated, because he feels that he was unjustifiably — and I intend to prove this — detained, harassed, assaulted, beaten, battered and arrested. And he sustained injuries. So he is here in this courtroom today.

In regard to June 12th of 1978, Mike Horak, who had for a long time been a driver and trainer of horses, in fact, had first gotten involved in it in 1959, was going to the track because he was looking for a horse in order to breed to a mare in order to produce a colt that he could then train and drive. In the last few years before 1978, he had only been mildly involved in training and driving because he had devoted his duties full-time to his job as a trucker. In 1979, I intend to prove his pension was going to be due. His intentions were to stop trucking and go into harness racing full-time.

See, in June of 1978 he was at this end and coming to the racetrack (indicating). He didn't get to the racetrack until the seventh race and this particular incident arose out at the ninth race at Sportsman Park. He was there to look at the horse, make sure he still liked the horse because he had seen it earlier, and to place a bet on the horse. He got to the track. He watched the horse. The horse's name was Phase-Out. Watched Phase-Out warm up. He had a good warm-up. Mike Horak had seen him race earlier that year and knew he was a good horse. After he watched him warm up, he placed a $1,000.00 bet on Phase-Out, and then he returned back to the track in order to watch the race. I should note here we intend to prove it was not unusual for Mike Horak to bet that amount of money. He did it maybe four, five times a year, very selectively because he had a knowledge of horse racing and a knowledge of horses and therefore a knowledge of betting.

What you see here is a very crude idea of the layout of Sportsman Park. I think the evidence will show that generally this area here is the Clubhouse area. This area here is the security shack where the beating took place. This area here is the Grandstand. This area is the Paddock and in case you couldn't tell, this area is the racetrack itself, where the horses would run. This area here is where the horses would enter in order to go out and begin the race. However, when they finished the race, the horses would be brought back to the barn, which is off here, and the horses would come — jockeys would come out to the dressing area here. The name of the driver of Phase-Out on that particular evening was Daryl Busse. Mr. Busse was involved in horse racing, I think the evidence will show that, for some time and this particular race, the ninth race at Sportsman Park's track on that evening was only a five-horse race. The odds on Phase-Out were three to five. He was heavily favored to win the race.

Mike Horak began to watch the race and being a driver himself, he began to watch the way that Daryl Busse drove that horse. And I think the evidence is going to show that Mike Horak saw Daryl Busse whipping that horse at the beginning of the race and laying back at the horse at the end of the race. At any rate, the horse finished dead last in a five-horse race, even though it went off as a three to five favorite.

I think you are going to find from testimony, and I think you are also going to find from some other means that Mike Horak did not like injustices, things that he thought were unfair. And when that occurred, he made sure that the person that was being unjust knew about it. And in regard to this particular instance, he was going to let Daryl Busse know that he did not like the way that Daryl Busse drove that race and drove that horse. We will prove that after the race, Mike Horak watched the race over here, walked over to the Paddock area where Daryl Busse would be passing in order to talk to Busse about the way he raced that horse that night.

When Busse passed by, Michael Horak told him in a loud tone of voice, "Busse, if I couldn't drive a horse any better than that, I'd tear up my license." At that point, Busse made some lewd gestures to Mike Horak, then Busse went in and dressed. Mike Horak having only come for that ninth race for this specific purpose to see the horse and to bet on the horse, then began to leave because he parked over here on Laramie Avenue, which is on the Clubhouse side of the park. As he walked from the Paddock area and began to walk along the fence here, in order to get through the Grandstand, he was approached by two security guards, one of these guards was Eugene Oliver, the defendant in the case. As they approached him, Oliver said, "Mike there's some people"—your Honor, please, could you please advise Mr. Bishop not to talk during my opening statement, I'd appreciate that.

MR. BISHOP: I didn't say a word.

JUDGE LASSERS: Did anybody say anything?

MR. BISHOP: My client whispered a message to me and I don't understand the dramatics. I wish to be heard outside the presence of the jury.

MR. FARES: I am going to object to this in my opening statement.

JUDGE LASSERS: Let's just move on.

MR. FARES: Mike Horak began to walk over here in this area to leave the race track. When he did that, he was approached by Oliver. Eugene Oliver came up to him and said, "Mike, the officials want to see you." And Michael Horak at that point said, "Okay," and began to walk towards the Grandstand area where the officials' officers were.

As he walked towards that area, Oliver said, "No, we are going to the security office." And Mike Horak obliged him and began to walk to the security office with Eugene Oliver. At that point, Mike heard Eugene talking to his Walkee-Talkee saying, "We're bringing Horak in." They walked into the security office area. There was no physical contact of any nature between the time that Horak was approached and the time that they got to the security office.

This is a crude depiction of what the security office looked like on that evening. What we intend to prove, that on the evening at the security office, this office was somewhere in the area of ten feet by fifteen feet, that there was a door that entered at this side of the office. There was a window that was here and there was a window that was here (indicating).

We further intend to prove that at the time that Mike Horak entered the office, the blinds were pulled on these two windows. As he entered into the office, he was followed by Oliver and the other security guard or the other investigator. Oliver was on his right side at all times and behind him and the other security guard on the other side. When he got inside the door, there's a gate here. There is a counter and there's a gate here that he can enter in and out of. He was nudged in towards the gate on his right side. As Mike turned around to see, Eugene Oliver had a gun in his hand. He was nudged through the gate to a desk which was sitting on this side of the office where Steve Bajovich was sitting. There was a conversation that took place between Horak and Bajovich concerning an alleged disturbance at the Paddock area. Bajovich said, "We heard that you have been bothering the drivers at the Paddock area." And Horak said, "Who said this? I haven't done anything."

Bajovich said — at that point the phone rang. Bajovich picked up the phone, mumbled some words, slammed the phone down and said to Horak, "I want your license," referring to his track driver's license, not to his truck driving license. As Horak reached into his pocket to hand the license over, all of a sudden, again from the right side, an arm grabbed him around the throat and threw him to the ground on his back. He was dazed for a minute. He looked up and he saw Oliver standing over him beginning to kneel. Oliver kneeled on Mike Horak's left arm and grabbed his right arm. At that point his face was completely covered. He got kicked by the other two or three security guards who were sitting in the office. Incidentally, these are all plain-clothes security guards. They didn't have on any uniform. They all carried guns. He began to get kicked. As he was being kicked, he was rolled over onto his belly. His arms were yanked up behind his hands and somebody started to put handcuffs on him.

One of the security guards — and we believe it's Joseph McCarthy — sat on Mike Horak's legs. Oliver sat over his neck and head area. Finally the kicking stopped. He was on his belly, his hands were in cuffs in such a manner (indicating) and at that point, there was a moment or thirty seconds or ten seconds of silence. Remember, Mike Horak's a little dazed at this point. Following the silence, Mike felt a sharp blow to his left elbow with a blunt instrument, an electro-cutting sensation went through his body and he lost consciousness.

The next thing he knew, he was up sitting in the benches that were either in this area or this area of the office (indicating). As he was sitting there, he looked up and he saw another person being dragged in by the throat and his chest being pounded by Oliver. At that particular point, he said, "Watch out, 'cause he has a witness." They laid off this person, who you will hear testifying, incidentally. His name is Richard White, and they finally frisked White and sat him down next to Oliver where certain conversations ensued.

Mike Horak at this point, his elbow began to swell, his arm began to swell. The handcuffs were starting to make him bleed here because they were put on so tight. The Cicero

Police were called. He was taken to the Cicero Police Station. He was fingerprinted. He was booked. They kept him there for three hours. Finally he was let go on a hundred dollars bond. He went to Court in regard to this matter. There was a hearing before a Judge, Gene Oliver was there to testify. Mike Horak was found not-guilty of the charges. They had brought, incidentally, disorderly conduct charges against him arising allegedly out of some scuffle that occurred in this security office. At any rate, he was found not-guilty on those charges.

At that point, Mike Horak undertook self-treatment. As I already said, he was a trainer of horses. So he's used to strain injuries and muscle injuries and ligament injuries in treating his horses. And, in fact, he had certain bandages that he used to treat horses called Gelo-cast Bandages, which was like an Ace Bandage that you wrap around your arm, only it was dipped and soaked in medication and he wore that for two or three days. At night he put a heating pad on it.

That morning when he got home he soaked it in ice. That was the first thing he did. In soaking it in ice, he remembers being up until the sun came up. So he soaked it for some period of time. We will prove that then finally on the sixteenth of June, three days after he had gotten home on the thirteenth of June, he went to MacNeal Memorial hospital. At MacNeal he was X-Rayed, he was given a sling for his arm. Told to come back at ten o'clock in the morning. At ten o'clock he went back. He saw Dr. Asok Ray, an orthopedic surgeon.

Dr. Ray looked at the X-Rays and put Mike Horak's arm in a cast that ran up here all the way down to his wrist with his arm in a bent position. He stayed under Dr. Ray's treatment for two weeks. When Dr. Ray removed the cast from his arm, he did not return to see Dr. Ray after that. He continued at that point with his self-treatment with Gelo-cast Bandages, with putting a heated pad on it every night, icing it from time to time, also using an Ace Bandage, also having a prescription that Dr. Ray prescribed for him, taking that for the pain he experienced.

After five or six months, the condition of the elbow was

not improving. He was still experiencing swelling in the elbow, he wasn't able to move the elbow and so he went and saw Dr. Kamel Mikhail. Dr. Mikhail is a general physician who had a residency in orthopedics. That was on February 5th, 1979, about seven months later. At that time, Dr. Mikhail undertook treatment of Mike Horak. He's seen him in this period of time from 1979 until today's date approximately 80 to 85 times. Mr. Mikhail will be called here to testify as will Dr. Ray. Dr. Mikhail will testify that he undertook conservative treatments of his elbow. He has a limitation of extension in his arm, as well as a limitation of flexion.

Now, I intend to prove what we mean by that, that he can't put his arm all the way out, nor can he touch his shoulder. Flexion, that hand also goes so far. I think Dr. Mikhail is going to testify that that is as a direct result of this accident.

I think also, Dr. Mikhail is going to testify for you concerning where on Mike Horak's elbow the injury occurred. This is the — I think he will use this model to testify also. This is the left elbow. This bone right here that is sticking out when your palm is face up, this one here, this nob here is called the medial epicondyle. This particular bone here, which is at the base of this long bone, that is called the olecranon process.

You should pay particular attention because it is going to be one of the most telling pieces of evidence in regard to this case. If these arms are up in handcuffs and they are hit with a blunt instrument such as the butt of a gun or something of that nature, what are the two bones that are going to be affected by that, the medial epicondyle and the olecranon (indicating). Let's bring them back, those are the two very bones that Dr. Ray and Dr. Mikhail are going to testify were injured in regard to this beating that Mike Horak took from these security guards.

Most importantly, you are going to hear testimony from Dr. Mikhail, as well as testimony from Mike Horak himself, that he is not physically capable of returning to driving horses again. We will prove that it was Mike Horak's intention on that date before this incident occurred, and on getting his pension from trucking in 1979, less than a year and a half later, to return to horse driving and training because that is the one thing that he loved to do. That is the one thing that he had dedicated a greater part of his life to and with that blow to his elbow, that dream that he had was shattered.

Now, I think I have related all the relevant facts that I have to relate to you. You will hear a little bit more in detail about how Mike trained horses, the kind of training he gave them, the horses he owned, the horses he raced, when he started and how he did it and all that. But now I am finished with my opening statement and you people have to hear Mr. Bishop give his. You are going to start listening to the testimony in this case. I want you to remember a couple of things. First of all, this is Michael Horak's only day in Court. This is the only time he has to be compensated for the wrongs that were done to him. Second of all, judging means that you have a willingness to listen. And in choosing this jury and talking with you, discussing with you, my decisions mainly were based on whether or not you had that willingness to listen. I trust that throughout this case, you will do that and at the end of the case, when it comes time to give your judgment, that you will reach into your hearts and your souls, you will find out what you had in regard to that willingness to listen, what that tells you, and you will come out with a verdict and I wish you luck in that regard. Thank you very much.

JUDGE LASSERS: Thank you very much.

MR. BISHOP: Your Honor, ladies and gentlemen, counsel, you should know by now my name is Ron Bishop and I represent all of the defendants in this lawsuit. And if I may, your Honor, I would like to introduce Mr. Daniels Groth, who is one of the defendants in the lawsuit. As the case goes on, I will have the other defendants move in and move out so you can see them, recognize them as being on the defense side of the case. Of course I'm sure you will hear some if not all of them as witnesses in this case. I have elected not to have the four individual defendants sit here throughout the trial.

MR. FARES: I will object at this point for these reasons. Those actions speak for themselves.

JUDGE LASSERS: Overruled, go ahead.

MR. BISHOP: Or have a representative sit here throughout the trial for the two club defendants, that is the National Jockey Club and the Fox Valley Trotting Association.

Let's start very easily and very quickly. There was on the night in question an altercation. And involved in that altercation were a number of security guards working at Sportsman Park Racetrack, working for my clients. Those gentlemen are defendants in this lawsuit. They are trained police officers, then and now. The evidence will show that they were additionally trained in racetrack security. The evidence will further show that their function and duties and training at the time of this particular occurrence that we're here about was not the type of training that you see of a uniformed security guard when we go to an amusement park such as Cubs Park or Sox Park. We are talking about security people dressed in soft or plain clothes. We are talking about trained and armed security officers. We are talking about, and the evidence will show, that some of those security guard police officers were involved in the very early stages of what was known as or what is known as the Illinois Bureau of Racetrack Police.

We will bring before you the evidence as to how the security force, the soft clothed force, was put together at Sportsman Park and how it operated and what its function and purpose was. We will bring before you their training, their experience, and a general idea of what their function is at other racetracks or was at other racetracks throughout the area, recognizing we are talking about 1978.

The evidence will further show that the security force not only worked at this particular racetrack but moved onto other racetracks and the force would change somewhat, but basically the hard shell was there.

On the evening in question, there was a disturbance in the Paddock area. A request for assistance for security was received in the security office because of a disturbance involving Mr. Horak. Security officers did in fact go the Paddock area and did in fact encounter Mr. Horak where they said, “Mr. Horak, we want to speak with you in the security office.” The evidence will further show that the security force recognized and knew who Mr. Horak was. The evidence will further show that at the inception of this meeting and discussion, that Mr. Horak didn't seem to think it was very serious, but yet he did agree, “Yes, I will come with you.”

The evidence will further show that there were no laying hands on at that time or guiding or taking into physical restraint-type custody. It was merely, “Mr. Horak, we would like you to come to the security office.” And he did in fact do that.

The evidence will further show that as Mr. Horak got closer and closer to and then inside of the security office, his demeanor changed from that kind of a joke to a serious matter because he began to realize that they were really taking him into custody, the realization finally came to his head. He then arrived in the security office and was standing by the counter when he was asked for his license. And you know what license we're talking about. He reached for his license and then he started to push and shove and got into a tugging match with one of the security Guards, that was Mr. McCarthy. Mr. McCarthy is presently with the Chicago Police Department as a full-time police officer. He was doing at that time the second job that some of us had in our lifetime as a security officer at Sportsman Park for the National jockey or the Fox Valley Trotting.

Because of his hostility with Mr. McCarthy and Mr. McCarthy trying to control the situation, they fell to the floor. The hostility by Mr. Horak continued whereupon Mr. Oliver got into it and they did in fact ultimately succeed in restraining Mr. Horak, placed him in handcuffs and sat him down on a chair and called the police department in Cicero, and had them come and pick up Mr. Horak on an appropriate charge.

The testimony will further show that several days later, Mr. Horak did in fact go to the hospital. I think this happened on a Monday Evening, June 12th, and he went to the hospital I think it was Friday, Thursday or Friday. He did see the doctor and he did receive some treatments for his elbow and I'm pretty sure there isn't any doubt about it. I know what's in the records. He wore a cast for several weeks.

The evidence will further show that there were other problems to his elbow, both prior and subsequent to the date of this accident. The evidence will further show that reasonable force, that reasonable measures, that appropriate measures were taken in the situation of Mr. Horak's disturbance in the Paddock area on the evening of the occurrence.

The evidence will show that on prior occasions where he was leading up to this event, that also at those times appropriate and reasonable care was taken by the security officers at Sportsman Park with reference to Mr. Horak. We hope to bring before you some of the people who were not security people at Sportsman Park at the time of the occurrence. I would like you very much to listen to what the witnesses have to say. Don't believe what I say. Decide this case on the facts and on the law. Thank you very much.

JUDGE LASSERS: Thank you very much, Mr. Bishop. That is the end of the opening statements, ladies and gentlemen. We are now ready to move on to the next phase of the trial and that is the presentation of Plaintiff's case. Mr. Fares?

Chapter 30

The Trial

MR. FARES: At this time I call the plaintiff, Mr. Horak.

JUDGE LASSERS: Before we move onto that, I am going to take a 30-second adjournment. I will be right back folks.

(Whereupon, the following proceedings were held in chambers outside the presence of the jury:)

MR. BISHOP: Your Honor, I feel compelled, your Honor, during counsel's opening statement, he went a long, long way away from what the evidence would show and I made three separate objections and I recognize the eagerness for the Court to have the matter proceed in an expeditious manner, but I am placed in a situation, I don't get a ruling on the record and I must get a ruling on the record. I don't mind if you overrule my objection, I really don't mind whether you overrule me, but I absolutely must have a ruling.

JUDGE LASSERS: I think it was pretty apparent what the ruling was

MR. BISHOP: In the reviewing courts they don't see it that way. One other thing, I feel highly prejudiced in this matter from the conduct of the counsel screaming and shouting in front of the jury and accusing me of talking during his opening statement. That conduct was totally uncalled for.

JUDGE LASSERS: Apparently, as I piece it together now, your client said something.

MR. BISHOP: He whispered in my ear.

JUDGE LASSERS: It was more than that.

MR. BISHOP: I didn't hear what he said.

JUDGE LASSERS: That may be, but I heard something. It was sort of a disturbance. We are at the beginning now of a trial that is going to go on for another week. Things have all been very pleasant and nice up to this point. Let's try to keep the good relationship to a minimum.

MR. BISHOP: I agree wholeheartedly. I am thoroughly convinced that the one in charge of that courtroom is the Judge. If I make an objection, don't feel bad about turning me down, but please get it on the record.

MR. FARES: I will be brief. First of all, in regard to the whispering that was going on, it wasn't whispering, well I heard it. It was distracting the jury. I was looking in the juries' eyes. It was something that it followed conduct by counsel constantly interrupting my opening statements, his objections concerning my opening statement. I have a right to talk to the jurors briefly about what their duty is. That is the law in the State of Illinois. I am not only presenting the facts, and I just want the record to reflect that (Whereupon, the following proceedings were held in open court in the presence of the jury:)

JUDGE LASSERS: Mr. Fares.

MR. FARES: I will call the plaintiff, Mr. MICHAEL HORAK, to the stand.

MR. FARES: May I approach the bench. Are you going to give them the instructions about note taking?

JUDGE LASSERS: Now, ladies and gentlemen, from this point on you folks have the right to take notes during the course of the trial. Looseleaf books have been provided for your convenience. Please place your name on the first page. You do not have to take notes. I have no preference one way or the other. You may use your notes to refresh your memory. Your notes are for your use only and not for any other juror's. Do not show them to anyone else at anytime and this includes the time when you are deliberating your verdict. You should rely on your own memory of the evidence. If someone's notes conflict with your memory or if someone else's notes conflict with your memory, you are free to use your own memory of the evidence.

Just because a juror has taken notes does not mean that his or her memory of the evidence is better than the memory of a juror who has not taken notes. Your notes must not leave the courtroom. They will be collected by Deputy Smith when you leave for lunch and at the close of the court day. At the end of the trial your notes will be collected and destroyed. No one will be allowed to look at the notes before they are destroyed.

(Witness sworn.)

MICHAEL JOHN HORAK, called as a witness on his own behalf, having been first duly sworn, was examined and testified as follows:

DIRECT EXAMINATION by Mr. Fares:

MR. FARES: Would you please state your name and address.

MICHAEL HORAK: Michael John Horak, 3227 Cleveland Avenue, Brookfield, Illinois.

MR. FARES: Let me direct your attention to June 12th, 1978. Did anything unusual occur on that day?

MICHAEL HORAK: Yes. I was beaten up by a security guard, Eugene Oliver, and three other security guards at Sportsman Park racetrack.

MR. FARES: On that evening, approximately what time did

you arrive at the track?

MICHAEL HORAK: It was between nine and nine-thirty in the evening.

MR. FARES: What was the weather like that evening?

MICHAEL HORAK: The weather was cool and dry.

MR. FARES: What were you wearing, how were you dressed?

MICHAEL HORAK: I was in a light brown turtleneck sweater, brown slacks, brown shoes, that's it.

MR. FARES: The turtleneck sweater, was it long-sleeved or short-sleeved?

MICHAEL HORAK: It was long-sleeved.

MR. FARES: Now, when you came to the track, how many parking lots are there at that track, sir?

MICHAEL HORAK: There's two big ones and one little one.

MR. FARES: Describe for me — this was Sportsman Park, correct?

MICHAEL HORAK: Sportsman Park racetrack

MR. FARES: Where is it located?

MICHAEL HORAK: In between Laramie Street on the west and Cicero Avenue on the East. They take up that whole area, four-block area.

MR. FARES: Now, when you got there that evening and you came in at the Grandstand entrance, where did you go?

MICHAEL HORAK: I walked immediately to the Paddock area and stood there and waited until Phase-Out came from the barn area to go to the track.

MR. FARES: When you say you walked to the Paddock area at that point, where in the Paddock area did you walk?

MICHAEL HORAK: Stood right about in the middle, right up in there.

MR. FARES: Between the actual Paddock fence and the racetrack fence?

MICHAEL HORAK: Oh, yes, that's where all the patrons and everybody go.

MR. FARES: When you got there, then what did you do?

MICHAEL HORAK: I waited for Phase-Out to come out and warm up.

MR. FARES: You waited for Phase-Out to come out?

MICHAEL HORAK: Yes.

MR. FARES: Did Phase-Out come out and warm up?

MICHAEL HORAK: Yes. He came out after the sixth race.

MR. FARES: Incidentally, when you got there what race was it?

MICHAEL HORAK: I'm pretty sure it was about the fourth race.

MR. FARES: Now, Phase-Out, why were you particularly interested in this horse, if you were?

MICHAEL HORAK: I understood from the people that owned him, Donner Packing Company in Milwaukee, this horse was going to be retired at the end of the meet. And they were going to stand him for stud.

MR. FARES: What does that mean, stand him for stud?

MICHAEL HORAK: To mate mares with him.

MR. FARES: Go Ahead.

MICHAEL HORAK: And he was the best, in my opinion, of any horse on that track at Sportsman Park at that meet. I saw this horse a couple of years before when he was younger, and in my estimation, he was good.

MR. FARES: Do you remember what race Phase-Out was scheduled to race in on that evening?

MICHAEL HORAK: It was the ninth race.

MR. FARES: Were there any other horses or races that you came to see on that particular evening.

MICHAEL HORAK: No.

MR. FARES: Did Phase-Out then come out to the Paddock area?

MICHAEL HORAK: Yes.

MR. FARES: What did you do then.

MICHAEL HORAK: I watched him warm up.

MR. FARES: When you watched him warm up, where did you stand?

MICHAEL HORAK: By the fence at the Paddock turn there.

MR. FARES: When you watched him warm up that evening, what did you notice about him?

MICHAEL HORAK: The horse was on the iron, which means he was full of run, wanting to go faster.

MR. FARES: Then what?

MICHAEL HORAK: I went back to the Paddock fence and watched the groom unhook him from the sulky and sponge him off.

MR. FARES: How did he look then?

MICHAEL HORAK: He looked real fresh.

MR. FARES: What happened next?

MICHAEL HORAK: Well, after he covered him up, I went to the Grandstand, I got a Coke.

MR. FARES: Where in the Grandstand would that have been generally.

MICHAEL HORAK: On the East end there, there's concession stands there on one side.

MR. FARES: Again, when you say the East end, East, West, South and North, correct (indicating)?

MICHAEL HORAK: Yes.

MR. FARES: On the east end of the Grandstand, the Blue building, that's where you went and bought a Coke?

MICHAEL HORAK: Yes.

MR. FARES: Then what did you do?

MICHAEL HORAK: Then I walked back out into the middle of the grandstand. I didn't go all the way to the Paddock because the horses were coming onto the track, so I stayed just on the West side of the little gate where they would come out onto the track.

MR. FARES: During that period of time, did you place a bet?

MICHAEL HORAK: Not yet.

MR. FARES: So when you say you walked into the West side, you are talking —

MICHAEL HORAK: Yes, I stood right there because that is where the horses passed onto the track and you can see them when they're walking out.

MR. FARES: While this was going on, were there any other races running?

MICHAEL HORAK: No. The race prior to that had been ten minutes before.

MR. FARES: So we are now between what races?

MICHAEL HORAK: We are between the eighth and ninth.

MR. FARES: After you walked back there, then what did you do next.

MICHAEL HORAK: After Phase-Out got on the track, I watched him parade by, and you have ten minutes left before they go to the post.

MR. FARES: What do they do when they get on the track?

MICHAEL HORAK: They just kind of jog around lightly, just to kind of loosen up again, because they've been standing for forty-five minutes in the stall.

MR. FARES: They go all the way around the track?

MICHAEL HORAK: Then the staring gate will be lined up at the top of the stretch.

MR. FARES: Now, how long a track is Sportsman Park?

MICHAEL HORAK: Five-eighths of a mile in circumference.

MR. FARES: What did you do then?

MICHAEL HORAK: Well, I took my time going to the betting windows. They are on the East end of that Grandstand. There's a whole row of windows from one end of the Grandstand all the way to the West end of that Grandstand, different types of betting at that time. Now it's all the same windows.

MR. FARES: All we are concerned about now is how it existed at that time. So there were windows at the West end at that time?

MICHAEL HORAK: Yes.

MR. FARES: What did you do when you got to the windows?

MICHAEL HORAK: I made my wager.

MR. FARES: How much did you wager?

MICHAEL HORAK: I bet a thousand dollars.

MR. FARES: Now, is that the only race you bet that night?

MICHAEL HORAK: Yes.

MR. FARES: Tell me what you observed when you saw the ninth race, specifically in regard to Phase-Out, on June 12th or 1978.

MICHAEL HORAK: They were all going behind the gate. The gate pulled away, and the horses were on their way. The gate pulls away to the side of the track. Now you have five horses straight across the track with the turn coming up ahead. They let them go in the middle of the backstretch. Right away, the horse Phase-Out, he actually shoots right out. I mean just like a bolt of lightning, he's out in front by three lengths, but the driver is already whipping him, even before he gets away from the field.

MR. FARES: Who is the driver?

MICHAEL HORAK: Daryl Busse.

MR. FARES: Did you know that when you placed the bet?

MICHAEL HORAK: Oh, yes.

MR. FARES: Is there anything unusual about treating a harness horse that way, in your opinion as a driver?

MICHAEL HORAK: Very much.

MR. FARES: What is unusual about it?

MICHAEL HORAK: Well, any horse, Thoroughbred or harness, is only good for three-eights of a mile of full blast speed. Some will have a little more, but very seldom. This particular horse in all of his races that I have watched in three years, he's always raced from out of the pack. He starts slow and finishes fast. He never went to the front. Never in his life did he go to the front. With a small field, he would have had no problem. Normally, if there had been nine horses he might have had to shoot out there a little bit to get away from some of the slower horses in the race. He had no problem. I was under the impression in such a short field, he could start dead last.

MR. BISHOP: Objection Your Honor, impressions.

JUDGE LASSERS: Sustained.

MR. FARES: So he started to whip the horse very quickly?

MICHAEL HORAK: And he pulled out to a fast lead.

MR. FARES: How do you describe "a lead" in harness racing?

MICHAEL HORAK: Each length is the length of a horse.

MR. FARES: What do you call — (Indicating from a picture)?

MICHAEL HORAK: The sulky. You can call them buggies, but sulky is the proper name.

MR. FARES: How much of a lead did he break out to, for Daryl Busse, while he was driving Phase-Out?

MICHAEL HORAK: Before the turn, he was three lengths in front.

MR. FARES: Now, you said that — How long after the race did Mr. Busse continue to whip the horse?

MICHAEL HORAK: All the way until he got in the stretch.

MR. FARES: He took it from the backstretch where the race started, got to the stretch and gave the horse all he had in that time?

MICHAEL HORAK: Well, in other words, he whipped him for three-eighths of a mile that I saw from the point where I was at.

MR. FARES: Then what happened, after he whipped him?

MICHAEL HORAK: Then the other horses started catching up to him, 'cause he was out there pretty good.

MR. FARES: Then what happened?

MICHAEL HORAK: Then I saw him throw the lines loose at the horse. You could see them just flopping, the driving lines that he controls the horse with.

MR. FARES: What happened to Phase-Out then?

MICHAEL HORAK: The rest of the horses passed him up and he just followed them on home then.

MR. FARES: Did Daryl Busse ever tighten the lines up again

from the backstretch to the finish line?
MICHAEL HORAK: As he came around the Paddock turn where all the people were standing out in the fence yelling and screaming, then he took out his whip again and he started swinging his whip. I don't know what that was for he was already dead last.

MR. FARES: At the point that he got around here about to the entrance from the Paddock to the track itself, he was already fifth?

MICHAEL HORAK: Yes.

MR. FARES: How far was he behind the fourth horse in the race?

MICHAEL HORAK: Seven, eight lengths.

MR. FARES: At any point during the race itself, while Phase-Out was running and Busse was driving, what were you doing during the race?

MICHAEL HORAK: Well, for a moment or two I stood there in disbelief because a top-notch horse like that getting a race like that, and everybody else is screaming, I heard a little vulgar language going on, but you're going to hear screaming and yelling at a racetrack, just like a ball game, they'll say, "Kill the umpire." I went to White Sox Park and heard that.

MR. BISHOP: Objection.

JUDGE LASSERS: Sustained.

MICHAEL HORAK: I'm sorry.

MR. FARES: You say that race was run in about two minutes?

MICHAEL HORAK: Yes.

MR. FARES: About where, generally, did Phase-Out finish the race?

MICHAEL HORAK: Well, he was dead last by some fifteen lengths.

MR. FARES: How many minutes or minutes and seconds did he finish the race in?

MICHAEL HORAK: Well, he probably finished in about two minutes and three seconds.

MR. FARES: Each second is?

MICHAEL HORAK: Five lengths for each second of the clock.

MR. FARES: He finished about fifteen lengths behind the winner?

MICHAEL HORAK: Yes.

MR. FARES: At that point then when Busse got off the sulky and gave it to the groom and came into the gate, what did you do?

MICHAEL HORAK: As I watched him coming up to the Paddock area, I saw the groom there, I knew the groom real well, name was Brown, and I went over to see what was wrong with the horse at first.

MR. FARES: So you walked from where to where?

MICHAEL HORAK: Right from that X and just about twenty feet over to the gate there.

MR. FARES: When you say the gate, you are here?

MICHAEL HORAK: Yes, then I walked to the entrance gate of the Paddock.

MR. FARES: In which direction?

MICHAEL HORAK: Straight across. That's where they first came in off the track.

MR. FARES: What did you do then.

MICHAEL HORAK: I looked the horse over. The horse was just — a different horse altogether. He was all beat up. He had welt marks on his back, red marks on both of his sides. You hit a horse with a whip, they show just this kind of welt marks on the hide.

MR. FARES: Is it unusual after a race that there will be welt marks on a horse?

MICHAEL HORAK: Very unusual.

MR. FARES: What happened then?

MICHAEL HORAK: As Busse was approaching me on the other side of the fence, he was walking West into the Paddock.

MR. FARES: And what happened?

MICHAEL HORAK: As he got within three feet of me, I yelled out, I said, "Busse, you gave that horse one lousy ride!"

MR. FARES: Anything else?

MICHAEL HORAK: I said, "If I couldn't drive better than that, I'd tear up my driver's license," meaning my harness license.

MR. FARES: Did you follow Phase Out after this race?

MICHAEL HORAK: After this race, yes.

MR. FARES: Did you follow his performance?

MICHAEL HORAK: Yes.

MR. FARES: What were his performances after this race on 6/12/78?

MICHAEL HORAK: After he finished dead last in the Sportsman Park race, the owners changed drivers and put a different driver on his horse.

MR. FARES: What were his performances?

MICHAEL HORAK: He won the next three races.

MR. FARES: What did you do next? Where were you going, where were you intending on going?

MICHAEL HORAK: I was going back to the West parking lot to get my car and go home.

MR. FARES: In going back to the West parking lot, which route did you use?

MICHAEL HORAK: I just walked towards the fence and then straight West.

MR. FARES: What is the next thing that happened?

MICHAEL HORAK: I got middle-way in that Grandstand area, Oliver and another fellow was with him at the time — I didn't know him. I knew Oliver from knowing him from being at the track — they approached me.

MR. FARES: Now, describe for me what Mr. Oliver looks like?

MICHAEL HORAK: Well, he's a big, heavy-set fellow. I would say about 350 pounds, six foot.

MR. FARES: At least that's how he looked on that day?

MICHAEL HORAK: Yes.

MR. FARES: I am going to show you, Mr. Horak, which has previously been marked Exhibit Number 3-A for purposes of identification and ask you if you can identify that person in the picture.

MICHAEL HORAK: Eugene Oliver.

MR. FARES: Does that generally truly and accurately depict how Mr. Oliver looked on or about June 12th or 1978?

MICHAEL HORAK: About.

MR. FARES: Any distinguishing features from that picture as to how he looked, anything different?

MICHAEL HORAK: No.

MR. FARES: Now, you had known Mr. Oliver before this, had you not?

MICHAEL HORAK: Years before.

MR. FARES: How long had you known Mr. Oliver?

MICHAEL HORAK: Oh, 1966, 1967, about ten years before.

MR. FARES: Why would Mr. Oliver be in the barn area, if you know, during those times?

MICHAEL HORAK: Well, a couple times he stopped by my stall. He was just walking through, but he'd stop by asking for a few horses that I knew had a chance of winning, so he could place a bet on them.

MR. FARES: Did he have any position at the track at that time?

MICHAEL HORAK: I just knew he was a security guard. That's what I understood he was. I didn't know for sure what he did.

MR. FARES: In all the times that you saw him at the track from 1967 until this date in 1978, had you ever seen him in a uniform?

MICHAEL HORAK: Never, no.

MR. FARES: How many times, as best as you can, would you estimate you saw him during that period of time?

MICHAEL HORAK: I'd run into him every time I was at the Grandstands.

MR. FARES: Could you describe what Mr. Oliver's partner looked like?

MICHAEL HORAK: He was short, about five foot seven, five, in that area.

MR. FARES: His weight?

MICHAEL HORAK: About 135 pounds, maybe a little more. I didn't pay too much attention.

MR. FARES: Did you ever come to find out that man's name?

MICHAEL HORAK: No, I never did.

MR. FARES: Before this incident or this meeting with Eugene Oliver on June 12th, 1978, had you ever — had you known Mr. Oliver?

MICHAEL HORAK: Yes, I've known him quite a few years.

MR. FARES: Now, what was the nature of your relationship with him?

MICHAEL HORAK: When I'd go to the Grandstand to see the races years before or once in a while he'd be walking through the barn area and the stable area.

MR. FARES: Let's say within the thirty days before June 12th of 1978, had you had any conversations with Mr. Oliver in his capacity as a security guard at the track.

MICHAEL HORAK: About two weeks before this incident at the track.

MR. FARES: Where did those conversations — where did that conversation take place?

MICHAEL HORAK: In the Grandstand by the fence between the Paddock and Grandstand, right West of that little gate there going onto the track.

MR. FARES: Along the fence?

MICHAEL HORAK: Right there. I had a lady friend with me that night.

MR. FARES: Who else was present?

MICHAEL HORAK: That was it.

MR. FARES: Your lady friend, what was her name?

MICHAEL HORAK: Laura Nichalosa.

MR. FARES: What was the conversation you had with Eugene Oliver on that evening?

MICHAEL HORAK: The horses had just come out onto the track for the ninth race.

MR. BISHOP: I fail to see any relevancy.

JUDGE LASSERS: What is the relevance?

MR. FARES: Your Honor, this simply goes to the prior relationship between these Defendants and the plaintiff as well as certain prior incidents, all of which your Honor has already ruled on concerning this particular area.

JUDGE LASSERS: You claim that this is linked somehow to this later incident?

MR. FARES: Yes, your Honor.

JUDGE LASSERS: I will overrule the objection.

MR. FARES: Go ahead Mr. Horak.

MICHAEL HORAK: I was watching the horses come out and the driver by the name of Connell Willis, who I know quite well. I yelled at him to watch out for the seven horse because she was real lame and a front runner.

MR. FARES: In this particular race?

MICHAEL HORAK: Yes. He was driving the five horse.

MR. FARES: Who was the seven horse?

MICHAEL HORAK: Ocala Star Craft.

MR. FARES: Why did you tell him to look out for the 7 horse?

MICHAEL HORAK: I knew she was lame.

MR. FARES: How did you know that?

MICHAEL HORAK: Two and a half months previous I was in Florida at Pompano Park racetrack. I saw this particular horse. They were trying to sell her. That's why I was paying attention to her. She had led for half a mile in the race, all of a sudden, she just pulled up suddenly and stopped and she reared up in the air and stopped. The field went around her. After the race they had to take this horse off the track in a horse ambulance because she was unable to walk.

MR. FARES: On that particular evening other than this

conversation you had with Eugene Oliver, did you have any conversations with anybody else employed by Sportsman Park or Fox Valley concerning that horse, Ocala Star Craft?

MICHAEL HORAK: Yes, about three minutes before the race.

MR. FARES: Who did you have a conversation with?

MR. BISHOP: If the Court pleases, I still object. I fail to see any relevancy.

JUDGE LASSERS: We are getting pretty far afield now, Mr. Fares.

MR. FARES: Your Honor, May I be heard on that for just a moment then?

(Whereupon, the following proceedings were had in chambers outside the presence of the jury:)

JUDGE LASSERS: Where is all this going?

MR. FARES: It's one of my client's contentions that part of the motive for his beating that he took, was related to the fact that two weeks prior there was this incident at the racetrack wherein he mentioned to the Paddock Judge that this horse Ocala Star Craft was going to break down. The Paddock Judge, Frank Pennino, told him to mind his own business and indeed the horse broke down that night. It caused a terrible accident where six horses went falling to the ground crippling some of the drivers. Further, there has been indication by Mr. Bishop that he is going to bring in testimony concerning Mr. Horak's prior involvement with other drivers that led up to this incident and I assume as well as prior statements by security concerning this incident as to why they brought him in on this particular evening.

And although I don't feel all of that may be necessarily admissible, what I'm trying to show is that he had no prior contact with Eugene Oliver concerning any warnings or anything of that nature concerning misconduct. I think that's relevant to the issue of whether or not there is any provocation as they claim.

JUDGE LASSERS: As I understand, the incident two weeks ago, two weeks before the major incident, Mr. Horak has testified simply that he told another driver to watch out for a horse, but there's no — there's nothing said between Oliver and Horak.

MR. FARES: Not as of yet, Judge. I haven't gotten to the conversation between Oliver and Horak.

JUDGE LASSERS: Why don't you get to that conversation, but when you start to get into events that happened previously, it seems to me that you're really going far afield.

MR. FARES: That's fine, Judge.

MR. BISHOP: I have no difficulty with the proposition that there had been previous contact, verbal contact between Mr. Horak and Mr. Oliver as well as Mr. Horak and many, many other security people at the track.

JUDGE LASSERS: Let's get back to that.

(Whereupon, the following proceedings were had in open court in the presence of the jury:)

MR. FARES: Mr. Horak, this conversation that you had with Mr.. Oliver, what did that consist of?

MICHAEL HORAK: Oliver was about twenty feet away from me and he called over to me, I guess seeing that I was with a lady friend, "Michael John, I want to talk with you."

MR. FARES: What did you say?

MICHAEL HORAK: I walked over to him and he says, "You

can't be yelling at these drivers."

MR. FARES: What did you say?

MICHAEL HORAK: I said, "I was just yelling at Connell Willis to watch the seven horse, he might cause a problem in the race."

MR. FARES: Did the number seven horse ultimately cause a problem in the race.

MR. BISHOP: Objection, your Honor.

MR. FARES: I will leave this area.

MR. BISHOP: I have an objection, your Honor. This is totally immaterial to the issues of why we're here.

JUDGE LASSERS: I overrule the objection. Go ahead.

MR. FARES: Did the seven horse, Ocala Star Craft ultimately break down in the race?

MICHAEL HORAK: Yes. She did the same thing she did in Florida. The rest of the field plowed into her and only one horse finished the race. The track looked like a bloody battlefield.

MR. BISHOP: I fail to see the relevancy.

JUDGE LASSERS: The answer is she did cause a problem.

MR. FARES: Other than that conversation that you had with Eugene Oliver on May 31st, approximately two weeks before, 1978, had you had any other prior conversations concerning — with Eugene Oliver concerning your conduct at the track.

MICHAEL HORAK: None whatsoever.

(After many stupid questions, Mr. Fares finally got down to

the main topic as to the damage done by Sportsman Park management. As I was now in the security office standing in front of Bajovich's desk.)

MR. FARES: What happened then?

MICHAEL HORAK: I got up to the desk. Mr. Bajovich, he said, "We understand you've been causing a lot of problems at the Paddock, a lot of trouble."

MR. FARES: What did you say?

MICHAEL HORAK: And the only thing I could think of at that moment is that I said, "Well, if it's about the way Daryl Busse drove that last race, I told him, 'Busse, you give that horse a lousy drive. If I couldn't do better than that, I'd tear up my license.'"

MR. FARES: What happened next?

MICHAEL HORAK: Then I also said, "If you don't believe that story, Busse's up in the driver's room right now changing his clothes." I told him to call him.

MR. FARES: What did he say, if anything?

MICHAEL HORAK: He said, "We're running this racetrack."

MR. FARES: At this point, where was Eugene Oliver?

MICHAEL HORAK: He was still standing behind me.

MR. FARES: On what side?

MICHAEL HORAK: On the right side.

MR. FARES: How about his partner?

MICHAEL HORAK: He was standing on the left side of me.

MR. FARES: And the other two security guards, do you remember where they were?

MICHAEL HORAK: One was on the side of the desk.

MR. FARES: Which side?

MICHAEL HORAK: On the North side of the desk and the other one was against the wall.

MR. FARES: Then what happened?

MICHAEL HORAK: Then the telephone rang.

MR. FARES: What did you observe?

MICHAEL HORAK: The man behind the desk picked up the phone, he answered it and he started mumbling something. I couldn't understand what he was saying, he was mumbling so I wouldn't understand him, I guess.

MR. BISHOP: Objection, Your Honor, move it to be stricken.

JUDGE LASSERS: All right.

MR. FARES: He was mumbling into the phone?

MICHAEL HORAK: He was talking. I couldn't understand what he was saying.

MR. FARES: So what happened?

MICHAEL HORAK: He slammed down the phone. He said, "I want to see your harness owner driver's license now."

MR. FARES: What did you do?

MICHAEL HORAK: I was standing there and I reached in my back pocket with my right hand, I pulled out the billfold and opened it up, I had my hand out like this, just as I got the license out (indicating).

MR. FARES: What happened?

MICHAEL HORAK: I felt an arm go around my neck real quickly, started choking me, and pulling me backwards on the right side in the direction where Eugene Oliver was standing.

MR. FARES: Where you able to determine where the arm came from?

MICHAEL HORAK: Came up back here. His other arm this way, and pulled me back like that in an arm lock and just choking me (indicating).

MR. FARES: You were then thrown to the floor?

MICHAEL HORAK: Yes.

MR. FARES: How did you land?

MICHAEL HORAK: I landed on the back of my head.

MR. FARES: What did you notice about yourself at that point?

MICHAEL HORAK: I was a little dazed from the knock on the floor and I was just laying there.

MR. FARES: When you were laying there, what did you see, if anything?

MICHAEL HORAK: Well, about that time, I looked up and here's Eugene Oliver kneeling on my left arm reaching over, my other arm was out here someplace, he was reaching over to grab it. In the meantime somebody was grabbing my ankles. I don't know who was grabbing my ankles and holding my feet down. Eugene Oliver laid across the upper part of my body.

MR. FARES: At that point what was your position?

MICHAEL HORAK: I was laying on my back at that time.

MR. FARES: Was your face covered?

MICHAEL HORAK: After he laid on top of me, yes.

MR. FARES: What happened next then?

MICHAEL HORAK: Then I started feeling, getting kicked or hit with something or being kicked quite a few times.

MR. FARES: Where?

MICHAEL HORAK: My side of my legs, my lower ribs, and just another part of my lower body. I was yelling out, "What the Hell are you guys doing, I hadn't done anything!"

MR. FARES: Was there any other conversation during this period?

MICHAEL HORAK: Somebody yelled out, "We're going to fix you."

MR. FARES: Do you know who that was?

MICHAEL HORAK: No.

MR. FARES: Anything else that was said?

MICHAEL HORAK: Well, I started yelling, and trying to have him let me go. I don't know what I said. I probably used some swear words, anything I could do to get them to stop.

MR. FARES: Did they stop?

MICHAEL HORAK: Just enough — Eugene Oliver got up off my upper body, grabbed this arm and pulled me over. As he was pulling me over to get me on my back, somebody yelled out, "Don't kick him in the face."

MR. FARES: Do you know who that was?

MICHAEL HORAK: No.

MR. FARES: Were you still being kicked?

MICHAEL HORAK: Yes. I got kicked good one time in the stomach.

MR. FARES: Then what happened?

MICHAEL HORAK: They had me on my stomach, my face was laying sideways on the floor. Then someone grabbed my arms behind my back, just jerked them back and put a pair of handcuffs on me real tight.

MR. FARES: Do you know where Eugene Oliver was at the time your arms got grabbed behind your back?

MICHAEL HORAK: He had a hold of my arm.

MR. FARES: You were laying on you face?

MICHAEL HORAK: Right.

MR. FARES: Now, where was Eugene Oliver?

MICHAEL HORAK: I don't know.

MR. FARES: Was anybody else sitting on you at that point?

MICHAEL HORAK: Well, then the person let go of my ankles at the time when I was being turned over, I felt a lot of weight on them, I just assumed that they sat on them or was holding me down. I couldn't move.

MR. FARES: What happened next?

MICHAEL HORAK: Well, after — I don't know how many times I got kicked or whatever they were doing —

MR. BISHOP: Objection, Your Honor, non-responsive answer.

JUDGE LASSERS: I think it is. Overruled.

MR. FARES: What happened then, Mr. Horak?

MICHAEL HORAK: Well, then everything stopped. The room got real quiet. Nobody was saying anything, and —

JUDGE LASSERS: Get a glass of water.

MICHAEL HORAK: I'll be all right. Then I felt a crushing blow under the left elbow.

MR. FARES: What did it feel like?

MICHAEL HORAK: I don't know. Must have been some kind of a blunt object 'cause I never felt pain like that in my life and the pain just went through my whole body like electric shock.

MR. FARES: Then what happened?

MICHAEL HORAK: Well, everything got cloudy and I don't know what happened.

MR. FARES: Just before you felt this blow, was anybody sitting on any part of your body?

MICHAEL HORAK: Yes. Someone was either laying on my head or sitting on my head.

MR. FARES: Do you know who that was?

MICHAEL HORAK: No, I don't.

MR. FARES: It was after this that you felt a blow?

MICHAEL HORAK: Yes.

MR. FARES: What is the next thing you remember after losing consciousness?

MICHAEL HORAK: Well, I was sitting in the chair against the wall, that South wall.

MR. FARES: And what did you notice? Were you still in cuffs at that point?

MICHAEL HORAK: Yes, the handcuffs were behind my back.

MR. FARES: Incidentally, when this crushing blow was struck to your left elbow, what part of your elbow was hit, as you recall?

MICHAEL HORAK: The inner part.

MR. FARES: Show us, please?

MICHAEL HORAK: Right in here, in this area right here (indicating).

MR. FARES: At the time that you got struck that crushing blow, your arms were still behind your back cuffed?

MICHAEL HORAK: Yes.

MR. FARES: Were you cuffed during that whole time?

MICHAEL HORAK: Yes. I was laying on my stomach.

MR. FARES: When you awoke, what did you see sitting in a chair?

MICHAEL HORAK: Well, first thing I remember, there was

a lot of pain coming from my left elbow. I was sweating, yet I couldn't figure it out 'cause I was shaking from being cold. And I noticed the left hand right by the wrist was just throbbing and the whole hand was just — felt like it was asleep or numb. It was a tingling feeling. The right arm wasn't that way and I couldn't figure that one out at the time.

MR. FARES: Then what happened after you noticed the condition of your left arm.

MICHAEL HORAK: I was sore all over. My ribs ached. I went to cough and it just hurt me when I tried to cough.

MR. FARES: Then what happened?

MICHAEL HORAK: About that time, I noticed there was a little scuffle or commotion coming in through that door.

MR. FARES: Which door are you referring to?

MICHAEL HORAK: That door there.

MR. FARES: The same door you entered through?

MICHAEL HORAK: Yes.

MR. FARES: What did you see?

MICHAEL HORAK: First I saw somebody being brought in with Eugene Oliver had an arm lock around his neck and he was pushing him through that little hallway door.

MR. FARES: What else did you see?

MICHAEL HORAK: He was punching him a few times in the chest and I yelled out, "You better stop beating on that guy, he's got a witness."

MR. FARES: Then what happened?

MICHAEL HORAK: They stopped.

MR. FARES: What did they do with the guy?

MICHAEL HORAK: They marched him over, put him in a chair to sit next to me.

MR. FARES: Did you later come to find out the name of the guy that Oliver brought in by the throat?

MICHAEL HORAK: Yes. He had a pair of handcuffs on him also.

MR. FARES: What was his name.

MICHAEL HORAK: Richard White.

MR. FARES: What then happened with Richard White?

MICHAEL HORAK: Nothing happened at that time. We just sat there, must have been a half hour.

MR. FARES: During that period of time, other than what you said, "You better let him go, he's got a witness", was there anything else said by you during the period of time that you were sitting in the security office with your handcuffs on?

MICHAEL HORAK: I said in a loud voice to the man behind the desk, I said, "These handcuffs are killing me. How about loosening them up?"

MR. FARES: When you say the handcuffs were killing you, what do you mean?

MICHAEL HORAK: The left hand was throbbing and it was just sore.

MR. FARES: Go ahead?

MICHAEL HORAK: The circulation seemed like it was almost stopped on the left hand.

MR. FARES: Then what happened?

MICHAEL HORAK: Then he sent Eugene Oliver over to look at my handcuffs behind my back.

MR. FARES: And what happened?

MICHAEL HORAK: Eugene Oliver took a look, he went back to the desk, said something, I don't know what it was, came back, and started to proceed to take the handcuffs off of me completely.

MR. FARES: Was anything said at this time?

MICHAEL HORAK: Well, somebody across the room said, "I wouldn't take them handcuffs off of him."

MR. FARES: One of other guards?

MICHAEL HORAK: Yes.

MR. FARES: Do you remember which one it was?

MICHAEL HORAK: No, I don't.

MR. FARES: Was there any response?

MICHAEL HORAK: Yeah, Oliver said, "He won't be using that arm anymore."

MR. FARES: Other than that, was there any other conversation between you and the guards on that evening?

MICHAEL HORAK: No. They took the handcuffs off.

MR. FARES: After you were sitting in the chair there, other than what you've already told us you said and other than what you may have said to Richard White, did you do any screaming of any nature?

MICHAEL HORAK: After the handcuffs were off I told them, "There will be some severe repercussions on this matter."

MR. FARES: Who did you say that to?

MICHAEL HORAK: I just said it to anybody in the room. I was looking at the desk when I said it, though.

MR. FARES: Anything other than that?

MICHAEL HORAK: Couple of guys got a big laugh out of it, they said, "There will be some concussions all right." They got a big laugh out of it.

MR. FARES: Do you know who it was?

MICHAEL HORAK: It was at least two or three of them laughing, I didn't bother looking up.

MR. FARES: During that period of time, did you say anything to Richard White?

MICHAEL HORAK: I told him that I got —

MR. BISHOP: I will object to this unless he indicates who else was a party to or overheard that conversation.

JUDGE LASSERS: What?

MR. BISHOP: Unless he could indicate who else was present.

MR. FARES: He wants a foundation, Judge. I will give him that. Mr. Horak, you said you did say something else to Richard White?

MICHAEL HORAK: Yes.

MR. FARES: Was there anybody else present while you were

talking to Richard White?

MICHAEL HORAK: No. Just the security people. They just ignored me then. So they weren't even paying attention to me anymore.

MR. FARES: What did you tell Richard White?

MICHAEL HORAK: I just told him I got the same treatment, only a little bit worse.

MR. FARES: Anything else?

MICHAEL HORAK: I said, "It's probably lucky that I was here because I think he would have got worse too."

MR. BISHOP: Objection.

JUDGE LASSERS: He is relating conversation.

MICHAEL HORAK: He said, "I'm sure glad you were in there."

MR. FARES: Did you have any further conversation with Richard White at that point?

MICHAEL HORAK: No.

MR. FARES: What happened then when the Cicero police came?

MICHAEL HORAK: Well, they took us to the Cicero police station.

MR. FARES: What occurred at the police station?

MICHAEL HORAK: Well, I got there, when they were making out the report, I told them I'd like to go to the hospital, have my arm checked. I was hurting all over.

MR. FARES: What happened next.

MICHAEL HORAK: The officer behind the desk said, “You'll only be here a few minutes.”

MR. BISHOP: Objection to what he said to somebody at the police station.

JUDGE LASSERS: What is the objection?

MR. BISHOP: It's hearsay.

JUDGE LASSERS: Overruled.

MR. BISHOP: This is the Cicero police station he is testifying to here now.

JUDGE LASSERS: Overruled.

MICHAEL HORAK: He said, “You'll only be here a few minutes, then you can go to the hospital, you wouldn't have to come back here to be booked. We have to book you right now.”

MR. FARES: About what time was it when you finally got to the Cicero police station, if you remember?

MICHAEL HORAK: 11:30, at least. It was 11:30. It was in that area.

MR. FARES: What time did you finally leave the Cicero police station?

MICHAEL HORAK: It was after three in the morning.

MR. FARES: While you were there, what did they do to you, or what occurred?

MICHAEL HORAK: They just booked me and I guess fingerprinted me, put me in a cell.

MR. FARES: How did you get out of the cell that night?

MICHAEL HORAK: Well, someone came, said they were sorry, but they had a lot of paperwork to do and that was the reason why they kept me so long.

MR. FARES: Did you have to pay a bond to get out?

MICHAEL HORAK: Yes, I put up a thirty-five dollar bond.

MR. FARES: They let you out finally at about 3:00?

MICHAEL HORAK: Yes.

MR. FARES: Now let me ask you one more thing. From the time that you left Sportsman Park and were put into custody of the Cicero police until the time that you got to the Cicero police station, did you say anything to Richard White?

MICHAEL HORAK: Well, I said —

MR. FARES: Did you say anything?

MICHAEL HORAK: Yes.

MR. FARES: Was there anybody else present at that time?

MICHAEL HORAK: No.

MR. FARES: What did you say?

MICHAEL HORAK: I said, "We'll probably have to put up bond, I don't know what the charges are going to be."

MR. FARES: Any other conversation concerning your injuries or anything of that nature?

MICHAEL HORAK: I told him my arm was just falling asleep on me. It was just numb.

MR. FARES: Is that the extent of you conversation with Richard White on the way to the police station?

MICHAEL HORAK: I asked him if he had any money to post his bond.

MR. FARES: What did you do at that point?

MICHAEL HORAK: He said, "No." I said, "I'll put up your bond for you."

MR. FARES: When you got to the police station, did you put up his bond?

MICHAEL HORAK: No, because some of my money was missing. I had only $115.00 in my billfold.

MR. FARES: You mean when you got to the police station?

MICHAEL HORAK: Yes.

MR. FARES: When you got to the security office, how much did you have in your billfold?

MICHAEL HORAK: It was a little over eight hundred dollars.

MR. FARES: Do you know where that money went during that period of time?

MICHAEL HORAK: No, I don't, but I have a real good guess.

MR. FARES: Do you remember what you were charged with at the Cicero police station?

MICHAEL HORAK: I think it was disorderly conduct, something like that.

JUDGE LASSERS: What is your exhibit number?

MR. FARES: Number nine. I am going to show you what's previously been marked Plaintiff's exhibit number nine for purposes of identification, and ask if you can identify that for me.

(Plaintiff's exhibit number nine so marked)

MICHAEL HORAK: Yes, that's the charge they had on me signed by Eugene Oliver.

MR. FARES: That is disorderly conduct?

MICHAEL HORAK: Yes.

MR. FARES: Were you ever, incidentally, charged with battery arising out of this incident?

MICHAEL HORAK: None, just the disorderly conduct.

MR. FARES: Did you go to court on the charges?

MICHAEL HORAK: Yes, later on.

MR. FARES: Did you have to pay an attorney to represent you?

MICHAEL HORAK: Yes, I hired the law firm of Mr. Burken.

MR. FARES: How much did you pay him for their representation in regard to this charge?

MICHAEL HORAK: A thousand dollars.

MR. FARES: Did you have a trial when you went to court?

MICHAEL HORAK: Yes.

MR. FARES: Who was there to testify in regard to that trial?

MICHAEL HORAK: Eugene Oliver.

MR. FARES: Did Mr. Oliver give testimony there?

MICHAEL HORAK: Yes, he did.

MR. FARES: Did the Judge make a ruling.

MICHAEL HORAK: Yes.

MR. FARES: What did you plead in regard to the disorderly conduct charge?

MICHAEL HORAK: Not guilty.

MR. FARES: What was the Judge's finding in regard to that?

MICHAEL HORAK: Not guilty.

MR. FARES: You got back home at three o'clock in the morning after the police station, we are back now to June 13th of 1978?

MICHAEL HORAK: Yes.

MR. FARES: What was the condition of your left arm at that time?

MICHAEL HORAK: It was swollen up all the way to the hand by now.

MR. FARES: From where to where was it swelling?

MICHAEL HORAK: From in this area all the way to the hand and the fingers were puffed up.

MR. FARES: What about the rest of your body, what was the condition of the rest of your body?

MICHAEL HORAK: It was just sore.

MR. FARES: Were you having any pain at this time?

MICHAEL HORAK: Pain in my elbow was the main thing.

MR. FARES: What kind of pain was it at that time?

MICHAEL HORAK: It was a sharp pain.

MR. FARES: Did you go to the hospital at that time?

MICHAEL HORAK: I was in too much of a dazed condition to think about hospitals.

MR. BISHOP: Objection, Your Honor, move that it be stricken.

MR. FARES: I think it's responsive, Your Honor.

MR. BISHOP: Self-serving statement.

JUDGE LASSERS: That may be. I will let it stand. Go ahead.

MR. FARES: What did you do, if anything, for your condition at that time?

MICHAEL HORAK: When I got home I got a plastic dish pan and filled it half full of water, got four trays of ice cubes out of the refrigerator and bought two more bags of ice cubes from the store.

MR. FARES: What did you do then?

MICHAEL HORAK: I put the whole elbow into the water, ice water, soaked it.

MR. FARES: How long did you soak it?

MICHAEL HORAK: About an hour and a half.

MR. FARES: At home there?

MICHAEL HORAK: Yes.

MR. FARES: What is the next thing you did, if anything?

MICHAEL HORAK: Well, then I dried it off and I had a couple boxes of bandages and medicine from the horses. I knew a

Gelo-cast Bandage is a real good bandage to put on something in that predicament.

MR. FARES: What is a Gelo-cast Bandage?

MICHAEL HORAK: It is a medicated bandage we use on horses with swollen legs. And it will take the heat and soreness out of a leg in three or four days if you leave it on.

MR. FARES: I am going to show you what has previously been marked Plaintiff's exhibit number twelve for purposes of identification, and ask you if you can identify that?

(Plaintiff's Exhibit Number twelve so marked.)

MICHAEL HORAK: Yes, that is the type of bandage we use. It's medicated. You keep it sealed. It is moist, then when you wrap it around your hands, you wrap it every quarter inch, just keep on going right up.

MR. FARES: You did that about 5:00 in the morning, 4:30?

MICHAEL HORAK: Yes.

MR. FARES: You had used these things previous to this in your training of horses?

MICHAEL HORAK: Oh yes, I had a whole case of them at all times.

MR. FARES: What else did you do for your arm at that time, if anything?

MICHAEL HORAK: Well, I wrapped the bandages, then I put a role of cotton over the top of that and an Ace elastic bandage around the top of that.

MR. FARES: The Gelo-cast, is that like an Ace Bandage?

MICHAEL HORAK: No. Because this will get a little hard

once it's put on, but you still have a little flexibility, that's why they call it a Gelo-cast, it's a cast but not a hard cast. Once it dries, then I put the Ace Bandage around it to keep the medication from going onto my clothes or whatever.

MR. FARES: The next day, that morning, what did you do, if anything?

MICHAEL HORAK: I took off the Gelo-cast bandage but the swelling and the pain was still there. I put a poultice, Numotizine poultice on my entire arm.

MR. FARES: What kind of poultice?

MICHAEL HORAK: It's a poultice like a paste and you put it on and then you wrap plastic paper around it and then put a bandage on it, it also will draw out heat and soreness.

MR. FARES: So you did that that night. This was the night of the 13th?

MICHAEL HORAK: First I soaked it in some more ice water. I dried it off. I put the poultice on about a quarter-inch thick around the whole arm. I had a bigger bottle though. They sell it in quart jars.

MR. FARES: Since June 12th of 1978, have you tried to drive a race horse?

MICHAEL HORAK: It's impossible.

MR. FARES: Why is it impossible?

MICHAEL HORAK: I wouldn't be able to control the horse with my left arm and trying to drive with one hand. All you're going to do — the horse is going to go from side to side, you're going to cause a wreck.

MR. BISHOP: Objection to what's going to happen. Speculation.

MR. FARES: I don't think he's speculating.

JUDGE LASSERS: The man has a lot of experience. Overruled.

MR. FARES: Go ahead.

MICHAEL HORAK: Well, then any pressure on the arm, by extending the arm out, I just don't do it because I would get an extreme amount of pain from doing so.

MR. FARES: What was the condition of your elbow when you got home?

MICHAEL HORAK: The elbow was getting worse now.

MR. FARES: What do you mean, "It was getting worse"?

MICHAEL HORAK: The swelling was a lot bigger. The three fingers, they were swelled up a good third of the size normal.

MR. FARES: What happened then, Mr. Horak?

MICHAEL HORAK: Well, then I decided I better do something. I went to the hospital and had my arm X-rayed.

MR. FARES: That evening you went to which hospital?

MICHAEL HORAK: Berwyn, MacNeal Hospital in Berwyn, Illinois.

MR. FARES: You went to the emergency room?

MICHAEL HORAK: Yes.

MR. FARES: When you got there, what did they do for you?

MICHAEL HORAK: They removed the bandages first that I had on, they took the X-rays, and they put the arm in a sling and picked a doctor for me stating that I should be sure to come down Saturday morning at ten o'clock and he would be there waiting for me.

MR. FARES: Who was the doctor?

MICHAEL HORAK: Dr. Asko Ray.

MR. FARES: Did you see Dr. Asko Ray the next morning?

MICHAEL HORAK: Yes, I was there at ten o'clock.

MR. FARES: When you saw Dr. Ray, what if anything did he do for you?

MICHAEL HORAK: He was checking the X-rays, and he looked over the whole arm and everything. About twenty minutes later, he came back into the room and said —

MR. BISHOP: Objection, Your Honor, hearsay.

JUDGE LASSERS: Sustained.

MR. FARES: What did he do, Mr. Horak?

MICHAEL HORAK: He put a hard cast on the arm.

MR. FARES: Where did that hard cast run from?

MICHAEL HORAK: It ran from the lower part of my arm, right in here all the way down to my wrist.

MR. FARES: When you say a hard cast, describe it for us, please.

MICHAEL HORAK: It was just a hard cast that put my arm in a bent position. I've never had a cast on, I don't know what they call it, a regular cast they would put on for a fracture.

MR. FARES: It was a white cast?

MICHAEL HORAK: White hard cast.

MR. FARES: I'm going to show you what's previously been marked as Plaintiff's Exhibit Number ten for purposes of identification. Can you describe that for us?

(Plaintiff's Exhibit Number ten so marked.)

MICHAEL HORAK: That was at Balodimas' Restaurant. He just took that picture. He just took it at that time.

MR. FARES: What does it show?

MICHAEL HORAK: I was sitting at the counter of his restaurant and he took the picture with his camera.

MR. FARES: Is that the cast Dr. Ray put on?

MICHAEL HORAK: Yes.

MR. FARES: Does that truly and accurately depict the cast as it existed on or after June 17th or 1978?

MICHAEL HORAK: Yes. This was a Sunday morning, the day after Dr. Ray put the cast on.

MR. FARES: Now, how long did the cast remain on?

MICHAEL HORAK: Two or three weeks, replaced with other new casts put on after that.

MR. FARES: There was still swelling in your hand during that period of time?

MICHAEL HORAK: The swelling was all the way into the fingers now.

MR. FARES: What else did you notice about yourself during that two- or three-week period of time?

MICHAEL HORAK: Well, I just felt a lot of pain and swelling and I couldn't move my arm anymore because of the cast.

MR. FARES: If you couldn't pick up a knife or a fork, how did you eat?

MICHAEL HORAK: Well, James Balodimas at his restaurant is a personal friend of mine. I would eat at his restaurant every night. He actually came over and cut my food for me up.

MR. FARES: You ate then with your right hand?

MICHAEL HORAK: Yes.

MR. FARES: Finally, Mr. Horak, on or about February fifth of 1979, you saw Dr. Mikhail, is that true?

MICHAEL HORAK: Yes.

MR. FARES: What was the condition of your elbow at that time and your arm generally, your left?

MICHAEL HORAK: The swelling left the hand and was just a puffiness in the inner part of the elbow.

MR. FARES: What about the pain?

MICHAEL HORAK: Well, the sharp pain was there, but now I noticed there was still a numbness in my fingers and some kind of a tingling sensation.

MR. FARES: In what fingers?

MICHAEL HORAK: In the two lower fingers. The other three seemed to be all right (indicating).

MR. FARES: The baby finger and the ring finger you are indicating?

MICHAEL HORAK: Yes, these two fingers here.

MR. FARES: Why did you go see Dr. Mikhail at that time?

MICHAEL HORAK: Dr. Ray said it would be six to eight months before this would heal and it never — seven months went by and the only difference I noticed was that I got the swelling out of my hand, but I still had the pain and I thought I had better get a second opinion.

MR. FARES: You saw Dr. Mikhail at his office?

MICHAEL HORAK: Yes, in Berwyn.

MR. FARES: On that first visit, generally what did he do for you?

MICHAEL HORAK: He had me go to MacNeal, take more X-rays the next day, and he just looked over my arm and took measurements of it and I showed him how I could bend it. The arm wouldn't go back to normal position like that. (Indicating)

MR. FARES: Before your elbow was hit, struck on June 12th of 1978, could your arm go back to normal position?

MICHAEL HORAK: Oh, yes, it could go back, anything.

MR. FARES: What did Dr. Mikhail do for you then?

MICHAEL HORAK: Well, he had me come back three days later when he went to MacNeal to get the X-rays.

MR. FARES: What did he do for you?

MICHAEL HORAK: He gave me an injection shot of cortisone to relieve the pain, prescribed pain pills, took measurements of the arm, and generally just checked me out the rest of the way.

MR. FARES: How long of a period of time did you continue to see Dr. Mikhail after you saw him in 1979?

MICHAEL HORAK: Well, my last visit was December, 1985.

MR. FARES: During that period of time from February fifth or 1979 until today's date, approximately how many times did you see Dr. Mikhail?

MICHAEL HORAK: Between sixty to eighty office visits.

[END THIS PORTION OF TRANSCRIPT]

Mr. Fares's remaining questions to me dealt with how I started with my beginning of horses in my early years up to the present date of the trial. Mr. Fares finished with me at noon on January 31st, 1986.

Judge Lassers called for a recess until 1:30 p.m. He said that we would resume the trial at that time.

Mr. Bishop called me to the witness stand for cross-examination. For the entire afternoon, he kept pounding me with many of the same questions of what took place on the night of June 12th, 1978, over and over. Not once did Mr. Fares object to his badgering tactics.

At five o'clock, Judge Lassers intervened. He said, "Mr. Bishop., I have patiently sat here as well as these jurors all afternoon. It seems as though you are stuck in a rut of questions. I've heard some as much as six or seven times and you always receive the same answer from Mr. Horak, Now let's get on with the case."

Mr. Bishop started to raise his voice at Judge Lassers, but he was ready for him. He quickly stated, "Mr. Bishop, if you can't conduct yourself in a professional manner, I'm sure we can go into my chambers to find out who's in control of these court proceedings." Bishop's six-foot frame seemed to shrink to five-foot, as he meekly said, "Your Honor, I was only trying to get a few facts into the open." Judge Lassers, looking at his watch said, "I believe that we are already a half-hour late in going home for the week-end." He said, "This court is in recess until Monday morning, February 3rd, 1986 at nine-thirty in the morning."

The jurors rose and slowly filed out, handing their notebooks and pens to the Bailiff for safe-keeping. Each of their names were on the front covers.

Mr. Fares and I were the last to leave the courtroom. As he finally said, "Michael John, you did real good on the stand this afternoon," I wanted to ask him if he had fallen asleep thus giving Bishop free reign of the courtroom. However, I decided to wait and give him a little more rope, maybe he would hang himself.

Continuing to walk down the long, empty hall way to the elevators, we walked around the corner where they were. There, pressed up next to the wall pretending to be looking over some papers, was, you guessed it, Mr. Ronald Bishop. There was no doubt that he had been there for at least fifteen minutes waiting for Mr. Fares and myself so he could listen to our conversation in the hallway. At that time of the evening, everyone else had left, therefore, our voices could be clearly heard. This clown didn't miss a trick! He was always out there punching away. That was a lot more than my fair-weather lawyer was doing.

After my train ride and long walk home in the blizzard-like conditions, I called Ted then I called Jim Karubas. I filled them both in on the proceedings. Bishop was to continue with his cross-examination of me on Monday morning. I needed a good night's sleep and a relaxing week-end. If Mr. Bishop couldn't break me on the witness stand and I didn't get excited, then just maybe I would have a chance of winning the lawsuit. I sure wasn't getting much help from Fares. I just wondered who wrote his opening statements to the jury. Lord only knows he sure didn't.

February 1, 1986: With the telephone disconnected, I was able to obtain ten hours of sleep with the help of three sleeping pills. After breakfast, I drove to Jack's Men's store in LaGrange and bought two new suits, one tan and the other dark blue. I also got two new pair of shoes, some white shirts, ties and cuff-links. I also added a few extra dollars just to be sure that the tailor would have one of the suits ready by closing time. At least when I faced Mr. Bishop on Monday morning, he would know that I still had a coupe of quarters to my name.

February 3rd, 1986: This had to be the coldest winter for February. The outer storm windows were completely frosted making it impossible to see anything out of them. I knew that the frozen snow would be on the ground for the next few weeks. Buying the two new suits with all of the extras brightened my outlook on that frigid and snowy morning. I was looking forward to the occasion. I carefully placed the new dark-blue suit in a leather suit bag along with a white shirt, light blue tie and new shoes. I would change in the lawyer's small room off the courtroom. The neatly-pressed suit should help my appearance on the witness stand. Walking through the deep snow and riding in a train would have made my clothing somewhat wrinkled and shabby-looking so the extra effort would also make me feel better.

The sidewalks were still snow-packed over a foot deep, making a difficult early-morning walk to the train station a mile away. Having a hot bowl of oatmeal with raisin toast warmed me up during my walk to the Daley center after getting off the train. I also stopped at a restaurant for a cup of hot tea with a spoon of honey.

I waited in the lobby of the Daley Center for my fair-weather lawyer, Mr. Fares at 8:45 a.m. while reading my *Chicago Tribune* newspaper. At 9:15 a.m., he arrived. Before walking in his direction, I waited to be sure he wasn't with his buddy Bishop. That day he was alone. The first thing he said to me was that Bishop said that he had a surprise witness that would win his case so easily that the jurors wouldn't even leave the courtroom to give their decision. He also stated that we should consider closing the case with a small settlement. I quickly told Fares, "You know how I stand on the subject. You tell him that I said that he's bluffing and for him to buy a shovel to do some snow removal from the sidewalks. I said that that was all he would accomplish at that late stage of the trial.

9:30 a.m.: Judge Lassers called the court to order and I was back on the witness stand with Bishop taking a few extra looks at my attire. Compared to his wrinkled suit, his look alone made my day. I knew that there was no way I would let him ruffle my feathers. Try, as he did, all morning and afternoon, he was running out of questions. He was again repeating the same ones over and over. I had to give him credit, he was trying to use every trick in the book. Sportsman Park must have promised him a large bonus if he won, for I hadn't ever seen a lawyer work so hard on a case. Bishop had exhausted every question in the book. Judge Lasser broke up the proceedings at 5:00 p.m.

Mr. Bishop stormed from the courtroom even before the judge had left. Seeing this, gave me the satisfaction of knowing he didn't accomplish all he had planned to do with me. I thought that maybe he would meet with Mr. Fares for dinner later. I couldn't care less.

I hadn't eaten any lunch that day, so I owed myself a delicious Greek dinner. The only restaurant in town for that would be Rodiety's near Adam and Halstead streets. A short cab-ride later, and I was shaking hands with the owner Perry. Two hours later, I boarded the train home. Opening my front door, I heard the phone ringing. I answered it and it was Jim Karubas. He wanted to know when he would be called to testify as Fares hadn't called him or the others. I said, "So what else is new? You know those lawyers think they are some sort of Gods!" Jim remarked, "I know what kind of Gods they are — dammed fools." I said, "Now, Jim, calm down. What goes around, comes around!"

I then spoke with him for over an hour about the events of the day. I told him that I figured he should be finished with Dr. Asko Ray and Dr. Kramel Mikhail after the next day. I also explained that Mr. Fares had already received over $3,000 from me just for the expenses of the doctors' round-trip airline tickets for the court case. The money also was to pay for a motel and rental car for Richard White for when he came from California.

In closing our conversation, I thought that Jim should plan on being called for Thursday. I told him that I would get after Fares to be sure he would call him. With a hearty "Cheers!" I gently hung up the telephone. I made a large cup of hot chocolate and went to bed, setting the alarm for six the next morning.

February 4th, 1986: Mr. Fares called Doctor Asok Ray to the stand. His testimony dealt with the medical aspects of the case. His professional conclusion was of his medical diagnosis of my left elbow. He explained that I "would never be able to use my damaged left arm to any degree as I did in the past." Dr. Asok Ray was on the witness stand for only about twenty minutes by each attorney. This was probably due to the fact that he had only treated me for such a short time.

A five-minute recess was called by Judge Lassers.

Chapter 31

The Trial Continued

At ten-thirty that morning, Dr. Kamel Mikhail was called to the witness stand. At 11:45, many questions were asked of Dr. Mikhail. He gave explanations of the stacks of X-Rays he had presented. The following are excerpts from Dr. Mikhail's testimony:

(WHEREUPON, the witness was duly sworn.)

Dr. Kamel Mikhail, called as a witness herein on behalf of the Plaintiff, having been first duly sworn, was examined and testified as follows:

DIRECT EXAMINATION by Mr. Fares:

MR. FARES: Would you please state your name.

DR. KAMEL MIKHAIL: Kamel, K-A-M-E-L, Mikhail, M-I-K-H-A-I-L.

MR. FARES: What's your profession?

DR. KAMEL MIKHAIL: M.D.

MR. FARES: Are you licensed to practice in the State of Illinois?

DR. KAMEL MIKHAIL: Yes.

MR. FARES: How long have you been licensed to practice in Illinois?

DR. KAMEL MIKHAIL: Since 1959.

MR. FARES: What medical school or schools did you attend?

DR. KAMEL MIKHAIL: I attended medical school in Cairo, Egypt.

MR. FARES: When did you attend that?

DR. KAMEL MIKHAIL: From 1948 to 1955.

MR. FARES: Did you serve any internships?

DR. KAMEL MIKHAIL: Yes.

MR. FARES: Where did you serve internships?

DR. KAMEL MIKHAIL: I served internships in Egypt for six months, England for twenty-two months, and the Unites States for two years.

MR. FARES: Were those internships concentrated in any specific area?

DR. KAMEL MIKHAIL: England mostly orthopedic.

MR. FARES: How long did you serve in England?

DR. KAMEL MIKHAIL: About two years.

MR. FARES: Any residencies?

DR. KAMEL MIKHAIL: They were — the residencies were in England and in the United States.

MR. FARES: When you referred to "internship", you were using that as a like term?

DR. KAMEL MIKHAIL: Six months in Egypt and one year in

the United States.

MR. FARES: Doctor, in preparation for your testimony today, in general, your treatment of Michael Horak, have you had occasion to review the records of MacNeal Hospital, Dr. Asok Ray as well as your own records?

DR. KAMEL MIKHAIL: Yes.

MR. FARES: From time to time, will it be necessary for you to refer to those records in order to refresh your recollection regarding the treatment of Mr. Horak?

DR. KAMEL MIKHAIL: That's correct.

MR. FARES: When you do so, if you would note that you were referring to your records at that time to recall specifically what you were talking about. Did you have occasion to see Michael John Horak on or about February 5th, 1979?

DR. KAMEL MIKHAIL: Yes.

MR. FARES: Where did you see him at that time?

DR. KAMEL MIKHAIL: At my office.

MR. FARES: Did you obtain a history from him?

DR. KAMEL MIKHAIL: Yes.

MR. FARES: And what was the history?

DR. KAMEL MIKHAIL: He was hit on the medial side, that's the inside of the elbow, on June 12th, 1978, at about 10:30 in the evening with a blunt object that felt like a steel rod.

MR. FARES: He was hit on what side of the elbow?

DR. KAMEL MIKHAIL: The inside.

MR. FARES: The medial side?

DR. KAMEL MIKHAIL: The medial side.

MR. FARES: Did you have any history at that time that he had seen anybody for medical treatment before February 5th, 1979?

DR. KAMEL MIKHAIL: Yes, he mentioned that he saw Dr. Ray before.

MR. FARES: Do you know what brought Michael Horak to your office at that time?

DR. KAMEL MIKHAIL: I believe he was recommended by another patient of mine.

MR. FARES: What subjective complaints did he have?

DR. KAMEL MIKHAIL: He was complaining of pain in the medial epicondyle of the left elbow, e-p-i-c-o-n-d-y-l-e, of the left elbow. And flexion of the elbow as bending the elbow was very painful and the grip was weak because of the pain.

MR. FARES: Flexion means what?

DR. KAMEL MIKHAIL: When you bend the elbow.

MR. FARES: And the grip was weak?

DR. KAMEL MIKHAIL: Was weak.

MR. FARES: Why?

DR. KAMEL MIKHAIL: This is more or less universal attachment of muscle in that part of the elbow of the bone. And when you bend the elbow, when you bend the wrist when you grip, the muscle pulls on that part.

[END OF TESTIMONY]

Dr. Kamel Mikhail was on the witness stand for the next hour and a half, bringing his closing remarks in the following court transcript excerpt:

MR. FARES: Let's go back to February 5th, 1979, what treatment at that time did you prescribe for Michael Horak?

DR. KAMEL MIKHAIL: I saw him again on February 15th, after the X-Rays were made and I injected his elbow.

MR. FARES: You did what?

DR. KAMEL MIKHAIL: I injected his elbow.

MR. FARES: What did you inject his elbow with?

DR. KAMEL MIKHAIL: Local anesthetic and steroid clinically known as cortisone.

MR. FARES: What does that do, Doctor? What is the purpose?

DR. KAMEL MIKHAIL: Brings the inflammation down. And I put him on some anti-inflammatory medication.

MR. FARES: What was that?

DR. KAMEL MIKHAIL: Neperson, N-e-p-e-r-s-o-n.

MR. FARES: At that point, did you formulate a preliminary diagnosis.

DR. KAMEL MIKHAIL: Yes.

MR. FARES: What was your preliminary diagnosis?

DR. KAMEL MIKHAIL: Severe contusion of the left elbow.

MR. FARES: And what does that mean, "severe contusion of the left elbow"?

DR. KAMEL MIKHAIL: It's like an injury sustained by a blunt instrument.

MR. FARES: And what is a characteristic of the left elbow, severe contusion?

DR. KAMEL MIKHAIL: Swelling number one, swelling and the skin swells the muscles underneath right down to the bone. Depends on what it is and just pain and discomfort.

MR. FARES: When did you see him next after July 19th?

DR. KAMEL MIKHAIL: It was February 26th, 1979.

MR. FARES: I'm sorry. And on February 26th, 1979, what was Mr. Horak's condition?

DR. KAMEL MIKHAIL: He was better than the time before though he was sore over the medial epicondyle still.

MR. FARES: What did you do for him on that occasion?

DR. KAMEL MIKHAIL: I injected his elbow again.

MR. FARES: Again with the same thing?

DR. KAMEL MIKHAIL: Same medication, yes.

MR. FARES: What else, if anything, did you prescribe?

DR. KAMEL MIKHAIL: Continue on the same medication as before.

MR. FARES: Did you prescribe home treatment for him?

DR. KAMEL MIKHAIL: No, not at that point.

MR. FARES: When did you see him next after February 26th?

DR. KAMEL MIKHAIL: March 12th, 1979.

MR. FARES: March 12th, 1979, what was his condition?

DR. KAMEL MIKHAIL: He was much better but still some tenderness. Sometimes you can break blood vessels there and have them ridge inside the joint and wind up with more problems. That's why we don't like to do it unless it becomes very, very essential.

MR. FARES: After then, what was the next time you saw him?

DR. KAMEL MIKHAIL: January 10th, 1980.

MR. FARES: And at that time what was his condition?

DR. KAMEL MIKHAIL: He had severe pain in the same area. That's the medial epicondyle. The grip was weak. The flexion extension was just about the same.

MR. FARES: Did extension change?

DR. KAMEL MIKHAIL: No.

MR. FARES: What did you do for him?

DR. KAMEL MIKHAIL: Gave him another injection there in the arm.

MR. FARES: The next time you saw him after that?

DR. KAMEL MIKHAIL: Was April 21st, 1980.

MR. FARES: What was his condition at that time?

DR. KAMEL MIKHAIL: He was still tender in the same area and flexion and extension was all the same, no change.

MR. FARES: When you note he was much better that was

not in regard to flexion and extension?

DR. KAMEL MIKHAIL: No, I mean pain-wise.

MR. FARES: When did you see him next after then?

DR. KAMEL MIKHAIL: July 26th, 1984.

MR. FARES: And what was his condition at that time?

DR. KAMEL MIKHAIL: No change since last visit. Still very tender over the medial epicondyle. I gave him some different pain medication.

MR. FARES: What did you give him then?

DR. KAMEL MIKHAIL: Darvoset N-100, non-narcotic medication.

MR. FARES: Pardon?

DR. KAMEL MIKHAIL: Non-narcotic medication.

MR. FARES: When did you see him after that?

DR. KAMEL MIKHAIL: October 11th, 1984.

MR. FARES: Where did you see him then?

DR. KAMEL MIKHAIL: At my office.

MR. FARES: What did you do for him?

DR. KAMEL MIKHAIL: He was still very tender over the medial epicondyle of the left elbow.

MR. FARES: Did you prescribe anything for him at that point?

DR. KAMEL MIKHAIL: No, just continue the physical therapy.

He had skin complaints at that time, unrelated. So I gave him some medication for that.

MR. FARES: When did you see him after October 11th?

DR. KAMEL MIKHAIL: December 11th, 1984. He had pain in the left elbow over the medial epicondyle for four days with numbness of the ring or the fifth finger, the little one and weakness of the grip. Central nervous system was intact except for hypothesia of the ulnar nerve distribution.

MR. FARES: The weakness of the grip — to what do you attribute that at this point?

DR. KAMEL MIKHAIL: The injury still, the pain.

MR. FARES: After December 11th, when did you see him next?

DR. KAMEL MIKHAIL: January 29th, 1985.

MR. FARES: And what was his condition at that time?

DR. KAMEL MIKHAIL: That's when I tagged him a left ulnar neuropathy inflammation of the left ulnar nerve.

MR. FARES: Why did you formulate that diagnosis at that time?

DR. KAMEL MIKHAIL: He was getting worse. He was not letting up at all and I made an entry here, "Maybe will need ulnar nerve transposition." That's when we bring the ulnar nerve from behind the elbow as I showed you that groove and bring it out in front.

MR. FARES: And what does that do, Doctor?

DR. KAMEL MIKHAIL: Avoids the adhesions that were forming here and makes the distance of it shorter so it doesn't get caught when he stretches his arm.

MR. FARES: So at that point you were considering ulnar nerve transplant?

DR. KAMEL MIKHAIL: Yes.

MR. FARES: Why didn't you perform one at that time?

DR. KAMEL MIKHAIL: Well, we don't like to do it unless it's necessary and really becomes a problem.

MR. FARES: When did you see him next after January 29th, 1985?

DR. KAMEL MIKHAIL: He had hypothesia, which is numbness of the left finger and the ring finger and he was very tender over the medial epicondyle of the left arm quite tender over the left ulnar nerve, too, in the elbow.

MR. BISHOP: What was that?

DR. KAMEL MIKHAIL: He was quite tender over the ulnar nerve at the elbow.

MR. BISHOP: The date?

DR. KAMEL MIKHAIL: That's March, 1985.

MR. BISHOP: Thank you.

MR. FARES: When did you see him after March 19th, 1985?

DR. KAMEL MIKHAIL: That was May 7th, 1985.

MR. FARES: What was his condition then?

DR. KAMEL MIKHAIL: His range of motion was the same as in March of 1985.

MR. FARES: What was that?

DR. KAMEL MIKHAIL: That was the flexion was 63 degrees and the extension was 154 degrees. So he lost some degrees in the extension here.

JUDGE LASSERS: 60 on the —

DR. KAMEL MIKHAIL: 63 on the flexion and 154 on extension.

MR. FARES: Doctor, can you demonstrate for us approximately what 154 extension is?

DR. KAMEL MIKHAIL: 63 would be approximately this much, (indicating). And 154 would be that much, (indicating).

MR. FARES: Okay. All right. When you saw him on May 7th, 1985, flexion and extension were the same. What else did you —

DR. KAMEL MIKHAIL: I noted here, "The grip is poor on the left."

MR. FARES: I'm sorry.

DR. KAMEL MIKHAIL: The grip was poor.

MR. FARES: When did you see Michael Horak next?

DR. KAMEL MIKHAIL: The last time I saw him was December 16th, 1985, that was before Christmas.

MR. FARES: His condition at that time?

DR. KAMEL MIKHAIL: His left arm was the same, no change in it with no improvement since the last exam in October. He was tender in the medial, lateral epicondyle. He was starting to have numbness of the fingers again.

MR. FARES: Now, this tenderness, Doctor, that you spoke

of throughout your treatment of Mike Horak over that medial epicondyle, to what do you attribute that it's continued so long?

DR. KAMEL MIKHAIL: It is tendinitis. You see when you have a muscle attached to bone and an injury to that attachment and you keep using that muscle because there is no way that you can stop it always will continue to bother, sometimes for years.

JUDGE LASSERS: It always will what?

DR. KAMEL MIKHAIL: Bother for years, for a long time.

MR. FARES: Now, you noted, Doctor, earlier on the X-Rays taken in 1984 a narrowing of the bone?

DR. KAMEL MIKHAIL: Joint space.

MR. FARES: And sclerotic changes as well as cystic changes?

DR. KAMEL MIKHAIL: Yes.

MR. FARES: Are those in any way related to the tenderness that he continues to experience in that area of his arm?

DR. KAMEL MIKHAIL: They're not related to the tenderness. They're related to the accident itself, the injury itself, but in themselves they will give him pain.

MR. FARES: Okay. What is it at this time, Doctor, your diagnosis regarding Michael John Horak?

DR. KAMEL MIKHAIL: Severe tendinitis and arthritis of the elbow joint.

MR. FARES: You mentioned earlier that there was — you would consider ulnar nerve transplant?

DR. KAMEL MIKHAIL: Ulnar neuropathy, I was just going to

add.

MR. FARES: In relation to the possibility of ulnar nerve transplant, what is your opinion at this time concerning that issue?

MR. BISHOP: Object to the form of the question, Your Honor.

DR. KAMEL MIKHAIL: Strictly speculative.

JUDGE LASSERS: Overruled.

MR. BISHOP: Objection. Pardon me, Your Honor.

JUDGE LASSERS: Overruled.

DR. KAMEL MIKHAIL: Strictly speculative he could, he could not — depending on how much symptoms he have, how much problem he has with that numbness if he starts having numbness and pain on rest then he certainly will need something done.

MR. FARES: That has not occurred as of yet?

DR. KAMEL MIKHAIL: No.

MR. FARES: Only with use?

DR. KAMEL MIKHAIL: Only with use.

MR. BISHOP: Pardon me. Can I have the reporter read the answer back?

(WHEREUPON, the record was read by the reporter as requested.)

MR. BISHOP: I move to strike the question and answer as speculative as indicated by the doctor.

JUDGE LASSERS: The question appropriates the answer. Overruled.

MR. FARES: Thank you. Doctor, based upon your examination and treatment, your review of records and X-Rays in regard to Michael Horak and to a reasonable degree of medical and surgical certainty, do you have an opinion as to whether or not the condition of ill-being as described by you and as currently being experienced by Mr. Horak might or could be related to the incident of June 12th, 1978?

DR. KAMEL MIKHAIL: Could very well be, yes.

MR. FARES: Your opinion is?

DR. KAMEL MIKHAIL: It could be.

MR. FARES: Do you have an opinion based upon a reasonable degree of medical and surgical certainty and again all those other things, review of records, review of X-Rays, your treatments as to whether or not this condition of ill-being as has been described by you and is being experienced by Mr. Horak might or could cause present pain?

DR. KAMEL MIKHAIL: Yes, it would.

MR. FARES: And what type of pain is it that it might or could cause.

DR. KAMEL MIKHAIL: Degree or pain?

MR. FARES: Yes.

DR. KAMEL MIKHAIL: Well, it depends how bad it is at the time. Sometimes they can flare up and rather uncomfortable, very severe pain. Sometimes they just ache.

MR. FARES: Knowing Mr. Horak's condition and again based upon your treatment and what not, do you have an opinion based upon the reasonable degree of medical and surgical certainty as to whether or not Mr. Horak might or could experience pain when he attempts to flex that arm too far or when he attempts to extend that arm too far?

DR. KAMEL MIKHAIL: You mean forceful extension and flexation?

MR. FARES: Yes.

DR. KAMEL MIKHAIL: He couldn't do it.

MR. FARES: He couldn't?

DR. KAMEL MIKHAIL: He couldn't do it, no. The pain would have been severe.

MR. FARES: Pardon me?

DR. KAMEL MIKHAIL: The pain would have been severe for him.

MR. FARES: Okay. Do you have any history, Doctor, of Michael John Horak being a harness race driver?

DR. KAMEL MIKHAIL: He mentioned that to me, yes.

MR. FARES: As he described to you generally and through your own personal knowledge, do you know what's involved in driving a harness horse?

DR. KAMEL MIKHAIL: He does the driving with his left arm.

MR. FARES: Based upon, again, your treatment, your review of X-Rays, review of medical records and to a reasonable degree of medical and surgical certainty, do you have an opinion as to whether or not Michael John might or could engage in the driving of harness horse races at this time?

DR. KAMEL MIKHAIL: Well, I'm not exactly a harness race fan. I've never seen it except once and that was last year because when he was complaining I said I better go and see myself what do they do, how much effort. And apparently from what I have seen, the drivers exert considerable amounts of effort in controlling that animal in front of them.

MR. FARES: So what is your opinion as to whether or not he can engage in the driving of harness racing?

DR. KAMEL MIKHAIL: Under the present circumstances, I doubt it.

MR. FARES: Do you have an opinion based upon a reasonable degree of medical and surgical certainty as to whether or not this condition as described by you and as experienced by Mr. Horak would be permanent?

DR. KAMEL MIKHAIL: Well, from my own experience these are very, very frustrating to a physician as well as the patient because they just don't quit, period. They just can go on and on and on. This is the reason we find patients jumping from one physician to another, one clinic to the other not getting any results. It's a very frustrating problem.

MR. FARES: Is it your opinion that it's a permanent condition?

DR. KAMEL MIKHAIL: I would say, yes.

MR. FARES: Again, do you have an opinion based upon your treatment, your examination and to a reasonable degree of medical and surgical certainty as to whether or not this condition of ill-being as experienced by Mr. Horak and as described by you might or could cause future medical expenses to be incurred.

DR. KAMEL MIKHAIL: It could.

MR. FARES: Do you have an opinion, Doctor, as to what types of future medical expenses would be incurred by — are likely to be incurred by Mr. Horak?

DR. KAMEL MIKHAIL: Physical therapy would be the most considerable one. Surgery maybe considered too.

MR. FARES: Up to this point —

DR. KAMEL MIKHAIL: Medication.

MR. FARES: — you have Mr. Horak on home therapy?

DR. KAMEL MIKHAIL: Yes.

MR. FARES: Why have you not up to this point prescribed physical therapy at the hospital for —

DR. KAMEL MIKHAIL: Because I felt he can do just as good at that time at home instead of incurring the cost of the hospital but, of course, if things change and he deteriorates he will need the hospital care.

MR. FARES: If he were required to go through future physical therapy do you have an estimate as to what cost of that would be in regard to Mr. Horak's condition?

MR. BISHOP: Objection, Your Honor, I think we ought to know what type of surgery we're talking about.

MR. FARES: I didn't mean surgery. I meant physical therapy. Did I say surgery? Scratch surgery, make it physical therapy.

DR. KAMEL MIKHAIL: It is my understanding — don't quote me one way or the other here —

MR. BISHOP: I have to object, Your Honor. If the doctor knows, fine. If he doesn't, tell us.

JUDGE LASSERS: I have to sustain the objection.

MR. FARES: Do you have an opinion, Doctor?

DR. KAMEL MIKHAIL: Each visit costs about $30.00 take or

leave $20.00 one way or the other and three visits can go from 20 to 100. You know, but I don't know how many visits he'll need but the visits are expensive.

MR. FARES: And the type of surgery that you've talked about that might be necessary that is what type of surgery?

DR. KAMEL MIKHAIL: It's transposition of the nerve, taking the nerve from it's home base and putting it in the front.

MR. FARES: You mentioned earlier that at one form of treatment might be to anesthetize the patient and break the adhesions?

DR. KAMEL MIKHAIL: Yes.

MR. FARES: Is that something that in your treatment and in your opinion you were considering Michael Horak might need to have done?

DR. KAMEL MIKHAIL: Not at this time.

MR. FARES: Then in regard to the transposition of the ulnar nerve, do you have an opinion as to what the estimated cost of that would be?

DR. KAMEL MIKHAIL: I can't. I don't do that surgery myself, so I can't tell you what the surgeon would charge and he probably would be in the hospital for a couple of days.

MR. FARES: Do you know what the hospital charges would be in relation to that?

DR. KAMEL MIKHAIL: Probably about $2,000.00 or $3,000.00.

MR. FARES: Doctor, do you have an opinion based upon a reasonable degree of medical and surgical certainty and again based upon your treatment and review of X-Rays as to whether or not the condition as experienced by Mr. Horak and as treated by you and seen by you might or could cause future pain?

DR. KAMEL MIKHAIL: Yes, very likely.

MR. FARES: I have no further questions. Thank you.

[END OF TRANSCRIPT]

At 1:30 p.m., court resumed after an hour lunch break.

Mr. Bishop continued with Doctor Mikhail on the witness stand going over the same questions that Mr. Fares had asked earlier, hoping to obtain some sort of different answers. Try as he might, Dr. Mikhail stood fast. After two hours of questioning, Mr. Bishop stated that he had no further questions. A short recess was then called until 3:45 that afternoon. The following excerpt is from the court transcript:

MR. FARES: Your Honor, at this time, the Plaintiff would call Mr. James Balodimas.

(Witness sworn.)

JAMES BALODIMAS, called as a witness herein, having been first duly sworn, was examined and testified as follows:

DIRECT EXAMINATION by Mr. Fares:

MR. FARES: Would you state your name and spell it, please?

JAMES BALODIMAS: James Balodimas. B-A-L-O-D-I-M-A-S.

MR. FARES: All right, and your address, Mr. Balodimas?

JAMES BALODIMAS: 1698 North Bloomingdale Road.

MR. FARES: What city is that?

JAMES BALODIMAS: Glendale Heights.

MR. FARES: And what is your occupation, sir?

JAMES BALODIMAS: I was restauranteur. Now I'm retired. Nothing to do.

MR. FARES: When you were — a restaurant owner, what restaurant did you own?

JAMES BALODIMAS: The last one was the Chariot Restaurant. You want the address?

MR. FARES: No. That's okay right now. The — do you know Michael Horak, the Plaintiff in this case?

JAMES BALODIMAS: Yes, sir, I know him before, so around —

MR. FARES: How long have you known him?

JAMES BALODIMAS: Oh, between ten to fifteen years.

MR. FARES: What's the nature of your relationship with him?

JAMES BALODIMAS: Well, as a customer and a friend, daily, every other day, to my store like the other customers too.

MR. FARES: Did you know him on or about June 12th of 1978?

JAMES BALODIMAS: Yes, sir.

MR. FARES: All right. And what was the name of the restaurant, if any that you were operating on or about June 12th, 1978?

JAMES BALODIMAS: Chariot Restaurant, Inc.

MR. FARES: Where was that located?

JAMES BALODIMAS: 16th Street and Harlem Avenue in Berwyn.

MR. FARES: Did you see Mr. Horak on June 13th, 1978?

JAMES BALODIMAS: Thirteen?

MR. FARES: Yes.

JAMES BALODIMAS: Yeah, I saw him.

MR. FARES: Where did you see him on June 13th?

JAMES BALODIMAS: He — my place. He come in one night when I was ready to close, late. And I saw his hand is a little swell up, and I tell him, "What happened?"

MR. BISHOP: Objection, Your Honor.

JUDGE LASSERS: Sustained.

MR. FARES: All right. What did you notice about him? What did you notice? What did you see about him, not what was said?

JAMES BALODIMAS: He came as I was ready to close for the day.

MR. FARES: When you were ready to go and close up and you saw him —

JAMES BALODIMAS: Yes, sir.

MR. FARES: — what did you notice about his person, about his condition?

JAMES BALODIMAS: His left hand was bandaged up past his elbow and his fingers were swelled up. He was in terrible pain.

MR. FARES: And that was about June 13th of 1978?

JAMES BALODIMAS: Right, yes, sir.

MR. FARES: All right. When is the next time after that that you saw him?

JAMES BALODIMAS: Oh, about three, four days later, he come.

MR. FARES: And where did you see him then?

JAMES BALODIMAS: Again in my place. That was Sunday, I believe.

MR. FARES: And what was his condition then, did you notice?

JAMES BALODIMAS: Then I saw him with a cast on his arm. And then I was wondering, "What happened to you, Michael?"

MR. FARES: Okay. Don't tell me what he said because there will be an objection. All right. And at that time after you saw him that following Sunday with the cast on his arm, how often did you see him over the next couple of weeks?

JAMES BALODIMAS: That's almost every day, because that particular time, he couldn't use his arm. So he ask me if I can cut his food so he can eat. I said "Okay." From then on, I was doing the same thing until he had the cast off.

MR. FARES: Okay. Thank you, Mr. Balodimas. That's all I have, Your Honor.

JUDGE LASSERS: Thank you.

CROSS-EXAMINATION by Mr. Bishop:

MR. BISHOP: Mr. Balodimas, what was the address of your restaurant?

JAMES BALODIMAS: 7151 West 16th Street.

MR. BISHOP: And that's right near Harlem Street?

JAMES BALODIMAS: It's corner. Harlem and 16th.

MR. BISHOP: Thank you, sir. Thank you very much.

JAMES BALODIMAS: You're welcome.

JUDGE LASSERS: That's it.

MR. BISHOP: That's it, Your Honor.

JUDGE LASSERS: Thank you, Mr. Balodimas.

MR. FARES: At this time, Your Honor, the Plaintiff would call as an adverse witness, Mr. Daniel Groth, one of the Defendants in this cause.

(Witness sworn)

DANIEL GROTH, called as an adverse witness herein, having been first duly sworn, was examined and testified as follows:

CROSS-EXAMINATION by Mr. Fares:

MR. FARES: Sir, your name and address, please?

DANIEL GROTH: My name is Daniel Robert Groth, G-R-O-T-H. My address is Post Office Box 158, Crete, Illinois.

MR. FARES: Are you currently employed?

DANIEL GROTH: Yes, I am.

MR. FARES: What is your current position?

DANIEL GROTH: My current position is vice-president and general manager of Balmoral Racing Club, Inc.

MR. FARES: Now, on or about June 12th of 1978, you were on duty at Sportsman Park, were you not?

DANIEL GROTH: Yes, sir.

MR. FARES: And at that time you were the head of security at Sportsman Park?

DANIEL GROTH: Yes, sir.

MR. FARES: And your employer was the Fox Valley Trotting Association, correct?

DANIEL GROTH: I believe so.

MR. FARES: And in your duties as head of security, you also carried a weapon at all times, did you not?

DANIEL GROTH: Yes, sir.

MR. FARES: All right. And what kind of weapon were you carrying on or about June 12th of 1978?

DANIEL GROTH: I was either carrying a .38 caliber Colt with a four-inch barrel or a .38 caliber Smith and Wesson with a two-inch barrel.

MR. FARES: Now, on that date you allege that you didn't see Mr. Horak until, on that evening, until you saw him handcuffed and sitting on a bench in the security office?

DANIEL GROTH: That's correct.

MR. FARES: All right. And where was that bench located?

DANIEL GROTH: It would be, as you walk through the door, it would be on my left, which would be, I believe, in a, in a Southerly direction.

MR. FARES: It was a gate-type thing?

DANIEL GROTH: A gate, yes.

MR. FARES: Okay. Now, when you walked in, the shades and the windows in the security office were closed so the view to the outside was obliterated, isn't that true?

DANIEL GROTH: That's true.

MR. FARES: And when you got to the office, Gene Oliver, Joe McCarthy and Steve Bajovich were there?

DANIEL GROTH: As best I recall, yes.

MR. FARES: When you got into the office, where was Joe McCarthy?

DANIEL GROTH: He was within the area on the, on this side of the counter.

MR. FARES: When you say — let's use directions. This is an upside down E for —

DANIEL GROTH: He would be East of the counter.

MR. FARES: All right. And he was here in relation to Mr. Horak when he testified he was sitting here, correct?

DANIEL GROTH: That's correct.

MR. FARES: All right. And where was Mr. McCarthy in relation to Mr. Horak?

DANIEL GROTH: He would have been between the counter, the East wall, somewhere in proximity to Mr. Horak.

MR. FARES: Close to Mr. Horak?

DANIEL GROTH: In proximity.

MR. FARES: Where was he — when you say proximity —

DANIEL GROTH: He was in the room. How close he was, I don't know, counselor.

MR. FARES: I mean as close as you are to me?

DANIEL GROTH: No, the room is not that wide so I doubt that it would be — much closer than that.

MR. FARES: Five feet?

DANIEL GROTH: I don't know.

MR. FARES: What was McCarthy doing when you walked in?

DANIEL GROTH: I believe he was standing there.

MR. FARES: And where was Oliver?

DANIEL GROTH: He was also in that area.

MR. FARES: Same area?

DANIEL GROTH: Yes, sir.

MR. FARES: And how about Bajovich?

DANIEL GROTH: Bajovich was in the other area behind the counter, probably sitting behind the desk, if my recollection is correct.

MR. FARES: And you don't remember if anybody else was in there, do you, at that time?

DANIEL GROTH: No, I don't.

MR. FARES: You don't know if there was another patron that was sitting there handcuffed either, do you?

DANIEL GROTH: I have no recollection of another patron being there.

MR. FARES: Okay. It was after you arrived, correct, that you instructed Mr. Bajovich at that point to type up a complaint against Mr. Horak?

DANIEL GROTH: I don't recall.

MR. FARES: You remember giving your deposition on or about January 21st of 1981, correct?

DANIEL GROTH: Yes, sir.

MR. FARES: And a representative from Mr. Bishop's office was there —

DANIEL GROTH: I believe so.

MR. FARES: — in your representation?

DANIEL GROTH: Yes.

MR. FARES: And a Mr. Richard Rock on Behalf of Michael Horak was there?

DANIEL GROTH: I believe so.

MR. FARES: And there were a number of questions asked of you?

DANIEL GROTH: Yes, sir.

MR. FARES: And you gave a number of answers, correct?

DANIEL GROTH: Yes.

MR. FARES: And was this question asked and did you give this answer?

"Question: Okay, What happened next?

Answer: I probably directed Steve Bajovich to type up a complaint for disorderly conduct based on what he told me about his conduct. The complaint was signed."

MR. FARES: And that was on your arrival after Mr. Horak was already handcuffed?

DANIEL GROTH: Mr. Horak was obviously in custody when I arrived in the office, that is correct, a little bit afterwards.

MR. FARES: Okay. But at that time, likewise, none of the security guards reported to you that they had any physical contact whatsoever with Mr. Horak on that evening?

DANIEL GROTH: That's correct.

MR. FARES: In the normal course of operations, in frisking and arresting a patron, it would be typical to take that person's personal property such as a wallet?

DANIEL GROTH: It would depend on the situation. What do you mean by "take it", please? You mean remove it?

MR. FARES: Yes.

DANIEL GROTH: And do what with it? And place it on the counter area?

MR. FARES: It would be normal to remove something such as a wallet from the person, isn't that true?

DANIEL GROTH: Sometimes, yes.

MR. FARES: Okay. As to these particular detectives — let's start with Joe McCarthy. When did you first hire him?

DANIEL GROTH: Probably about, some time in late 1977, early 1978.

MR. FARES: How long did he work for you?

DANIEL GROTH: Approximately one year.

MR. FARES: How did you know Joe McCarthy?

DANIEL GROTH: I worked with him in the 18th Police District.

MR. FARES: Did Fox Valley Trotting or you as head of the department of security, provide any training for Joseph McCarthy in regard to his duties at the track?

DANIEL GROTH: Yes, sir.

MR. FARES: What training did you provide?

DANIEL GROTH: We — we had a manual that indicated the type of activities that might occur at a racetrack, and we also give them some training in the rules and regulations of horse racing and the statutory requirements under the Illinois Horse Racing Act. But again, Joe McCarthy was a captain in the Chicago Police Department and well-trained.

MR. FARES: All right. I'm talking about the racetrack in particular. Was this, by the way, some type of a class that Joe McCarthy would attend?

DANIEL GROTH: That would be — as relates to the rules and regulations, he would have been provided with a copy of the statute as it relates to the Illinois Horse Racing Act. Plus, there was a, a guide that indicated, would tell a new employee what the duties were as it relates to either uniformed guard or a detective.

MR. FARES: So those would all be provided to him?

DANIEL GROTH: That's correct.

MR. FARES: And he'd be instructed to read that?

DANIEL GROTH: Yes, sir.

MR. FARES: Was he ever given any test regarding those?

DANIEL GROTH: Not to my knowledge.

MR. FARES: How about Eugene Oliver? Did you hire Eugene Oliver there at the track?

DANIEL GROTH: Yes, I did?

MR. FARES: And when did you hire him?

DANIEL GROTH: I am going to say 1968 or 1969.

MR. FARES: Let's go back to Joe McCarthy for a minute. Other than these manuals that you provided for him, the statute and the manual and whatnot, was there any training provided him by Fox Valley Trotting Association as opposed to the training that you may have provided him with in the manuals?

DANIEL GROTH: Well, we were working under the auspices of Fox Valley Trotting and the National Jockey Club. This material was routinely part of the function of the security office when he worked for Fox Valley or National Jockey Club.

MR. FARES: So, what you're telling me, the answer to my question is "no", there was nothing more that Fox Valley or National Jockey provided than what you yourself provided?

DANIEL GROTH: Than what we provided, that is correct.

MR. FARES: How about Eugene Oliver, did you provide him with those manuals?

DANIEL GROTH: Eugene Oliver had been a detective at this time, probably ten years on the racetrack. He had originally been trained under the Illinois Bureau of Racetrack Police as a uniformed guard. One of his responsibilities was policing racetracks, so this would — I didn't hire him myself until 1968 to work directly for me.

MR. FARES: Would that pre-exist 1968 that he —

DANIEL GROTH: Yes, sir.

MR. FARES: So is that how you knew Eugene Oliver?

DANIEL GROTH: Yes, sir.

MR. FARES: That's how you came into direct contact with him?

DANIEL GROTH: Yes, sir.

MR. FARES: Do you know what type of training he was provided, what was that?

DANIEL GROTH: Illinois Bureau of Racetrack Police.

MR. FARES: Illinois Bureau of Racetrack Police?

DANIEL GROTH: Yes, sir.

MR. FARES: What type of training was he provided?

DANIEL GROTH: He would have been providing training, in, again, the rules and regulations set forth by the Illinois Racing Board and also by statute, the Illinois Horse Racing Act, report writing, mob and bomb control. There was about

10 or 12 categories that they were provided training in.

MR. FARES: Was this classroom instruction?

DANIEL GROTH: Some of it was, yes.

MR. FARES: How much of it?

DANIEL GROTH: I would say, initially, several hours.

MR. FARES: Incidentally, before you walked into the security office and saw Mike Horak there, where were you?

DANIEL GROTH: I was either in the Grandstand or the Clubhouse, in the buildings.

MR. FARES: You don't remember specifically?

DANIEL GROTH: I was throughout the plant, as I would do on a nightly basis, as I do on a regular basis. I was somewhere within the plant.

MR. FARES: How about Steven Bajovich? What was he on that evening?

DANIEL GROTH: Steve, that evening, was acting as office manager or secretary.

MR. FARES: Would that give him a position in terms or hierarchy above Oliver and McCarthy?

DANIEL GROTH: Probably above, yes. He would be making assignments that evening.

MR. FARES: How long had he been there employed at the track?

DANIEL GROTH: Approximately four years.

MR. FARES: Did you hire him?

DANIEL GROTH: Yes, I did.

MR. FARES: How did you come to know Steve Bajovich?

DANIEL GROTH: He made application.

MR. FARES: You didn't know him before he made application.

DANIEL GROTH: I don't believe I did.

MR. FARES: How did you make physical contact with Michael Horak on that night?

DANIEL GROTH: You're talking about contact, sir.

MR. FARES: Did you physically eject him?

DANIEL GROTH: If I don't see him physically, I certainly can't eject him, can I?

MR. FARES: That's what physically eject means to me.

DANIEL GROTH: When I walk up to him, I see him physically. If I don't see him, obviously he's not there physically.

MR. FARES: Hold on just a minute here. Did Mr. Langley tell you, "If you physically see Mr. Horak, eject him from the racetrack"?

DANIEL GROTH: If I see Mr. Horak, eject him from the racetrack.

MR. FARES: He told you if you see Mr. Horak, you were to physically eject Horak from the track, correct?

DANIEL GROTH: I don't recall the exact language, counselor.

MR. FARES: I have nothing further. Thank you, Mr. Groth.

JUDGE LASSERS: All right. Do you wish to question him at this point?

MR. BISHOP: Oh, you bet I do, Your Honor.

Chapter 32

More Witnesses

MR. FARES: Your honor, please, I object and move that counsel's remarks be stricken.

JUDGE LASSERS: Mr. Bishop, if you could just answer without commenting, okay? All right.

REDIRECT EXAMINATION by Mr. Bishop:

MR. BISHOP: When you went by the office and saw that the shades were closed, why did you go inside?

DANIEL GROTH: I saw the shades were closed; that indicated to me that there was a problem of some kind. I wanted to go in and find out what it was.

MR. BISHOP: What I'm getting at, was there a usual practice and procedure at that track as well as other tracks you worked at —

MR. FARES: Objection, Your Honor, as to the other tracks.

JUDGE LASSERS: Sustained.

MR. BISHOP: I'll confine it to this track. Was there a usual practice at this track as to when the shades would be pulled up and when the shades would be pulled down?

DANIEL GROTH: If you had a prisoner or an unruly customer, you would pull up the shades so the person would not be in the public view.

JUDGE LASSERS: So what?

DANIEL GROTH: So the person would not be within view of the public.

JUDGE LASSERS: I see. Okay.

MR. BISHOP: And that was the usual and customary practice back in 1978 at Sportsman Park?

DANIEL GROTH: Yes, sir.

MR. BISHOP: And when you saw that condition, walking by the security office, that told you that there was a problem?

DANIEL GROTH: That's correct.

MR. BISHOP: Someone was in custody for one reason or another?

DANIEL GROTH: Not necessarily someone in custody but there was a problem.

MR. BISHOP: And is that why you went into the office at that time?

DANIEL GROTH: Yes, sir.

MR. BISHOP: Had those shades been pulled up and closed, would there be any reason for you to go in there at that time?

DANIEL GROTH: I probably would not have gone in; just passed by and waved to them or something.

MR. BISHOP: I have nothing further.

(The following proceedings were held in open court where Mr. Fares called Aristotle Glazos to the witness stand for examination.)

DIRECT EXAMINATION by Mr. Fares:

MR. FARES: Sir, can you state and spell your last name.

ARISTOTLE GLAZOS: Spell my last name?

MR. FARES: State your full name.

ARISTOTLE GLAZOS: Aristotle Glazos. G-L-A-Z-O-S.

MR. FARES: All right. And do you use any nicknames?

ARISTOTLE GLAZOS: Ted, T-E-D.

MR. FARES: And your occupation?

ARISTOTLE GLAZOS: I'm retired.

MR. FARES: Okay. And how long have you been retired?

ARISTOTLE GLAZOS: Since 1983.

MR. FARES: Now, sir, do you have any or have you had any experience or relationship with harness racing?

ARISTOTLE GLAZOS: How's that?

MR. FARES: Have you had any — let me get a little closer.

ARISTOTLE GLAZOS: I'm a little hard of hearing.

MR. FARES: Have you had any experience or relationship with harness racing?

ARISTOTLE GLAZOS: Well, I started racing in 1957, 1958.

MR. FARES: In what — how did you start racing? What was your capacity?

ARISTOTLE GLAZOS: Well, I had two partners, and we

bought two or three horses at the sale, three it was.

MR. FARES: All right. Now, your relationship throughout this period of time, say, from 1957, you were never a driver of harness horses?

ARISTOTLE GLAZOS: No, strictly an owner.

MR. FARES: All right. And how long did you continue to own horses, harness horses?

ARISTOTLE GLAZOS: Until 19, the Fall of 1959. That was a period of a year.

MR. FARES: All right. And after that time, did you own any more harness horses?

ARISTOTLE GLAZOS: No, I got interested in the restaurant business, and I re-entered harness racing in 1967.

MR. FARES: All right. And then you were involved in owning harness horses from 1967 until what time?

ARISTOTLE GLAZOS: Oh, I sold out about 1979, 1980, right in there.

MR. FARES: Why did you sell out at that time?

ARISTOTLE GLAZOS: I had a heart attack and an operation and I was advised to get out.

MR. FARES: Do you know Michael John Horak?

ARISTOTLE GLAZOS: Yes.

MR. FARES: And how long have you known Michael John Horak?

ARISTOTLE GLAZOS: Since 1968.

MR. FARES: And what was your relationship with him?

ARISTOTLE GLAZOS: Strictly friends, acquaintances at that time.

MR. FARES: During the years that you first met Mr. Horak, have you come to know him as a trainer of horses?

ARISTOTLE GLAZOS: Yes.

MR. FARES: And what have you come to know about him in that capacity.

ARISTOTLE GLAZOS: Well, we got acquainted when he was at Sportsman Park. That was in 1968. And of course, visiting him all the time. He had a nice spot on the South end of the first barn area. We used to talk. And, of course, I had my own horses. And over a period of time, why I got to know his training habits and his methods and so forth, and I liked him.

MR. FARES: Okay. Did he ever train a horse for you through 1979?

ARISTOTLE GLAZOS: No, he's never trained any of my horses.

MR. FARES: All right. Did you, at any point before 1979, attempt a business venture with Mr. Horak?

ARISTOTLE GLAZOS: Well, we got started on it. We got started in about 19, oh, '77, in '76, in '75 or '76 my trainer died and I continued training with his father-in-law because he had a farm up in Wisconsin in which I had some mares, and I was racing colts.

MR. FARES: All right.

ARISTOTLE GLAZOS: So I felt an allegiance to him and I continued with him for a year or two. And then we started to look for colts, Michael John and I.

MR. FARES: All right. And where did that hunt or looking for colts bring you?

ARISTOTLE GLAZOS: Well, we first went to Brandywine.

MR. FARES: Where's Brandywine?

ARISTOTLE GLAZOS: Maryland.

MR. FARES: All right. Go ahead. What did you see there?

ARISTOTLE GLAZOS: Well, we heard that Joe Brian had a tar heel colt there by the name of Lincoln and he was going pretty cheap, so we went to look at him. We saw him race. In fact, we flew there to watch him race.

MR. FARES: Yourself and Michael John Horak?

ARISTOTLE GLAZOS: Yes, we went together. We flew there.

MR. FARES: Okay. What year was that?

ARISTOTLE GLAZOS: That was 19, oh, '76, '77, right in there.

MR. FARES: All right. And what was your purpose in bringing Michael John along with you at that time?

ARISTOTLE GLAZOS: Well, I wanted to buy some colts.

MR. FARES: Did you buy Lincoln?

ARISTOTLE GLAZOS: No, we didn't. He ran a very poor race so we decided against him.

MR. FARES: All right. Did you look at any other horses with Michael John?

ARISTOTLE GLAZOS: We went to Pompano. We looked at some Bret Hanovers and some Nordon Grand Slam colts.

MR. FARES: What are those things?

ARISTOTLE GLAZOS: Well, Nordon Grand Slam is a sire, very good sire and Bret Hanovers, of course, was a champion. And colts, you know, develop a little minor problem, and these grand circuit driver's don't want them, they want to sell them off. So we thought we might pick up a bargain there.

MR. FARES: And what did you find in Pompano? When did you go to Pompano?

ARISTOTLE GLAZOS: We went to Pompano, I think it was about that same time. It was all in the same year that we started to look. As soon as my trainer died, why then thereafter, we started making plans to maybe start racing a few horses —

MR. FARES: All right.

ARISTOTLE GLAZOS: — with Michael John.

MR. FARES: What then happened in Pompano.

ARISTOTLE GLAZOS: Nothing. The colts were too high-priced.

MR. FARES: All right.

ARISTOTLE GLAZOS: They were asking 50, 60 thousand for them, and that was out of our range.

MR. FARES: Where else, if anywhere, did you go?

ARISTOTLE GLAZOS: Well, we went to Lexington, I believe. Then, of course, we looked at a lot of colts in Sportsman Park.

MR. FARES: All right. Thank you Mr. Glazos. That's all I have.

MR. BISHOP: No questions at all. Thank you very much, sir.

JUDGE LASSERS: All right. Thank you Mr. Glazos.

(Mr. Fares then called James Karubas as a witness)

(Witness sworn)

JAMES KARUBAS,called as a witness herein, having been first duly sworn, was examined and testified as follows:

DIRECT EXAMINATION by Mr. Fares:

MR. FARES: Sir, would you state your name, please?

JAMES KARUBAS: Jim Karubas.

JUDGE LASSERS: How do you spell that?

JAMES KARUBAS: K-A-R-U-B-A-S.

MR. FARES: All right. And your address?

JAMES KARUBAS: 2418 East Martindale Drive.

MR. FARES: And your occupation?

JAMES KARUBAS: Food manager.

MR. FARES: Do you know the Plaintiff in this cause, Michael Horak?

JAMES KARUBAS: Yes, I do.

MR. FARES: And how long have you known him?

JAMES KARUBAS: For about 20 years.

MR. FARES: And what's the nature of your relationship with him?

JAMES KARUBAS: We were in the horse business together.

MR. FARES: Now, you said that you were in the horse business together with Mr. Horak. When would that have been?

JAMES KARUBAS: 1965.

JUDGE LASSERS: Are you finished?

MR. FARES: Judge, I have one more question.

JUDGE LASSERS: Sure, go ahead.

MR. FARES: Mr. Karubas, you gave some testimony on cross-examination concerning the length of time that the horses were in business and what-not and also the way that Michael Horak trained the horses. Knowing all those things in 1978, you were again ready to go into business with Michael John Horak as your trainer, co-owner and driver?

MR. BISHOP: Object to the leading nature of the question, Your Honor.

JUDGE LASSERS: I think — I am going to sustain it. You really covered in on direct.

MR. FARES: Well, let me rephrase it then, Your Honor, please. At that time, in 1978, you were willing to go back into business with Mr. Horak as an owner and trainer and driver of your horses?

JAMES KARUBAS: Yes, we were.

MR. BISHOP: Same Objection, Your Honor.

JUDGE LASSERS: Overruled. All right.

MR. FARES: Thank you Mr. Karubas. I have nothing further.

RECROSS EXAMINATION by Mr. Bishop:

MR. BISHOP: If I understand what you told us, you were in business with Mr. Horak for six years; that's 1972 to this plan you said you had in 1978, is that right?

JAMES KARUBAS: Yes.

MR. BISHOP: No further questions.

JUDGE LASSERS: You can step down. Thank you for your coming down.

MR. FARES: Your Honor, at this time, the Plaintiff would call to the stand as an adverse witness, Mr. Joe McCarthy.

(Witness sworn)

JOSEPH McCARTHY, called as an adverse witness herein, having been first duly sworn, was examined and testified as follows:

CROSS-EXAMINATION by Mr. Fares:

MR. FARES: Your name, sir?

JOSEPH McCARTHY: Joseph McCarthy.

MR. FARES: And you're one of the Defendants in this case, are you not?

JOSEPH McCARTHY: That's correct.

MR. FARES: Your address, Mr. McCarthy?

JOSEPH McCARTHY: 5009 West Balmoral.

MR. FARES: And where is that, sir?

JOSEPH McCARTHY: In Chicago.

MR. FARES: Now, directing your attention to June 12th, 1978, on that night you were on duty at Sportsman Park as a private security guard or private investigator, is that true?

JOSEPH McCARTHY: That's correct.

MR. FARES: All right. And at that time also, you were a Chicago policeman?

JOSEPH McCARTHY: I was employed —

MR. FARES: You were also employed as a Chicago policeman?

JOSEPH McCARTHY: That's correct.

MR. FARES: But you were not on duty as a Chicago policeman at that time?

JOSEPH McCARTHY: No, I wasn't.

MR. FARES: And you weren't acting in your capacity as a Chicago policeman.

JOSEPH McCARTHY: No, I wasn't.

MR. FARES: And at that time, you were employed by Fox Valley Trotting Association?

JOSEPH McCARTHY: That's correct.

MR. FARES: All right. And Fox Valley, at that time, employed security guards, is that correct?

JOSEPH McCARTHY: That's my understanding, yes.

MR. FARES: And were you carrying a weapon on that evening?

JOSEPH McCARTHY: Yes, I was.

MR. FARES: What kind of weapon were you carrying?

JOSEPH McCARTHY: A .38 Colt snub-nose.

MR. FARES: Now, you allege that you did not see Michael John Horak that particular evening until he came into the security office.

MR. BISHOP: Objection, Your Honor.

MR. FARES: What's the basis?

MR. BISHOP: This man is a Defendant. He's made no allegations at all. Object to the form of the question.

JUDGE LASSERS: Why don't you reframe the question?

MR. FARES: You didn't see Michael John Horak on 6/12/1978 on that evening until he came into the security office, is that true?

JOSEPH McCARTHY: The best of my recollection, yes.

MR. FARES: So your partner on that night was Eugene Oliver, is that correct?

JOSEPH McCARTHY: That's correct.

MR. FARES: But you did not go with Eugene Oliver to pick up Mr. Horak?

JOSEPH McCARTHY: The best of my recollection, no, I didn't.

MR. FARES: What time was it then, that you first saw Mr.

Horak in the security office?

JOSEPH McCARTHY: Some time after eight o'clock in the evening.

MR. FARES: And Eugene Oliver brought him in, isn't that true?

JOSEPH McCARTHY: That's correct.

MR. FARES: Who else was with Eugene Oliver when he brought him in?

JOSEPH McCARTHY: I don't know.

MR. FARES: There was somebody else?

JOSEPH McCARTHY: I'm not sure.

MR. FARES: That security office is separated, isn't it, by a counter?

JOSEPH McCARTHY: That's correct.

MR. FARES: There was a desk behind the counter?

JOSEPH McCARTHY: Correct.

MR. FARES: And when Michael John Horak was brought in by Eugene Oliver, Michael John Horak stayed on the East side of the counter, correct?

JOSEPH McCARTHY: Yes, correct.

MR. FARES: You were also on the East side of the counter?

JOSEPH McCARTHY: That's correct.

MR. FARES: And Eugene Oliver walked around, behind the counter?

JOSEPH McCARTHY: That's correct.

MR. FARES: And Steve Bajovich was also there that evening?

JOSEPH McCARTHY: Yes, he was.

MR. FARES: And where was Steve Bajovich sitting?

JOSEPH McCARTHY: I think he was sitting at the desk.

MR. FARES: And what was he doing, do you remember?

JOSEPH McCARTHY: No, I don't.

MR. FARES: Do you remember what Michael Horak was doing?

JOSEPH McCARTHY: At which point?

MR. FARES: When he first came in.

JOSEPH McCARTHY: My first recollection is that he was at the security — at the counter.

MR. FARES: At this counter?

JOSEPH McCARTHY: Right.

MR. FARES: About where at the counter was he?

JOSEPH McCARTHY: Approximately in the middle.

MR. FARES: Here someplace? (Indicating.)

JOSEPH McCARTHY: Yes.

MR. FARES: And where were you when he first came in, at the counter?

JOSEPH McCARTHY: I believe I was to his right.

MR. FARES: How close to him?

JOSEPH McCARTHY: Several feet.

MR. FARES: Three feet?

JOSEPH McCARTHY: More than that, five feet.

MR. FARES: Five feet?

JOSEPH McCARTHY: Five feet, six feet.

MR. FARES: And to his right?

JOSEPH McCARTHY: Yes.

MR. FARES: Where were you standing when the door first opened?

JOSEPH McCARTHY: I don't recall.

MR. FARES: You were on this side of the counter, though.

JOSEPH McCARTHY: Yes, I was.

MR. FARES: Did you know Mike Horak was coming in?

JOSEPH McCARTHY: No, I didn't.

MR. FARES: Was there anybody else in the security office other than Bajovich, Oliver, yourself and Horak at that time?

JOSEPH McCARTHY: I don't recall.

MR FARES: In reference to Michael Horak's arrest, the arrest occurred prior to any struggle that you claim occurred that evening?

JOSEPH McCARTHY: Yes.

MR FARES: Correct?

JOSEPH McCARTHY: Yes.

MR FARES: You told Horak, allegedly, to empty his pockets and you got no response?

JOSEPH McCARTHY: That's correct.

MR FARES: Then you started to frisk Mr. Horak?

JOSEPH McCARTHY: That's correct.

MR FARES: Correct?

JOSEPH McCARTHY: Correct.

MR FARES: How did you begin to frisk him?

JOSEPH McCARTHY: Probably, depending on how he was dressed — I don't recall at the time — but I would normally start at the top and pat down.

MR FARES: Okay. Do you recall — would it refresh your recollection if I told you there had been testimony that he had on a light turtleneck shirt that night?

JOSEPH McCARTHY: No, it wouldn't.

MR FARES: Okay. I don't want a "probably". Do you know how you began to frisk him that night?

JOSEPH McCARTHY: I either started at the chest here or at the waistline.

MR FARES: All right. But you don't recall specifically where you started?

JOSEPH McCARTHY: No, I don't.

MR FARES: And then what did you do in your frisking?

JOSEPH McCARTHY: Mr. Horak grabbed my arm.

MR FARES: Oh, wait a minute. In your frisking, what did you do?

JOSEPH McCARTHY: I frisked him.

MR FARES: All the way down?

JOSEPH McCARTHY: I never got that far.

MR FARES: Okay. And at that point Michael Horak, according to your claim —

MR. BISHOP: Objection, Objection.

MR FARES: — grabbed your right arm with his left arm, with his left hand.

MR. BISHOP: Object to the form of the question, Your Honor. This man has claimed nothing.

JUDGE LASSERS: Oh, he gave a deposition.

MR. BISHOP: I know he gave a deposition, but he has claimed nothing. He has responded to questions.

JUDGE LASSERS: All right. That may be. That may be. All right. Go ahead.

MR FARES: Thank you, Judge. You were standing behind Mike Horak at this time, correct?

JOSEPH McCARTHY: Correct.

MR FARES: And he was still standing at the counter?

JOSEPH McCARTHY: That's correct.

MR FARES: Correct? And you were relatively close to him, I assume?

JOSEPH McCARTHY: Yes, I was?

MR FARES: All right. And you claim that he grabbed your right arm with his left arm?

JOSEPH McCARTHY: That's correct.

MR FARES: So he would be reaching over in this type of fashion? (Indicating)

JOSEPH McCARTHY: He half turned.

MR FARES: Like this? (Indicating)

JOSEPH McCARTHY: He half turned.

MR FARES: Okay. And the impetus of this contact, him grabbing your left arm, made you both fall to the ground?

JUDGE LASSERS: He grabbed which arm?

JOSEPH McCARTHY: He grabbed my right arm.

JUDGE LASSERS: With his —

JOSEPH McCARTHY: I believe it was his left arm.

MR FARES: Let me withdraw that last question and ask you one before that. At that point you grabbed both of Horak's arms?

JOSEPH McCARTHY: I attempted to grab his arms, yes.

MR. FARES: Well, did you grab them or did you attempt to grab them?

JOSEPH McCARTHY: I remember grabbing one. I don't

remember if I had both the —

MR. FARES: And then the impetus of the contact made you both fall to the ground?

JOSEPH McCARTHY: That's correct.

MR. FARES: All right. You fell on your right side?

JOSEPH McCARTHY: Correct.

MR. FARES: Correct? And Horak fell to his right side or face down?

JOSEPH McCARTHY: To the best of my recollection, that's correct.

MR. FARES: And you're sure of that?

JOSEPH McCARTHY: Yes.

MR. FARES: And then as soon as he hit the ground, one way or the other he was turned face down?

JOSEPH McCARTHY: That's correct.

MR. FARES: And you got on his back?

JOSEPH McCARTHY: Correct.

MR. FARES: Where did you get on his back, what part of his body.

JOSEPH McCARTHY: On his back.

MR. FARES: Right here? (Indicating)

JOSEPH McCARTHY: His lower back.

MR. FARES: Sat on it, laid on it, what did you do?

JOSEPH McCARTHY: Sat on it.

MR. FARES: And you told him at that time to put his hands behind his back?

JOSEPH McCARTHY: That's correct.

MR. FARES: And he put his hands behind his back voluntarily?

JOSEPH McCARTHY: The best of my recollection, he did.

MR. FARES: And this is the same man that was pounding and hollering and grabbing at you that voluntarily put his hands behind his back?

JOSEPH McCARTHY: Yes, he was the same man.

MR. FARES: Horak never pushed you, did he?

MR. BISHOP: Your Honor, now I move to strike the dialogue for the reason that it is not inconsistent with what the witness has already testified to. That's exactly what he told us.

JUDGE LASSERS: I don't think it's inconsistent.

MR. FARES: Your Honor, it's not inconsistent except that then again in the same deposition —

JUDGE LASSERS: I can't hear you.

MR. FARES: Then again, in the same deposition, Mr. McCarthy goes on to state that there was — that Michael Horak grabbed his arm. There is nowhere in this deposition that he says that he pushed him, nowhere.

JUDGE LASSERS: That's not a significant difference between grabbing and pushing.

MR. FARES: Your Honor, may I be heard on this point now or after Mr. McCarthy testifies?

JUDGE LASSERS: Go on. But really, I'll sustain the objection.

MR. BISHOP: Thank you your honor.

MR. FARES: Your Honor, it is an important point to this case, and I'd like to be heard after Mr. McCarthy's testimony.

JUDGE LASSERS: All right. Great. Okay. Go ahead. Next question.

MR. FARES: In regard to this handcuffing of Michael Horak and the grabbing and the wrestling, no one else assisted you at any time, is that true?

JOSEPH McCARTHY: Not that I recall.

MR. FARES: And to the point that Mike Horak was put in a chair or a bench in the security office, no one else assisted you, is that true?

JOSEPH McCARTHY: Before he was put in the chair, he was searched.

MR. FARES: And you did the searching?

JOSEPH McCARTHY: Yes, I did.

MR. FARES: Nobody else helped you to search him?

JOSEPH McCARTHY: I don't recall if anyone else did or not.

MR. FARES: And you didn't find a weapon on him, did you?

JOSEPH McCARTHY: No, I didn't.

MR. FARES: He had a wallet?

JOSEPH McCARTHY: Yes, he did.

MR. FARES: And you took the wallet out of his pocket?

JOSEPH McCARTHY: Yes, I did.

MR. FARES: And according to you, Michael Horak made no complaints of pain whatsoever following this incident?

JOSEPH McCARTHY: None that I —

MR. BISHOP: Objection, Your Honor. He's assuming there is an injury, and that's an issue very much present in this case.

JUDGE LASSERS: Overruled, overruled.

MR. BISHOP: I'm objecting.

JUDGE LASSERS: Overruled.

MR. FARES: Thank you, Your Honor.

JUDGE LASSERS: All right, go ahead.

MR. FARES: He made no complaints of pain whatsoever following this incident?

JOSEPH McCARTHY: None that I recall.

MR. FARES: And during the period of time that this all occurred, Daniel Groth was in the office some time, but you don't remember specifically when?

JOSEPH McCARTHY: That's correct.

MR. FARES: You don't remember either if the shades were up or down on that evening?

JOSEPH McCARTHY: No, I don't.

MR. FARES: Did you sign a complaint for battery against Mr. Horak?

JOSEPH McCARTHY: No, I didn't.

MR. FARES: Well, from what you just told us occurred, that was a battery, was it not?

MR. BISHOP: If the Court pleases, that calls for a legal conclusion.

JUDGE LASSERS: Well, I think so. I —

MR. FARES: He's testified —

MR. BISHOP: Objection, Your Honor.

JUDGE LASSERS: Sustained.

MR. FARES: Your Honor, he's testified that —

MR. BISHOP: Objection, Your Honor. The Court has ruled.

JUDGE LASSERS: Just a moment. The man is entitled to speak, Mr. Bishop.

MR. BISHOP: He is not entitled to argue with the Court's ruling.

JUDGE LASSERS: That's up to me, not up to you, Mr. Bishop. Now, go ahead, Mr. Fares.

MR. FARES: Your Honor, this man has testified that he was a police officer for the city of Chicago. He knows what a battery is and when there is grounds —

JUDGE LASSERS: That may be. It's a matter of fact whether he signed a complaint or he didn't sign a complaint, all right?

MR. FARES: Why didn't you sign a complaint for battery.

JOSEPH McCARTHY: I didn't think it was serious enough to sign a complaint for battery.

MR. FARES: That's all I have, thank you.

(The following is an excerpt from Mr. Bishop's examination of Joseph McCarthy:)

MR. BISHOP: Now, you had frisked people before, had you not, sir?

JOSEPH McCARTHY: Yes, I have.

MR. BISHOP: And you went about the usual and customary procedure in frisking Mr. Horak that you had followed on other occasions, hadn't you?

JOSEPH McCARTHY: Yes.

MR. FARES: Your Honor, I am going to have to object to the leading of the witness.

JUDGE LASSERS: Sustained, Sustained. Don't lead your witness. Just a moment, Mr. Bishop. Don't lead your witness.

MR. BISHOP: I agree, Your Honor. How did you go about frisking Mr. Horak?

JOSEPH McCARTHY: Well, generally you start at the top —

MR. FARES: Your Honor, I am going to ask — he's asking him specifically what he did, and he's answering in general.

JUDGE LASSERS: I'll overrule it. Go ahead.

JOSEPH McCARTHY: Generally, you either start at the top or depending how he is dressed, maybe you might start at the waist and pat down.

MR. FARES: Your Honor, again I am going to object. He testified three times he doesn't remember with Mr. Horak other than he just started.

JUDGE LASSERS: Overruled.

JOSEPH McCARTHY: I'm not sure.

MR. BISHOP: Did you get to the waistline?

JOSEPH McCARTHY: I — I'm not positive. I don't know.

MR. BISHOP: You indicated something about Mr. Horak turning and grabbing you, isn't that correct?

JOSEPH McCARTHY: That's correct.

MR. BISHOP: With his left hand?

JOSEPH McCARTHY: He reached around with his left —

MR. BISHOP: Would you stand up in the witness stand there and describe for the ladies and gentlemen of the jury, the best you can recall, the movement that Mr. Horak made when you attempted to frisk him?

JOSEPH McCARTHY: (Indicating)

MR. BISHOP: He turned to his right and reached — sit back down again — and reached with which hand?

JOSEPH McCARTHY: His left hand.

MR. BISHOP: And when he reached with his left hand, where did he make contact with your body?

JOSEPH McCARTHY: With my right arm.

MR. BISHOP: Where on your right arm?

JOSEPH McCARTHY: I think the upper part.

MR. BISHOP: And when that happened, what did you do?

JOSEPH McCARTHY: I grabbed for him.

MR. BISHOP: Okay. And did you succeed in grasping him with both hands or only with one hand?

JOSEPH McCARTHY: I'm not sure. I know I hit him with one hand.

MR. BISHOP: What happened next?

JOSEPH McCARTHY: We both fell down.

MR. BISHOP: Landed on the floor?

JOSEPH McCARTHY: That's correct.

MR. BISHOP: When you landed on the floor, what parts of Mr. Horak could you see?

JOSEPH McCARTHY: His back.

MR. BISHOP: And seeing his back, what was the first thing you did?

JOSEPH McCARTHY: I pushed, either pushed my gun on top of his back and told him to put his hands behind his back.

MR. BISHOP: And did you slide up on top of him?

JOSEPH McCARTHY: Yes, I did.

MR. BISHOP: So you kind of pushed him over and slid up on top of him?

MR. FARES: Your Honor, again leading and repeating testimony.

JUDGE LASSERS: Sustained.

MR. BISHOP: You were then up on top of Mr. Horak?

JOSEPH McCARTHY: That's correct.

MR. BISHOP: And then what did you do?

JOSEPH McCARTHY: I told him to put his hands behind his back.

MR. BISHOP: And what occurred?

JOSEPH McCARTHY: And he did.

MR. BISHOP: You put on the handcuffs?

JOSEPH McCARTHY: Yes.

MR. BISHOP: Then what did you do?

JOSEPH McCARTHY: We got up, I helped him up and we — I searched him.

MR. BISHOP: How long did this whole series of events take from the starting to frisk until you and Mr. Horak got back up off the floor? What kind of a time schedule are we talking about?

JOSEPH McCARTHY: Five, ten seconds, I guess.

MR. BISHOP: In connection with that, did you say anything to Mr. Horak or did he say anything to you right after you got the handcuffs on him or got back up?

JOSEPH McCARTHY: I don't recall.

MR. BISHOP: You don't recall saying anything to him?

MR. FARES: Asked and answered, Your Honor.

MR. BISHOP: Do you recall him saying —

JUDGE LASSERS: What?

MR. FARES: Your Honor, this has been asked and answered. He asked him if he said anything to Horak, and he said he doesn't recall. And now he's asking the same questions again.

JUDGE LASSERS: What was your last question?

MR. BISHOP: Did he say anything to Mr. Horak, and he said he doesn't remember. Now I'm asking, Did Mr. Horak say anything to you?"

MR. FARES: Your Honor, may we have the court reporter read it back from the point of the first question?

JUDGE LASSERS: It's not that significant. Did Horak say anything to you?

JOSEPH McCARTHY: I don't recall if he said anything to me.

JUDGE LASSERS: All right. Next question.

MR. BISHOP: There was also mention, then, of a search. What were the things that were taken from Mr. Horak's pocket? Where were they placed?

JOSEPH McCARTHY: They were placed on the counter.

MR. BISHOP: And at that time, where was Mr. Horak standing?

JOSEPH McCARTHY: I think he was back up by the counter where the incident started.

MR. BISHOP: I have nothing further. Thank you, sir.

JUDGE LASSERS: All right, is there any additional adverse?

MR. FARES: About five questions, Judge.

JUDGE LASSERS: All right

RECROSS EXAMINATION by Mr. Fares:

MR. FARES: You stated that you had a conversation or that Mr. Horak and Eugene Oliver were having a conversation. You don't recall what was said during that period of time, do you?

JOSEPH McCARTHY: No.

MR. FARES: And you said specifically in your testimony on direct examination — on cross-examination by me earlier, that when Horak fell, he fell — that number one, you fell to your right side, correct?

JOSEPH McCARTHY: (Nodding)

MR. FARES: You have to answer out loud, sir.

JOSEPH McCARTHY: Yes.

MR. FARES: And that Horak also fell either to his right side or face down, correct?

JOSEPH McCARTHY: That's what I said, yes.

MR. FARES: Now, you just — stand up once more, if you will, and show us how you grabbed — how Mr. Horak turned and grabbed your right arm with his left arm.

JOSEPH McCARTHY: Around like this. (indicating)

MR. FARES: Now, earlier when you did that, you brought that left leg around, didn't you?

JOSEPH McCARTHY: He turned halfway and took, with his left arm, grabbed my right arm.

MR. FARES: And you — and you were then — he turned and you were then facing him, in effect, is that true?

JOSEPH McCARTHY: I was facing his side, yes.

MR. FARES: So you were kind of like — he was kind of like parallel to you?

JOSEPH McCARTHY: He was turning like this, and I was right here. (indicating)

MR. FARES: Okay. Hold that position in your mind. Now show me in relation to Horak where you where?

JOSEPH McCARTHY: Back here. (indicating)

MR. FARES: That far away?

JOSEPH McCARTHY: No, I was right behind him.

MR. FARES: The chair is in your way. I just want to make sure. And you fell on your right side. And when you fell, did Horak still have a grab on your left arm — on your right arm?

JOSEPH McCARTHY: No, I don't think so.

MR. FARES: What happened to that?

JOSEPH McCARTHY: I think the impetus made him let go.

MR. FARES: Okay, I have nothing more, Your Honor.

JUDGE LASSERS: Are we all done?

MR. BISHOP: Yes, sir.

JUDGE LASSERS: All right. Thank you very much.

MR. FARES: Thank you Mr. McCarthy.

JUDGE LASSERS: All right. Fine. Let's see if we can get in another witness before lunch.

MR. FARES: Your Honor, at this time the Plaintiff will call Mr. Richard White.

(Whereupon, the witness was duly sworn)

RICHARD WHITE, called as a witness herein on behalf of the Plaintiff, having been first duly sworn, was examined and testified as follows:

DIRECT EXAMINATION by Mr. Fares:

MR. FARES: Sir, would you please state your name?

RICHARD WHITE: My name is Richard White.

JUDGE LASSERS: How do you spell the last name?

RICHARD WHITE: W-H-I-T-E.

MR. FARES: And your address, Mr. White?

RICHARD WHITE: 1906 South Overland in Los Angeles.

MR. FARES: California?

RICHARD WHITE: California.

MR. FARES: And what's your occupation, sir?

RICHARD WHITE: I'm a project manager.

MR. FARES: What does that mean? What do you do?

RICHARD WHITE: I have an engineering degree and I oversee projects. Basically build tanks for gasoline and mainly I work for a pipeline company.

MR. FARES: Are you married?

RICHARD WHITE: No, I'm single.

MR. FARES: Any children?

RICHARD WHITE: No.

MR. FARES: Mr. White, I'm going to direct your attention to the evening of June 12th, 1978, did anything unusual occur that evening?

RICHARD WHITE: Yes.

MR. FARES: What happened?

RICHARD WHITE: What happened to me?

MR. FARES: Yes, sir.

RICHARD WHITE: I was arrested that evening.

MR. FARES: Where?

RICHARD WHITE: Sportsman Park Race Track.

MR. FARES: What time did you get to Sportsman Track on that evening?

RICHARD WHITE: Before the first race. I believe post time was about 8:00 p.m. So probably around 7:30.

(End of court transcript)

For the next hour, Mr. Fares and Mr. Bishop continued to question Richard White about his activities on the night of June 12th, 1978.

Richard White testified that he accidentally bumped into a lady while hurrying to make a wager on a horse that was about to race. He explained that two of Sportsman Park security guards happened to see the incident, and immediately escorted him to the security office. There, they physically assaulted him until I yelled at them to stop. The horrible events that followed concluded his testimony.

Chapter 33

Eugene Oliver

MR. FARES: The Plaintiff will call as an adverse witness, Mr. Eugene Oliver.

(Witness sworn)

EUGENE OLIVER, called as a witness herein, having been first duly sworn, was examined and testified as follows:

CROSS-EXAMINATION
by Mr. Fares:

Eugene Oliver

MR. FARES: State your name, please.

EUGENE OLIVER: Eugene A. Oliver.

MR. FARES: And your address?

EUGENE OLIVER: 2822 74th Avenue, Elmwood Park, Illinois.

MR. FARES: Do you also go by the nickname Gino?

EUGENE OLIVER: That's correct, sir.

MR. FARES: On 6/12 of 1978, you were on duty as a security investigator at Sportsman Park, is that correct?

EUGENE OLIVER: Yes, sir.

MR. FARES: And your employer at the time was National Jockey Club.

EUGENE OLIVER: That's correct.

MR. FARES: And were — you were carrying a nine millimeter automatic weapon at that time, correct?

EUGENE OLIVER: Yes, sir.

MR. FARES: All right. Now, directing your attention again to 6/12 of 1978, on that evening the first time you saw Michael John Horak, he was, according to you, he was at a gate near the Paddock area where horses entered the track, correct?

EUGENE OLIVER: Yes, sir.

MR. FARES: Now, referring to Plaintiff's Exhibit Number 1, already admitted into evidence, this is a representation of the layout of the track, this being the Paddock area, the Grandstand the security office, the Clubhouse, and this being the track itself with this representing the fence. Is that a fair description?

EUGENE OLIVER: If that's the way you put it there.

MR. FARES: I'm asking you, sir, if it's a fair description?

EUGENE OLIVER: The Grandstand, yes, that's — Paddock, Grandstand.

MR. FARES: It's not to scale.

EUGENE OLIVER: Yes.

MR. FARES: Generally, the horses would come out of the Paddock here and enter the track at a gate which is located approximately here? (indicating)

EUGENE OLIVER: Right.

MR. FARES: In relation to this gate, where did you first see Michael Horak?

EUGENE OLIVER: At the fence line next to the track.

MR. FARES: All right. And this is when — which side of this gate?

EUGENE OLIVER: It would be on the west.

MR. FARES: On this side of the gate? (indicating)

EUGENE OLIVER: That's correct.

MR. FARES: And how close to this?

EUGENE OLIVER: Maybe ten feet.

MR. FARES: This area someplace generally, correct? (indicating)

EUGENE OLIVER: Right.

MR. FARES: And where were you when you first saw him?

EUGENE OLIVER: I was walking on the outside of the Grandstand walking towards the Paddock.

MR. FARES: In this area here someplace? (indicating)

EUGENE OLIVER: It's an apron. Call it an apron. The building inside is the Grandstand area on the first floor. They have an apron and then the track. Up on the second floor is the seating area of the Grandstand. I was walking —

MR. FARES: On the lower floor?

EUGENE OLIVER: On the apron of the first floor Grandstand.

MR. FARES: When you first saw Michael Horak, how far were you from him?

EUGENE OLIVER: Oh, approximately, maybe a hundred yards, fifty yards, something like that.

MR. FARES: And at that time, according to you, Joseph McCarthy was with you?

EUGENE OLIVER: I believe so.

MR. FARES: You're sure he was with you?

EUGENE OLIVER: That's who I believe was with me.

MR. FARES: This was after the eighth race?

EUGENE OLIVER: It was sometime during that period.

MR. FARES: Now, you received, on that evening — the reason why you were going to look for Mr. Horak is because you received a radio call that there was a disturbance involving Mr. Horak?

EUGENE OLIVER: That's correct.

MR. FARES: The Paddock judge on that night was Frank Pennino?

EUGENE OLIVER: That's correct, yes.

MR. FARES: And the Paddock judge has an office in the Paddock area, is that correct?

EUGENE OLIVER: Correct.

MR. FARES: And he was in the Paddock building on that

evening?

EUGENE OLIVER: He goes inside the Paddock and outside the Paddock.

MR. FARES: Well, when you say “outside”, you mean into the Paddock area?

EUGENE OLIVER: He walks up to the fence area then goes back into the office and walks into the Paddock area where the horses are being readied for the races.

MR. FARES: And, according to you, drivers — some drivers, that being Busse and Paisley, complained to the Paddock judge that Michael Horak was creating a disturbance; the Paddock judge called the general manager, Phil Langley. Langley then called Steve Bajovich, who was in the security office, and Bajovich radioed to you to go and pick up Mr. Horak?

EUGENE OLIVER: I — I don’t recall where the complaint originated from. All I can recall is that I received a call from our office, stating that there was an incident at the Paddock area with Mr. Horak.

MR. FARES: Has your memory been completely exhausted regarding that?

EUGENE OLIVER: If you maybe refresh my memory, maybe I can help you. I don’t —

MR. FARES: Let me mark this.

JUDGE LASSERS: All right. This now is a deposition?

MR. FARES: This is the deposition of Gene Oliver, and for these purposes, I’ll mark it Plaintiff's Exhibit —

JUDGE LASSERS: What was the date of the deposition?

MR. FARES: The date of the deposition being May 9 of 1980.

JUDGE LASSERS: All right. You're going to — what number is that?

MR. FARES: The number, I think is 35.

(Plaintiff's Exhibit Number 35 was marked for identification.)

MR. FARES: I'll ask you to refer to this area and ask you if that refreshes your recollection.

EUGENE OLIVER: Where at, counselor? Which one?

MR. FARES: Here.

EUGENE OLIVER: Ten?

MR. FARES: Yes.

EUGENE OLIVER: Yes, sir.

MR. FARES: Okay. Does that refresh your recollection then as to —

EUGENE OLIVER: That's what I stated.

MR. FARES: Then —

MR. BISHOP: If the Court please, Your Honor, I have an objection as to point of time that this information came into this man because we know he received the message over a radio, but we —

JUDGE LASSERS: Why don't you clarify the time then, Mr. Fares?

MR. FARES: All right. You received the message over the radio before you saw Mr. Horak, as you earlier testified here, over by the gate, correct?

EUGENE OLIVER: Would you repeat that, sir?

MR. FARES: You want to read it back, sir?

(Record read)

EUGENE OLIVER: That's correct.

MR. FARES: And that was the call that came from the Paddock judge to Phil Langley and then to Bajovich?

EUGENE OLIVER: Not to my knowledge, not at that time. I wasn't aware of where it originated from.

MR. FARES: You later learned that though, didn't you?

EUGENE OLIVER: I—I must have learned that later if I said it in that deposition there.

MR. FARES: You did say it in the deposition?

EUGENE OLIVER: What does it say in the deposition there?

MR. FARES: Deposition, page 16, line 7 through 14.

> "Question: Okay. Do you know who it was that contacted the security office to tell the desk men to have someone go down there?"
>
> "Answer: It was a report that I learned after where the complaint came from, that the drivers complained to the Paddock judge. The Paddock Judge, in turn called the general manager, and the general manager, in turn called the security, and then the security called office called us."

EUGENE OLIVER: That's correct, sir.

MR. BISHOP: Your Honor, I will adopt that in view of the fact that the answer said that —

MR. FARES: Your Honor, it's not his to adopt. If he's got an objection, let him make his objection.

MR. BISHOP: Your Honor, I don't know whether this is impeachment. I don't know whether this is refreshing his recollection, I —

JUDGE LASSERS: It's refreshing his recollection. Let's put the next question.

MR. FARES: Thank you, Judge. And from the time that you got the radio call until the time that you got to the Paddock area, that took you about two minutes?

EUGENE OLIVER: Approximately.

MR. FARES: And when you got there, Michael Horak was hollering at Daryl Busse and Walter Paisley who were two drivers, and he was waiving his arms?

EUGENE OLIVER: That's correct.

MR. FARES: And at that time, Busse and Paisley were still on the track after the race that had just been run, coming back to the Paddock area?

EUGENE OLIVER: That's correct.

MR. FARES: And, as I understand, the running of a race — and you have been there for a period of time, haven't you? You know how the races are run, correct?

EUGENE OLIVER: Yes, sir.

MR. FARES: The race come around, finishes at the finish line, correct? And then the drivers take the horses around and get off, and either a groom or hot walker takes them back to the barn, correct?

EUGENE OLIVER: That's right.

MR. FARES: So how could it have been then, that these drivers, Busse and Paisley, who were just in that race, had complained to Frank Pennino, Pennino complained to Langley, Langley had complained to the security office, the security office called you, and it took you two minutes to get there and those horses were still — and those drivers were still on the track after the race and hadn't come in yet?

MR. BISHOP: If the Court please, I object to the form of the question, and if counsel has those questions, they should be more properly addressed to the people who performed this conduct that he claimed they performed. This witness testified as to what he did, not what somebody else did.

JUDGE LASSERS: I think that's an appropriate question. Overruled. Go ahead.

EUGENE OLIVER: You want to repeat that question again?

MR. FARES: Sure.

JUDGE LASSERS: Let's have it read back. It's a long question.

(Record read)

MR. BISHOP: I have a further objection, Your Honor. I don't think we know when the complaint was made by Mr. Busse or Mr. Paisley or whoever it was that made the complaint. I don't know whether it was before the race or —

JUDGE LASSERS: You can go into that. Overruled. Go ahead.

EUGENE OLIVER: That area where they dismount and turn the horses over to the groom or hot walker or their assistant trainer isn't that far from the entrance to the Paddock.

MR. FARES: Okay. How could all of that time expire between the time that Horak was hollering and the time that the — and yet the driver's still on the track there?

EUGENE OLIVER: Okay.

MR. BISHOP: If the Court please, this witness has not testified as to what Mr. Horak was doing before he got there.

JUDGE LASSERS: That's —

MR. BISHOP: I don't know how he can know what Mr. Horak was doing before he got there, and I object to the form of the question.

JUDGE LASSERS: Overruled. Do you understand the question, Mr. Oliver?

EUGENE OLIVER: Yes, sir.

JUDGE LASSERS: Okay. Go ahead.

EUGENE OLIVER: They get off their horse. They get off by the — off of the trotting horse, and they turn it over to a groom or hot walker or assistant trainer, and then they walk into the Paddock area.

MR. FARES: When they walk into the Paddock area, Mr. Oliver, they don't walk in at this gate over here, do they? (indicating)

EUGENE OLIVER: Yes, they do.

MR. FARES: There's another gate further down there, isn't there?

EUGENE OLIVER: That's correct.

MR. FARES: And generally, they walk in here, don't they? (indicating)

EUGENE OLIVER: Not Generally.

MR. FARES: Well, do they walk in there?

EUGENE OLIVER: They walk in both gates.

MR. FARES: But at the time that you arrived, Busse and Paisley were still on their horses, weren't they?

EUGENE OLIVER: No.

MR. FARES: And then at this time, when you first saw Horak, any patrons that were in the area were moving away from the area after the race, isn't that true?

EUGENE OLIVER: Moving away from where the shouting was coming from.

MR. FARES: From this area here, sir? (indicating)

EUGENE OLIVER: From where Mr. Horak was standing.

MR. FARES: Right.

EUGENE OLIVER: Pardon me, sir?

MR. FARES: They were moving away from that area, true?

EUGENE OLIVER: Yes, they were moving away from Mr. Horak.

MR. FARES: They were moving away from the area?

EUGENE OLIVER: They were moving away from Mr. Horak.

MR. FARES: Your Honor, I am going to object to that answer and ask that it be stricken as being non-responsive to my question.

MR. BISHOP: Your Honor, he's asked the question, the same question four times.

JUDGE LASSERS: Well, I think it is. Go ahead. Put another question.

MR. FARES: What was the ruling, Judge? I'm sorry.

JUDGE LASSERS: I think it's responsive. Go ahead. Put another question.

MR. FARES: All right. You didn't talk to any of those patrons?

EUGENE OLIVER: No, sir.

MR. FARES: So you don't know why they were moving away from that area, do you?

EUGENE OLIVER: To me it appeared —

MR. FARES: Not what it appeared.

MR. BISHOP: Objection, Your Honor. Let the witness answer.

JUDGE LASSERS: All right. This is — you're asking him now and he is giving you the basis of his last answer. Okay. All right.

EUGENE OLIVER: To me it appeared that the people were turning around looking at Mr. Horak and moving away from him.

MR. FARES: But you didn't talk to any of these people?

EUGENE OLIVER: That wasn't what I was sent down there for.

MR. FARES: I understand that, Mr. Oliver. You didn't talk to him, is that correct?

EUGENE OLIVER: To the patrons?

MR. FARES: Right.

EUGENE OLIVER: That's correct.

MR. FARES: And this was after a race?

EUGENE OLIVER: Yes, sir.

MR. FARES: And after a race, people move away from the fence to cash in their tickets or look at their books or get a refreshment or something of that nature before the next race, don't they. It's not an uncommon thing?

EUGENE OLIVER: No, sir.

MR. FARES: And in regard to — incidentally, you claimed that when you first saw Mr. Horak, he was swearing and raising his arms and things of that nature, correct?

EUGENE OLIVER: That's correct, sir.

MR. FARES: But you don't recall any swear words that he used, do you?

EUGENE OLIVER: I can't recall, no, sir.

MR. FARES: And you approached him and asked him to come to the security office?

EUGENE OLIVER: Yes, sir.

MR. FARES: And what did he say?

EUGENE OLIVER: He said, "For what reason?"

MR. FARES: And what did you say?

EUGENE OLIVER: I said, "We want to try to solve this problem here that's — that you're causing a problem here. So come on down to the security office and let's see if we can work this out."

MR. FARES: And what did he say?

EUGENE OLIVER: "Okay."

MR. FARES: Page 19, lines 14 through 20, or 14 through 22. Again, you remember being at your deposition in May of 1980?

EUGENE OLIVER: I remember a deposition.

JUDGE LASSERS: There was one deposition. It's the same deposition.

MR. FARES: I don't think we went through this, Judge.

JUDGE LASSERS: Not with Mr. Oliver. All right. Go ahead. Lay your foundation.

MR. BISHOP: Is this page 17?

MR. FARES: Page 19.

MR. BISHOP: I'm sorry. What lines are you talking about?

MR. FARES: There was an attorney there on behalf of Mr. Horak, Mr. —

EUGENE OLIVER: I don't know who the people were.

MR. FARES: There was a lawyer representing you there?

EUGENE OLIVER: I imagine there was, sir.

MR. FARES: And a lawyer representing Mr. Horak?

EUGENE OLIVER: I — I have no idea if he has a lawyer or not. I imagine it was. If it's down there it was a lawyer, then he was a lawyer.

MR. FARES: He was asking questions?

EUGENE OLIVER: I imagine so, sir.

MR. FARES: And you were giving answers?

EUGENE OLIVER: That's correct, sir?

MR. FARES: And did you — were these questions asked and were these answers given?

> "We asked Mr. Horak if he would mind coming down to the security office.
>
> "Question: What was his response?
>
> "Answer: And he started hollering and waiving his arms again. I told Mr. Horak, 'We can't settle nothing out here. If you have any complaints.'
>
> "Question: Who was he hollering to at this point?
>
> "Answer: Just hollering in general, hollering at myself, hollering at my partner, just hollering."

MR. BISHOP: If the Court please, I move to strike the dramatics.

JUDGE LASSERS: Strike what?

MR. BISHOP: The dramatics, the way in which the question was asked of the witness.

MR. FARES: Your Honor, I —

MR. BISHOP: Your Honor, I think that —

MR. FARES: Well, Your Honor, if he moves to strike the dramatics, Mr. Bishop is —

JUDGE LASSERS: Counsel, counsel, one at a time. I don't think there was any undue dramatics.

MR. BISHOP: I also move to strike the question and answer. It's not the least bit inconsistent with what the witness said.

JUDGE LASSERS: There is a certain inconsistency here.

MR. BISHOP: No, Your Honor. I must take exception. But you're the boss.

JUDGE LASSERS: Okay. All right. Overruled.

MR. FARES: His objection is noted. May I go ahead, Your Honor?

JUDGE LASSERS: Yes, overruled. We're getting toward the lunch hour, so find an appropriate time to wind up.

MR. FARES: You want me to rush, Judge?

JUDGE LASSERS: No, no, the farthest thing from my mind. But just find an appropriate breaking point. That's all.

MR. FARES: When you got to the security door, you don't recall who went in first or if you went in first or Mr. Horak or your partner, whoever that was, you don't recall?

EUGENE OLIVER: I can't recall, sir, no.

MR. FARES: And at that time, Daniel Groth was in the office, wasn't he?

EUGENE OLIVER: I believe that he was in the office then.

MR. FARES: When you arrived?

EUGENE OLIVER: When I — yes.

MR. FARES: And at that time, Steve Bajovich was in the office also, is that correct?

EUGENE OLIVER: That's correct.

MR. FARES: And was Joe McCarthy in the office?

EUGENE OLIVER: Yes.

MR. FARES: Now, where was Dan Groth when you arrived in the office? Let's — you've seen this as you have been sitting here, haven't you?

EUGENE OLIVER: Yes, sir.

MR. FARES: Pretty fairly depicts the way the security office was set up?

EUGENE OLIVER: I would have to make changes there.

MR. FARES: What changes would you make?

EUGENE OLIVER: Well, I would have to make the desk all the way over to the wall with a typewriter.

MR. FARES: This desk all the way over here? (indicating)

EUGENE OLIVER: Right.

MR. FARES: What other changes?

EUGENE OLIVER: Typewriter right behind it.

MR. FARES: Behind the desk here?

EUGENE OLIVER: Right.

MR. FARES: Okay.

EUGENE OLIVER: And a big file cabinet against the back wall right there. Okay. And a big garbage can right against the side wall.

MR. FARES: Somewhere here? (indicating)

EUGENE OLIVER: Closer to — well, it isn't really that — it isn't that wide either, you know —

MR. FARES: The office —

EUGENE OLIVER: There's not that much room.

MR. FARES: The office is about 12 by 15, isn't it?

EUGENE OLIVER: I wouldn't say that.

MR. FARES: How big was the office?

EUGENE OLIVER: I would say maybe 13 by 13, something like that.

MR. FARES: Judge, I think this is an appropriate place to stop for now.

JUDGE LASSERS: All right. Let's adjourn now until 1:30 okay? See you all then.

(Court recessed until 1:30 p.m.)

MR. FARES: Okay. Also when you approached Mr. Horak you said that there were Daryl Busse and Walter Paisley present at that time, is that true?

EUGENE OLIVER: I didn't say that, sir.

MR. FARES: Were they present at that time?

EUGENE OLIVER: I can't recall.

MR. FARES: Do you recall if any drivers were present?

EUGENE OLIVER: I really don't recall. I know there was shouting there by Mr. Horak.

MR. FARES: Now, when you got into the security office, where did you go?

EUGENE OLIVER: I came in through the doorway.

MR. FARES: This doorway? (indicating)

EUGENE OLIVER: That's correct. Came in through the swinging door.

MR. FARES: How long did that take you?

EUGENE OLIVER: Matter of seconds.

MR. FARES: You walked in here, and then where did you go?

EUGENE OLIVER: I went behind the counter.

MR. FARES: Behind this counter? (indicating)

EUGENE OLIVER: Yes.

MR. FARES: Which way did you face?

EUGENE OLIVER: I faced Mr. Horak.

MR. FARES: At that point then, how long did it take you to get from here to here? (indicating)

EUGENE OLIVER: A matter of a second or two.

MR. FARES: And at that point then when you turned and

faced Mr. Horak, where was he standing?

EUGENE OLIVER: Right in front of me.

MR. FARES: He was on the other side of the counter?

EUGENE OLIVER: That's correct.

MR. FARES: Had anybody up to that point touched Mr. Horak in any way?

EUGENE OLIVER: No, sir.

MR. FARES: He came in willingly, correct?

EUGENE OLIVER: Yes, just hollering.

MR. FARES: And he was standing there willingly?

EUGENE OLIVER: Hollering and banging on the counter.

MR. FARES: He was there willingly? That's my question.

EUGENE OLIVER: I imagine he did come willingly. I imagine we asked him to come in there, sir.

MR. FARES: He was there willingly, correct?

EUGENE OLIVER: I imagine so.

MR. FARES: And he was standing right across from you?

EUGENE OLIVER: That's correct.

MR. FARES: Where was Joe McCarthy then?

EUGENE OLIVER: Joe McCarthy was on the right-hand side of Mr. Horak.

MR. FARES: And at that point when you first got to the

counter, how far was Joe McCarthy behind Mr. Horak?

EUGENE OLIVER: I believe that he was right behind him.

MR. FARES: Like a foot, two feet away?

EUGENE OLIVER: Two feet maybe, approximately.

MR. FARES: And just to Mr. Horak's right side?

EUGENE OLIVER: I believe so.

MR. FARES: On your way in, do you recall if Mr. McCarthy was — On the way in from the time that you left the Paddock area to the time that you got to the counter, did you have any conversation with Mr. McCarthy?

EUGENE OLIVER: I don't recall, sir.

MR. FARES: Do you recall if Mr. McCarthy said anything to you?

EUGENE OLIVER: I can't recall.

MR. FARES: Okay. And at that point where was Steve Bajovich?

EUGENE OLIVER: At what point, sir?

MR. FARES: The point that you were right at the corner.

EUGENE OLIVER: He was behind the desk facing the doorway.

MR. FARES: So this desk, as you testified earlier —

JUDGE LASSERS: Just a moment. Excuse me.

(Whereupon, there was a short interruption.)

MR. FARES: As you testified earlier, this desk was moved over further?

EUGENE OLIVER: Correct.

MR. FARES: And Steve Bajovich was sitting behind the desk?

EUGENE OLIVER: Correct.

MR. FARES: Facing the door?

EUGENE OLIVER: Correct.

MR. FARES: Was there anything of a physical nature in between you and Steve Bajovich other than this desk?

EUGENE OLIVER: Physical nature between myself and Mr. Bajovich? The desk.

MR. FARES: Other than the desk.

EUGENE OLIVER: Not that I can recall.

MR. FARES: The desk is about this high, maybe? (indicating)

EUGENE OLIVER: Standard desk table, yes.

MR. FARES: At that time the shades were drawn in the office? They were closed, correct?

EUGENE OLIVER: I can't recall.

MR. FARES: Again, I show you what's been marked as Plaintiff's Exhibit Number 35, for purposes of identification. That being the deposition. I ask you to refer to page 29, lines 15 — lines 13 through 16. Does that refresh your recollection as to whether or not —

EUGENE OLIVER: Wait, 13?

MR. FARES: 13.

EUGENE OLIVER: Okay.

MR. FARES: Does that refresh your recollection as to whether or not the shades were drawn at that time?

MR. BISHOP: At what time?

JUDGE LASSERS: At the time —

MR. BISHOP: Will you get a point of reference in time, Your Honor?

MR. FARES: Your Honor, I'm talking —

JUDGE LASSERS: I do not think it is necessary.

EUGENE OLIVER: Would you repeat it, sir. I'm sorry.

MR. FARES: Does that refresh your recollection as to whether or not the shades were drawn?

EUGENE OLIVER: No, it doesn't.

MR. FARES: Now, after you were with Mr. Horak at the counter, at some point you told him that he was arrested, and then instantly after that, you turned your back on him, is that true?

EUGENE OLIVER: No, that's not true.

MR. FARES: Are you saying that you never told Mr. Horak that he was arrested?

EUGENE OLIVER: No, I didn't say that.

MR. FARES: Then at some point after you first got at that

counter, you told Mr. Horak that he was arrested?

EUGENE OLIVER: After I got to that counter —

MR. FARES: Wait a minute.

MR. BISHOP: If the Court please, Your Honor —

JUDGE LASSERS: This man is giving an answer.

MR. FARES: Your Honor, this is cross-examination.

JUDGE LASSERS: I understand that, but you asked a question. Mr. Oliver was starting to answer, and then you cut him off.

MR. FARES: I'm sorry.

EUGENE OLIVER: Do you want to repeat the question?

MR. BISHOP: Can we have the reporter read the question, Your Honor?

JUDGE LASSERS: Would you read the question?

(Whereupon, the record was read by the reporter as requested.)

EUGENE OLIVER: No, I didn't.

MR. FARES: You're confusing me because you just said that you did tell him that he was arrested. Now, you're saying that you didn't.

EUGENE OLIVER: You asked me —

MR. BISHOP: If the Court please, Your Honor. I'm objecting to the argumentative nature of the question.

MR. FARES: Judge, I wasn't arguing.

JUDGE LASSERS: Overruled.

MR. BISHOP: Yes, Your honor.

JUDGE LASSERS: Overruled the objection. Go ahead.

EUGENE OLIVER: You asked me if I stated to Mr. Horak that he was under arrest at that time? Is that what you asked me before?

MR. FARES: Let me repeat it once more. At some time after you walked up to the counter, you told Mr. Horak that he was arrested. Is that true?

EUGENE OLIVER: Yes, I did.

MR. FARES: How much time transpired between the time that you told Mr. Horak that he was arrested?

EUGENE OLIVER: No more than a minute or so.

MR. FARES: It could have been less than a minute?

EUGENE OLIVER: It might have been.

MR. FARES: Or maybe a little more than a minute?

EUGENE OLIVER: Either way.

MR. FARES: Joe McCarthy never asked you if Mr. Horak was under arrest as you recall?

EUGENE OLIVER: Pardon me?

MR. FARES: Joe McCarthy never asked you if Mr. Horak was under arrest as you recall, did he?

EUGENE OLIVER: Yes, he did.

MR. FARES: Is that when you told Mr. Horak he was under

arrest?

EUGENE OLIVER: I can't recall, sir.

MR. FARES: Let's use this as a point of reference. You told Mr. Horak a minute or so after you got behind the counter that he was under arrest, correct?

EUGENE OLIVER: I believe so.

MR. FARES: Now, in relation to that time when you told Mr. Horak that he was under arrest, when did Joe McCarthy ask you if he was under arrest?

EUGENE OLIVER: When Mr. Horak. was still creating a disturbance in the office.

MR. FARES: I'll object and move that it be stricken as non-responsive, Your Honor. I used a specific point in time for him to reference it from.

JUDGE LASSERS: I think no. I think it is non-responsive. Now, do you want to hear the question again, Mr. Oliver?

(Whereupon, the record was read by
the reporter as requested.)

EUGENE OLIVER: Maybe not even a minute after that.

MR. FARES: And during the period of time from when you first came through this door here, this swing door, and the time that you told Mr. Horak that he was under arrest, Joe McCarthy was standing two feet behind him and to his right side, correct?

EUGENE OLIVER: That's correct. Approximately two feet.

MR. FARES: And then after that point that you told Mr. Horak he was under arrest you turned away from Mr. Horak, correct?

EUGENE OLIVER: That's correct.

MR. FARES: And you said something to Steve Bajovich to start typing out a complaint?

EUGENE OLIVER: That's correct.

MR. FARES: And where did you go to at that point after you turned around and told Steve Bajovich that?

EUGENE OLIVER: Just — You can't go too much. There's not that much room there. So you have to just turn around, and he was right on the other side of the desk. I just turned around and told him to start getting the complaint typed.

MR. FARES: And what did you do at that point?

EUGENE OLIVER: Just turned around from the counter.

MR. FARES: Right here? (indicating)

EUGENE OLIVER: Turned around, right.

MR. FARES: How many feet would you say it is from here to here? (indicating)

EUGENE OLIVER: Not more than maybe six, seven feet from the wall to the counter.

MR. FARES: So you're saying from the wall to the counter about this distance? (indicating)

EUGENE OLIVER: Up to where, sir?

MR. FARES: Where I'm standing.

EUGENE OLIVER: To what point here?

MR. FARES: To where you are, sir.

EUGENE OLIVER: To where I'm sitting right here?

MR. FARES: Yes, sir.

EUGENE OLIVER: That would be the wall, the chair, the desk. Maybe, yes, right. It's about like this, maybe. Maybe a half a foot or more closer. There's not much room in that office.

MR. FARES: So there's a wall here?

EUGENE OLIVER: Correct?

MR. FARES: And then there's a chair?

EUGENE OLIVER: There's a chair.

MR. FARES: And there's the desk?

EUGENE OLIVER: Then there's the desk.

MR. FARES: Standard desk?

EUGENE OLIVER: Table desk. It's a table desk combination.

MR. FARES: About the size of those? (indicating)

EUGENE OLIVER: No, sir. That's too wide.

MR. FARES: It's too wide this way. How wide was it?

EUGENE OLIVER: I have no idea. I couldn't even guess. It wasn't that wide, though.

MR. FARES: This wide? (indicating)

EUGENE OLIVER: I couldn't guess. It's not a big office, sir.

MR. FARES: You don't remember?

EUGENE OLIVER: I said I can't guess. I can't guess at it.

MR. FARES: I don't want you to guess. You don't recall then, true?

EUGENE OLIVER: I'm not saying I don't recall. I said I can't tell you how big it was or wide it was.

MR. FARES: Okay. And at that point that you turned around you weren't able to see Mr. Horak at that time?

EUGENE OLIVER: No, sir.

MR. FARES: Okay. And then what did Bajovich start to do?

EUGENE OLIVER: Started to take the complaint form out to start typing up a disorderly conduct form.

MR. FARES: At any point up until this point that Steve Bajovich took the complaint form out to type the disorderly conduct, did you question Mr. Horak concerning his identification, his age, address or ask him for any pieces of identification?

EUGENE OLIVER: I may have. I can't recall. I may have asked him to put his identification out.

MR. FARES: Are you sure that all this didn't occur here in front of the desk?

EUGENE OLIVER: No, sir.

MR. FARES: You're not sure?

EUGENE OLIVER: No, I said it didn't happen in front of the desk. Mr. Horak was on the other side of the counter.

MR. FARES: And then at that point you went to where Steve Bajovich was typing the complaint and started to talk to him about the complaint to show him the complaint?

EUGENE OLIVER: Go where, sir?

MR. FARES: To where Steve Bajovich was typing?

EUGENE OLIVER: I was on the other side of the desk.

MR. FARES: Over here? (indicating)

EUGENE OLIVER: Right.

MR. FARES: So you had to move to the front of the desk?

EUGENE OLIVER: I was in the front of the desk.

MR. FARES: So you turned around and Steve Bajovich was there in that chair? That's the chair, say, that Mr. Bajovich was sitting on.

EUGENE OLIVER: The desk was in front of him, is that correct? Is that what you're telling me?

MR. FARES: No. You said he was typing, and you earlier said there was a typing stand over here on the other side of the desk, not on the desk.

EUGENE OLIVER: Right. On the side of the desk is right.

MR. FARES: And then you were standing here?

EUGENE OLIVER: I'm standing in front of the desk.

MR. FARES: Like this? (indicating)

EUGENE OLIVER: That's correct.

MR. FARES: And you started to talk to Bajovich about the complaint, itself?

EUGENE OLIVER: That's correct.

MR. FARES: What did you tell him about the complaint?

EUGENE OLIVER: I got the Chapter 38 out of the State's Attorney's Complaint Book. Then I gave Mr. Bajovich the copy of the complaint out to type it.

MR. FARES: Then you got the complaint, not Mr. Bajovich?

EUGENE OLIVER: He got the complaint forms. I got the complaint, itself, the book.

MR. FARES: So then you walked to the file cabinet to get it?

EUGENE OLIVER: It may not have been the file cabinet. It may have been in the box behind the counter.

MR. FARES: Where do you remember that it was?

EUGENE OLIVER: I don't remember going to the file cabinet, sir, so it must have been by the — in the box behind the counter.

MR. FARES: Well, if your deposition said that you went out and got the Chapter 38 out of the file cabinet and brought it back to the desk, would that be correct?

EUGENE OLIVER: If it says it in there then it's correct.

MR. FARES: Then you did go to the file cabinet as you recall?

EUGENE OLIVER: If it says it in there.

MR. FARES: All I want is your recollection, Mr. Oliver.

JUDGE LASSERS: What is your question?

MR. BISHOP: Objection, Your Honor.

JUDGE LASSERS: Just put your question, Mr. Fares.

MR. FARES: As you sit there now, what is your recollection? Did you walk to the file cabinet or did you simply turn around?

EUGENE OLIVER: I don't recall. If it states in my deposition there then that's what I must have done.

MR. FARES: As you sit there now, you don't recall?

EUGENE OLIVER: I said I don't recall now.

MR. FARES: How far is the file cabinet from the desk?

EUGENE OLIVER: Maybe three feet, two or three feet.

MR. FARES: And then as Mr. Bajovich was typing the complaint, you were reading the complaint over his shoulder?

EUGENE OLIVER: No, I don't know if I was reading. I can't recall.

MR. FARES: Let me again show you Plaintiff's Exhibit Number 35, page 25, lines 20 through 23, on through 23.

MR. BISHOP: This is recollection?

MR. FARES: Yes, this is to refresh your recollection.

EUGENE OLIVER: Okay.

MR. FARES: Does that refresh your recollection as to whether or not you were reading that complaint while Steve Bajovich was typing?

EUGENE OLIVER: It states there, yes.

MR. FARES: Now, you recall that you were doing that?

EUGENE OLIVER: I don't recall it, but it stated there. So I

must have recalled it then.

MR. FARES: In order for you to be reading that complaint at the time that Steve Bajovich was typing it you had to be behind Steve Bajovich, didn't you?

EUGENE OLIVER: No.

MR. FARES: You mean you were reading — The typing table is here? (indicating)

EUGENE OLIVER: That's correct.

MR. FARES: The desk is here? (indicating)

EUGENE OLIVER: That's correct.

MR. FARES: And you were reading the complaint from over here? (indicating)

EUGENE OLIVER: That's correct.

MR. FARES: Incidentally, Mr. Oliver, how tall are you?

EUGENE OLIVER: Five eight and a half, five eight.

MR. FARES: And how much do you weight?

EUGENE OLIVER: About 350.

MR. FARES: and was that —

MR. BISHOP: Do you mean then or now?

MR. FARES: I was just going to clarify that. Was that about your height and weight at the time that this incident occurred?

EUGENE OLIVER: I can't recall. At one time I was 520 pounds. So I don't know if that's the time I was 520 pounds.

MR. FARES: But somewhere in there is correct?

EUGENE OLIVER: Or around between then and now. The weight I am now. I don't know.

MR. FARES: So you weren't less than 350 pounds at that time?

EUGENE OLIVER: I could have been. I could have been 280. I just had an operation, a gastro bypass. So I don't know if that's —

MR. FARES: At that time you did?

EUGENE OLIVER: Right around that. Probably that area of time. I really don't know when it was.

MR. FARES: Okay. Incidentally, again when you first came in the office and came around the counter, bringing you back to that point, when you first came in again. Do you understand where we are now? Where was Dan Groth at that time?

EUGENE OLIVER: I believe Dan Groth was right at the door of the security office.

MR. FARES: Over here some place? (indicating)

EUGENE OLIVER: No, no. In the doorway of the security office.

MR. FARES: The counter swinging —

EUGENE OLIVER: In the entrance door of the security office.

MR. FARES: In here? (indicating)

EUGENE OLIVER: Yes. That is the door opening that you got there?

MR. FARES: Yes.

EUGENE OLIVER: Right there, yes. That door was flush against the other wall.

MR. FARES: You mean after you brought Mr. Horak in?

EUGENE OLIVER: No, as we were bringing Mr. Horak in.

MR. FARES: This door was already open?

EUGENE OLIVER: That's correct.

MR. FARES: It stayed open the whole time he was in there?

EUGENE OLIVER: No, I don't believe it did, no.

MR. FARES: Do you know when it was closed?

EUGENE OLIVER: Probably when Mr. Groth went out the door.

MR. FARES: How much later was that?

EUGENE OLIVER: Right away.

MR. FARES: Now, after that first time that you turned your back on Mr. Horak in order to tell Mr. Bajovich to start typing the complaint and then either you went to the file cabinet or you didn't; after the first time that you turned, how long of a period of time inside before you turned back in the direction of the front counter?

EUGENE OLIVER: Matter of maybe 15, 20 seconds.

MR. FARES: And during that 15 to 20 second period of time, what you did was you turned from the counter. You either walked over to the file cabinet in order to get out the book. You brought the book back over to Mr. Bajovich who was sitting here, and then Mr. Bajovich had started to type the complaint and you looked over Mr. Bajovich's shoulder in order to watch him start typing the complaint?

EUGENE OLIVER: I didn't look over Mr. Bajovich's shoulder.

MR. FARES: Or well, from the other side of the desk?

EUGENE OLIVER: That's correct.

MR. FARES: I assume to some extent you had to look over his shoulder, didn't you?

EUGENE OLIVER: No. He was just sitting sideways, and I was standing like this. Just like we're doing right there. So, I wouldn't be.

MR. FARES: You were even this way. (indicating) Is that what you're saying? You were standing here? (indicating)

EUGENE OLIVER: I'm not — I could have been on a little angle. I could have been in front of him. All I know is that I wasn't looking over his shoulder.

MR. FARES: Okay. Maybe we're talking semantics. I don't want to confuse the issue. But, at any rate, during that period of time, that's what you did in those 15 to 20 seconds?

EUGENE OLIVER: I believe so.

MR. FARES: And all of that took 15 to 20 seconds in order for you to do?

EUGENE OLIVER: I believe so.

MR. FARES: And then you did turn back around towards the counter?

EUGENE OLIVER: Did I turn facing the counter?

MR. FARES: Yes.

EUGENE OLIVER: When I heard a commotion.

MR. FARES: You heard a commotion?

EUGENE OLIVER: Uh-huh.

MR. FARES: During the time that you left the counter and got the book and went to Bajovich's, looked at the complaint as he was typing it; during that period of time, was Mr. Horak doing anything?

EUGENE OLIVER: Yes, he was banging on the counter and yelling.

MR. FARES: All right. And then you heard a commotion. What did you hear that made you turn around if he was banging and hollering anyway? What more of a commotion did you hear?

EUGENE OLIVER: I heard a — got a bigger roar. Like a bigger commotion, and then in a matter of seconds, I turned around and I see Mr. —

MR. FARES: Don't tell me what you saw yet.

EUGENE OLIVER: You asked me.

MR. FARES: No, I asked —

MR. BISHOP: If the Court please. He asked him what he saw. I'd like him to be able to tell us

MR. FARES: That's not my question.

JUDGE LASSERS: Let's hear the question.

(Whereupon, the record was read
by the reporter, as requested.)

JUDGE LASSERS: The answer was, "a bigger commotion." What is your next question?

MR. FARES: What did you do then?

EUGENE OLIVER: I can't recall. I just turned around. I don't know if — Do you mean completely?

MR. FARES: Did you turn your whole body around, shifting your legs?

EUGENE OLIVER: I can't recall. I don't know.

MR. FARES: Did you just turn your head? You don't remember what you did?

EUGENE OLIVER: I turned around, but I don't know if I turned my whole body around or not.

MR. FARES: And at that point, you saw Mr. Horak push Mr. McCarthy?

EUGENE OLIVER: No.

MR. FARES: You did not see Mr. Horak push Mr. McCarthy at that point?

EUGENE OLIVER: No.

MR. FARES: The deposition, page 25, lines 20 through 24 and on page 26, line one:

> "Question: Okay. And what happened next?
>
> "Answer: Steve was typing up the complaint, showing him the complaint. We heard a scuffle."
>
> Twenty-four:
>
> "Question: What did you see?"

> "Answer: Turned around and I seen Mr. Horak arguing and pushing the other investigator, Joe McCarthy."

Are those the answers you gave to the questions that were asked back on May 9th, 1980?

EUGENE OLIVER: If that's what is says in the deposition, then that's what I said.

MR. FARES: Well, then did you see —

MR. BISHOP: Objection, Your honor.

JUDGE LASSERS: Let me hear the question.

MR. BISHOP: Your Honor. The witness has answered the question in the affirmative. That ends the subject.

JUDGE LASSERS: Is it a new question?

MR. FARES: I think it was.

JUDGE LASSERS: Put your question.

MR. FARES: As you sit here now, do you remember seeing Michael Horak push Joe McCarthy?

EUGENE OLIVER: If I said it in the deposition, it must have happened that way then.

MR. FARES: What about what you do remember now?

EUGENE OLIVER: I can't recall.

MR. FARES: Do you feel, Mr. Oliver, that your recollection of the events that occurred on June 12, 1980, was fresher in your mind as you sit there today?

EUGENE OLIVER: Fresher in my mind in 1980.

MR. FARES: Then for purposes of our discussion — Take your time.

EUGENE OLIVER: Excuse me.

MR. FARES: That's okay. That's no problem. Are you finished? For the purposes of discussion here, you did see Mike Horak push Joe McCarthy?

MR. BISHOP: Same objection, Your Honor.

EUGENE OLIVER: No.

JUDGE LASSERS: Really, the question has been asked and answered. Go on to something else.

MR. FARES: Right after that happened, after whatever you don't recall happened, you turned around again. You turned your back to the counter again, didn't you?

EUGENE OLIVER: After what happened, sir?

MR. FARES: Well, you said you turned around, correct? And in your deposition in 1980 you said you saw Mr. Horak push Mr. McCarthy. That's what you said in the deposition. You said that was fresher in your mind then. Then right after that you turned back around again?

EUGENE OLIVER: Does it state that in the deposition?

MR. FARES: I'm asking you what you recall.

EUGENE OLIVER: I don't recall. I don't recall if I did.

MR. FARES: Okay. Let me withdraw the question and back up just a minute. When you turned around, you heard Joe McCarthy say to Mr. Horak that he was under arrest and that he was going to be handcuffed, is that true?

EUGENE OLIVER: Did I say it there, sir? I don't recall it

now. I don't know. Did I say it in my deposition?

MR. FARES: I'll get to that.

MR. BISHOP: If the Court please. I would like the record to reflect that counsel has the deposition in front of him and appears to be reading from it. I'd like to know the page that he's referring to.

MR. FARES: Page 26, Mr. Bishop. I think you know the page pretty well.

MR. BISHOP: I object to that, Your Honor.

JUDGE LASSERS: That is inappropriate. Just a moment please, folks. Now, counsel may not engage in any by-play between themselves. All the remarks have to be addressed to the Court. The Court is the official.

MR. BISHOP: May I make a point for the record?

JUDGE LASSERS: No, no. Let's just move on.

MR. FARES: Thank you, Judge.

JUDGE LASSERS: We will follow strictly by the book, Mr. Fares.

MR. FARES: Then after that point, there was some scuffle between Mr. McCarthy and Mr. Horak?

EUGENE OLIVER: After what point, sir?

MR. FARES: After the point — let's go over here. Again, page 26. Do you want to read lines one through seven for purposes of refreshing your recollection? Does that refresh your recollection?

EUGENE OLIVER: What was the question, now?

(Whereupon, the record was read
by the reporter as requested.)

MR. FARES: And then you said, "What point?" And now I'm referring back to the point where Mr. McCarthy said that Mr. Horak was under arrest.

MR. BISHOP: Objection, Your honor. The witness never testified that he heard Mr. McCarthy say the witness was —

MR. FARES: That's fine. I'll withdraw that question. Does this refresh your recollection after reading those lines as to whether or not Mr. McCarthy, after you saw this push, said to Mr. Horak that he was under arrest? Does that refresh your recollection?

EUGENE OLIVER: If it's down there, I must have stated it.

MR. FARES: Okay. And then after that point, there was some scuffling that you heard. Is that true?

EUGENE OLIVER: No.

MR. FARES: Because you turned your back?

EUGENE OLIVER: That's correct.

MR. FARES: You saw Mr. Horak push Mr. McCarthy. Wouldn't it be natural for you to go to Mr. McCarthy's aid?

MR. BISHOP: Objection, Your honor. Argumentative. And it goes to state of mind.

MR. FARES: Your Honor —

MR. BISHOP: Most importantly, state of mind, Your honor.

JUDGE LASSERS: I'll let him answer. Go ahead. Go ahead.

EUGENE OLIVER: There was no need for it. I wouldn't think so.

MR. FARES: You were a security guard at this track for how many years?

EUGENE OLIVER: Up to this date now?

MR. FARES: Up to 1978.

EUGENE OLIVER: '78, I was —

MR. FARES: Or an investigator, I'm sorry, security guard.

EUGENE OLIVER: For about, oh, 17 years.

MR. FARES: And in your widespread experience as an investigator, isn't it practice that if another investigator is in a scuffle you go to his aid in order to subdue the patron or the prisoner or whatever it is he's involved in a scuffle with?

EUGENE OLIVER: Yes, I would go there to prevent anybody from getting hurt.

MR. FARES: But you didn't go to Mr. McCarthy's aid?

EUGENE OLIVER: No, there was just no need for it.

MR. FARES: Okay, thank you. When you turned around after you said you saw the push, then you turned around and then you heard a further scuffle. When you turned around, did you sit down?

EUGENE OLIVER: I don't recall.

MR. FARES: 26, line 13.

MR. BISHOP: For what purpose?

MR. FARES: Refresh his recollection. Line 26, 13, 14 and 15.

MR. SHERIFF: Excuse me. One of the jurors doesn't feel well.

JUDGE LASSERS: We will take a recess.

(Whereupon, there was a short recess.)

MR. FARES: Okay. And then after that point, you saw a push. You turned back around towards Bajovich, and then you turned around again. And at that point Mr. Horak had handcuffs on?

EUGENE OLIVER: I believe that's correct, sir.

MR. FARES: And where was Mr. Horak at that time?

EUGENE OLIVER: Standing in front of the counter.

MR. FARES: Which way was he facing?

EUGENE OLIVER: He might have been facing myself or the desk or the counter or the wall or Mr. McCarthy. I can't recall.

MR. FARES: You don't remember. Do you remember how close he was to the counter?

EUGENE OLIVER: I believe he was no more than a foot away.

MR. FARES: Incidentally, that security office, as it existed on June 12th, 1978, it's not there anymore, is it?

EUGENE OLIVER: No, sir.

MR. FARES: So there's a completely different security setup now at Sportsman Park, correct?

EUGENE OLIVER: That's correct, sir.

MR. FARES: And when was this particular security office was disassembled or taken away from that building?

EUGENE OLIVER: When the plant was rehabilitated as far as the entrances and the lobby or entrance-ways there. I don't know which it was just maybe three years ago, four years ago, maybe it was changed. Something like that. We made an elevator to the Clubhouse area right over where the offices were.

MR. FARES: At the time that you heard the scuffle between Mr. McCarthy and Mr. Horak, were the shades drawn at that time?

EUGENE OLIVER: I believe they were.

MR. FARES: Do you know who drew the shades or —

EUGENE OLIVER: I may have. I don't know. I can't recall.

MR. FARES: You don't know? Do you know if Daniel Groth was involved in the scuffle?

EUGENE OLIVER: He wasn't.

MR. FARES: He was not?

EUGENE OLIVER: No, sir.

MR. FARES: Are you certain of that?

EUGENE OLIVER: He was in the room only a matter of seconds. That's all I can recall.

MR. FARES: Deposition page 29, line 24, page 30, lines 1 through 8:

> "Question: What was Mr. Groth doing during the scuffle between McCarthy and Horak?
>
> "Answer: I don't know.
>
> "Question: Was he involved in it in any way?

"Answer: I don't know.

"Question: Was there anyone else in the room from the time that you came in with Horak and the time that he was handcuffed and sitting on the bench?

"Answer: I can't recall if there was or not."

MR. FARES: Were those the questions that were asked and the answers you gave on that day when you gave your deposition in May of 1980?

EUGENE OLIVER: If it's there in the deposition, then those are the answers I gave.

MR. FARES: Does that refresh your recollection as to whether or not Mr. Groth was in the office at that time?

EUGENE OLIVER: No. I stated there and I stated here what I thought.

MR. FARES: To your knowledge, the only person that came into contact with Mr. Horak was Joe McCarthy?

EUGENE OLIVER: That's correct.

MR. FARES: You never did?

EUGENE OLIVER: No, sir. Physically.

MR. FARES: Yes, sir.

EUGENE OLIVER: Is that what you're referring to, physically?

MR. FARES: Yes, sir.

EUGENE OLIVER: Yes, sir.

MR. FARES: And then Mr. Horak was seated on a bench on

which side of the counter?

EUGENE OLIVER: Was Mr. Horak on the bench.

MR. FARES: He was seated on a bench.

EUGENE OLIVER: Yes, sir.

MR. FARES: On which side of the counter?

EUGENE OLIVER: On the — is that the east side?

MR. FARES: Yes, that's a backwards "E".

EUGENE OLIVER: South wall, east side.

MR. FARES: And at that time you came, Mr. Horak was still hollering?

EUGENE OLIVER: Yes, he was still. Still stating that he couldn't be arrested and started yelling and that's —

MR. FARES: Okay. And you stayed in the office, the security office, the whole time from the time you came in with Mr. Horak until the police came and took him away?

EUGENE OLIVER: I don't believe that I stayed there the whole time, no.

MR. FARES: Did you leave at some point?

EUGENE OLIVER: I may have left the office to go and check the entrances for pickpockets at the end of the, like the breaking of the last race we would check the area of the entrances. And then we would move our — some of our investigators to the main money rooms because we would be transporting money from the different divisions throughout the track. That's what our duties are at the end of the racing night.

MR. FARES: Do you recall whether you did that for certain or not or —

EUGENE OLIVER: I, I can't be certain. I probably did, but I can't recall.

MR. FARES: In any event, you didn't go out to get any other patrons or —

EUGENE OLIVER: Get any other patrons for what?

MR. FARES: Patrons who might have been causing a disturbance?

EUGENE OLIVER: No, sir.

MR. FARES: You took no one else into custody that night after Mr. Horak?

EUGENE OLIVER: I, myself?

MR. FARES: You did not?

EUGENE OLIVER: No, sir.

MR. FARES: And at some point while Mr. Horak was seated on the bench there he was complaining that his handcuffs were too tight, wasn't he?

EUGENE OLIVER: I can't recall. He may have. I may have said that in my deposition.

MR. FARES: And to your knowledge, Mr. Horak's wallet was not taken during the time that he was in the security office? Wasn't physically taken from his body?

EUGENE OLIVER: I can't recall.

MR. FARES: You, sir, pressed disorderly conduct charges against Mr. Horak, correct?

EUGENE OLIVER: Yes, sir.

MR. FARES: This is Plaintiff's exhibit Number 9, already admitted into evidence. And that's a copy of the complaint that you signed against Mr. Horak, isn't it?

EUGENE OLIVER: That's correct, sir.

MR. FARES: You can keep it if you want it.

EUGENE OLIVER: There you are.

MR. FARES: You didn't file battery charges against Mr. Horak though, did you?

EUGENE OLIVER: Myself?

MR. FARES: Right.

EUGENE OLIVER: No.

MR. FARES: You saw him push Mr. McCarthy?

EUGENE OLIVER: Why shall I press — put charges against for battery? He didn't commit a battery on me.

MR. FARES: And to your knowledge, Mr. Horak as a result of this incident there, was not charged with battery, was he?

EUGENE OLIVER: No.

MR. FARES: Okay. And then you went to Court and testified against Mr. Horak in regard to his disorderly conduct charges?

EUGENE OLIVER: That's correct, sir.

MR. FARES: You testified before a Judge?

EUGENE OLIVER: That's correct.

MR. FARES: Judge Salerno?

EUGENE OLIVER: I don't recall who the judge was.

MR. FARES: There was a State Attorney who was asking you questions?

EUGENE OLIVER: That's correct.

MR. FARES: And there was a lawyer there on behalf of Mr. Horak who also asked you questions?

EUGENE OLIVER: That's correct, sir.

MR. FARES: And the case was discharged, wasn't it?

EUGENE OLIVER: That's correct, sir.

MR. FARES: Mr. Horak pleaded "Not guilty", didn't he?

EUGENE OLIVER: I believe he did.

MR. FARES: Now, before June 12th, 1978, other than — give me just a second. Before June 12th, 1978, you never had any altercation or problem with Michael John Horak before that date, did you?

EUGENE OLIVER: I can't recall.

MR. FARES: 39, 1 through 10. Let me show you for purposes of refreshing your recollection page 39, 1 through 10. Does that refresh your recollection as to whether or not before that date you had any altercation or problems with Michael John Horak?

EUGENE OLIVER: Right.

MR. FARES: It does?

EUGENE OLIVER: It states, "If I did have any contact with

him that he being the owner, trainer, driver, I may have come in contact with him in the stable area or something if he was"

MR. FARES: In the stable area.

EUGENE OLIVER: Or anywhere on the racetrack grounds.

MR. FARES: That would be arising out of him being a trainer or a driver of horses, correct?

EUGENE OLIVER: Trainer, driver, owner.

MR. FARES: Because at one point you were assigned to stable area?

EUGENE OLIVER: I am assigned to all the track property grounds, stable, Grandstand, Clubhouse, parking lot.

MR. FARES: You never came into contact with him prior to June 12th, 1978, Mr. Oliver, wherein Mr. Horak was screaming or yelling at drivers?

EUGENE OLIVER: I couldn't recall.

MR. FARES: I have nothing further, Your Honor.

JUDGE LASSERS: All right.

Chapter 34
Steve Bajovich

JUDGE LASSERS: Good morning, ladies and gentlemen. Well, I'm sure you will be pleased to know that Deputy Smith called Miss Strock this morning. She got home safe and sound. She is feeling better. We are starting late this morning. I understand one of the jurors had a traffic accident this morning, and that he had to have his car towed, but he wasn't hurt. I understand nobody was hurt, right?

JUROR: Yeah.

JUDGE LASSERS: That is the reason for getting started late this morning. Now we are ready to roll and the ball is in your court, Mr. Fares.

MR. FARES: I'd like to call, Your Honor, Mr. Steve Bajovich as an adverse witness.

(Witness sworn)

STEVE BAJOVICH, called as an adverse witness by the Plaintiff herein, having been first duly sworn, was examined and testified as follows:

EXAMINATION BY Mr. Fares:

MR. FARES: Would you state your name, please?

STEVE BAJOVICH: Steve J. Bajovich.

JUDGE LASSERS: How do you spell your last name?

STEVE BAJOVICH: B-A-J-O-V-I-C-H.

JUDGE LASSERS: Your first name?

MR. FARES: Steve, Steve not Steven.

STEVE BAJOVICH: Steve, S-T-E-V-E.

MR. FARES: Your address?

STEVE BAJOVICH: 3536 South 58 Avenue, Cicero.

MR. FARES: On or about June 12th of 1978, you were on duty, were you not, at Sportsman Park?

STEVE BAJOVICH: Yes, I was.

MR. FARES: And at that time you were employed as supervisor of security?

STEVE BAJOVICH: That's correct, sir.

MR. FARES: As supervisor at that time you were employed by Fox Valley Trotting Association?

STEVE BAJOVICH: I believe that's correct, yes.

MR. FARES: Also, as supervisor of security, generally your duties consisted of managing the desk in the security office?

STEVE BAJOVICH: That's correct.

MR. FARES: Also, at that time, at all times you carried a weapon?

STEVE BAJOVICH: Yes, I do.

MR. FARES: What kind of weapon did you carry?

STEVE BAJOVICH: Smith and Wesson snub-nose revolver, five shot.

MR. FARES: Now, on that date you didn't have a beard, did you?

STEVE BAJOVICH: No, sir, I didn't.

MR. FARES: Did you have a mustache?

STEVE BAJOVICH: No, sir.

MR. FARES: Also, at that time, you were a Cicero police officer, correct?

STEVE BAJOVICH: That's correct, sir.

MR. FARES: Assigned to, as I recall, the Mayor's liquor commission.

STEVE BAJOVICH: As the liquor license officer.

MR. FARES: And you made your own hours with your job with Cicero, correct?

STEVE BAJOVICH: I worked 40 hours a week, yes.

MR. FARES: Ultimately in regard to Mr. Horak, it was the Cicero police that came in order to pick Mr. Horak up?

STEVE BAJOVICH: That's correct, sir.

MR. FARES: Now, in regard to Mr. Horak — incidentally, at that time, aside from being employed by Fox Valley, were you also employed by the National Jockey Club?

STEVE BAJOVICH: When the National jockey Club held it's meet, yes.

MR. FARES: I'm talking about June 12, of 1978?

STEVE BAJOVICH: No, sir.

MR. FARES: Only Fox Valley?

STEVE BAJOVICH: Whatever the meet was, that's who I was employed by.

MR. FARES: You allege that on June 12 of 1978 you received a call from the Paddock area regarding a disturbance at the Paddock area, correct?

STEVE BAJOVICH: That's correct.

MR. FARES: You were at the desk of the security office at that time?

STEVE BAJOVICH: That's correct.

MR. FARES: You don't recall who called you?

STEVE BAJOVICH: No, sir, I don't.

MR. FARES: Nor do you recall who was involved in the disturbance?

STEVE BAJOVICH: No, I don't remember who it was.

MR. FARES: And then you say you sent Eugene Oliver and Joseph McCarthy to the area?

STEVE BAJOVICH: I radioed the officer to respond to the disturbance.

MR. FARES: Who did you radio, specifically?

STEVE BAJOVICH: We use call numbers, I radioed 201. 201 is Eugene Oliver's number.

MR. FARES: Well, what was Mr. McCarthy's number?

STEVE BAJOVICH: I don't remember.

MR. FARES: Do you remember radioing McCarthy?

STEVE BAJOVICH: No. McCarthy didn't have a radio. Eugene Oliver had the radio.

MR. FARES: So you don't know as you sit there whether or not McCarthy went with Oliver to investigate the disturbance or not, do you?

STEVE BAJOVICH: Well, Mr. McCarthy was Eugene's partner. I assume Mr. McCarthy went with Eugene when I radioed Oliver.

MR. FARES: You don't know that for sure?

STEVE BAJOVICH: No, sir.

MR. FARES: At that time that you made the call, you did not know who was creating the disturbance in the Paddock area?

STEVE BAJOVICH: No, sir.

MR. FARES: You are sure of that?

STEVE BAJOVICH: Yes, sir.

MR. FARES: The next thing — did you receive any further radio communications between the time that — concerning the incident in the Paddock area — between the time that Oliver — you radioed Oliver to go investigate the occurrence and the time that Mike Horak entered into the security office?

STEVE BAJOVICH: I don't recall. There could have been. I don't recall.

MR. FARES: At any rate, Mike Horak at some point after that

came into the office, the security office, correct?

STEVE BAJOVICH: Yes.

MR. FARES: Who was with him at that time?

STEVE BAJOVICH: With Mike Horak?

MR. FARES: Yes, sir.

STEVE BAJOVICH: Mr. Oliver and Mr. McCarthy.

MR. FARES: Did McCarthy come in from the outside?

STEVE BAJOVICH: I believe he did.

MR. FARES: You are sure of that?

STEVE BAJOVICH: I'm not sure, but he came into the office.

MR. FARES: And at that time the office was — the security office is no longer there, correct?

STEVE BAJOVICH: That's correct.

MR. FARES: But at that time, the size of the office was 12 feet by 15 feet, wasn't it?

STEVE BAJOVICH: Approximately, yes.

MR. FARES: And that would be 12 feet — referring to the exhibits which I'm sure you have seen, correct, Plaintiff's exhibit number 8 — 12 feet running in a North-South direction, and 15 feet running in an East-West direction, correct?

STEVE BAJOVICH: Yes.

MR. FARES: And this area, which is right off the entrance door, which I will call the east side of the counter for our purposes, this area was not — was smaller than the area behind the counter, isn't that true?

STEVE BAJOVICH: Possibly, yes.

MR. FARES: So the area behind the counter — to the West side of the counter, it is bigger than the East side of the office?

STEVE BAJOVICH: Not by much.

MR. FARES: 12 by 15, bigger than the security box?

STEVE BAJOVICH: Well, maybe a little bit, yes.

MR. FARES: When Mike Horak came into the office, the shades were open according to you, correct?

STEVE BAJOVICH: Yes.

MR. FARES: So you could see to the outside?

STEVE BAJOVICH: Yes.

MR. FARES: According to you, you don't know of any reason why during the whole time Mr. Horak was in the office those shades would have been closed?

STEVE BAJOVICH: Could you repeat that once again, please?

MR. FARES: I am referring to a period of time from when Mr. Horak first came into the office until the time ultimately the Cicero police came and picked Mr. Horak up and took him out of the office. In regard to that period of time you don't know of any reason why anybody would have closed the shades during that period of time, do you?

STEVE BAJOVICH: Well, yes.

MR. FARES: You do?

STEVE BAJOVICH: Yes.

MR. FARES: What reason would that be?

STEVE BAJOVICH: Well, a disturbance erupted in the office.

MR. FARES: What happens in that instance?

STEVE BAJOVICH: Well, somebody, inevitably closed — drew the shades.

MR. FARES: You remember them being drawn?

STEVE BAJOVICH: They were pulled eventually, yes.

MR. FARES: They were closed?

STEVE BAJOVICH: No; they were open when he came in.

MR. FARES: Ultimately before he left when a disturbance ensued somebody closed them?

STEVE BAJOVICH: Yes.

MR. FARES: You are sure?

STEVE BAJOVICH: Yes, I am.

MR. FARES: Why are you so sure about that?

MR. BISHOP: Objection, Your Honor, arguing with the witness.

JUDGE LASSERS: Overruled.

STEVE BAJOVICH: The shades were closed. I remember — I'm sure that someone closed the shades.

MR. FARES: You remember giving your deposition on or about June 22, 1981?

STEVE BAJOVICH: Yes.

MR. FARES: You were there, and a Mr. Jack Armstrong from Mr. Bishop's firm was there, correct?

STEVE BAJOVICH: Correct.

MR. FARES: There was an attorney, Mr. Richard Rock on behalf of Mr. Horak there?

STEVE BAJOVICH: I believe that's right, sir.

MR. FARES: Certain questions were asked of you and you gave certain answers to those questions?

STEVE BAJOVICH: Yes.

MR. FARES: Page 19 — let's start on page 18, line 20, and go through page 19, line 8.

MR. BISHOP: Your Honor, I'm objecting to the preliminary. It is consistent with what the witness has already testified to. We know there were shades. It is not impeaching. It is not—

MR. FARES: I was doing that for your purposes, Mr. Bishop. If you don't want the preliminaries, that's fine with me. So there was a question asked you, page 18 line 24:

> "Question: The shades were down?
>
> Answer: Yes. Well, our shades we pull up, not down. They were at the bottom and you pull the shades up. The shades weren't closed. You were able to look at the windows.
>
> Question: Did they remain open during the entire

time Mr. Horak was in the office?

Answer: I don't remember. I wouldn't have any reason to close them. No, I don't think so."

Were those questions asked and did you give those answers on that day?

STEVE BAJOVICH: If those were the questions that were asked in that deposition, then those are my answers.

MR. BISHOP: Now, I wish to have the question and answer stricken for the reason that the witness said he would not have any reason to close them.

JUDGE LASSERS: Let me see it.

MR. BISHOP: It is not inconsistent with what the witness said.

MR. FARES: You can start, Judge, on page 18, line 24, then over to line 8 of the next page.

(The Court examined the transcript.)

JUDGE LASSERS: I am going to let it stand, possibly inconsistent.

MR. BISHOP: Pardon me, Your Honor.

MR. FARES: He will allow it to stay. Possibly inconsistent. Those questions were asked and you gave those answers, correct?

STEVE BAJOVICH: Yes.

MR. FARES: Now, you just said now that you were sure those shades were drawn, correct?

STEVE BAJOVICH: I believe that's what I said, yes.

MR. FARES: And you also just said that when a disturbance is created, the shades are always drawn?

STEVE BAJOVICH: No, sir, I didn't say that.

MR. FARES: Well, is it or is it not a procedure or was it at the time a procedure to draw those shades when there was any type of disturbance in the security office?

STEVE BAJOVICH: It would be up to the individual officer coming into the security office.

MR. FARES: So there was no procedure?

STEVE BAJOVICH: We had no procedure on drawing shades, no.

MR. FARES: Was your memory better back in June of 1981 concerning this incident or is it better now?

STEVE BAJOVICH: Better at that time.

MR. FARES: But now you say that the shades were closed.

MR. BISHOP: Objection, Your Honor, argument.

JUDGE LASSERS: It's been asked and answered several times.

MR. BISHOP: You are sustaining the objection, Your Honor?

JUDGE LASSERS: Yes.

MR. FARES: According to you, Horak was not under arrest when he first came into the security office?

STEVE BAJOVICH: That's correct, sir.

MR. FARES: When Horak came in you were typing, trying to finish some work?

STEVE BAJOVICH: Yes, sir.

MR. FARES: You remember what that work was?

STEVE BAJOVICH: No, sir, I don't remember.

MR. FARES: When Horak came in, who was there. Who was in the office?

STEVE BAJOVICH: Who walked in with Horak?

MR. FARES: No. You already said that McCarthy and Oliver walked in with Horak?

STEVE BAJOVICH: I was there alone.

MR. FARES: Nobody else was in there?

STEVE BAJOVICH: I don't remember if there was anybody else.

MR. FARES: I am going to show you, Mr. Bajovich, which has previously been marked Plaintiff's exhibit number 36 for purposes of identification.

(Plaintiff's Exhibit Number 36, so marked.)

Take a look at that, please. This man here, do you know him?

STEVE BAJOVICH: Yes, I do.

MR. BISHOP: Objection, Your Honor. I'm going to request an appropriate foundation be laid for the photograph, that is, when and where it was taken.

MR. FARES: Your Honor, I'm not at this time attempting to admit that exhibit into evidence.

JUDGE LASSERS: Identify it. Overruled.

MR. FARES: What is that man's name?

STEVE BAJOVICH: Ray Rubino.

JUDGE LASSERS: Ray who?

STEVE BAJOVICH: Rubino, R-U-B-I-N-O

MR. FARES: And in the year of 1978, how did you know Ray Rubino?

STEVE BAJOVICH: We were friends and associates and he also was employed by Sportsman Park.

MR. FARES: What capacity?

STEVE BAJOVICH: Investigator.

MR. FARES: Same capacity as Oliver and Bajovich, correct?

STEVE BAJOVICH: That's correct.

MR. FARES: How big a man is he?

STEVE BAJOVICH: How big?

MR. FARES: Yes, sir.

STEVE BAJOVICH: I don't recall.

MR. FARES: About my size?

STEVE BAJOVICH: I don't think so.

MR. FARES: Bigger?

STEVE BAJOVICH: Probably a little bigger, yes.

MR. FARES: A Little heavier?

STEVE BAJOVICH: Yes.

MR. FARES: About my height, though?

STEVE BAJOVICH: I don't recall.

MR. FARES: Was he on duty on June 12th of 1978?

STEVE BAJOVICH: I don't remember.

MR. FARES: Do you notice anybody else in that photograph?

STEVE BAJOVICH: Two Andy Frain ushers, a subject standing there, and another person.

MR. FARES: Who is this man here?

STEVE BAJOVICH: I don't know who he is.

MR. FARES: That is not Eugene Oliver?

STEVE BAJOVICH: I can't identify him.

MR. FARES: Does this picture truly and accurately depict Sportsman Park Racetrack as it existed on or about June of 1978?

STEVE BAJOVICH: It looks like it.

MR. FARES: I move at this time, Your Honor, for admission of Exhibit number 36 into evidence.

JUDGE LASSERS: Any objection?

MR. BISHOP: Yes, Your Honor. No foundation. When was it taken?

MR. FARES: I think when we admit a photograph into evidence, we don't have to call the photographer to say when it was taken. All we need to do is establish that it truly and accurately depicts the scene as it existed on or about the date in question, June of 1978. I think our witness has testified to that.

MR. BISHOP: No, Your Honor, he hasn't.

JUDGE LASSERS: Let me talk to the lawyers.

(Whereupon, the following proceedings were had in chambers outside the presence of the jury.)

JUDGE LASSERS: What do you want to establish with this picture?

MR. FARES: I want to establish, number one, Mr. Horak testified that there was a smaller man that went with Eugene Oliver in order to pick up on that evening, not Joe McCarthy, as they claim.

JUDGE LASSERS: Who testified?

MR. FARES: Horak. He claims McCarthy picked him up. There was a smaller man about five-foot seven that weighed about 150 pounds that came with Oliver to pick him up.

JUDGE LASSERS: Not McCarthy?

MR. BISHOP: He identified in the courtroom because we had officer McCarthy stand up, and Mr. Horak said that is not the man who was with Mr. Oliver.

MR. FARES: Now we got a little guy. I'm five-seven, 122 pounds, for the record, he was a little bigger than me, with Eugene Oliver standing with him investigating something. It goes as some proof, number one, that those two worked as partners.

JUDGE LASSERS: Wait a minute. First of all, in your Exhibit Number 36, who is it that you are trying to identify?

MR. FARES: He's already identified that guy as Ray Rubino.

JUDGE LASSERS: Is Rubino a defendant?

MR. BISHOP: No, Your Honor.

MR. FARES: Your Honor, because he wasn't disclosed in discovery.

JUDGE LASSERS: What is it you hope to prove by this photograph?

MR. FARES: Your Honor, I hope to lend corroboration to my client's story that indeed there's another guard that works with Oliver. I don't have the evidence here. All the evidence is in the hands of those four men out there as to who was in the office, why they were in that office and what occurred. All I have is one man. This is some evidence that goes — that would go to show my client's side of the story and I think it is more than cumulative evidence when my client is telling a story against four other witnesses.

JUDGE LASSERS: Just a minute, you lost me. What is it that you want to show.

MR. FARES: That Oliver went to pick up Horak with another man other than Joseph McCarthy as he testified. That's already been brought into issue because McCarthy testified he didn't go and pick up Horak.

JUDGE LASSERS: Just a moment. Horak testified that it was not McCarthy?

MR. FARES: Right.

JUDGE LASSERS: McCarthy testified that he was with Oliver?

MR. BISHOP: No.

JUDGE LASSERS: McCarthy hasn't testified?

MR. BISHOP: McCarthy testified that he was not with Oliver.

MR. FARES: He never was with Oliver.

JUDGE LASSERS: Please, folks, you sort of overwhelmed me. McCarthy says he wasn't with Oliver?

MR. FARES: Right.

JUDGE LASSERS: Horak says McCarthy was not with Oliver?

MR. FARES: Right.

JUDGE LASSERS: Okay. Now, when was this photograph taken?

MR. FARES: The photo was taken a month later, Judge, June of 1978 or July of 1978.

JUDGE LASSERS: Why is it this old?

MR. FARES: I'm sorry. It was used in the Plaintiff's deposition, that's why there's markings on the back.

JUDGE LASSERS: Please, I still don't understand what it is that you want to try to prove with this photograph.

MR. FARES: Judge, I want to try to prove that there is a cover-up story going on here. All the evidence, Judge, is in the hands of the defendants.

JUDGE LASSERS: I understand that, but get down to the specific, what specific —

MR. FARES: The specifics is that this man — I am referring to the man identified as Rubino — and this man Oliver were partners on this particular evening, that it's plausible they were partners on the evening in question. Rubino is five-foot seven, just as Mr. Horak testified, about 155 pounds, and that Rubino was in that office that night. Nobody is talking about him. They made up a story, Judge, and they are trying to stick by it and they are leaving everything out.

JUDGE LASSERS: Let's suppose that it was Rubino — Oh, wait. What did Oliver say was the man who was with him?

MR. FARES: McCarthy.

MR. BISHOP: He said he thought it was McCarthy.

JUDGE LASSERS: Oliver says he thinks it was McCarthy. McCarthy says it wasn't him, Horak says it wasn't McCarthy.

MR. FARES: He says there's two guards.

MR. BISHOP: Let the Judge get it.

JUDGE LASSERS: Please, Horak says it wasn't McCarthy.

MR. FARES: Bingo.

JUDGE LASSERS: Let's suppose that it was Rubino, Rubino isn't a defendant here.

MR. FARES: That's true, as affects Rubino. I am not going to be able to bring Rubino in at this time. What does that show? It corroborates Mike Horak's testimony, or is some evidence that may corroborate Horak's testimony that there were more than the four defendants in the office.

JUDGE LASSERS: Just a moment. You never asked Horak if Rubino accompanied Oliver.

MR. FARES: Because Horak didn't know the name of the guy. We didn't find out until this man just said his name is

Ray Rubino. But Horak does say a man of about five-foot seven, 150 pounds.

JUDGE LASSERS: But you took Bajovich's deposition.

MR. FARES: I didn't.

JUDGE LASSERS: You took it some time in the '80s.

MR. FARES: Yes.

JUDGE LASSERS: You never asked Horak if the man here in the shirt-sleeves was the man who accompanied Oliver?

MR. FARES: Not yet, Judge.

JUDGE LASSERS: You have Horak on and off the stand?

MR. FARES: This photo just came to my attention in those terms.

JUDGE LASSERS: I am going to refuse it.
(Whereupon, the following proceedings were held in open Court in the presence of the jury.)

JUDGE LASSERS: Go ahead, Mr. Fares.

MR. FARES: Now, you say when Mike Horak first got into the office, you then walked up to the counter, came up to the counter, correct?

STEVE BAJOVICH: That I came up to the counter?

MR. FARES: Mike Horak came up to the counter?

STEVE BAJOVICH: Yes.

MR. FARES: On the East side of the counter?

STEVE BAJOVICH: That's correct.

MR. FARES: And Eugene Oliver came around the other side of the counter?

STEVE BAJOVICH: That's correct.

MR. FARES: In relation to this counter, is this a fair depiction of where Mike Horak was standing, or if not, where was he standing?

STEVE BAJOVICH: That's approximate, yes, that's about right.

MR. FARES: You recall that at the time, Mike Horak was shouting, correct?

STEVE BAJOVICH: Yes.

MR. FARES: But you don't recall what he was saying because you were paying attention to your typing?

STEVE BAJOVICH: That's right.

MR. FARES: And then Oliver came around the counter and started to ask Mike Horak for identification of some sort?

MR. BISHOP: May I get that question read back?
(Whereupon, the desired portion was read.)

STEVE BAJOVICH: You mean around behind the counter?

MR. FARES: Oliver was behind the counter, as you already testified, in front of Horak correct? Horak was here and Oliver was here? (Indicating.)

STEVE BAJOVICH: Yes.

MR. FARES: And Oliver asked Horak for some sort of identification, correct?

STEVE BAJOVICH: I believe so, yes.

MR. FARES: Horak was still shouting at this time?

STEVE BAJOVICH: Yes, he was.

MR. FARES: You were still paying attention to your typing?

STEVE BAJOVICH: Yes.

MR. FARES: At any time during the period that Mike Horak was in the office, did you answer the telephone?

STEVE BAJOVICH: I don't remember?

MR. FARES: At some point Joe McCarthy asked Oliver something, correct?

STEVE BAJOVICH: Possibly he did, yes.

MR. FARES: You don't remember, though, what it was that McCarthy asked Horak?

STEVE BAJOVICH: No.

MR. FARES: During the period of time that Horak first came in, you said he was hollering, and the time that Joe McCarthy asked Horak something but you don't remember what it was, during that period of time was Horak shouting the whole time?

STEVE BAJOVICH: Yes.

MR. FARES: Sir?

STEVE BAJOVICH: The noise level steadily rose with Horak.

MR. FARES: Did Horak stop hollering when McCarthy asked him a question?

STEVE BAJOVICH: I don't remember if he did or didn't.

MR. FARES: Page 22, lines 22 through 24. I am going to show you a copy of your deposition, which has been marked Plaintiff's Exhibit number 37 for purposes of identification. I will ask you to look at it, read lines 22 to 24 and see if that refreshes your recollection.

(Plaintiff's Exhibit number 37, so marked.)

MR. FARES: Does that refresh your recollection as to whether or not Mike Horak stopped shouting when Joe McCarthy asked him a question?

STEVE BAJOVICH: If that's what I said in the deposition, that's what happened.

MR. FARES: I just want to know if that refreshes your recollection?

STEVE BAJOVICH: Somewhat, yes.

MR. FARES: He did stop shouting?

STEVE BAJOVICH: Probably very briefly.

MR. FARES: Then very briefly Mike Horak started shouting all over again?

STEVE BAJOVICH: Yes.

MR. FARES: And at that point you stood up and you saw Horak push McCarthy?

STEVE BAJOVICH: Yes, correct, yes.

MR. FARES: How did he push him?

STEVE BAJOVICH: From my observation, I seen Horak swing to the right and push McCarthy, I believe with his elbow.

MR. FARES: Then you saw Horak — after you claim you saw Horak push McCarthy and then as McCarthy went down you claim Horak came down too, correct?

STEVE BAJOVICH: Yes.

MR. FARES: And at that time Horak was between the wall and McCarthy, is that true?

STEVE BAJOVICH: I didn't see them when they were on the floor.

MR. FARES: At the point that they went down.

STEVE BAJOVICH: Would you repeat that question once again?

MR. FARES: Let me go back a little to clarify. Mr. Horak was standing there, McCarthy was where when you heard the moment of silence?

STEVE BAJOVICH: Directly behind him and somewhat to his right.

MR. FARES: Okay. Then you claim you saw the push?

STEVE BAJOVICH: Yes.

MR. FARES: And they both went down?

STEVE BAJOVICH: Yes.

MR. FARES: You say just before that push, Horak was between the wall and McCarthy?

STEVE BAJOVICH: I don't remember.

MR. FARES: You don't remember if he was between the wall and McCarthy?

STEVE BAJOVICH: I don't remember.

MR. FARES: Again the deposition, page 25 lines 5 through 10, and I ask you to read those and see if that refreshes your recollection.

STEVE BAJOVICH: Yes.

MR. FARES: All right. Now, do you remember whether or not Horak was between the wall and McCarthy?

STEVE BAJOVICH: If that's what was stated in the deposition, that's what I said.

MR. FARES: I'm not asking you what you said then. Now, do you remember whether or not Horak was between the wall and McCarthy

STEVE BAJOVICH: Yes, just as it states.

MR. FARES: Horak was between which wall and McCarthy?

STEVE BAJOVICH: I don't remember that.

MR. FARES: What is the next thing you noticed after they fell?

STEVE BAJOVICH: They both got up right away.

MR. FARES: Was Horak handcuffed at that time?

STEVE BAJOVICH: Yes, he was.

MR. FARES: Did you continue to watch the whole time?

STEVE BAJOVICH: I sat down later. I stood up matter of seconds and when they got up I sat back down.

MR. FARES: So there's a matter of seconds they went down, came back up again and then you sat back down?

STEVE BAJOVICH: Yes.

MR. FARES: You didn't sit down until they came back up?

STEVE BAJOVICH: I don't think so. I don't really remember that.

MR. FARES: It was only at that point then that Oliver told you to draw a complaint against Horak for disorderly conduct?

STEVE BAJOVICH: That's true.

MR. FARES: After they got back up?

STEVE BAJOVICH: I believe that's correct.

MR. FARES: At any point before you stood up, did Oliver turn around from the counter?

STEVE BAJOVICH: I don't remember.

MR. FARES: Was there anybody else in the office at the time that you stood up and then sat back down which took a matter of seconds, was there anybody else in the office other than yourself, McCarthy, Oliver and Mr. Horak?

STEVE BAJOVICH: Mr. Groth popped in momentarily and left.

MR. FARES: During the time of the scuffle?

STEVE BAJOVICH: I don't remember. I remember him just popping in and leaving.

MR. FARES: Do you remember if he was there when Mr. Horak was first brought in?

STEVE BAJOVICH: I just remember Mr. Groth popping in and leaving.

MR. FARES: You don't remember when at all, correct?

STEVE BAJOVICH: I just remember him popping in and leaving.

MR. FARES: I have nothing further at this time.

Chapter 35

Phillip Langley

MR. FARES: Your Honor, at this time I call Mr. Phillip Langley as an adverse witness.

(Witness sworn.)

PHILLIP LANGLEY, called as an adverse witness by the Plaintiff herein, having been first duly sworn, was examined and testified as follows:

EXAMINATION BY Mr. Fares:

MR. FARES: State your name, please?

PHILLIP LANGLEY: Phillip Langley.

MR. FARES: Your address, sir?

PHILLIP LANGLEY: 20831 Greenwood, Olympia Fields.

MR. FARES: On or about June 12 of 1978, were you employed?

PHILLIP LANGLEY: Yes.

MR. FARES: Where were you employed?

PHILLIP LANGLEY: Sportsman Park Racetrack.

MR. FARES: Well, who were you employed by? Sportsman Park, as Mr. Bishop pointed out, was only a name.

PHILLIP LANGLEY: At that time I was employed by Fox Valley Trotting Club that was running the meet.

MR. FARES: Were you employed in any way, shape, or form for the National Jockey Club.

PHILLIP LANGLEY: At that time?

MR. FARES: Yes, sir.

PHILLIP LANGLEY: No.

MR. FARES: Have you ever been employed by National Jockey Club?

PHILLIP LANGLEY: Yes. When they are conducting a meeting or when no one is conducting a meeting at Sportsman Park, I am employed by National Jockey Club.

MR. FARES: At this time, Fox Valley was running a meet?

PHILLIP LANGLEY: Yes.

MR. FARES: What capacity are you employed?

PHILLIP LANGLEY: Director of racing.

MR. FARES: What did your duties include?

PHILLIP LANGLEY: As director of racing, I do all the work connected with putting on the races, with getting the horsemen at the track, deciding what the purses are, coordinating the back-stretch and the racetrack activities, hiring the officials, just about everything. I'm in charge —

MR. FARES: Including the financial aspects?

PHILLIP LANGLEY: To some extent.

MR. FARES: On that date, you employed, did you not, Mr.

Daniel Groth as chief of security?

PHILLIP LANGLEY: Yes.

MR. FARES: So Fox Valley employed him?

PHILLIP LANGLEY: Yes.

MR. FARES: Under him was Joe McCarthy, who was also employed by Fox Valley, correct?

PHILLIP LANGLEY: I don't recall Joe McCarthy. He was only there for a short time.

MR. FARES: How about Eugene Oliver?

PHILLIP LANGLEY: Eugene Oliver was there.

MR. FARES: He was employed by Fox Valley?

PHILLIP LANGLEY: Yes.

MR. FARES: Also at that time by National Jockey Club?

PHILLIP LANGLEY: I only know that he was employed by Fox Valley.

MR. FARES: At that time, Fox Valley?

PHILLIP LANGLEY: Right.

MR. FARES: Your Honor, I need a minute here and I ask that we adjourn this jury at this time. It appears this is going to take longer than I originally anticipated.

JUDGE LASSERS: We will adjourn.

(Whereupon, the following proceedings were held in chambers outside the presence of the jury:)

MR. FARES: Let me state so the record is clear, Judge. Earlier in the week, Mr. Bishop asked me if I minded there was a man named Mr. McHugh, who was the accountant for both Fox Valley and National Jockey, who testified in his deposition that Eugene Oliver was employed by National Jockey as well as Fox Valley and that the other guys were employed by Fox Valley. He said that this guy's gone out of town and would I mind if he substituted Langley for that purpose as well as to go over the financial statements of Fox Valley. I told him, "No, I don't mind as long as he'll testify to the same thing."

Now, Mr. Langley doesn't know if McCarthy was employed. He is not saying Eugene Oliver was employed by National Jockey Club. I don't know if he's capable of testifying to the financial statement of the National Jockey Club. I am kind of put in a bind. If we could clear it up, let's do it.

MR. BISHOP: I will solve his bind for him right now. Even Mr. McHugh, who is not the accountant but the comptroller, if you put him on the witness stand today and asked him who he worked for, would say, "I work for the National Jockey Club." And if you would ask him, "Don't you work for Fox Valley Trotting?", he would say, "No, because Fox Valley Trotting is not running the meets."

I will stipulate for the record and will straighten out Mr. Langley because he hasn't got the slightest idea of where you're coming from. He has risen to the point of vice president. Eugene Oliver worked for the National Jockey Club and the differentiation is when the track is leased out, National Jockey owns the premises. When the premises are leased out to another meet and the State of Illinois provides that other people can use our tracks, they get dates through the State of Illinois Racing Commission, if they want to pay the rent.

When somebody else comes in and uses our National Jockey Club tracks, we retain the parking lot, the responsibility for the parking lot. Eugene Oliver is paid off a parking lot payroll, that's why he testified from the witness stand that he's employed by National Jockey. The Grandstands, themselves, where the patrons come into the race, all those people involved with that are paid off a payroll from the Fox Valley Trotting. I will stipulate to that right here and now.

JUDGE LASSERS: Okay. Is that agreeable?

MR. FARES: I need to know, Judge, because Eugene Oliver — I need to know if he's going to stipulate to an agency relationship between National Jockey Club and Fox Valley because the testimony is that Oliver takes orders from Mr. Groth who is employed by Fox Valley and not Jockey Club. Mr. Groth takes orders from Mr. Langley. It's kind of a situation where I'm caught in a bind.

MR. BISHOP: I won't stipulate to something legal, a legal conclusion, but I certainly will stipulate, and I think it is clearly on the record that when this meet is being run and that this was a Fox Valley meet, that Mr. Groth was paid by the Fox Valley Trotting Association and every security person on those premises, with the exception of the State of Illinois racing people, they all answered to him and it didn't matter whose payroll they were on. If Eugene Oliver and other people were being paid off the payroll of the National Jockey Club because they were concerned with parts of the premises that were not leased, so be it, but they still were agents or they were still responding to Mr. Groth.

MR. FARES: I don't have any objection if he goes over the testimony with his witness over lunchtime. Could you clear that up?

MR. BISHOP: I will clear that up.

MR. FARES: That's no problem.

MR. BISHOP: He answered his question right. As far as the financial net worth is concerned, you asked Mr. McHugh, he is now in an executive position with one or both of the corporations, as soon as Fox Valley starts trotting, he assumes that other hat as he knows the financial data, if you ask him the right question.

MR. FARES: I will show him the exhibit. I am going to ask if the net worth was $945,000.00 as of November 30 of 1984.

MR. BISHOP: Here is the problem.

JUDGE LASSERS: Is this Fox Valley or National Jockey Club?

MR. FARES: Both.

JUDGE LASSERS: You work it out, will you? If you have a problem then come to me, right?

MR. BISHOP: Off the record.

(Whereupon, a discussion was had off the record.)

(Whereupon, said proceedings were continued to February 6, 1986, at 1:30 p.m.)

(Whereupon, the following proceedings were held in open court in the presence and hearing of the jury, to-wit:)

JUDGE LASSERS: Mr. Langley, I will remind you that you are still under oath.

PHILLIP LANGLEY: Thank you, Your Honor.

Phillip Langley, called as a witness herein, having been previously duly sworn and having testified, resumed the stand, was examined and testified further as follows:

EXAMINATION by Mr. Fares:

MR. FARES: Mr. Langley, over the noon hour, you had an opportunity to check some of the records of Fox Valley National Jockey, correct?

PHILLIP LANGLEY: Yes, sir.

MR. FARES: And in regard to that, let me go over a couple questions that I already asked you this morning. On the date in question, 6/12/78, you were the — say it once more?

PHILLIP LANGLEY: Director of racing.

MR. FARES: Director of racing, okay. And under you came Daniel Groth?

PHILLIP LANGLEY: Yes, sir.

MR. FARES: He was chief of security at that time?

PHILLIP LANGLEY: That's right.

MR. FARES: And you were subject to the direction and control as to your job, the types of things you did and whatnot from, at that time, Fox Valley Trotting Association?

PHILLIP LANGLEY: That's correct.

MR. FARES: Correct, okay. And Daniel Groth, who came under you, was subject to your direction and control at that time?

PHILLIP LANGLEY: That's correct.

MR. FARES: And then under Daniel Groth, in regard to this specific case, there was Joseph McCarthy?

PHILLIP LANGLEY: Yes, sir.

MR. FARES: And he was subject to the direction and control of Daniel Groth.

PHILLIP LANGLEY: Yes.

MR. FARES: And he was also employed at that time, in other

words, paid by, Fox Valley?

PHILLIP LANGLEY: Yes.

MR. FARES: And then there was Eugene Oliver?

PHILLIP LANGLEY: Yes, sir.

MR. FARES: And Eugene Oliver was subject to the direction and control of Daniel Groth?

PHILLIP LANGLEY: Yes.

MR. FARES: And also of you?

PHILLIP LANGLEY: Yes.

MR. FARES: But Eugene Oliver, although being subject to the direction and control of Fox Valley, was paid by National Jockey Club?

PHILLIP LANGLEY: He — I checked on that this noon and he was paid by National Jockey Club.

MR. FARES: And then there was also Steve Bajovich?

PHILLIP LANGLEY: Yes, sir.

MR. FARES: And Steve Bajovich was subject to the direction and control of Daniel Groth?

PHILLIP LANGLEY: Right.

MR. FARES: Daniel Groth was subject to your direction and control and you were subject to the direction and control of Fox Valley?

PHILLIP LANGLEY: Right.

MR. FARES: And Steve Bajovich was paid by Fox Valley?

PHILLIP LANGLEY: Yes.

MR. FARES: And this arose out of a contention that National Jockey Club was running the parking lot as in effect landlords of Sportsman Park?

PHILLIP LANGLEY: That's right.

JUDGE LASSERS: This was National Jockey that did that?

PHILLIP LANGLEY: Yes, sir.

MR. FARES: And Fox Valley was running the meet?

PHILLIP LANGLEY: Yes, sir.

MR. FARES: So they did all those other things or National actually got the horses to run and organize the races and things like that at that time?

PHILLIP LANGLEY: Right.

MR. FARES: And generally in this time period you as director of racing would switch from being employed by Fox Valley if they were running the meet to National Jockey Club if they ran the meet to Suburban Downs, is it?

PHILLIP LANGLEY: Chicago Downs.

MR. FARES: Chicago Downs if they ran the meet, correct?

PHILLIP LANGLEY: Right.

MR. FARES: So you were kind of a free agent but your job was always the same?

PHILLIP LANGLEY: Right.

MR. FARES: You always did the same thing, okay. At this time, what's your position?

PHILLIP LANGLEY: I'm with National Jockey Club. I'm assistant to the president. With Fox Valley, I'm vice president and with Chicago Downs I'm director of racing.

MR. BISHOP: Could we finish up with Mr. Langley tomorrow?

JUDGE LASSERS: Just a moment. We can go off the record.

(Whereupon, there was a discussion off the record.)

(Whereupon, the following proceedings were held in open court in the presence and hearing of the jury:)

JUDGE LASSERS: Ladies and gentlemen, let me give you an update now. When we adjourned, I was in chambers with the lawyers, and we have to work out an important matter with respect to one portion of the testimony and where we come out is this. I am going to have to spend some time reading some cases. I do not want to have you folks just sitting here and twiddling your thumbs. I do not think that is fair to you and counsel or course. So we are going to dismiss you folks now. I ask you to come back. Now, as we see it, at this point, we are going to have a full day of testimony tomorrow. Then we are going to have to work on the instructions, and that is going to take us a matter of several hours. We are going to do that on Monday. So, therefore, the way it looks now, I will give you a definite word on this, we will not have a session with the jury on Monday. We will ask you to come back Tuesday morning. Tuesday morning the slate will be that we are going to have our closing arguments. I will read you the instructions, and then you will retire to consider your verdict. And we will probably wind that all up by noon, maybe shortly before noon depending upon the time we set for oral argument. And that way you folks would get the case Tuesday shortly before noon or noon.

I mention now that on the day that the case goes to the jury, the county supplies lunch. I make no further comment on that. So don't make any plans with friends. There is no need to brown-bag it that day.

So, that is our schedule, and I will let you know if there is any possibility that we can proceed on Monday to wind it up. I would not be optimistic about that. So that is it then for this afternoon. We will see you all back here tomorrow and the way it looks is that we may have some brief testimony on the part of the Plaintiff. That may or may not be. But the chances are that the day will be devoted mostly to the presentation of defense's case by Mr. Bishop. Okay.

(Whereupon, court was adjourned.)

February 7, 1986, 1:15 p.m.:

(Whereupon, the following proceedings were held in open court in the presence and hearing of the jury, to-wit:)

JUDGE LASSERS: Good afternoon, ladies and gentlemen. Okay. Mr. Bishop, another witness.

MR. BISHOP: Mr. Langley, I'd like you to resume the stand, if you would, sir.

JUDGE LASSERS: Okay. I remind you once again, you are under oath, Mr. Langley.

PHILLIP LANGLEY: Okay.

Phillip Langley, called as a witness herein, having been previously duly sworn and having testified, resumed the stand, was examined and testified further as follows:

DIRECT EXAMINATION By Mr. Bishop:

MR. BISHOP: Now, Mr. Langley, just to get some starting point. Would you tell us again what your position is with the Fox Valley Trotting Association?

PHILLIP LANGLEY: I am the director of racing, vice president and racing secretary.

MR. BISHOP: And what is your position with the National Jockey Club?

PHILLIP LANGLEY: I'm assistant to the president.

MR. BISHOP: And on June 12th, 1978, what was your position with the Fox Valley Trotting Association?

PHILLIP LANGLEY: I was director of racing and racing secretary.

MR. BISHOP: What were the duties of the director of racing and the racing secretary for the Fox Valley Trotting Association on June 12th, 1978? In short, what did you do?

PHILLIP LANGLEY: In short, I was in charge of bringing the horses to Sportsman Park and putting the races together and deciding what persons should be paid to each race, what nights the races went, what order the races went, and who the drivers were to be on the grounds and who the trainers were to be and in hiring the officials for the racing, the racing officials. Most everything that had to do with the racing end of the operation on the race track.

MR. BISHOP: Did that include the gathering and having available the information in the program of the type that's marked as Defendant's Exhibit Number 10, for identification?

PHILLIP LANGLEY: That was under my supervision, yes.

MR. BISHOP: You don't do all this work yourself. You had a group of people assisting you?

PHILLIP LANGLEY: Yes.

MR. BISHOP: And all those people worked under your direction and supervision, isn't that so?

PHILLIP LANGLEY: Yes, sir, that's correct.

MR. BISHOP: Sir, at the present time you are also associated with another organization, are you not?

PHILLIP LANGLEY: I'm —

MR. BISHOP: Specifically, the United States Trotting Association?

PHILLIP LANGLEY: Yes, sir, I'm a director of the United States Trotting Association.

MR. BISHOP: Sir, and what is the United States Trotting Association?

PHILLIP LANGLEY: It's basic purpose is to maintain the records. The records in the United States. All the statistics on all the horses and the drivers and the owners and a certain amount of rule making, supervision, suggestions. But each state is autonomous as far as the rule goes so, but it is the main record keeping organization in the country.

MR. BISHOP: And was that so in June of 1978?

PHILLIP LANGLEY: Yes, it's been so since 1939.

MR. BISHOP: I would like the record to reflect that I'm marking this document Defendant's Exhibit number 11, for identification.

(Whereupon, said document was marked Defendant's Exhibit Number 11, for identification, as of 2/7/89.)

MR. BISHOP: And, sir, I am handing you what is marked as Defendant's Exhibit number 11, for identification. I ask you to look at it and tell us what it is.

PHILLIP LANGLEY: It is — appears to be a copy of a printout by the United States Trotting Association on the horse Phase Out, which lists the races he participated in 1978.

MR. BISHOP: Is that the type of print-out that you use from time to time in the course of your activities when you're working at Sportsman Park?

PHILLIP LANGLEY: Yes, we have a print-out like this. Actually, we have an original availability paper like this on every horse that races at Sportsman Park. So we deal with hundreds of them daily.

MR. BISHOP: That is a print-out of what?

PHILLIP LANGLEY: Of the United States Trotting Association racing record of the horse.

JUDGE LASSERS: The horse, I see.

PHILLIP LANGLEY: Right.

MR. BISHOP: So that is the copy of the official record for that horse for that year.

PHILLIP LANGLEY: Yes, sir.

MR. BISHOP: 1978?

JUDGE LASSERS: What horse?

PHILLIP LANGLEY: Phase-Out.

JUDGE LASSERS: 1978?

PHILLIP LANGLEY: Yes, sir.

MR. BISHOP: Sir, now as you sit here, you don't have any specific recollection of the horse Phase-Out, do you or don't you?

PHILLIP LANGLEY: Yes, I remember the horse very well.

MR. BISHOP: Fine. Did you schedule that horse to race on

June 12, 1978?

PHILLIP LANGLEY: He raced on June 12, 1978.

MR. BISHOP: I see I have assumed something. How does it come about — what are the mechanics for a horse getting in a race such as Phase-Out on June 12, 1978?

PHILLIP LANGLEY: Some time prior to that date, usually a week or two ahead of time, I will schedule the potential races for the next two weeks or the next week, whatever the case may be. And at that time, trainers of horses will look over the schedule and pick out the races that they think their horses would fit in. In this particular horse's case, he was limited to one race that he could go in because we have horses that are called "Invitational Horses", and we have three or four invitational groups, which are the best horses on the track, and I pick out the horses that go in those races. So in this particular case, I selected the horses he would race against. I might have selected seven or eight and only five of them entered the race, but he was limited to the races he could go in at that time.

MR. BISHOP: And why was he limited in the race he could go in at that time?

PHILLIP LANGLEY: Because of the top, probably the top 16 horses at the track. I took those 16 or 18 horses and broke them down into three groups that I thought would be the most competitive and told those people which race they had to go in. If I could only do three or four races a week, the rest of them had to be given an option where they can go, but the very top horses, you can pick what race they go in, and I can tell them they have to go in that race.

MR. BISHOP: I kind of get the impression from what you said the horses fit into various classes for the purposes of racing?

PHILLIP LANGLEY: Yes, many, many different levels of races.

MR. BISHOP: And it's up to you as the director of racing —

MR. FARES: Your Honor, let me object to the leading of the witness.

JUDGE LASSERS: Sustained. Really, Mr. Bishop.

MR. BISHOP: Is it up to you as a director of racing to decide which class a horse can race in?

PHILLIP LANGLEY: It is up — no.

MR. BISHOP: How is that determined?

PHILLIP LANGLEY: I write certain types of races, schedule certain types of races, and with the exception of the top 20 horses, they can pick the race that they think their horse fits the conditions of whether it's a claiming race or a different kind of conditioned race.

MR. BISHOP: And what kind of a race was this that Phase-Out was in?

PHILLIP LANGLEY: He was in an invitational race for a purse of $11,000.

MR. BISHOP: And who was the jockey on that horse that day?

PHILLIP LANGLEY: Well, we call them drivers in harness races. That was Daryl Busse.

MR. BISHOP: And what were the odds on that horse?

PHILLIP LANGLEY: He was 70 cents to a dollar which is about three to five. It means if you bet a dollar and you win, you get your dollar plus 70 cents back.

MR. BISHOP: And how did he come out?

PHILLIP LANGLEY: He came out fifth.

MR. BISHOP: How many horses in the race?

PHILLIP LANGLEY: Five.

MR. BISHOP: How come only five?

PHILLIP LANGLEY: Often times, in the very best race, we go with five or six horses and I — since June 12th was a Monday night, probably that was all I could get to go in that race and reuse on the night when the crowd wasn't so big.

MR. BISHOP: Who was first in the race?

PHILLIP LANGLEY: A horse called "Pacing Robin".

MR. BISHOP: Who was second?

PHILLIP LANGLEY: A horse called "Chief Debonair".

MR. BISHOP: I have nothing further, Your Honor.

JUDGE LASSERS: Cross-Examination.

MR. FARES: Thank you, Your Honor.

CROSS-EXAMINATION By Mr. Fares:

MR. FARES: You said earlier that you knew Phase-Out. You remember that horse very well?

PHILLIP LANGLEY: Yes, sir.

MR. FARES: Why is that?

PHILLIP LANGLEY: I just remember horses like people remember baseball players.

MR. FARES: How long did Phase-Out continue to run after

1978?

PHILLIP LANGLEY: I think he raced another year and then they retired him to stud.

MR. FARES: How long did he race before that?

PHILLIP LANGLEY: Well, he was — in 1978 he was a five-year old. He raced as a three-year old in 1976.

MR. FARES: Incidentally, the three following races after 6/12/78, Phase-Out won, all three with different drivers than the one on 6/12, isn't that true?

PHILLIP LANGLEY: Yes.

MR. FARES: On 6/12, Busse drove Phase-Out, Daryl Busse?

PHILLIP LANGLEY: He drove him, yes.

MR. FARES: And then the next three it was another driver?

PHILLIP LANGLEY: Yes, it was a different driver, two different drivers drove him in those three races.

MR. FARES: In the three after, are you saying, two different drivers drove Phase-Out and he won all three races?

PHILLIP LANGLEY: Yes, sir.

MR. FARES: I have nothing further, Your Honor.

(End of transcript)

Phillip Langley slowly walked from the witness stand to the table where Mr. Bishop was seated. He had a dejected look across his face as he passed Mr. Fares's table where I was sitting. This made me feel quite a lot better. I thought that just maybe, Mr. Bishop hadn't pulled enough strings for a guaranteed victory. Judge Lassers called for a ten-

A very depressed Phil Langley leaving the court.
(Photo by Rory Martin)

minute recess, in order for Mr. Bishop to confer with his next witness in the hallway.

To my astonishment, my fair-weather attorney, on one of his rare occasions, sat down next to me at the attorney's table, overlooking the courtroom. Leaning closer, he whispered that Bishop was about to spring his Ace-in-the-hole witness that would win the case. Fares then said that I should now settle for the small amount of money that Sportsman Park officials were willing to pay. I gave him a cold look and said, "Don't even think about it!" I thought to myself, "Regardless of the outcome of this lawsuit, I made a terrible choice in choosing this law firm." Had I known before-hand, I wouldn't hire Fares to defend me on a parking ticket.

At that moment, the courtroom door opened. All of the spectators turned their attention to watch the little, old man enter, followed by Mr. Bishop as they headed towards the witness stand. At first glance, I guessed the witness's age to be in the seventies. It was difficult for me to comprehend Bishop's motive in bringing in a witness in the condition that guy was in.

His long, stringy, gray hair hung over a badly-worn red flannel shirt that was tucked into a a pair of soiled Levi's. His pants' cuffs were overlapping a pair of muddy cowboy boots. The inch-long gray beard covered his entire face except for the cheek bones that stuck out sharply making his bloodshot eyes look more recessed into his skull.

I was unable to recognize the individual as he slowly walked past my table to the witness stand. I was about to get the shock of my life for never in my wildest imagination could I ever believe that a person could have his features alter so drastically in a matter of a couple of years. I almost dropped my water glass when he gave his name as Daryl Busse, age 43.

Chapter 36

Daryl Busse

MR. BISHOP: Your Honor, I call to the stand Mr. Daryl Busse.

(Witness sworn)

Daryl Busse, called as a witness herein, having been first duly sworn, was examined and testified as follows:

DIRECT EXAMINATION By Mr. Bishop:

Daryl Busse at the race track.

MR. BISHOP: Sir, would you speak up nice and loud so everybody in the Courtroom can hear you.
Tell us what your name is and spell your last name.

DARYL BUSSE: My name is Daryl Busse, B-U-S-S-E.

MR. BISHOP: Where do you live, Mr. Busse?

DARYL BUSSE: I live in Kingston, Illinois.

MR. BISHOP: How old a man are you.

DARYL BUSSE: 43.

MR. BISHOP: What is your business or occupation?

DARYL BUSSE: I'm a harness horse owner, trainer and driver.

MR. BISHOP: How long have you been in that business, sir?
DARYL BUSSE: Since about 1960.

MR. BISHOP: Sir, owning, training and driving is your primary occupation, is it not?

DARYL BUSSE: Yes, it is my only occupation.

MR. BISHOP: You have no other occupation at all, is that right, sir?

DARYL BUSSE: No.

MR. BISHOP: Are you familiar with what it costs either now in 1986 or what the cost was in the year 1978 to maintain a trotting horse of the type that's used in and around the fair and usual tracks of the State of Illinois?

DARYL BUSSE: Yes.

MR. FARES: Judge, I object at this point. Number one, to relevance, and number two, it can't lead to anything relevant.

JUDGE LASSERS: Maybe not, but go ahead.

MR. BISHOP: Would you tell us what it generally cost to maintain a horse for the purposes of trotting on the fair and usual tracks, either now or in 1978?

DARYL BUSSE: For an average horse right now, it would probably cost you anywhere from $12,000.00 to $15,000.00 a year to keep it racing with all the costs. Back in 1978, it would have been slightly less. Maybe around $10,000.00. But right now it's about $12,000.00 to $15,000.00, I would imagine to keep a horse.

MR. BISHOP: You have books and records and you're confronted in your business with that all the time, aren't you?

DARYL BUSSE: Yes, sir.

MR. BISHOP: Sir, do you have any independent recollection of driving in one or more races at Sportsman Park in June of 1978?

DARYL BUSSE: I had no recollection until I had seen that program.

MR. BISHOP: I would like the record to reflect that I'm marking this document Defendant's Exhibit Number 10 for identification.

(Whereupon, Defendant's Exhibit Number 10 was marked for identification.)

JUDGE LASSERS: Do you have a question?

MR. FARES: I'm looking at the exhibit.

JUDGE LASSERS: I see. This is the program?

MR. BISHOP: Yes, sir, Your honor.

MR. FARES: Your Honor, at this point I have no objection depending on what purpose Mr. Bishop intends to use this document.

MR. BISHOP: Sir, I hand you what has been marked Defendant's Exhibit Number 10 for identification and ask you to look at it and tell us whether or not it's a program for June 12th, 1978 at Sportsman Park.

DARYL BUSSE: Yes, it is.

MR. BISHOP: And is a program such as what you have in

your hand something that's available for every race or every day that races are run?

DARYL BUSSE: Yes, sir.

MR. FARES: Your, Honor, at this point I am going to voice an objection. Apparently, this document is being used to refresh this man's recollection concerning some specific date, or whatever, and it's not being used for that purpose at this point.

JUDGE LASSERS: It's used to refresh his recollection but now he's asking other questions about it. Overruled. Go ahead.

MR. BISHOP: The point I am trying to get at is that a program is not something that you're unfamiliar with?

DARYL BUSSE: No, I am very familiar with it.

MR. BISHOP: As you sit here, now, do you recall whether on June 12th, 1978, you drove a horse known as Phase-Out?

DARYL BUSSE: Yes, I did. It was in the ninth race.

MR. BISHOP: In the ninth race?

DARYL BUSSE: Yes, sir.

MR. BISHOP: And how many other horses were in that race?

DARYL BUSSE: Four other ones. Five all together.

MR. BISHOP: Sir, did you also drive in the tenth race?

(Witness perusing document.)

DARYL BUSSE: Yes, sir. I drove Strong Arm in the tenth race.

MR. BISHOP: How many horses were in the tenth race?

DARYL BUSSE: Nine.

MR. BISHOP: Did you know the Plaintiff in this lawsuit before June 12th, 1978 — Mr. Michael John Horak, the gentleman sitting there?

DARYL BUSSE: Yes, sir. Yes, sir.

MR. BISHOP: On the evening of June 12th, 1978, at Sportsman Park Race Track did you ever encounter Mr. Michael John Horak?

DARYL BUSSE: Yes, I did?

MR. BISHOP: Could you tell us, to the best of your recollection, when your first contact with Mr. Horak was that evening?

DARYL BUSSE: Well, the first contact that I had with him of any, besides just seeing him, was after the ninth race.

MR. BISHOP: And where did that contact take place?

DARYL BUSSE: It was in the Paddock area up on the — by the west end of the Paddock by the Paddock Judge's office. He was standing outside, I was standing inside.

MR. BISHOP: And what, if anything, brought your attention to the fact that Mr. Horak was there at that time?

DARYL BUSSE: Well, he was being rather abusive to me, I guess, because of this race.

MR. BISHOP: Could you describe to the ladies and gentlemen of the jury what you mean by "abusive"?

DARYL BUSSE: Threatening me, calling me names. He made a certain statement considering, you know, different things like that. Being rather —

MR. FARES: Your Honor, at this point —

DARYL BUSSE: — bad, abusive.
MR. FARES: — at this point, I'm going to object for foundational reasons. He's talking about statements, threats being made, and he hasn't laid a foundation for any of this concerning conversation.

JUDGE LASSERS: You want to —

MR. BISHOP: I'm only asking the witness what happened.

JUDGE LASSERS: He's relating a conversation, but we know the time, we know the place. We don't know who else was present. Why don't you ask that?

MR. BISHOP: Who else was present, if you recall?

DARYL BUSSE: Well, the Paddock Judge was present.

MR. BISHOP: What was his name?

DARYL BUSSE: Frank Penino.

MR. BISHOP: How old a man is Mr. Penino?

DARYL BUSSE: Back then, let's see. He would have probably been 70 to 75 years old.

MR. BISHOP: That would make him about in his 80s now?

DARYL BUSSE: 80s, yes, sir.

MR. BISHOP: Do you recall anybody else by name who was present?

DARYL BUSSE: Stanley Banks was present.

MR. BISHOP: Anybody else — who is Stanley Banks?

DARYL BUSSE: He is a harness race driver.

MR. BISHOP: Did you recall anybody else that was present?

DARYL BUSSE: Not offhand.

MR. BISHOP: What about the patrons? Were there patrons right outside to Paddock area at that time?

DARYL BUSSE: Yes, they're right around that area the closest to the Grandstand where all the fans are and if anybody wants to come down to the Paddock, most generally, that's the biggest congregated place where there's people, fans on the outside. Of course, the grooms and the owners come in to see the horses and stuff like that. It's the most easy — acceptable place for people from the Grandstand to see the Paddock closest to the Grandstand, I should say.

MR. BISHOP: Sir, when you say Mr. Horak was making threats at you at that time, would you kindly, to the best of your recollection, tell us the nature or form of the threats?

DARYL BUSSE: He was calling me rather bad names, being rather loud about it. S.O.B. so on, so forth. 'Somebody ought to break your damn leg,' that kind of stuff, only with a little bit stronger language than that.

MR. BISHOP: You —

DARYL BUSSE: I have been abused at the track many times because I've lost lots of times, but this —

MR. FARES: Objection, Your Honor. No question pending.

MR. BISHOP: No, he's answering the question.

JUDGE LASSERS: You're not relating what was said.

MR. BISHOP: At this time, what happened?

MR. FARES: Your Honor, I'm going to object. If there's a question, let him put it to him.

MR. BISHOP: At this time what happened?

DARYL BUSSE: At this time after the race?

MR. BISHOP: Right.

DARYL BUSSE: He was real abusive. That's what concerned me. Because he was loud. Like I say, he used real bad language to me, "Somebody ought to break your legs", that kind of stuff.

MR. FARES: Objection, Your Honor. This has been asked and answered now three times.

JUDGE LASSERS: What else?

DARYL BUSSE: Conversation just like that, real loud. I mean, to the people around him were —

MR. FARES: Objection, Your honor. This is the same testimony.

JUDGE LASSERS: Just a moment.

MR. FARES: — Your Honor.

JUDGE LASSERS: That wasn't part of the question.

MR. BISHOP: Did you observe the other — the reactions of the other people in the area at that time?

DARYL BUSSE: Yes, sir.

MR. BISHOP: What did they do?

DARYL BUSSE: They tried to get away from him.

MR. BISHOP: Did you say anything to Mr. Horak at that time?

DARYL BUSSE: I can't possibly recall whether I did or didn't.

MR. BISHOP: After the end of that ninth race when you went into the Paddock — where did you go then?

DARYL BUSSE: Well, I went into the Paddock after the ninth race, walked down toward the other end of the Paddock where Mr. Horak was.

MR. BISHOP: Then what happened?

DARYL BUSSE: That's when he was starting to get very abusive.

MR. BISHOP: In what form did the abuse take at that time?

DARYL BUSSE: What?

MR. BISHOP: Have you already told us about that abuse?

DARYL BUSSE: That's what I was telling you about before.

MR. BISHOP: After that, where did you go?

DARYL BUSSE: Well, I got a little nervous. The guy was being —

MR. FARES: Objection. Objection as to what his mental state was. Asked to strike. It's non-responsive.

MR. BISHOP: May the witness be able to answer the question?

JUDGE LASSERS: Folks, one at a time. The portion with the

answer about Mr. Busse's mental state will be stricken as non-responsive. All right. Now —

MR. BISHOP: What did you do after you walked away from where Mr. Horak was?

DARYL BUSSE: I talked to Stanley Banks.

MR. BISHOP: Then what did you do?

DARYL BUSSE: I asked him what he thought.

MR. FARES: Objection to any conversation as being hearsay.

MR. BISHOP: Your Honor, it's not conversation. I object to the constant interruption. He's telling us what he said.

JUDGE LASSERS: He —

MR. FARES: He said Stan Banks said, Your Honor.

MR. BISHOP: No, he did not, Your honor.

JUDGE LASSERS: Just a moment counsel. Now, we can hear what Mr. Busse said because that's not hearsay. All Right. Now, go ahead.

MR. BISHOP: What did you say to Mr. Banks?

DARYL BUSSE: I asked him what he thought I should do.

MR. BISHOP: You can't tell us what somebody else told you, that's hearsay. Just what you did. Then what did you do after that?

DARYL BUSSE: I called Phil Langley.

MR. BISHOP: Who is Phil Langley?

DARYL BUSSE: He's a director of racing at Sportsman Park.

MR. BISHOP: That is the gentleman seated down here in the brown blazer?

DARYL BUSSE: Yes, sir.

MR. BISHOP: What did you say to Mr. Langley?

DARYL BUSSE: I asked him to please get the security down there.

MR. BISHOP: Did you call him anything else?

DARYL BUSSE: I just said the guy was coming off the wall.

MR. BISHOP: Did you name the guy?

DARYL BUSSE: Yes.

MR. BISHOP: What name did you say?

DARYL BUSSE: Michael John.

MR. BISHOP: Who is Michael John?

DARYL BUSSE: Michael John Horak. Fellow over there (indicating).

MR. BISHOP: You then rode in the next race, that is the tenth race?

DARYL BUSSE: Yes, sir.

MR. BISHOP: What horse did you drive in the tenth race?

DARYL BUSSE: Strong Arm.

MR. BISHOP: And the physical make-up of the Paddock really isn't clear to the ladies and gentlemen of the jury. Is the Paddock where the horses get ready, is that inside or outside?

DARYL BUSSE: Paddock is inside.

MR. BISHOP: Inside of a building?

DARYL BUSSE: Well, inside of a building with a fence enclosure to enclose the Paddock to keep the fans on one side.

MR. BISHOP: The fans can stand outside the fence and see into the Paddock.

DARYL BUSSE: Similar to that rail you got there, only it's a lot taller and the bottom part of it is all solid.

MR. BISHOP: We're just not talking about a door in the Paddock such as the door of the Courtroom; we're talking about something wider so the spectators and patrons can actually look all the way in?

DARYL BUSSE: There's an opening on each side of the Paddock.

MR. BISHOP: And what is your — what is the practice that you have to follow when you're getting ready to go out and drive in the next race such as on this evening? You drive in the tenth race? What do you do?

DARYL BUSSE: You can do several different things. But a minute before the horses go out, the Paddock Judge says, "One minute," before we go out.

MR. BISHOP: And at that time, where was your horse for the tenth race?

DARYL BUSSE: Well, let's see. First, second, third — the horse for the tenth race was down at the other end of the Paddock which would be the east end.

MR. BISHOP: Stalls in there?

DARYL BUSSE: Yes, sir.

MR. BISHOP: He would be in stall?

DARYL BUSSE: Yes, sir.

MR. BISHOP: And at that one-minute point, where would you go?

DARYL BUSSE: I would go up to my horse where the trainer would be?

MR. BISHOP: Then what would you do?

DARYL BUSSE: Ask the trainer —

MR. FARES: Your Honor, again I object to conversation — go ahead. I apologize.

MR. BISHOP: What happened?

DARYL BUSSE: I always ask the trainer how the horse was, how he would like me to race the horse, and then —

MR. BISHOP: Then what did you do after that?

DARYL BUSSE: The Paddock Judge would usually say, "Okay." We go out on the race track, so I would grab the lines, the groom would lead the horse out, I got out on the bike, get myself set, get the handles set, and we go out on the race track for a post parade.

MR. BISHOP: "Post Parade" is go around the track?

DARYL BUSSE: You go clock-wise around the race track and end up in front of the Grandstand where the announcer announces the name of the horses and down — you score the horse down twice.

JUDGE LASSERS: You what?

DARYL BUSSE: Score the horse down, what you call maybe a quarter-mile exercise time for the horse. You're on the race track for about ten minutes.

MR. BISHOP: When you take the horse from the stall in the Paddock out to the track proper, you have to go through this open area where the patrons are, don't you?

DARYL BUSSE: Yes, sir.

MR. BISHOP: Does a kind of aisle open up so you can ride through?

DARYL BUSSE: Yes, sir.

MR. BISHOP: Is there a fence where that aisle is or just open up so you can drive through?

DARYL BUSSE: When you walk, when you go out to the Paddock, they have two people there with two ropes and they take ropes outside of the aisle-way that you go out to the race track. The aisle-way is possibly a little wider, maybe twice as wide as that double door there (indicating).

MR. BISHOP: Sir, on that particular day in preparation for the tenth race, when you came out of the Paddock with your horse down the aisle, was Mr. Horak still out there in the patron area?

DARYL BUSSE: Yes, sir.

MR. BISHOP: And was there any dialogue by Mr. Horak at that time? Did he say anything?

DARYL BUSSE: Well, the same thing that he was saying before. I can't exactly give you his words but he was being very abusive.

MR. BISHOP: What about gestures? Were there any gestures?

DARYL BUSSE: Well, throwing his arms around, one thing and another, and hollering and screaming.

MR. BISHOP: What did you do?

DARYL BUSSE: I went out on the race track.

MR. BISHOP: Ran the race?

DARYL BUSSE: Yes, sir.

MR. BISHOP: And sir, after the race, you then came off the track —

DARYL BUSSE: Yes, sir.

MR. BISHOP: — is that correct? When you came off the track, was Mr. Horak still there?

DARYL BUSSE: Mr. Horak was up at the other end of the Paddock.

MR. BISHOP: When you say, "up at the other end of the Paddock", what do you mean?

DARYL BUSSE: He was up at the end of the Paddock that I described before by the — up at the end where the Paddock office is.

MR. BISHOP: In other words, there's one place you normally go onto the track with your horse?

DARYL BUSSE: Yes, sir.

MR. BISHOP: And there's one place you usually come off the race?

DARYL BUSSE: Yes, sir.

MR. BISHOP: When you finish the race, do you physically take the horse off the track or do you turn it over to a groom or —

DARYL BUSSE: Turn it over to a groom.

MR. BISHOP: Is that done when you're on the track proper?

DARYL BUSSE: You're on the edge of the race track, yes, sir.

MR. BISHOP: Where you usually stopped at that exit, let's call it, is there any kind of a gate or any kind of a fence that you walk through once you get off the race track proper and before you get to the Paddock?

DARYL BUSSE: There's a distance, probably a little longer, from here to the door that you walk from the race track to the Paddock that's unprotected that —

MR. BISHOP: That's where the patrons and general public come in?

DARYL BUSSE: Patron, yes, sir.

MR. BISHOP: That's not where Mr. Horak was?

DARYL BUSSE: No, sir.

MR. BISHOP: He was up at the entrance gate, is that correct?

DARYL BUSSE: To the best of my recollection, yes.

MR. BISHOP: Did he say anything to you at that time?

DARYL BUSSE: He still kept hollering and screaming.

MR. BISHOP: He apparently was some distance away,

wasn't he?

DARYL BUSSE: Well, yes. But I walked up at the other end of the Paddock where he happened to be and he kept screaming.

MR. BISHOP: It's not unusual for a driver to walk up in that area, is it?

DARYL BUSSE: Yes.

MR. BISHOP: You've done it many times?

DARYL BUSSE: Many times.

MR. BISHOP: When you realized Mr. Horak was still up there, what did you do?

DARYL BUSSE: Called Phil again?

MR. BISHOP: Then after — that didn't take place from the spectator area proper, you apparently were somewhere close to the phone, weren't you?

MR. FARES: I haven't been objecting to the leading nature of the questions of Mr. Bishop, but can we have him form proper questions?

JUDGE LASSERS: All right. Let's —

MR. BISHOP: When you called Mr. Langley did you use a phone?

DARYL BUSSE: Yes, sir.

MR. BISHOP: Where was the phone?

DARYL BUSSE: In the Paddock office.

MR. BISHOP: What did you tell Mr. Langley at that time?

DARYL BUSSE: "This guy's off the wall. We've got to have the security down there."

MR. BISHOP: I have nothing further. Thank you very much, sir.

JUDGE LASSERS: All right. Cross.

MR. BISHOP: Oh, I do have one or two other questions, Your Honor.

JUDGE LASSERS: Two questions, Mr. Bishop.

MR. BISHOP: Or maybe three.

JUDGE LASSERS: Three questions.

MR. BISHOP: Maybe four.

JUDGE LASSERS: Three.

MR. BISHOP: Sir, were there any precipitating events that you can recall on the previous occasions that led up to what happened on the evening on June 12th, 1978?

DARYL BUSSE: Well, I don't know if it led up to it.

MR. FARES: Your Honor, I'm going to object at this time pursuant to Your Honor's ruling in chambers and ask that a date be given before we get any alleged prior incidents.

JUDGE LASSERS: All right. What —

MR. BISHOP: I didn't.

JUDGE LASSERS: He said, "yes".

MR. BISHOP: I'm trying to find out if there was a precipitating event.

JUDGE LASSERS: Let's try to find out a date?

MR. BISHOP: Was there, if you can recall, a precipitating event at some previous occasion that led up to what happened on this date? Was there such an event —

DARYL BUSSE: Yes, there was.

MR. BISHOP: Can you tell us where that event occurred?

DARYL BUSSE: It took place at the Steak-n-Egger on Lake Street.

MR. BISHOP: Is that in Addison, Illinois?

DARYL BUSSE: I believe it's in Addison, yes.

MR. BISHOP: Can you tell us when that occurred in relation to this June 12th, 1978?

DARYL BUSSE: It was about a year before that, I believe.

MR. FARES: I'm going to object then, Your Honor, to any testimony concerning events that transpired prior to this particular area.

JUDGE LASSERS: Isn't that pretty far?

MR. BISHOP: No, sir.

JUDGE LASSERS: One year.

MR. BISHOP: One year, Your Honor. It's to the best of his recollection.

JUDGE LASSERS: Let me talk to the lawyers.

(Whereupon, a side bar was held.)

JUDGE LASSERS: What's the substance of the testimony,

Mr. Bishop?

MR. BISHOP: Pardon me, Your Honor?

JUDGE LASSERS: What's the substance of the testimony that we're going to hear?

MR. BISHOP: I think the witness is going to testify, Your Honor, that he was at the Steak-n-Egger on Lake Street in Addison, Illinois one evening when Mr. Horak came in and started the same kind of conduct. He was hollering, he was raving, he was shouting, he was waving his arms; and it's the impression and the understanding of this witness that this was precipitous of the events that occurred on the night of this occurrence. That's what he's going to testify to. Therefore, now if I could ask this witness about the conduct that observed Mr. Horak giving Mr. Busse is fair. I can ask about all sorts of conduct that Mr. Busse has been subjected to by Mr. Horak. All this is precipitous on the occurrence of this night. We finally have a man who said, "I had it. And he insulted my mother, he said all these things."

JUDGE LASSERS: All right.

MR. FARES: Judge, as I understand your ruling in Your honor's chambers, "is precipitous" meant something that led up to this particular incident then it's allowed in. Now we're talking about a course of action that may have been going on for years and years and may have been due to things that Busse did as well as things Horak did. How can you say something that happened a year prior is related to this particular incident.

(Whereupon, the following proceedings were held in chambers out of the hearing of the jury.)

MR. FARES: The horse Phase-Out that Busse drove in a race was far in advance of all of the horses in that field and yet finished last in a race where that horse was off with perfect odds and with the best odds and the horse with the worse odds came in first. There's no way it was precipitous.

MR. BISHOP: That's horse races.

MR. FARES: It's going to the character of Mr. Horak, and Your Honor is excluding me from using a character evidence. I don't think this type of character evidence should come in with Mr. Horak.

JUDGE LASSERS: What type of character witness —

MR. FARES: All that about Mr. Oliver, Mr. Oliver shooting, killing this other man, killing this young boy in the parking lot. I was going to have an I.B.A. Agent concerning cocaine use at the track. I had an I.B.A. agent to testify against Mr. Oliver about him taking money from pick-pockets so those pick-pockets could operate at the track. Now we left all that out, Judge, and he's going to start bringing in this garbage. It's unfair and it's unrelated.

MR. BISHOP: We have our ground rules and that's what the witness is prepared to testify to and that's exactly what Mr. Fares has known all along that the witness would testify to.

MR. FARES: Oh, absolutely not. Absolutely not.

JUDGE LASSERS: When you say precipitous —

MR. BISHOP: The man has demonstrated a course of conduct towards this witness who is not a party to this lawsuit, brought this witness to the point where he feared for his personal safety and he complained. He complained to the Paddock Judge and he complained to Mr. Langley after two races. He was concerned, he felt intimidated, he felt he was in jeopardy, and he complained and asked for help.

MR. FARES: So, his manner on this evening led him to believe that he was in danger for his safety? First of all, I think words are not provocation. I think that's a clear ruling of the law. Second of all, What do any words that happened a year before have anything to do with Mr. Busse's state of mind on this evening? What did they have to do with the fact that Michael John Horak got wacked on the elbow and can't drive horses anymore? Nothing.

MR. BISHOP: My only feeling is that Counsel for the Plaintiff and Mr. Horak wants to put Mr. Busse on trial in this case. It's not me. And now they don't want to hear what he has to say. I will confine it to that one event.

JUDGE LASSERS: I'll let you go.

MR. BISHOP: Thank you, Your Honor.

MR. FARES: Note my objections for the record, please.

JUDGE LASSERS: Surely.

(Whereupon, the following proceedings
were held in open Court:)

MR. BISHOP: Can you continue, Mr. Busse, telling us about your contact with Mr. Horak a year earlier.

DARYL BUSSE: I went in the restaurant to eat and Mr. Horak was in there. We started to talk about the race track, about around the race track. For some unknown reason, I guess he had his reasons —

MR. FARES: Object to the characterization, Your Honor.

MR. BISHOP: Just tell us what happened.

DARYL BUSSE: So he, all of a sudden, exploded.

MR. BISHOP: What do you mean by that?

DARYL BUSSE: Became rather abusive about that, talking about my character, my father's character. I got a little nervous.

MR. FARES: Objection, Your Honor.

JUDGE LASSERS: Sustained.

MR. BISHOP: What did you do?

DARYL BUSSE: I finally asked the fellow that was working behind the counter to call the police.

MR. BISHOP: Thank You, sir. No further questions.

JUDGE LASSERS: Cross-examination.

CROSS-EXAMINATION By Mr. Fares:

MR. FARES: Now, Mr. Busse, you drove in many, many, many races —

DARYL BUSSE: Yes, sir.

MR. FARES: — correct? Am I speaking loud enough for you to hear me?

DARYL BUSSE: Yes, sir.

MR. FARES: You're a true horseman, would you characterize yourself that way?

DARYL BUSSE: Yes, sir.

MR. FARES: It's your life, isn't it?

DARYL BUSSE: Yes, sir.

MR. FARES: And there's good things about your business and there's bad things about your business?

DARYL BUSSE: Yes, sir.

MR. FARES: Tell me something about those bad things about your business.

MR. BISHOP: Objection, Your Honor, I fail to see where this is relevant.

JUDGE LASSERS: I'm going to sustain that.
MR. FARES: Let me get more specific then, Judge.

(END OF TRANSCRIPT)

After many attempts, I was finally able to obtain The attention of Mr. Fares and have him come over to me and see what I had written on his yellow tablet in large printed letters.

"When are you going to stop pussy-footing around with this clown and let those jurors know that he is far from being the angel that he is trying to convince them of?" I had written. I continued, "Must I again remind you that I have the proof in an envelope in my pocket. Bishop has had enough help already!"

Fares's face had turned flush as though he had been caught with his hand in the formidable cookie jar. He abruptly turned and walked over towards the jury box.

(Start Transcript)

MR. FARES: Mr. Busse, you're familiar, are you not with incidents of drugging of race horses?

MR. BISHOP: Objection, objection, objection. Your Honor, I must be heard on this.

JUDGE LASSERS: Sustained, sustained, sustained.

MR. FARES: Mr. Busse, have you ever fixed a race or been involved in the fixing of an outcome of a race?

MR. BISHOP: Objection, Your Honor. An improper question unless he can prove it.

MR. FARES: I have the right to inquire.

MR. BISHOP: No, Your Honor, he does not.

MR. FARES: He's put this man on as an experienced driver and he's put him on as somebody high in the business and I think I have the right to inquire into this especially since part of our case is based on that very thing, Judge.

MR. BISHOP: If he proves this man of an unlawful act, he must come in with a certified copy of a conviction to prove it. Otherwise, he cannot answer the question. Mere accusations alone are not sufficient.

JUDGE LASSERS: I understand.

MR. BISHOP: Thank you, Your Honor.

JUDGE LASSERS: I will let him answer that question.

MR. FARES: Mr. Busse. Have you ever fixed a race or been involved in the fixing of an outcome of a race?

DARYL BUSSE: Yes, sir.

MR. FARES: Now, Mr. Busse, you said that until you saw that racing program that you had no recollection of driving Phase-Out on June 12th of 1978?

DARYL BUSSE: No, I didn't.

MR. FARES: Generally, did you have a recollection of June 12th, 1978?

DARYL BUSSE: Yes, I did.

MR. FARES: What is it you remembered about June 12th, 1978?

DARYL BUSSE: Well, I didn't recollect on that one date. I

recollected that Mr. Horak gave me the problems on or about that date.

MR. FARES: But you don't know for sure — Do you know for sure that it was the night that Phase-Out was involved in that race?

DARYL BUSSE: When I was reminded of the race, when I seen the race, then I remembered that that was the horse he was mad about.

MR. FARES: Now, you remember Phase-Out?

DARYL BUSSE: Yes, sir.

MR. FARES: Phase-Out won his next three races after that?

DARYL BUSSE: Yes, sir.

MR. FARES: Did you drive him in the next three races?

DARYL BUSSE: No, I didn't.

MR. FARES: In regard to that particular race, Phase-Out finished dead last?

DARYL BUSSE: Finished fifth, yes, sir.

MR. FARES: Phase-Out was the odds-on favorite when you were going off in this five-horse race?

DARYL BUSSE: Yes, sir.

MR. FARES: Did you remember what the odds were when Phase-Out went off?

DARYL BUSSE: According to that program, they're written alongside of it, the odds were 3 to 5.

MR. FARES: Do you know what horse won that race?

DARYL BUSSE: I'm not sure. I really didn't look that close at it to find out which horse won.

MR. FARES: Pacing Robin. Let's let you look at Pacing Robin. He won the race, didn't he?

DARYL BUSSE: Yes, he did.

MR. FARES: Do you know whether or not on your first call to Phil Langley, did security come?

DARYL BUSSE: Not that I can remember. They might have been on the way, but not that I can remember.

MR. FARES: Do you ever recall seeing security come?

DARYL BUSSE: I know they came — I know that they came later and took Mr. Horak away. I'm not sure -—

MR. FARES: Did you see them do that?

DARYL BUSSE: Yes, but I think — I can't remember seeing him, but I know that they took him away.

MR. FARES: You know that but you don't know from where you know that?

DARYL BUSSE: No.

MR. FARES: Somebody might have told you —

DARYL BUSSE: I know it happened that night. I know they took him away. I know he wasn't there anymore.

MR. FARES: Could have left?

DARYL BUSSE: I heard the security took him away.

MR. FARES: You heard that?

DARYL BUSSE: Yes, sir.

MR. FARES: You don't know that for sure?

DARYL BUSSE: No, sir.

MR. FARES: Was there anything that prevented you simply from walking away from Mike Horak and going to wait in your dressing quarters there?

DARYL BUSSE: No, there probably wasn't.

MR. FARES: Okay.

DARYL BUSSE: Except that I would have to race in the next race.

MR. FARES: Well, that's 20, 25 minutes now.

DARYL BUSSE: Yes, but then, of course —

MR. FARES: All right, fine. What did you do after the 9th race that Phase-Out finished last?

DARYL BUSSE: I got off the horse and walked up to the end, so that 20 to 25 minutes I think is probably 20 minutes — later I went to drive in the 10th race.

MR. FARES: How long does it take? A minute to walk to the end of the Paddock?

DARYL BUSSE: Anywhere from a minute to five minutes to where I was —

MR. FARES: Hold on. Did you stop to talk to anybody?

DARYL BUSSE: I can't remember whether I did or not.

MR. FARES: Okay. Now the second time that allegedly Mike Horak came up to you again in the Paddock or this was after the tenth race, correct?

DARYL BUSSE: I guess if you could call it the second time because he kept it going.

MR. FARES: At some point he left the Paddock area and you went on to the track.
DARYL BUSSE: But he kept it going between the ninth and kept it up after the tenth.

MR. FARES: You mean he walked to the fence? Is that what you're telling us?

DARYL BUSSE: He stood right there. We have to go by the spot right under the race track.

MR. FARES: Stood there?

DARYL BUSSE: Right. Right around that area. He kept it going after the ninth race from the time we walked by him with the horse to go out on the race track for the tenth race and until he was taken away by security.

MR. FARES: This is some distance from here to here, isn't it?

DARYL BUSSE: Not very far. It's only about, oh, I would say maybe a good 15 big steps from the Paddock to the race track.

MR. FARES: Maybe from where you're sitting to that wall outside the Courtroom on the other side of the hall?

DARYL BUSSE: Uh-hum. Approximately. A little shorter than that even.

MR. FARES: And then after he was talking to you here, then you walked?

DARYL BUSSE: He wasn't talking to me there. He was

screaming and hollering at me.

MR. FARES: Screaming and hollering.

DARYL BUSSE: Yeah.

MR. FARES: You took your horse out and raced it?
DARYL BUSSE: Yes, sir.

MR. FARES: You don't know if he stopped hollering at you or not because at some point you were over there at the race and couldn't hear him, could you?

DARYL BUSSE: Probably when he was screaming I could have been a lot further on that race track and still hear him.

MR. FARES: Mr. Busse, you have to answer my question.

MR. BISHOP: Objection to the argument with the witness.

JUDGE LASSERS: I think the answer was responsive.

MR. FARES: I would ask Your Honor to have him respond "yes" or "no" as any other witness.

JUDGE LASSERS: Put your next question.

MR. FARES: When you're riding in a race or warm up the horse, how many people were at the track that night?

DARYL BUSSE: I don't know. On a Monday night. Anywhere from 6,000 to 8,000 people.

MR. FARES: You don't know for sure?

DARYL BUSSE: I don't know for sure. Probably during that period of time it was fairly well-populated.

MR. FARES: Where you're over here, you can't hear Mike Horak hollering?

DARYL BUSSE: Probably not.

MR. FARES: You don't know if he stopped or not?

DARYL BUSSE: No, I don't.

MR. FARES: That fence now that you talked about at the Paddock area there, that high about?

DARYL BUSSE: Probably come to your shoulders.

MR. FARES: Up here?

DARYL BUSSE: Yeah.

MR. FARES: So it's about a five-foot fence?

DARYL BUSSE: Something like that.

MR. FARES: Fair?

DARYL BUSSE: Yes.

MR. FARES: When you say Mike Horak was hollering at you the first time, was he right up on the fence?

DARYL BUSSE: Close enough that I could see him.

MR. FARES: And you were now how far from him?

DARYL BUSSE: Probably four, five feet from it.

MR. FARES: And the Paddock Judge was there?

DARYL BUSSE: Yes, sir.

MR. FARES: The Paddock area's all closed off. In order to go out, you have to open a gate?

DARYL BUSSE: No.

MR. FARES: What?

DARYL BUSSE: There's an open gate at one end of the fence.

MR. FARES: Of which end?

DARYL BUSSE: At both ends. Paddock is open on both ends. Paddock — there's a security guard standing at each end.

MR. FARES: Over here and over here?

DARYL BUSSE: Yeah.

MR. FARES: So there was a security guard in the area?

DARYL BUSSE: Yeah.

MR. FARES: Do you know who that was?

DARYL BUSSE: No, not offhand.

MR. FARES: Well, did the security guard walk over to Mike Horak and say anything to him?

DARYL BUSSE: I really don't know.

MR. FARES: Did you go to the security guard and tell him what was going on?

DARYL BUSSE: No.

MR. FARES: Now, you weren't too far from this edge of the Paddock.

DARYL BUSSE: No.

MR. FARES: Why didn't you go to the security guard, Mr. Busse?

DARYL BUSSE: Usually, the security guards they have at Sportsman Park, are either older fellows or one thing or another that are there to keep the people without much force out of the Paddock. They — I wanted to go to somebody that would get something done right now, so I called Phil Langley who is the director of racing.

MR. FARES: Was he uniformed, the security guard?

DARYL BUSSE: I'm not sure if he was. Sometimes they are uniformed, sometimes they're not.

MR. FARES: You know Eugene Oliver?

DARYL BUSSE: (Pausing) Um, yeah, I believe I do.

MR. FARES: This is him sitting here?

DARYL BUSSE: Oh, is he? Okay. I know him. I'm sorry.

MR. FARES: He is a security guard for the track?

DARYL BUSSE: Yes, he is.

MR. FARES: Do you know Steve Bajovich?

DARYL BUSSE: I believe I do, but the name don't —

MR. FARES: Now, how many people did you say were in the area there?

DARYL BUSSE: I don't remember exactly how many people were there, but the Paddock is closest to the Grandstand and more accessible for the people to come. Sometime's they'll come up, sometimes they'll go down to the other end. Depends upon what race they want to see — but that is about the most accessible area to the Paddock where most of the people are up in the Grandstand.

MR. FARES: How many people were there, do you remember?

DARYL BUSSE: A pretty good crowd of people. I would say over 20.

MR. FARES: That was right after the race?

DARYL BUSSE: Yep.

MR. FARES: Now, lets go back to Addison about a year before. Can you be more specific than “a year before”?

DARYL BUSSE: No, I can’t. I don’t exactly remember what date it was, but I know that it was more than a year before that — this time.

MR. FARES: And did you race that night —

DARYL BUSSE: Yes, I did.

MR. FARES: — did you drive?

DARYL BUSSE: Yes, I did.

MR. FARES: Where did you drive?

DARYL BUSSE: I believe it was at Maywood Park. I believe it was. It might have been at one of the others. This is on my way home where I had something to eat at the Steak-n-Egger. I usually stopped at it on my way home.

MR. FARES: So, Maywood is where?

DARYL BUSSE: Maywood is — well, it’s into Melrose-Maywood Park area.

MR. FARES: And you live in Kingston, which is where?

DARYL BUSSE: Actually be right straight west of Maywood Park. It would be in the Melrose Park area. Right straight west about 55 miles.

MR. FARES: And Addison. How far is that from Maywood Park?

DARYL BUSSE: Addison from Maywood Park is only about 15 minutes drive time.

MR. FARES: And is there a particular street you use to get there, highway?

DARYL BUSSE: I come right down North Avenue and get on the — I think it's 290 By-Pass and get off and go to that Steak-n-Egger.

MR. FARES: So, on this particular evening, Mike Horak was there, you were sitting with him, talking with him?

DARYL BUSSE: I was sitting at the counter. I can't remember where Mike was at the time, but I know we engaged in a conversation.

MR. FARES: You said earlier, "I want to get it straight", you were at the Steak-n-Egger restaurant sitting there talking to him?

DARYL BUSSE: We engaged in conversation.

MR. FARES: What were you talking about?

DARYL BUSSE: Just general things. About the race track, about harness racing, one thing or another, which is the only thing we had in common.

MR. FARES: Anyone else present?

DARYL BUSSE: Man behind the counter, couple of waitresses there, there were, I know, at least a couple of other people there, two or three.

MR. FARES: In the Steak-n-Egger, two or three hundred people?

DARYL BUSSE: Two or three other people.

MR. FARES: I'm sorry. I misunderstood you, Mr. Busse. Thank you for your blessing. And at that point, what did he say and what did you say in this conversation?

DARYL BUSSE: The conversation was generally about around the race track. About horses and everything. What disturbed me about the conversation —

MR. FARES: I don't know that —

DARYL BUSSE: The conversation built up into Mike —

MR. FARES: Wait. Your Honor.

JUDGE LASSERS: There's no question pending. There's no question pending, Mr. Busse. No question pending.

MR. FARES: Move to strike, Your honor.

JUDGE LASSERS: Stricken.

MR. FARES: Thank you. What did you say and what did he say in this conversation you were having?

DARYL BUSSE: He got all wound up —

MR. FARES: Right. I'm not asking what you saw him do. I want to know if you remember what was said.

DARYL BUSSE: No, I don't.

MR. FARES: Did he strike you on that date?

DARYL BUSSE: No, he didn't.

MR. FARES: Did he have a weapon?

DARYL BUSSE: No, sir.

MR. FARES: Did he act like he was — strike that. Did he raise his fist to you in any manner?

DARYL BUSSE: No.

MR. FARES: How close was he to you?

DARYL BUSSE: Probably no further than right within shoulder distance at one time.

MR. FARES: Getting back to the night of June 12th, 1978. Can you give us some idea, with the sequence of events, if you rode in the ninth race on Phase-Out and the tenth race on the other — next horse, how much time would you have had in the Paddock?

DARYL BUSSE: Probably no more than ten minutes. Probably ten to fifteen minutes.

MR. FARES: Mr. Busse, I am going to show what's been marked as Plaintiff's Exhibit Number 41 for purposes of identification. Can you tell me what that is?

DARYL BUSSE: That is the cyclone fence that is on the outside of the race track. I'm looking from east to west along this fence.

MR. FARES: And it's truly and accurately — that's the Paddock in front of the Paddock area all the way down?

DARYL BUSSE: The fence that goes between the fans and the race track. It's the outside fence of the race track.

MR. FARES: This fence here?

DARYL BUSSE: Yes.

MR. FARES: All the way down?

DARYL BUSSE: Yes.

MR. FARES: Truly and accurately depicts it as of June 12th, 1978?

DARYL BUSSE: Yes.

MR. FARES: Mr. Bishop, I realize this is —

MR. BISHOP: That's Okay.

MR. FARES: I move to admit this, Judge, for purposes of identification. Let's get to the time once again, you're in this area here sometime between 10 to 15 minutes, is that correct?

DARYL BUSSE: Yes, sir.

MR. FARES: Then what you're saying is that on the evening Mike Horak stood there and hollered at you it was for 10 to 15 minutes?

DARYL BUSSE: I couldn't tell you exactly how long he was doing it but he was doing it for a large amount of time because I called security.

MR. FARES: Let me clarify it. I don't want to take up too much time. The first time you were here between races about 10 to 15 minutes, correct?

DARYL BUSSE: Correct.

MR. FARES: During that 10 to 15 minute period, you claim Mike Horak was standing, hollering at you the whole time after the 9th race and 10th race, is that correct?

DARYL BUSSE: Yes, sir.

MR. FARES: That's all I have.

MR. FARES: Yes, Your Honor.

JUDGE LASSERS: Let me talk to the lawyers. Mr. Busse, you're excused. Step down.

JUDGE LASSERS: Ladies and gentlemen, Mr. Bishop is now resting his case.

MR. BISHOP: That's correct, Your Honor, we will rest our case at this point.

JUDGE LASSERS: So you have heard all of the testimony on the part of the defense. I just spoke to Mr. Fares. He says he has rebuttal testimony that will take him 12 minutes. Can you folks bear with us? If you folks bear with us now, then we will send you home and we will re-call you on Tuesday, okay. Is that agreeable to everybody? All right. Good. Let's go.

MR. FARES: Mr. Bishop has rested, Your Honor?

JUDGE LASSERS: Yes, he has. Oh, yes, he has.

MR. FARES: Mr. Horak, would you like to take the stand?

JUDGE LASSERS: I remind you, you are still under oath.

MICHAEL HORAK: Thank you, Your Honor. Thank you.

MICHAEL HORAK called as a rebuttal witness herein on behalf of the Plaintiff, having been previously duly sworn and having testified, resumed the stand and testified further as follows:

DIRECT EXAMINATION By Mr. Fares:

MR. FARES: Mr. Horak, again, you are still under oath?

MICHAEL HORAK: Yes.

MR. FARES: I show you what's been marked as Plaintiff's Exhibit Number 46, for purposes of identification. Can you identify that for me?

MICHAEL HORAK: It's a map of the area 40 miles as around the Chicago area.

MR. FARES: And I think that we have previously marked that map, but would you indicate for me by making a very small "X" in the area of Maywood Race Track as it is on that map?

MICHAEL HORAK: Okay. Maywood Race Track is up here in between Melrose and Maywood, Illinois.

MR. FARES: Make an "X", please.

MICHAEL HORAK: Right about there.

MR. FARES: And in June of 1978, where were you living?

MICHAEL HORAK: June of 1978, I was living in Lyons, Illinois.

MR. FARES: And for how long had you lived in Lyons, Illinois as of June of 1978?

MICHAEL HORAK: For nine years.

MR. FARES: Would you mark on the map where Lyons is with an "X"?

MICHAEL HORAK: Okay. Lyons is right down here.

MR. FARES: All right. And would you finally mark on the map where Addison is?

MICHAEL HORAK: Addison is up here North someplace.

MR. FARES: Could you mark it with an "X"?

MICHAEL HORAK: Here it is right here (indicating).

MR. FARES: Now, you heard testimony from Daryl Busse that approximately one year before June 12th, 1978, you met him at Steak-n-Egger in Addison?

MICHAEL HORAK: Yes, that's what he said, isn't it.

MR. FARES: Have you ever been at Steak-n-Egger in Addison?

MICHAEL HORAK: I've never been in any restaurant, in Addison, Illinois.

MR. FARES: Do you remember ever having a conversation of the type that Mr. Busse spoke of on or about a year, give or take, before June 12th, 1978?

MICHAEL HORAK: Never, no. No conversation with Daryl Busse.

MR. FARES: And, in fact, in regard to if you had been at Maywood on a particular evening —

MR. BISHOP: Objection, Your Honor, if he had done something.

MR. FARES: Your Honor, there's been —

JUDGE LASSERS: Let's hear the question first.

MR. FARES: If you had been to Maywood Park on a particular evening —

MICHAEL HORAK: Here is Maywood, okay.

MR. FARES: — would it be necessary for you on your way home to pass by Addison?

MR. BISHOP: Same objection, Your Honor.

JUDGE LASSERS: Overruled.

MICHAEL HORAK: No, Lyons is down here. I would go straight South to get to Lyons. Addison is Northwest of Maywood Park Race Track. It's got to be some distance.

MR. BISHOP: Objection, Your Honor.

MICHAEL HORAK: Sorry.

MR. FARES: Mr. Horak, do you know any reason why Phase-Out after the race of June 12th, 1978, would not have raced for or would have to go into a qualifying race because he didn't race for thirty days?

MR. BISHOP: Objection, Your Honor. The witness testified he had not been back to the track for some considerable period of time thereafter. Therefore, the question is calculated to elicit a hearsay answer, and I object to it.

MR. FARES: Your Honor, he may know.

JUDGE LASSERS: Let's ask if he knows. Do you know?

MICHAEL HORAK: Know what. Why he didn't go back to the races after June 12th?

MR. FARES: Yes, for a period of time.

MICHAEL HORAK: The horse was badly beaten.

JUDGE LASSERS: Just a moment. Do you know why?

MR. BISHOP: Objection.

JUDGE LASSERS: That takes a "yes" or "no" answer.

MICHAEL HORAK: I would have to say "yes".

MR. FARES: Why?

MICHAEL HORAK: After I saw him coming back from the race —

MR. FARES: Which one? The one on June 12th?

MICHAEL HORAK: Yes. The one that Daryl Busse finished last. I saw him ten feet away from me. That was the first thing I looked at. I stated that I saw Phase-Out had welt marks all over him from the stifle area all the way to his hips. He had three welt marks over his back, and was brutally beaten. This was the only way that this horse could have lost the race.

MR. BISHOP: Objection, Your Honor.

JUDGE LASSERS: Overruled.

MR. FARES: After you have heard the defendants testify, has that changed your recollection in any way of the events that occurred on June 12, 1978?

MICHAEL HORAK: The truth can never be changed of what happened to me on June 12th, 1978.

MR. FARES: I have nothing further, Your Honor.

JUDGE LASSERS: Any cross?

MR. BISHOP: I have no questions.

JUDGE LASSERS: No cross. All right. You rest?

MR. FARES: I rest, Judge.

JUDGE LASSERS: Plaintiff rests.

MR. FARES: Less than 12 minutes.

JUDGE LASSERS: Settled, the jury will now go home and rest.

MR. FARES: I want to admit —

MR. BISHOP: I have no objection to his map, Your Honor.

MR. FARES: I wanted to admit the map.

JUDGE LASSERS: Any objection to the map? Okay, the map is in, Exhibit Number 46. That is received. All right. Goodnight, ladies and gentlemen, I will see you all on Tuesday at 9:30.

(Whereupon, Court was adjourned.)

Chapter 37

Closing Arguments

The recess break was just about over as I re-entered the now empty Courtroom and sat at my lawyer's table. A strange thought came over me then. "Suppose Fares hasn't any idea of the amount of damages he plans to have the jurors decide on," I thought. After all, within minutes he would be giving his closing arguments. Once he starts, there would be no possible way I could interrupt him.

I quickly went to the lawyer's room where I knew he was going over his notes. He seemed surprised when I entered, as though I didn't belong in there. I said, "This will only take a minute; what amount of damages are you going to ask the jurors for?" He looked stunned for a couple of seconds, then stuttering, he stated that he "thought he would ask for one hundred and thirty-five thousand dollars."

I raised my voice a tad and said, "Is that all you think my life and career are worth?" I continued, "You sound as though you are working for the officials at Sportsman Park or their attorneys!" I then stated, "Just to refresh your memory, the original lawsuit almost eight years ago was for five hundred thousand dollars." There was a knock on the door by the Bailiff telling us that the court session was about to begin. I gave my fair-weather lawyer a stern look as I opened the door noting that the jurors were filing in. Time would tell if I had made the right decision in the last few minutes.

I sat down at the table as Ted Glazos was coming into the courtroom to see the end of the trial. James Balodimas and Jim Karubas had stayed home due to the extreme cold and blowing snow.

Judge Lassers entered the courtroom as we stood, then

sat back down to hear both attorneys give their closing arguments. I was more nervous at that point than at any other time during the trial. Soon I would know if I was a lamb being led to be slaughtered, again.

Judge Willard Lassers announced to the jury that each attorney would be allotted forty-five minutes each to conduct their closing arguments.

I'll have to give O'le Ronald Bishop credit, he was still plugging away trying to convince the jury and probably himself, that he could build a brick house by using a stack of printed lies for a foundation. He repeated over and over, at the top of his voice, that Eugene Oliver, Phil Langley, Daryl Busse and the other track security guards were honest, law-abiding citizens and pillars of society.

I personally believe that Bishop would have a difficult task in locating an insurance company that would write him a policy on his new brick house that he had tried to build in that courtroom using materials made from the likes of those "pillars of society". Any insurance agent that would be able to pass kindergarten, would immediately drop him like a hot potato as a hazardous investment.

David Fares, on the other hand, went through the motion of talking to the jurors as though, no matter what decision they arrived at, he would still leave the courtroom smelling like a blooming rose. To this day, I still firmly believe that this is true. Lord only knows, he had presented me with enough facts throughout all of the preceding months that he had dragged his feet, pretending to be a lawyer, from day one to the next. Lucky for me, all the major paperwork had been completed by my first two law firms before he arrived for his hand outs.

He made no attempt to locate that fifth track security guard, nor did he even try to bring out the fact that Eugene Oliver had killed seventeen year-old Rodney Harris. I believe that this would have put a little doubt in the minds of the jurors about this maniac's credibility and of the other track officials. Fares had only touched the tip of the iceberg of the corruption in the horse racing industry. He also failed to note that these track officials would do anything to obtain a favorable ruling on the lawsuit. One thing I know for sure, he didn't make any waves. The ocean waters were as calm as water in a swimming pool.

My only concern was that, whatever the outcome the jury ruled on, the news media would inform the general public what they had witnessed during the trial. Only when the governor and track officials in each state notice a sharp decline in attendance, would they maybe attempt to curtail the disastrous abuse with illegal drugs on these beautiful animals. Maybe then they would do away with track officials and security guards who use Gestapo tactics on anyone who won't bow down to their warped minds as though they were back in Germany in the 1940s.

If this were accomplished, I would have won far more than I could have ever expected in this world.

Chapter 38
The Verdict

The last spectator departed from the courtroom that was crowded just minutes earlier. Ted Glazos walked over to Fares and me, and said, "Did you see how Phil Langley and Bishop bolted out of here?" I looked up and said, "It didn't surprise me one bit, knowing those two clowns." This caught Ted's attention enough to ask, "How do you account for that, Michael John?" "Well," I said, "they probably figured that if Judge Lassers had to look at them one minute more, he would have them held in contempt of court for over-acting!" We both gave out with a light chuckle. It did relieve a little tension that was thicker than ice-cold honey in a jar.

With that, I got up from my chair and said, "Let's get a cup of tea and a sandwich. It's already three-thirty, too late for lunch and too early for supper." The three of us walked out of the courtroom and into the elevator. As the door closed, I remarked, "I sure hope that this bus doesn't stop at every floor." I looked up to see how many lights were lit to answer my question. "Unbelievable," was all I could say as I nudged Ted to look at the only two numbers that the elevator was going to stop at: the seventeenth and the seventh floors. I then said, "If I ever needed an omen, I've got one now." Looking at Ted, I said, "Don't you remember? Since June 12th, 1978, it's taken me seven years, seven months, and seventeen days to get my lawsuit to this court." All Ted said was, "You sure have a point, for there is no way I would have bet that we would only make two stops at this time of day. Normally, we would have had at least ten."

Leaving the building, we walked across Randolph Street to a restaurant. Fares had nothing to say, nor did I need his conversation. The only thing I was thinking over and over was that there might have still been someone else on the jury that didn't belong, as in the first panel. I would bet my life on the fact that no one would have been able to influence Judge Willard Lassers in any way. I knew I had an honest judge. This I never doubted all through the trial.

Ted broke the silence by asking Fares if he had any idea as to how long the jurors would take in a case such as this. Fares just shrugged his shoulders saying that he didn't know. I put down my empty cup and waited.

A short time later, I said, "Well, its five-fifteen, let's get back to the courtroom where we can obtain a few more answers to all of our questions." We then left the restaurant and walked back across the street to the courthouse. The ride up that elevator felt to me as though I were riding in a ghost ship. I had closed my eyes until the door opened, non-stop to our destination.

We stepped out into the now-empty hallway where only a few lights were left on after the normal business hours were over. We walked down the long hallway, passing the many darkened-glass doors of the other courtrooms on that floor. It gave me a weird feeling that the only action going on was in the jury room of Judge Lassers' Court.

When we arrived, Fares went inside while Ted and I sat down on one of the marble slabs, in the middle of the hall way. My new shoes felt a little tight, being that I had them on all day, so I removed them. What a relief as I wiggled my toes. No sooner had I done this than Fares rushed out saying that the jurors were about to enter the courtroom. I hurriedly slipped on my shoes, not taking any precious seconds to tie the laces. As soon as we sat at our table, the jurors slowly started to file in. I strained my eyes, hoping to catch some kind of sign or expression on just one of the jurors' faces, but this was not to be.

I started to feel my heart pumping faster than I had ever felt it before. It was a good thing I was not standing. The last juror had been seated when Judge Lassers entered. Everyone stood up. My knees quivered just a little. In a quiet, slow-tone voice, Judge Lassers asked, "Ladies and gentlemen of the jury, have you reached a verdict?" A middle-aged man stood up and stated, "Yes, we have Your Honor." Then reading from a slip of paper, he continued, "We, the jury, find for the Plaintiff, two hundred sixty-thousand dollars in compensatory damages and another two hundred fifty-thousand dollars in punitive damages.

I stood there motionless, not fully understanding the whole meaning of what I believed I had just heard. Maybe my nerves were playing tricks on me, but when I heard Ronald Bishop's loud voice demanding to poll the jurors, I gave out with a sigh of relief. Only after hearing the twelfth juror, did Bishop slowly sit down at his empty table. No one else came from the comedy of errors of Sportsman Park Race Track to hear the outcome of the lawsuit. I thought that it was mighty strange, to say the least.

STATE OF ILLINOIS)
) SS
COUNTY OF COOK)

IN THE CIRCUIT COURT OF COOK COUNTY, ILLINOIS

COUNTY DEPARTMENT, LAW DIVISION

MICHAEL JOHN HORAK,
Plaintiff,
vs.
EUGENE OLIVER, STEVE BAJOVICH, JOSEPH McCARTHY, DANIEL GROTH, NATIONAL JOCKEY CLUB, INC., and FOX VALLEY TROTTING CLUB, INC.,
Defendants.

JUDGMENT ORDER - PLAINTIFF, JURY

After hearing the evidence, the jury found for the plaintiff MICHAEL JOHN HORAK and against the defendants, EUGENE OLIVER, STEVE BAJOVICH, JOSEPH McCARTHY, DANIEL GROTH, NATIONAL JOCKEY CLUB, INC., and FOX VALLEY TROTTING CLUB, INC and assessed damages as follows:

$ 260,000.00 in compensatory damages;

$ 250,000.00 in punitive damages; and

costs of this suit.

Chapter 39

Thankful Gratification

I looked around the courtroom and noticed that Fares had already departed. It was quite obvious to me that my fair-weather lawyer had overheard the negative responses Ted Glazos and I were receiving from the jurors. They were talking about the lack-luster presentation Fares gave my case. They felt as though he was representing someone else. They had formed the opinion that Fares was just waiting to see which way the case would bend, then follow in that direction.

Fares finally came to life in the closing hour of the trial. The Illinois Bar Association would be hearing from me on all of my four different lawyers who all stated, "Trust me". I hope to have these sleazy lawyers disbarred.

Fares was probably on the phone across Randolph Street, calling all of his friends, if he had any, to tell them how he alone had won this lawsuit. I've always said when I won a race that "it was the horse that won; all I did was hold on to the reins and enjoy the ride!"

Walking with the jurors to the elevators, we could see the snow falling against the huge windows along the empty hallways. They overlooked the other office buildings that had only a few of their lights on. It was dinner time and the personnel were already at home watching the six o'clock news. They had already experienced the weather report on their way home. Ted and the jurors would be doing likewise, along with myself during the next hour. I mentioned to the jurors that investigative reporter Pam Zekman would be on the 6:00 pm news tomorrow night on channel 2 with the results of this trial.

It had been a very stressful two weeks. I told Ted to plan

on having dinner at his restaurant in a couple of days and just maybe the weather would improve. He nudged me in the cab saying, "Michael John, you should have no trouble in picking up the dinner check." We both started to laugh. I replied, "I'll even go one better than that. I'll pay the cab fare to the train station." Then we both had the first good laugh in a very, very long time. We had to take different trains for Ted lived thirty-five miles north of Chicago, while I lived twenty miles west.

One hour later, I was stepping off the train into sub-zero cold, with a wind-chill of forty below and blowing snow. Only two other people got off at the same time, walking in the opposite direction. Just out of habit, I looked over my shoulder to see if I had any company at the deserted train station. It was indeed a strange feeling not seeing anything move on the sidewalks or streets. The cars that were parked were so covered with ice and snow, they looked like small igloos.

Obviously, walking was the only sure means of transportation that night. The mile-long walk would be very stimulating, giving me time to think. I slowly made my way through the deep snow as though I was the only person left on this Earth. It reminded me of the rainy Thanksgiving night I was driving Liberty Queen. when I thought everyone had left the racetrack.

My thoughts were flowing more easily, for at that moment, I realized that I had overcome the overwhelming odds that were stacked against me from the beginning.

Suddenly, a sensation of physical warmth circulated throughout my entire body. The happiness and satisfaction within me felt as though I was miraculously walking barefooted and splashing through the oncoming waves as they washed upon the sandy beaches. An abundance of wild orchids, along with hundreds of different varieties of brightly-colored flowers below the tall coconut palm trees truly enhanced the surroundings of this beautiful paradise island of Bora Bora, Tahiti, in the South Pacific.

A thought flashed in my mind back to my teenage years: **Dreams are nothing more than believing in yourself.**

The End.

Part III

An Update Summary

While the scallywags involved in my case have, for the most part, received the justice due them, the race horses — of all breeds — continue to be abused by their owners and trainers. As the following pages will show, the use of drugs in racehorses is on the increase.

Thirty-Sixth Governor,

DANIEL WALKER

(1922-)

Democrat

January 8, 1973 to January 10, 1977

The thirty-sixth Governor of Illinois, who was in office from Jan. 8, 1973 to Jan. 10, 1977, pleaded guilty to Bank Fraud, Misapplication of bank funds and Perjury. Illinois Judge Ann Williams sentenced ex-Governor Daniel Walker to seven years in prison and ordered him to pay $231,600 restitution to First American Bank. This was the second Governor of Illinois to be sent to prison.

The thirty-sixth Governor of Illinois, who was in office from Jan. 8, 1973 to Jan. 10, 1977, pleaded guilty to Bank Fraud, Misapplication of bank funds and Perjury. Illinois Judge Ann Williams sentenced ex-Governor Daniel Walker to seven years in prison and ordered him to pay $231,600 restitution to First American Bank. This was the second Governor of Illinois to be sent to prison.

The Greylord defendants

from the *Chicago Tribune*,
Wednesday,
October 5, 1988

Judges

Defendant	Position	Case status
John J. Devine	Associate judge	Convicted; 15 years
Daniel Glecier	Associate judge	Convicted
Martin F. Hogan	Associate judge	Convicted; awaiting sentencing
Reginald Holzer	Circuit judge	Convicted; 13 years
John Laurie	Associate judge	Acquitted
Richard LeFevour	Presiding judge*	Convicted; 12 years
Francis Maher	Circuit judge	Acquitted
John H. McCollom	Circuit judge	Convicted; 11 years
John J. McDonnell	Circuit judge	Indicted
Michael E. McNulty	Associate judge	Pleaded guilty; 3 years, $15,000 fine
John M. Murphy	Associate judge	Convicted; 10 years
James L. Oakey	Associate judge	Convicted; 18 months; awaiting trial on second indictment
Wayne W. Olson	Circuit judge	Pleaded guilty; 12 years, $35,000 fine
John F. Reynolds	Circuit judge	Convicted; 10 years, $33,000 fine
Frank Salerno	Circuit judge	Pleaded guilty; 9 years, $10,000 fine
Roger E. Seaman	Circuit judge	Pleaded guilty; awaiting sentencing
Raymond Sodini	Circuit judge	Pleaded guilty; 8 years

Court personnel

Defendant	Position	Case status
James Canoff	Ass't. corporation counsel	Pleaded guilty; 6 months work release
Harold Conn	Deputy traffic court clerk	Convicted; 6 years, $2,000
Alan Kaye	Holiday Court bailiff	Convicted; 5 years
Nick Lapalombella	Circuit Court clerk	Pleaded guilty; 60 days work release
Henry Lemanski	Deputy court clerk	Pleaded guilty; awaiting sentencing
Norman Vandigo	Ass't. corporation counsel	Charged in criminal information
Ernest Worsek	Court-appointed receiver	Pleaded guilty; 6 months

continued on the next page

The Greylord defendants, continued

Deputy sheriffs

Defendant	Case status
Gaetano Bianco	Pleaded guilty; 6 months probation
Al Hardin	Indicted; deceased
Leopoldo Hernandez	Pleaded guilty; 6 months work release
Paul Hutson	Pleaded guilty; 60 days work release
Jerome Kohn	Pleaded guilty; 18 months, $10,000 fine
Frank Mirabella	Pleaded guilty; 7 months, $15,000 fine
Lucious Robinson	Pleaded guilty; 3 years, $3,000 fine
Steve Ruben	Pleaded guilty; awaiting sentencing
Patrick Ryan	Pleaded guilty; 60 days work release
Nick Yokas	Pleaded guilty; 60 days work release

Police officers

Defendant	Case status
Ira Blackwood	Convicted; 7 years, $20,000
James Hegarty	Pleaded guilty; 3 years probation
James LeFevour	Pleaded guilty; 30 months
Arthur McCauslin	Pleaded guilty; 18 months
Lawrence McLain	Pleaded guilty; 15 months
James Trunzo	Pleaded guilty; 1 year, $10,000 fine
Joseph Trunzo	Pleaded guilty; 1 year, $10,000 fine
Joseph Yasak	Indicted

Lawyers

Defendant	Case status
Hugo Arquillo	Pleaded guilty; 2 months work release, $1,300 fine
Lee Barnett	Pleaded guilty; 6 months
Lebert Bastianoni	Pleaded guilty; 30 days work release, $5,000 fine
Harlan Becker	Convicted; 6 years, $60,000 fine
Jerry Berliant	Pleaded guilty; 20 weekends in jail
Neal Birnbaum	Pleaded guilty; awaiting sentencing
Dale Boton	Pleaded guilty; 90 days work release
John W. Brady	Pleaded guilty; awaiting sentencing
Howard Brandstein	Pleaded guilty; 1 year and 1 day
Blair Braverman	Pleaded guilty; awaiting sentencing
Houston Burnside	Pleaded guilty; 30 weekends, $3,000

continued on the next page

The Greylord defendants, continued

Bruce Campbell	Pleaded guilty; 1 year
James J. Costello	Pleaded guilty; 8 years
Robert Daniels	Convicted; 6 years
Vincent Davino	Pleaded guilty; 4 years
Thomas DelBeccaro	Pleaded guilty; $1,000 fine
David Dineff	Açquitted
Louis Dineff	Indicted
Thurman Gardner	Pleaded guilty; 6 months
Alphonse Gonzales	Pleaded guilty; 1 year, $2,000 fine
Richard Goldstein	Pleaded guilty; 1 year
Harry Jaffe	Convicted; 1 year and 1 day; deceased
William Kampenga	Pleaded guilty; awaiting sentencing
Melvin Kanter	Pleaded guilty; 90 days work release, $25,000 fine
Edward Kaplan	Pleaded guilty; 2 years
Paul Kulerski	Pleaded guilty; 3 months
Bernard Mann	Pleaded guilty; 6 months, $25,000 fine
Joseph McDermott	Pleaded guilty; 1 year and 1 day, $30,000 fine
Ralph Meczyk	Pleaded guilty; 30 days work release, $5,000 fine
Jay Messinger	Convicted; 2 years, $1,000 fine
James E. Noland	Pleaded guilty; 15 months, $15,000 fine
Edward Nydam	Pleaded guilty; reindicted; 6 months detox
Richard Pezzopane	Pleaded guilty; awaiting sentencing
Cary N. Polikoff	Pleaded guilty; awaiting sentencing
William Reilly	Pleaded guilty; 14 months, $5,000 fine
Mark Rosenbloom	Pleaded guilty; 2 years probation
Bruce Roth	Convicted; 10 years
Martin Schachter	Pleaded guilty; Probation
Fredric Solomon	Pleaded guilty; 2½ years
John J. Ward	Conviction overturned on appeal
Phillip Wertz	Pleaded guilty; awaiting sentencing
Dean Wolfson	Pleaded guilty; 7½ years, $3,000
Cyrus Yonan	Pleaded guilty; 1 year and 1 day, $15,000 fine
Arthur Zimmerman	Pleaded guilty; 3 years, $3,000 fine

Note: Thomas Kangalos, assistant corporation counsel, is believed to have fled to Greece after being indicted for accepting bribes from undercover FBI agent.
*Of 1st Municipal District; formerly supervising judge of Traffic Court.

Chicago Tribune Graphic; Source: News reports

Chicago Sun-Times, Wednesday, June 19, 1991

Helped exec defraud bank, lawyer admits

By Susan Chandler, Banking Writer

A Chicago attorney Tuesday admitted he was guilty of helping a First Chicago executive defraud the bank of more than $800,000 by submitting false invoices and work orders during a two-year period.

Bennett Alban pleaded guilty to two felony counts of bank fraud, which carry a total possible sentence of 40 years in prison and a $2 million fine. However, because he cooperated with the government, U.S. District Judge Ilana Rovner said she expected prosecutors to recommend a considerably lighter sentence.

Alban was the last of 10 defendants to plead guilty in the last two weeks to bank fraud charges arising from a yearlong federal investigation of the bank's administration department.

Eight separate schemes involving three bank executives were uncovered and are estimated to have cost First Chicago more than $1 million from 1979 to 1989.

Alban admitted to working with the former First Chicago Vice President Robert Olson to generate false work orders and invoices for construction and real estate work at the bank. As part of the scheme, Alban created bogus corporations to bill the bank for nonexistent work. Olson's role was to make sure the bank paid the fake bills, prosecutors said.

June 19, 1991

I knew if I waited long enough, I would be able to rejoice the happenings of this day. One of the four of my ex-attorneys finally got his fingers caught in the cookie jar. Chicago attorney Bennett Alban, pleaded guilty to two felony counts of Bank Fraud totalling over $800,000. There were nine other thieves involved, who also pleaded guilty to the same charges.

Bennett Alban quickly testified for the State against his fellow partners in crime, thus making a deal for a lighter prison term and fine. Ol' Alban was still in there looking out for Bennett Alban, no matter who he has to sell out!

Chicago Tribune, October 5th, 1989

Former Cicero official pleads guilty in thefts

By Andrew Fegelman

A former deputy liquor commissioner for Cicero, who was also a longtime lieutenant on the suburb's police force, pleaded guilty Wednesday in federal court to charges of skimming nearly $50,000 in liquor license fees from the town.

In addition to pleading guilty to tax evasion charges for failing to report the fees on his income tax returns, Steven Bajovich also pleaded guilty to charges that he tried to cover up the crime by taking the liquor license records to a Cicero racetrack and burning them.

Bajovich, who was the deputy liquor commissioner from 1975 until 1986, is scheduled to be sentenced Nov. 28 by U.S. District Court Judge James Zagel. Bajovich faces a maximum of 15 years in prison and a $600,000 fine.

Assistant U.S. Atty. William Hogan, who prepared the case, said he would ask Zagel to sentence Bajovich to a "substantial" period of time in prison. Hogan said a federal investigation of liquor licenses in Cicero was continuing, but he refused to say whether Bajovich was cooperating with authorities.

Two other men have been indicted as a result of the investigation. Charles Willis pleaded guilty Aug. 30 to charges that he lied to the grand jury about paying a $400 bribe to Bajovich to influence the issuance of a license. Willis is scheduled to be sentenced Oct. 19. A similar charge is pending against Theodore Tampas, who is expected to plead guilty this month.

Bajovich, 53, who is employed by a suburban beer distributor, hastily left the courtroom with his attorney George Pappas after the hearing and declined to comment.

Bajovich was indicted by a federal grand jury in April on five counts of tax evasion for failing to report $45,325 in embezzled liquor license

continued on the next page

continued from the previous page

fees on income tax returns between 1982 and 1986. He also was charged with one count of obstructing justice for destroying the records.

He pleaded guilty Wednesday to two tax evasion counts and the obstruction of justice charge. The other three charges were dropped.

Although the town president is legally responsible for issuing liquor licenses in Cicero, Bajovich handled most of the administrative chores.

Rather than requiring tavern and liquor store owners to come to the Town Hall to fill out applications and then pay the $400 to $975 license fee to the town collector, Bajovich personally delivered the licenses to the owners and the pocketed the fees, Hogan said.

Hogan said the liquor licenses are numbered and Bajovich was able to hide the embezzlement by using high numbered license forms that would usually go unused.

Hogan said that in 1986, after Bajovich learned he was the target of a federal grand jury investigation, he quit both his jobs in Cicero. According to witnesses whom prosecutors had planned to call to testify, Bajovich then burned liquor license records at Sportsman's Park in Cicero, where he worked as a security guard.

Attorney Bishop had said in his closing statements to the jury that Mr. Steve Bajovich was a "pillar of society," and tried to lead the jurors to believe that Bajovich was as honest as the day is long. Apparently, the days have gotten much shorter since Mr. Bishop first met him.

HORSE RACING

Unidentified body could be that of missing jockey Hansen

Authorities in Alameda, Calif., believe a body found Thursday could be the remains of jockey **Ron Hansen**, who mysteriously disappeared in early October. The badly decomposed body was found in the mud flats of Hayward, near the San Mateo Bridge. Positive identification, using dental records, could take more than 24 hours. Hansen, 33, a Northern California rider with nearly 3,700 career victories, was last seen Oct. 1.

From the *Chicago Tribune*, July 26th, 1984. In reference to the July 24th killing of teenageer Rodney Harris by Eugene Oliver

Racetrack killing of teenager probed

AN INVESTIGATION was underway Wednesday into the fatal shooting of a 17-year-old Chicago youth by a security guard at Sportsman's Park in Cicero. Police said Rodney Harris, of 5243 Gladys Ave., was shot in the head Tuesday night by Eugene Oliver, a Cook County deputy sheriff working as a guard at the racetrack. Police said Oliver caught Harris trying to break into a car in the track's parking lot and Harris allegedly resisted arrest. Assistant State's Atty. Jay Magnuson declined comment pending the completion of tests by the medical examiner and the state crime laboratory. David Copeland, Sheriff Richard Elrod's director of internal investigations, said prosecutors told him **no charges would be filed against Oliver.**

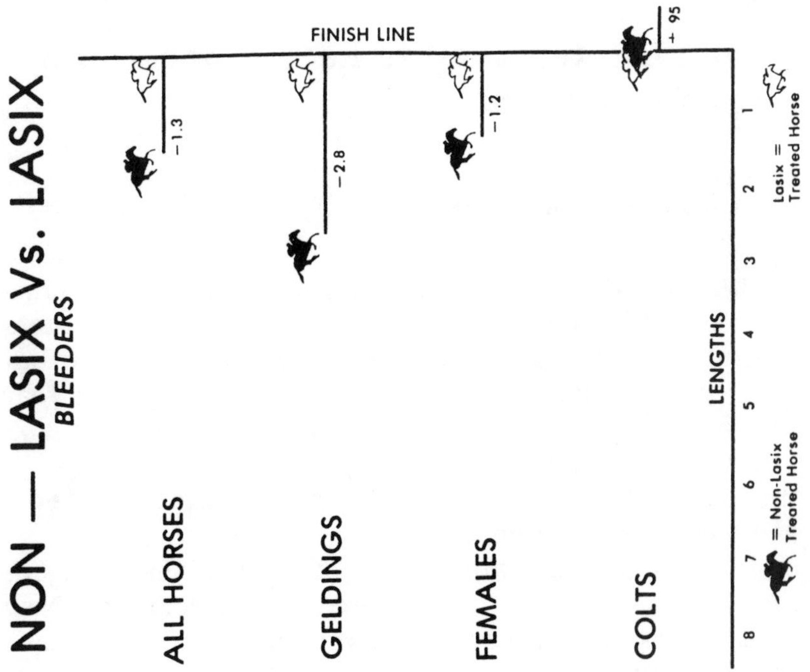
NON — LASIX Vs. LASIX
BLEEDERS
FINISH LINE
ALL HORSES
−1.3
GELDINGS
−2.8
FEMALES
−1.2
COLTS
+ 95
LENGTHS
8 7 6 5 4 3 2 1
= Non-Lasix Treated Horse
Lasix = Treated Horse

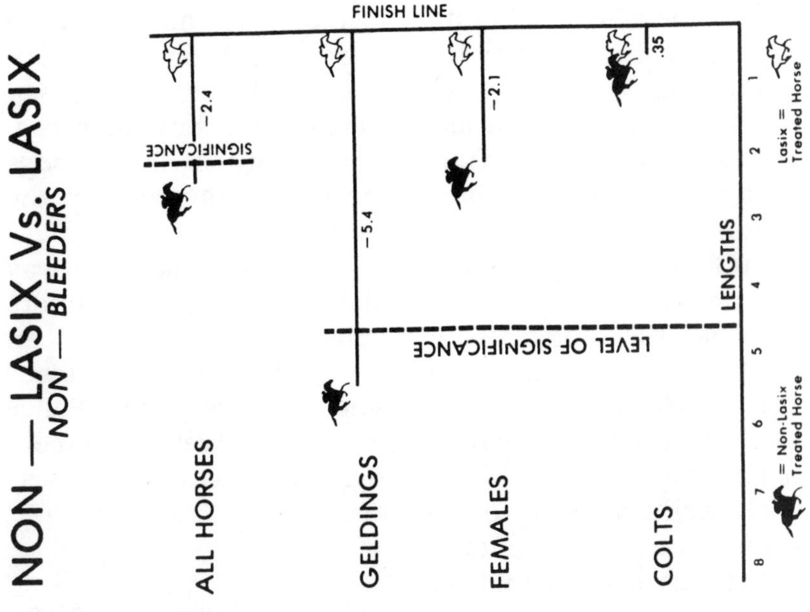
NON — LASIX Vs. LASIX
NON — BLEEDERS
FINISH LINE
ALL HORSES
−2.4
SIGNIFICANCE
GELDINGS
−5.4
LEVEL OF SIGNIFICANCE
FEMALES
−2.1
COLTS
.35
LENGTHS
8 7 6 5 4 3 2 1
= Non-Lasix Treated Horse
Lasix = Treated Horse

The Boca News, Boca Raton, Florida, December 23rd, 1990

Study: Lab tests fail to keep horse racing free of illegal drugs

by Frank Fitzpatrick
KNIGHT-RIDDER NEWSPAPERS

PHILADELPHIA — For two years now, lab technicians in Lexington, Ky., have been deliberately planting amphetamines, opiates and other illegal substances in the daily blood and urine samples collected from thoroughbreds at the nation's race tracks.

These tainted specimens are then mixed in with the normal shipments of samples sent to the 20 U.S. laboratories the racing industry has retained to search for illegal drugs in its horses. The labs are warned well ahead of time that their shipments may contain doctored samples — including which drugs and the amounts.

What the study discovered was that testing failed to detect the illegal drugs in the tainted samples 47 percent of the time.

It adds weight to the claims by a growing number of industry officials and veterinarians that the sport has lost its race with cheaters because a testing system that cost $27.6 million last year didn't catch them.

Designer drugs imported

In the last year, law-enforcement officials in New Jersey and elsewhere have intercepted large caches of designer drugs and illegal medications smuggled from Europe and Japan — substances investigators say were headed for race tracks. Few, if any, of these drugs are being uncovered in the tests.

"The horsemen are way ahead of us. The trainers know how much they can give and still pass the test," said New Jersey State Police trooper Walt Wells, who spent eight years with the department's Race Track Unit.

continued on the next page

continued from the previous page

Wells said part of the problem appears to be that most labs have been concentrating their efforts on detecting overdosages of phenylbutazone (Eute) and Lasix — drugs that, in limited quantities, are legal in most racing states — rather than for steroids, dangerous narcotics and stimulants.

"We're chasing rabbits, and the tigers are eating the natives," said Wells.

Credibility at stake

Carl Nafzger, the trainer of Unbridled, the 1990 Kentucky Derby and Breeders' Cup Classic winner, said the lack of credible testing could create a vicious cycle for the sport. Honest owners and trainers, convinced the testing system does not work, assume that they, too, must resort to creative chemistry in order to compete with the drug abusers.

"If we had testing that made it absolutely certain no medication at all was being used, you'd see a lot less problems," said Nafzger. "But the credibility of the labs is just not what it should be."

Financial pressures

Feeling the financial pinch, racing authorities have been reluctant to increase their investment in testing.

The average cost of tests in the United States is $14.

"A good test on a human, like the one done on Ben Johnson at the Olympics, probably would cost about $500," said Dr. Edward Murray, president of the American Association of Equine Practitioners.

Earlier this year at a small race track near Toronto, a rumor surfaced that a test for an illegal bronchial dilator, Robinal, had been developed.

"The next day, 16 horses were scratched, 14 others were trucked away and the horsemen's association voted to go on strike," said Frank Drea, chairman of the Ontario Racing Commission.

The Death of Jockey Rodney Dickens

Sportsman Park Race Track in Cicero, Illinois, had yet another disastrous tragic accident. A young teenager's hopes and dreams were suddenly left on the surface of this dangerous race track. Nineteen year-old Rodney Dickens was killed riding in a race on that Sunday afternoon.

Riding a horse named, Rough Rider, he was following a horse who was ridden by the leading rider, Fransisco Torres, at this track. As quick as lightning strikes, Torres' horse broke his leg, falling very quickly to the hard surface. Rodney Dickens had no chance of getting around the accident. His horse tried in vain to leap over the fallen horse, causing jockey Rodney Dicken's fall to the surface. He was hit by other horses that were behind him and who also tried to avoid the accident.

Jockey Rodney Dickens died at the hospital due to severe head injuries. Jockey Fransisco Torres was hospitalized in very critical condition. The horse he was riding, Special Little Guy, was put to sleep with an injection by the track veterinarian.

I have to wonder if any track official bothered to take the time to check veterinarian's records on Special Little Guy's medical charts for any lameness he might have had, and, if so, just how serious was it? I would also like to know if this horse was injected with the drug Lasix, or any other illegal drugs, before this race.

If this horse were lame before the race, like so many are, then Rodney Dickens was murdered, for the cards and odds were stacked against him or any other jockey who happened to be following Special Little Guy. Accidents don't just happen, they are caused.

Another case in point: A five year-old mare named Dance Appeal suffered a severely fractured leg as a two year-old in 1987. In returning to the races in 1990, she broke down again, causing three other horses to also fall to the surface of the race track. Jockey Benito Narvaez, 29 years old, was permanently paralyzed due to this "accident."

A jury found the racetrack negligent and solely responsible and awarded $4 million to Benito Narvaez. The case against the track was based upon whether or not a veterinarian checked Dance Appeal for complete soundness.

No matter how much money the jury awarded Narvaez, his whole future has been destroyed. No amount of money can buy it back.

continued on the next page

continued from the previous page

Returning to Toronto, Canada, on a pleasure trip in 1990, I learned that the Canadian Government had ordered a full investigation into the use on horses of the drug furosemide (Lasix). It was to consider legalizing this drug.

Afterward, they received reports from the University of Pennsylvania's School of Veterinary Medicine stating that furosemide improves the performance of horses that do not suffer from "bleeding" and exercise-induced pulmonary hemorrhage. They also stated that the drug failed to stop bleeding in over 60 percent of the horses which were designated as bleeders.

I sincerely hope that the Canadian government doesn't make the same horrible mistake as the United States government by legalizing this drug.

Chicago Sun-Times, Horse Racing,Thursday, Mar. 3, 1994

DAVE FELDMAN'S SPORTSMAN'S LINE / Thoroughbreds

Listed in handicap order. Post Time: 1 p.m.
Best Bet: Boldienne (5th). Long Shot: Ron Wood (6th).
Wednesday's Best Bet: Hotspyinthecity won.
★Lasix horses. ★★First time Lasix.
Post position numbers are not necessarily program numbers.

FIRST RACE—1m, 3-y-o up, f&m, allowance, pr. $25,960. 1:00

★Sweet Ophelia, Meier	116	6	2-1	Very best needed
★Empress Of All, Razo	116	3	3-1	Very dangerous
★Findalady, Guerra	116	1	6-1	Best could threaten
★Young Frost, Razo	116	5	9-2	Might surprise
★Twin Oaks Miss, Diaz	116	4	5-1	Could be close
Megan's Brass Band, Enriquez	116	2	6-1	Had some good races

SECOND RACE—1m, 3-y-o up, f&m, clm., $6,250, pr. $7,900. 1:25

★Shiney Saber, Guidry	113	6	7-2	Won her last
★Leading Sonnet, Meier	116	3	5-2	Best could take all
★Diamonds 'N Jazz, Nuesch	116	4	5-1	Rates a slice
★Mon Cadeau, Baird	116	5	5-1	Drop for best
Springtime Ballet, Smith	108	1	6-1	OK at times
Honesty Wins, Diaz	108	7	6-1	Ran with better
Really Misbehaving, Enriquez	116	2	15-1	Poor form

THIRD RACE—3/4m, 3&4-y-o, fils, mdns, clm.,$10,000, pr. $6,800. 1:49

Avalanche Blanche, Guerra	113	7	3-1	Ready for this
★Minstrel Style, Diaz	113	3	5-2	Best might win
R K Island, Meier	121	5	5-1	May get a slice
★Patrinka, Lasala	121	1	6-1	Could improve
Accuse Me Not, Sorrows	113	4	8-1	Always a price
★Bunny's Type, Baird	121	6	15-1	Shown very little
Amykin O'Malley, Silva	113	8	15-1	Blinkers off today
Pretty Cathy, Razo	113	2	15-1	Drop might help

FOURTH RACE—1 mile, 4-y-o up, clm., $4,000, pr. $5,300. 2:13

★Gone Twice, Diaz	122	5	7-2	Best should take all
★Winning Rainbows, Zuniga	122	6	5-1	Best would threaten
★Ringmere, Meier	122	4	7-2	Can run with these
★Premier Danseur, Retana	122	1	2-1	Last effort fine; rates
★Grand Colony, Silva	122	7	6-1	Needed last
Joi Toi, Woodley	122	3	10-1	Beat easier
★Charles Nite Out, Kurek	122	2	20-1	Pass

FIFTH RACE—3/4 mile, 4-y-o up, f&m, clm., $4,000, pr. $5,000. 2:37

★Boldienne, Silva	121	10	3-1	Well placed
★Social Means, Enriquez	121	9	8-1	Chance at a price
★Silent In The Rear, Meier	121	2	9-2	Not out of this
★Zen's Magic, Lasala	121	6	4-1	Bet on in last
★Adelphai's Cause, Kelber	121	4	8-1	Last was OK
★Preak Miss, Sayler	121	1	8-1	Must better last
Shirley's Play, Meza	121	3	15-1	Always a price
★Alomaha, Medina	121	8	15-1	Been idle
★Ten Stars, Retana	121	7	15-1	Poor form
★Visible Gal, Macias	121	5	20-1	Never wins

SCRATCHED: Big Nose Kate, Tobasco Baby, Never Grunk Again.

SIXTH RACE—34/4 mile, 3&4-y-o, mdns, clm, $10,000, pr. $6,800. 3:01

Ron Wood, Macias	122	2	7-2	Can last for all
Close To The West, Guerra	113	10	7-2	Big threat
Weevy, A. Razo	122	3	8-1	Longshot chance
Spend A Bundle, Diaz	122	1	2-1	Edge in tossup
General Stealth, Meier	113	6	6-1	First time starter
Fazoid, E.Razo, Jr.	122	4	8-1	Could improve
★Great Bouquet, Baird	113	9	10-1	Must show more
Mr. Tom T., Zuniga	113	8	15-1	May need the race
Stop Counting, Enriquez	113	7	15-1	Lone effort poor
Rebs Toy, Sorrows	113	5	10-1	Not too much

SCRATCHED: H.H. Express, D B's Bouquet, Zydeco Spell.

SEVENTH RACE—3/4 mile, 3-y-o up, clm., $5,000, pr. $5,800. 3:25

Sir Garth, Guidry	117	8	8-5	Best should win
★Many A Quest, Guerra	117	4	8-1	Ready
★Not To Be Matched, Meier	117	1	8-1	Could come to life
★Mertzies Boy, Enriquez	117	7	9-2	Can better last
★Mr. Prime Rate, Nuesch	117	3	6-1	Not too bad
Chad's New Friend, Murray	110	9	8-1	Trying to scratch
★Fortunate D., Smith	112	6	10-1	Not off last few
★aPatient Playful, Meier	117	1a	15-1	Recent form dull
Cigar Special, Zuniga	117	5	15-1	Best easier
Distinctive Honor, Silva	117	2	20-1	Not here

EIGHTH RACE—1m, 4-y-o up, clm., $12,500, pr. $13,100. 3:49

★Theo's Machine, Zuniga	117	5	3-1	Likes this track
★Tiblow Crossing, Guidry	117	1	5-2	Best may take all
★Run For Your Honey, Diaz	117	7	7-2	Can be a contender
★D'B Moment, Meier	117	2	6-1	Idle, and dropped
★Justabonus, Marquez	117	3	8-1	Good at one time
★This Time Tony, Baird	117	4	8-1	Beat easier
★Malibu Express, Macias	117	6	15-1	In tough

[redacted]

NINTH RACE—3/4 mile, 3-y-o up, f&m, allowance, pr. $20,000. 4:13

★Cozy Miss, Lasala	116	8	3-1	Well placed
★Dearest Dee, Guidry	116	1	5-1	Rider helps
★Equal To The Best, Razo	116	9	4-1	Best would threaten
Cody Pass, Baird	116	5	7-2	Main rival
Southern Paradise, Hunter	116	2	6-1	New York invader
★Gentle Imp, Marquez	116	3	8-1	Could surprise
★Quite A Quiver, Medina	116	4	8-1	Fine effort in last
★Trip The Load, Macias	116	7	15-1	May need the race
★Zsa Zsa's Hour, Meier	116	10	15-1	Could show speed
★Star Tiffany, Diaz	116	6	20-1	Not with these

Temperature

Normal today	39/23
Last year	43/34
Record high	80 *(1974)*
Record low	-6 *(1873)*
Yesterday *(through 6 p.m.)*	34/11

Precipitation

A year ago today	.02"
This month	None
Normal month-to-date	.18"
This year	4.33"
Normal year-to-date	3.09"
Yesterday	None

49 of 76 Horses Racing Have Been Injected With Lasix.

Chicago Sun-Times, p.88, Horse Racing Section, Saturday, April 30, 1994

DAVE FELDMAN'S SPORTSMAN'S LINE / Thoroughbreds

Handicap order. Post: 1 p.m. ★Lasix. ★★First time Lasix.
Best Bet: Polar Expedition (8th). Long Shot: Eskimo Slush (1st).
Friday's Best Bet: Walk The Chalk won.

FIRST RACE—1 mile, 3-y-o up, f&m, allowance, pr. $21,300.				1:00
★aCarey's Visit, CH Marquez, Jr	110	1a	9-5	4th in big stake, edge
★Eskimo Slush, Meier	116	6	5-1	Had three fine races
★★Ambitious Lady, A Marquez	116	3	4-1	In fine form
★Forty Niners Miss, Lasala	116	4	5-1	Last fine; rates
★aSue Sez, Bourque	121	1	9-5	Could improve
★Regal Runner, Baird	116	2	8-1	Must show more
Roil, Meza	116	5	15-1	Much later
SECOND RACE—3/4 mile, 3-y-o up, clm., $10,000, pr. $10,000.				1:27
★Mimi's Live Wire, Guidry	117	4	5-1	Class drop; has speed
★Focus, Meier	119	3	3-1	Chance on best
★Sharkspeare, Diaz	119	6	7-2	Big 2nd in last
★Island Thorn, E Razo, Jr	110	1	8-1	Not bad
★Improvisational, Valenzuela	117	2	10-1	Could be ready; good rider
★Pleasant Quest, Zuniga	119	5	8-1	Overdue; shot
★Dance For Choice, Silva	117	7	10-1	Overdue; shot
THIRD RACE—1 mile, 3-y-o up, f&m, clm, $4,000, pr. $5,300.				1:54
★Over Shoe, Silva	121	4	5-2	Best may take all
Bruness, Guidry	121	2	5-2	Tries; rates edge
★Ranvulera, A Marquez	121	8	6-1	Overdue
★Lovans Lethal Lady, E Razo Jr	121	1	10-1	Overdue
★Bellyachin' Babe, Sayler	121	7	15-1	Last few poor
★So Engaging, Meier	121	6	8-1	Been losing
★Robards, Sibille	121	5	15-1	Must show more
★December First, A Sorrows	121	3	15-1	Must show more
FOURTH RACE—3/4 mile, 3&up, allowance, pr. $24,530.				2:20
★Hotspyinthecity, Baird	122	2	1-1	High speed; won last
★Double Jeopardy, Silva	117	5	5-1	Big 2nd in last
Sound Of Angels, Lasala	117	3	3-1	Good speed
★Powerful Headache, Valenz	117	4	8-1	Always close
★Sunny's Sauce, Diaz	122	6	8-1	Won start before last
Count Zen, Sibille	117	1	6-1	Not too bad
★Lucky Find, Macias	117	7	15-1	In a bit tough
FIFTH RACE—1 mile, 4-y-o up, clm., $5,000, pr. $7,400.				2:47
Raid The Mint, Hunter	122	2	5-2	Almost lasted in last
★Prince Plaything, Bourque	122	5	3-1	Won start before last
★Bet On Blade, Meier	122	3	6-1	Needed last race
★Bid, Enriquez	122	1	8-1	Last few fair
★★Filipino Boy, Guidry	122	4	5-1	First time Lasix; beware
★You Regent You, Zuniga	122	8	4-1	Won last; threat
★Range Rider, Thomas	122	7	9-2	Big win in last
★Proper Exposure, Sibille	122	6	20-1	Maybe later
Classy Red, Murray	122	9	6-1	Ran with bit better
SIXTH RACE—3/4 mile, 3&4-y-o, ll. clm, $10,000, pr. $10,000.				3:13
★Richard Dan, A Sorrows, Jr	117	1	4-1	Improved in last
★Awesome Kyle, Guidry	119	3	5-2	Has sharp speed
★Dobe Sam, Silva	117	8	9-2	Edge off last 4th
Dani Jas, Zuniga	122	5	4-1	Beat easier in last
★Madderbythemoment, Guerra	117	4	8-1	Lost to better
Red Green Go, CH Marquez, Jr	108	6	12-1	Overdue
★Mom's Special Gift, Meier	113	7	4-1	Won last
★Facilatin Bud, Macias	122	2	3-1	Last races fair
Blazing Bobby, Sibille	119	9	12-1	Can run a bit

continued from the previous page

SEVENTH RACE—3/4 mile, 3&up, f&m, cl, $15,000, pr. $13,300.				3:40
★Petite D'Accord, Silva	116	8	3-1	Best might win, here
★Southern Paradise, Guidry	116	3	7-2	Barely lost last
Amy's Pistachio, Hunter	116	6	5-1	Ran with better
★Tune In Tonight, Lasala	116	1	5-1	Has sharp speed
★Fit Dancer, Bourque	116	2	6-1	Big second in last
★Tardy To Party, Diaz	116	4	8-1	Class drop
★Caramella, Meier	121	7	15-1	Last races fine
★Icanrun, A Razo	116	5	15-1	OK last year
EIGHTH RACE—1 1/8 miles, 3-y-o, Illinois Derby, pr. $500,000.				4:10
★Polar Expedition, Bourque	124	1	4-5	Pounds the best
Amathos, Guidry	114	5	3-1	Has class
Can't Slow Down, Martinez	117	2	10-1	Tries; in tough
★Rustic Light, Fires	117	4	8-1	Always close
★R Friar Tuck, Valenzuela	114	6	10-1	In tough spot
★★Bit Of Puddin, Davis	118	3	8-1	In good form
★Seminole Wind, Silva	112	7	15-1	Later
NINTH RACE—1 mile, 3-y-o, The Derby Trail, pr. $100,000. Simulcast from Churchill Downs				4:42
Numerous, McCannon	112	3	9-5	Ready for these
Exclusive Praline, Perret	119	1	3-1	Can run with these
Commanche Trail, Gomez	112	6	7-2	Big threat
Tarzans Blade, Day	122	2	8-1	In bit tough
Dynamic Asset, Sarvis	114	5	10-1	Always close
Crary, Sellers	114	4	8-1	Last two good ones
TENTH RACE—3/4 mile, 3-y-o up, clm., $25,000, pr. $18,000.				5:10
★Downtown Clown, Meier	122	9	3-1	Won last; poor p.p.; edge
★Position Of Power, Sibille	117	7	3-1	Last was OK
★Tidal Wave, Guidry	117	3	7-2	Big threat
★Cure Thyself, Silva	117	1	6-1	Always close
Ghostbucker, Davis	117	2	8-1	Good last year
★Lil Bit Deadly, Bourque	117	4	8-1	Bit outclassed
★Tory Sound, CH Marquez, Jr	122	5	10-1	Poor start in last
★Sham Topper, E Razo, Jr	117	6	12-1	In a tough spot
★Tumbleweed, Martin	117	8	15-1	Usually close
11TH RACE—3/4 mile, 3&4-y-o, allowance, pr. $18,000.				5:36
★Mutuality, Guidry	113	5	7-5	Class should tell
Ten Cent City, Diaz	108	4	3-1	Beat cheaper easily
★Big And Bold, E Razo, Jr	113	6	8-1	Maybe a slice
Amgroovy, CH Marquez, Jr	113	2	5-1	Beat easier
Sunset Slew, Bourque	117	1	8-1	In tough spot
★Silver Threads, Lasala	108	8	15-1	Good second in last
★Browneyehansumman, Murray	117	3	20-1	Not this trip
★Sea Galli, Sibille	110	7	20-1	Must improve
12TH RACE—1 mile, 3-y-o up, Il. allowance, pr.$20,790.				6:02
It's Inevitable, Guidry	117	2	3-1	Last two fair; rates
★Heart Beat Fault, Guerra	108	8	4-1	Forget last; threat
★Final Days, Valenzuela	117	1	8-1	Best may win
Twist Maneuver, A Razo	113	4	8-1	Had three good races
★Dont Quarrel, Sorrows, Jr.	117	3	10-1	In good form
★Don't Be Even, Lasala	117	7	5-1	Won last
★Big Bad Rolf, E Razo, Jr	117	10	12-1	Best may win, Tony
★Pesotum, Meier	117	9	10-1	Last few OK
Bmyone And Holy, A Marquez	113	6	15-1	Won start before last
★Mr. Socco, Focareto	113	5	15-1	Won last

Of the 89 horses racing on April 30, 1994, at Sportsman's Park track, 70 have been injected with the drug Lasix (Lasix horses' names preceded by★). This reflects a substantial increase in the percentage of horses racing under the influence of this dangerous drug.